Y0-BDG-786

THE EARLY HISTORY OF GLASTONBURY

The Early History of Glastonbury

An Edition, Translation and Study of William of Malmesbury's *De Antiquitate Glastonie Ecclesie*

JOHN SCOTT

THE BOYDELL PRESS

Published by
The Boydell Press, an imprint of
Boydell & Brewer Ltd., PO Box 9, Woodbridge, Suffolk IP12 3DF
Distributed in the USA by Biblio Distribution Services
81 Adams Drive, Totowa, NJ 07512

British Library Cataloguing in Publication Data

William, *of Malmesbury*
[De antiquitate Glastonie Ecclesie. *English*]
The early history of Glastonbury.
1. Glastonbury Abbey – History
I. Title II. The early history of Glastonbury
III. Scott, John
942.3'83 DA690.G45

ISBN 0 85115 154 X

Printed in Great Britain by
St Edmundsbury Press, Bury St Edmunds, Suffolk

Contents

Acknowledgements

IT will be obvious, from the notes and references, how dependent my work has been on the labour of other scholars. In particular, I would like to thank Dr M. Lapidge and Dr S. Keynes who allowed me to see unpublished work that they had produced. For help with proof-reading I would like to thank my colleague at the University of Tasmania, Dr M. Bennett. For reading numerous drafts of the work and allowing me to profit from his wide knowledge of William of Malmesbury my greatest thanks go to my friend and colleague at the University of Tasmania, Dr Rod Thomson. But for his continuing help and encouragement, at all stages of my work, this book either would not have appeared or would have been much inferior. He is not, of course, responsible for the errors that undoubtedly remain. Finally, I owe much to two inspiring teachers of history, Dr Bob Hind and Dr John Ward, from whom I have learnt much more than a love of history and a determination to study it honestly.

Abbreviations

AD	*Adami de Domerham Historia de Rebus gestis Glastoniensibus*, ed. T. Hearne, 2 vols (Oxford, 1727)
ASC	*The Anglo-Saxon Chronicle*, a revised translation ed. D. Whitelock with D. C. Douglas and S. I. Tucker (London, 1961)
ASE	*Anglo-Saxon England*
Birch	W. de Gray Birch, *Cartularium Saxonicum*, 3 vols and index (1885-99)
Carley	James P. Carley ed., *John of Glastonbury Cronica sive Antiquitates Glastoniensis Ecclesie*, British Archaeological Reports 47 (i) 1978
CCC	Corpus Christi College
DA	William of Malmesbury, *De Antiquitate Ecclesie Glastonie* (as herein edited)
DB	Domesday Book
EHR	*English Historical Review*
GP	*Willelmi Malmesbiriensis Monachi de Gestis Pontificum Anglorum Libri Quinque*, ed. N. E. S. A. Hamilton (RS, 1870)
GR	*Willelmi Malmesbiriensis Monachi de Gestis Regum Anglorum Libri Quinque*, ed. W. Stubbs (RS, 1887-9, 2 vols)
HA	Bede, *Historia Abbatum*, in *Venerabilis Baedae Opera Historica*, ed. C. Plummer (Oxford, 1896)
HE	Bede, *Historia Ecclesiastica Gentis Anglorum*, in *Venerabilis Baedae Opera Historica*, ed. C. Plummer (Oxford, 1896)
HN	*The Historia Novella by William of Malmesbury*, ed. K. R. Potter (Nelson's Medieval Texts, 1955)
HRB	Geoffrey of Monmouth, *The History of the Kings of Britain*, trans. Lewis Thorpe, (Harmondsworth, 1976)
Hardy, *Materials*	T. D. Hardy, *Descriptive Catalogue of Materials Relating to the History of Great Britain and Ireland to the end of the Reign of Henry VII*, (RS, 1862-71, 3 vols)
Hearne, *JG*	*Johannis . . . Glastoniensis Chronica sive Historia de rebus Glastoniensibus*, ed. T. Hearne, 2 vols (Oxford, 1726)
JEH	*Journal of Ecclesiastical History*
LC	'The Liturgical Calendar of Glastonbury Abbey', ed. F. Wormald in *Festschrift Bernard Bischoff* (Stuttgart, 1971), 325-45
MBV	P. N. Carter, *An Edition of William of Malmesbury's Treatise on the Miracles of the Virgin*, Ph.D. diss., Oxford University, 1959
MGH	*Monumenta Germaniae Historica*
MSD	*Memorials of St Dunstan*, ed. W. Stubbs (*RS*, 1874)
MO	D. Knowles, *The Monastic Order in England*, (Cambridge, 2nd edn., 1963)

PL	*Patrologiae cursus completus, series Latina*, ed. J. P. Migne, (Paris, 1852-1904)
PMLA	*Publications of the Modern Language Association of America*
PSANHS	*Proceedings of the Somerset Archaeological and Natural History Society*
RS	*Rolls Series*
RTAM	*Récherches de Théologie Ancienne et Médiévale*
S	P. H. Sawyer, *Anglo-Saxon Charters*, (Royal Historical Society, 1968). (References are to charter numbers)
SHE	J. Armitage Robinson, *Somerset Historical Essays*, (British Academy, 1921)
TRHS	*Transactions of the Royal Historical Society*
VCH	*Victoria County History*
VP	William of Malmesbury, Vita Patricii (no longer extant)
VSD	William of Malmesbury, *Vita Sancti Dunstani*, in *MSD*
Watkin	A. Watkin, *The Great Chartulary of Glastonbury*, 3 vols (Somerset Record Society, 1947-56). (References are to charter numbers)

References in the notes are by author's name (and short title if necessary) to the full details given in the bibliography, with the exception of items listed above.

1

William of Malmesbury at Glastonbury

WILLIAM of Malmesbury came to Glastonbury about 1129. A few years earlier Henry of Blois, a nephew of King Henry, had been appointed abbot of that monastery which at the time of Domesday had been the wealthiest in England.[1] Yet Henry, by his own account, found it on the point of ruin: its buildings reminded him of peasants' huts; its monks were struggling to obtain the necessities of life; and it had been deprived of many of its possessions.[2] An energetic and ambitious man, Henry at once set out to make his abbey once again a *locum . . . celeberimum* (sic).[3] To assist him to recover the monastery's lost estates, to restore its buildings and to reestablish economic stability he employed Robert of Lewes whose business ability had already been demonstrated,[4] while the historical and hagiographical works produced by William, complemented by the work of Caradoc of Llancarvan, can be seen as an endeavour to restore the reputation of Glastonbury as a place of great holiness and sanctity and to justify its claims to vast estates and other riches.

The traditions that the monastery maintained certainly justified a belief in its long and pious history. As early as the late tenth century the first biographer of Dunstan recorded his belief that the earliest church at Glastonbury had not been built by men but had been fashioned in heaven,[5] while William recounts a less fanciful but equally ancient foundation attributed to the disciples sent by Pope Eleutherius to King Lucius.[6] He even allows the possibility, no doubt in deference to the conviction of his hosts, of an apostolic origin for the church.[7] Over the centuries the holiness of the place was reinforced by the Irish pilgrims who frequented it, especially St Patrick, who was believed by William's day to have been the first abbot of the monastery. This tradition too can be traced back to the tenth century, possibly to St Dunstan himself, and there is liturgical evidence that not only Patrick but also Bridget, David and Gildas were venerated at Glastonbury during the eleventh century.[8] To confirm the high regard in which the monastery had been held in the past the Glastonbury traditions spoke also of the numerous kings, bishops and important nobles who had been associated with it throughout its history.[9] William was clearly justified, on the evidence presented to him, in speaking of Glastonbury as being 'redolent with divine sanctity'.[10]

An examination of the past of Glastonbury revealed more than a long tradition of holiness. It showed also that the monastery had been richly endowed by devout kings and nobles. William could trace grants of land back to the year 601, and the records showed that most of the kings of Wessex had favoured the house, with King Ine being the first of its great patrons and the kings of the tenth century enriching it with gifts of vast estates.[11] The reverses in the monastery's fortunes began in the eleventh century. Both Aethelweard (1027-1053) and Aethelnoth (1053-1077/8) appear as unsatisfactory abbots in the traditions of the monastery, the one alienating many of the abbey's estates and the other removing ornaments from within the church.[12] The monastery's difficulties had been aggravated by the incursions of the Danes and later by the Norman Conquest, particularly because the Conqueror had enfeoffed many of his vassals with its lands.[13] In the aftermath of the Conquest came other troubles for Glastonbury: the first Norman abbot, Thurstan, was involved in a serious conflict with his monks as a result of which at least two of them were killed, some of the rest removed to other houses and he himself sent back to Caen, whence he had come;[14] it was during Thurstan's reign too that the bishop of Wells made his first attempt to encroach upon the privileges of Glastonbury and so inaugurated a dispute that was to preoccupy the monks for the next century.[15] Thus despite the endeavours of abbot Herluin (1100-1118) Henry and the monks felt entitled to complain about the sad state of the abbey in 1126.[16]

Modern scholars, however, are more sceptical about both Glastonbury's illustrious early history and the extent of its impoverishment in 1126. An apostolic foundation is not accepted – William himself had referred to it only as a possibility – and it is known that the story of King Lucius and Pope Eleutherius, found in Bede and the *ASC*, arose from a misreading of the *Liber Pontificalis*. On the other hand, there is a case to be made out for a pre-Saxon settlement at Glastonbury. The possibility of Glastonbury having played a crucial role in trade with the Mediterranean by way of the Severn has been raised. More concretely, archaeological excavations have revealed the remains of a wattled chapel and an ancient cemetery of a type which corresponds to the traditional account of the foundation of Glastonbury. These discoveries, together with the cult of Celtic saints at Glastonbury, seem on balance to outweigh the fact that the only Roman or sub-Roman pottery found in the excavations at Glastonbury was in the clay brought to the site much later.[17] There is, in short, no doubt that there was some justification for the monks' claim that their monastery pre-dated the building of a new church by King Ine, remains of which have also been recovered.[18] The parade of holy men supposed to have been drawn to Glastonbury is similarly modified by modern scholars. The great Irish saints are not thought to have been associated with Glastonbury – in particular, there is no evidence for St Patrick ever having been there – but it seems likely that there were Irish scholars there in the tenth century and there is no doubt that as early as that Glastonbury was venerating Celtic saints.[19] If the traditions concerning the antiquity and holiness of Glastonbury have been questioned, so have its claims to extravagant wealth and privileges. It is quite clear that many of its charters are later forgeries.[20] At the same time a significant number are certainly authentic and Domesday reveals that the monastery did indeed possess many of the estates to which its charters refer.[21] This fact has made modern historians sceptical of the monks' complaints about the dilapidation and impoverishment of their monastery in the eleventh century. Although Glastonbury may have been more severely imposed on than other monasteries, whose common lament that they had suffered large losses of lands was not justified, it was after all, (despite the assessment of its knight service at 60) the wealthiest abbey in England at the time of the compilation of Domesday.[22]

Nevertheless many monks and abbots throughout England believed that their monasteries had suffered severely at the hands of the Normans and would have echoed the words of Hemming, the monk from Worcester, who complained of the violence of the Normans 'who by force, guile and rapine have unjustly deprived this holy church of its lands, villages and possessions, until hardly anything is safe from their depredations.'[23] Perhaps more fundamentally, the Conquest posed a threat to a whole monastic culture and religious tradition. The new Norman abbots, whose appointments not only denied English monks the chance of promotion but rendered obsolete the very language in which so many of their prayers and rituals were expressed, attacked some of the cherished beliefs and practices of the English monks. The ill-fated attempt by Thurstan to impose a new chant on the monks of Glastonbury, who forcibly resisted the move, was only the most striking instance of the policy.[24] More widespread, and even more of an affront to the English, was the disdain in which the new rulers held the Anglo-Saxon saints, whose sanctity they questioned and whose very existence, they asserted, was recorded only by local tradition. Lanfranc's suspicion of the English saints is well known; and other Norman abbots were even more peremptory in their treatment of treasured relics, among them Warin, abbot of Malmesbury, who had cast the remains of revered saints out of the church.[25]

One of the responses of the monks to this challenge to their way of life was a literary recreation of it, in the form of saints' lives, cartularies and histories. The innate conservatism of monks predisposed them to contemplation of the past and preservation of what had been gained in it, and it was never more important to record its beauties than when there were threats to it.[26] Hence the frenetic literary activity by English monks in the century after the Conquest, as they delved into old charters to establish their rights to lands and the early history of their monasteries, and laboured to recover the lives of their saints from ancient writings and oral traditions. Most of this research and writing was done by monks of the house concerned, but there was also a small band of professional historians and hagiographers whose skills were put at the service of a number of monasteries. The earliest of these was Goscelin who . . . *multo episcopatus et abbatias perlustrans tempore . . . innumeras sanctorum vitas recentium stylo extulit*, and so earned high praise from William.[27] Among William's own contemporaries, there were Osbert of Clare, who wrote a Life of St Eadburg for the monks of Pershore, some lections and hymns for the Festival of St Anne for the monks of Worcester, and the Miracles of St Edmund for abbot Anselm of Bury; and also Caradoc of Llancarvan, who wrote a Life of Gildas for Glastonbury, a Life of St Cadoc and probably also a Life of St Iltuit and a Life of St Cyngar for Wells.[28] William himself, even before his work at Glastonbury, had tried, in the *GP*, to record the history of the Anglo-Saxon church and preserve the local traditions which the monks passed on to him and had translated a Life of Wulfstan into Latin for the monks of Worcester.[29]

Consideration of this awakened historical consciousness suggests that William's visit to Glastonbury was not fortuitous. In fact the evidence indicates that he was commissioned by the monks to write Lives of a number of early Glastonbury saints in order to confirm the abbey's prestige both in the eyes of the monks and the thoughts of possible pilgrims and incidentally to counter the claim of the Canterbury monk Osbern that Dunstan had been the first abbot of Glastonbury.[30]

Thus the Preface to *DA* reveals that William has already written works on four Glastonbury saints and handed them over to the monks for correction.[31] In the only one of these works to survive intact, his *VSD*, William is even more explicit about the commission that he has received: he dedicates the book to the monks, who have provided him with writings to help him in his task; he speaks of fulfilling their expectations, submitting to their commands and following their orders; and finally he offers the work to them as the required token of his obedience.[32] It might be permissible at this point to speculate about the inducements offered to William for his labours. Stubbs, noticing long ago that in his *VSD* William speaks of himself as though he were a monk of Glastonbury, raised the possibility that William may have had letters of confraternity with the monks of that house.[33] Since we know that the institution of confraternity was common in England, being dealt with in fact by Lanfranc in his Statutes, this appears to be a most plausible hypothesis.[34] No doubt access to the abbey's archives, the opportunity to broaden his knowledge of the Anglo-Saxon past, and the kind hospitality which he must have encountered so often as he perambulated the country, were sufficient attractions for an enthusiastic historian such as William.[35]

Although we can confidently conclude that William had been hired by the monks, encouraged by Henry of Blois, to write saints' lives for them, it seems likely that they had not envisaged a work such as the *DA* when they engaged William to celebrate their famous saints and that the splendid archives of the house had suggested such an enterprise to the historian who needed to compensate the monks for his failure to fulfill all their expectations. Certain peculiar features of the preface to the *DA* favour this interpretation of its composition. After the dedication the preface rehearses, in language adapted by William from his own *Life of Wulfstan*, the arguments for writing the lives of saints, especially those who are compatriots.[36] A defence of hagiography seems out of place in this context, and in fact William relates it as a justification for his *Life of Dunstan*, written at the request of the Glastonbury monks. However, he goes on to say, he has also set down the history of their church, lest his zeal fail in its duty, and this ought not to be regarded as very different from their plan (*multum a proposito alienum*) since the honour of the church redounds upon Dunstan and praise of him upon the church.[37] These remarks imply a close relationship between the *VSD* and the *DA*. I suggest that William was expected to write a Life of Dunstan, celebrating the saint's connection with Glastonbury, that the *VSD* partly fulfilled that obligation but that the *DA*, justified as indirectly praising Dunstan, and hence Glastonbury his first house, was offered because the monks' plan, *propositum*, their wish, had been for something more.

The clue to what the monks had expected William to write can be found in a letter from Eadmer, the Canterbury monk and biographer of Dunstan, to the convent of Glastonbury, written about 1120.[38] Eadmer is concerned to counter the claim of the Glastonbury monks that their church now possessed the body of St Dunstan, as a result of rescuing it from Canterbury at a time when that church had been attacked and burnt by the Danes. Among other arguments, Eadmer taunts the monks with having no writings to prove their claim: *Habetis quaeso aliqua litterarum monimenta, quae haec ita se habuisse probent? videlicet quae ferant cadaver abbatis illius eo quo diximus modo redimitum.*[39] It is difficult to believe that the Glastonbury monks, conscious of the attraction to pilgrims of the relics of St Dunstan, would have been satisfied with an account of his life or the history of their monastery which did not provide written proof of his translation to their abbey. The fact that such proof was soon added to the *DA*, at considerable length, shows that the monks were not satisfied with what William had done.[40] William's resistance to their wishes can be adequately explained by his own close contacts with Canterbury,[41] the monks of which, as Eadmer's letter demonstrates, were jealous of their possession of the relics of one of the country's most famous saints.

This hypothesis explains not only the curious preface to the *DA* but also several other features of the work. The defensive character of the preface, with its insistence that the author has not betrayed his obligations and its reminder that the monks have approved of all the other works written for them and submitted to their inspection, is due to William's realisation that the work would not be well received.[42] The cursory notice of Dunstan in William's original version, which omitted details of his life or miracles, in sharp contrast to the treatment of less famous saints, is accounted for by the work being intended to supplement the *VD*. We can understand too why the work, originally written for the monks, was in the end dedicated to Henry of Blois from whom William hoped for a sympathetic hearing and whose support he hoped for *ne fructu laboris excidam.*[43]

William of Malmesbury's visit to Glastonbury, then, must be viewed in the context of a general unease which afflicted the Anglo-Saxon church striving to come to terms with its new Norman masters, and the particular perceptions of the abbot and monks of Glastonbury that their church had been deprived of wealth and prestige that rightfully belonged to it. This attitude led English churchmen to strive to recreate the glories of their past, and the convent of Glastonbury concentrated particularly on glorifying the holy men traditionally associated with it. They therefore encouraged William of Malmesbury to come and utilise their records and he did so, mostly to their satisfaction. But he could not accept their claim to possess the body of St Dunstan, one of their chief glories, and so the monks were dissatisfied with the *Life of Dunstan* which William wrote. In an attempt to allay their resentment he offered them the *DA* which, he argued, would add to the glory of both Glastonbury and St Dunstan. This gesture was apparently rejected and so William added a *Preface* appealing to the support of the abbot, Henry of Blois.

Although the Glastonbury monks were not impressed by the *DA*, modern historians admire the skill with which William constructed the work out of the disparate sources available to him. It is to those sources that I will now turn.

2

Sources and Models for the *De Antiquitate*

WILLIAM was not unacquainted with the history of Glastonbury when he arrived there about 1129, and he had included an account of its origins and its more famous relics in the *GP.*[1] It is possible – indeed the details he incorporated suggest it[2] – that he had visited the monastery before 1125, but if that were so the sources on which he later drew were either not convincing then or were not shown to him at the time (if they were not concocted between his two visits). The *GP* attributed the foundation of the monastery to King Ine, at the instigation of Aldhelm, and although it recognised many of the relics associated with the monastery, including those of Benignus, Indract and Patrick, it qualified the story of Patrick's return to Glastonbury after the completion of his missionary work with the phrase *si credere dignum.*[3] Yet within a few years the scepticism about Patrick had been abandoned and a much earlier foundation date for the monastery was acknowledged. What were the sources that caused William to revise the views he had expressed in his major work on the history of the English church?

It is clear that the one most to his purpose and the book that probably persuaded him to undertake the *DA* was the monastery's *Liber Terrarum*, a volume that collected the charters granted to Glastonbury from the time of King Cenwalh, c.670, to the reign of Aethelred. Although it is no longer extant, its contents were recorded about 1247, under the rubric *Carte contente in libro terrarum Glaston*, in MS R.5.33 from the Library of Trinity College, Cambridge (T), by the same scribe who was also responsible for copying William's *DA* and Adam of Domerham's history of the monastery.[4] There is no certainty about the date of the compilation of the *Liber Terrarum* and Keynes has pointed out that the assumption of a late 10th or early 11th century date – presumably on the grounds that there are no documents entered which belong to a reign later than that of Aethelred – cannot be convincingly sustained.[5] He argues, with some plausibility, for a post-Conquest date and it is possible – to extend his argument – that the cartulary was not put together until the third decade of the twelfth century, the time when forgery was becoming a popular weapon in the struggles of the English monasteries to recover lost estates and when, as we have seen, the monks of Glastonbury were pressing the claims of their monastery.[6] What is fairly certain is that the *Liber Terrarum* existed when William wrote the *DA.*[7] The significance of the *Liber Terrarum*, or rather the charters that it gathered together, the originals of which he may have had access to, was that they enabled William to construct a chronology of the abbots of the monastery and the lands with which they had been endowed. This *series abbatum* provided the framework of the *DA*. The precise use that William made of the charters he examined will be explored later.

Most of the rest of the new information about the early history of Glastonbury with which William filled out his chronological framework must have come from the writings with which the monks supplied him for his saints' lives. This is explicitly acknowledged in the prologue to the *VSD* where William records that he had learnt the truth about Dunstan from 'writings both in Latin and Anglo-Saxon' which the monks had found for him in a very old chest,[8] and we can imagine that the monks had documents pertaining to all their saints. In the *VSD* William explicitly refers to the earlier *Lives* of Dunstan by Osbern and the anonymous hagiographer known as 'B',[9] and he also made use of the *Life of Dunstan* by Adelard, the *Life of Odo* by Eadmer, the *Life of Aethelwold* by Wulfstan, the *Life of Edith* by Goscelin and an anonymous *Life of Oswald.*[10] These works were mainly relevant to the *VSD* and less directly to the *DA* – which I have suggested was meant to accompany the former – although, because of the saint's associations with the abbey, they do inevitably record some of the Glastonbury traditions, including the belief that Patrick was buried there.[11] Moreover their comprehensiveness suggests the dedication with which the Glastonbury monks collected material on their saints.

More immediately relevant to the composition of the *DA*, because William incorporated some of them into his account of the early history of the monastery, were the materials on which he based his *VP*. Although that work is no longer extant the sources for it can be reconstructed by reference to Leland's summary of it and to the extracts from it used by John of Glastonbury in his fourteenth-century account of Patrick, which drew heavily on William's work.[12] The researches of Slover and Bieler have established that William had access to two earlier Lives, a version of the *vita tertia* and a version of the *vita secunda-vita quarta* type,[13] and we can add that William also made use of Patrick's own *Confessio.*[14] Despite the range of writings that the monks had accumulated, none of them was satisfactory because they failed to establish the intimate connection between Patrick and Glastonbury, hinted at in 'B's' *Life of Dunstan* and confirmed for the house by William.[15]

If it is possible to identify the sources from which William obtained information about Patrick and his times it is not as easy to work with the materials relevant to the other Glastonbury saints about whom William wrote. His *Life of Benignus* is not extant and although we can reconstruct part of it from John of Glastonbury, little can be said about William's sources because there are no extant earlier Lives to which it can be compared.[16] We do know that he copied an inscription from a tomb reputed to be that of Benignus and that this identified him as a minister of St Patrick, a claim that William no doubt connected with an incident in the *vita tertia* in which the apostle to the Irish gave the name Benignus to a man he baptised who, the saint prophesied, would be the heir to his kingdom.[17] Probably the oral traditions of the monks enabled William to fill out his *Life* with more details and with the miracle stories that we know it contained;[18] and much of the information for his lost *Passio Martiris Indracti* must have come from the same source. In the case of Indract, however, William probably had a written source from which to work. This was an Old English Life which no longer survives but which was translated into Latin during the twelfth century and is extant in that form. It appears from a comparison between the extant Life of Indract and what we can reconstruct of William's Life (using John of Glastonbury and references in William's other writings) that the author of the former vividly embellished his Old English source to add local colour whereas William was content merely to adopt the account contained in his source.[19]

There is no doubt that, in addition to the scrupulous care which the monks took to collect writings about their history, they nurtured fertile stories about their glorious past and the famous saints who had illuminated Glastonbury by their pious presence. It is clear that William made use of these local legends to augment what he could learn from charters and saints' lives. Such stories were obviously the source of the account of St Patrick's arrival at Glastonbury and his posthumous appearance in a vision to a local monk as well as the heavenly warning to St David about the prior consecration of the church.[20] It will suffice here to record William's debt to oral tradition, leaving an analysis of the use which he made of it to the next chapter. Similarly, I only note here that William was conscious of the importance of archaeological evidence and did not fail to take note of monuments or paintings if they could add to his knowledge. His record of the inscription on the tomb of St Benignus, mentioned above, is but one example, and he supplemented the information derived from written and oral sources with careful observations of the physical monuments at Glastonbury. A fuller analysis of this is postponed to the next chapter.

Besides these various sources for the local history of Glastonbury and its saints, William, ever conscious of the whole of which Glastonbury was but a part, consulted larger works which enabled him to make some connections between the part and the whole. In particular his speculations about the foundation of Glastonbury are informed by a close acquaintance with its historical context. He knew about the contact between King Lucius and Pope Eleutherius from *bone credulitatis annales*, presumably the *ASC*,[21] and was able to conjecture intelligently and not implausibly, about the possibility of St Philip having sent disciples to Britain because of his familiarity with Freculph, a copy of whose history he would probably have been able to find in the library at Glastonbury.[22] Bede too provided William with some historical background, enabling him to locate the mission of St Patrick in the context of the journey to England of St Germanus.[23]

Yet the *DA* is emphatically a local history based on a great deal of information relevant to the antiquity of Glastonbury. The problem that confronted William was how to arrange this mass of information, and what shape to give to it. Of course, local history was an old and established genre of monastic historiography, but on the other hand earlier works had not drawn on quite the same sources nor had been fashioned with quite the same intentions. To a large extent William was forced to create his own type of history, as he was when he wrote the *GP*, the problems of which he described in words that could well have been applied to the task that he undertook with the *DA*: *Hic autem, pene omni destitutus solatio, crassas ignorantiae tenebras palpo, nec ulla lucerna historiae praevia semitam dirigo.*[24]

For all that, there were models to help William, and Bede, the master to whom he would look first, the historian whose successor he considered himself, that *vir maxime doctus et minime superbus* whom he so admired, had in fact produced a paradigm for local monastic histories in his *Historia Abbatum*.[25] Indeed we find, after making allowances for the different time spans covered by the two works and for the special problems encountered by William writing of a time lost to the memories of his contemporaries, that the structure and the content (in the sense of the matters considered worthy of record) of the *DA* and Bede's *Historia Abbatum* are similar. Bede constructed his account of the early years of Wearmouth and Jarrow around biographies of the first three abbots – William actually refers to the work as a *librum quem idem Beda composuit de vita eius (Benedict Biscop) et ceterorum abbatum suorum*[26] – and within that framework described the foundation of the monasteries, the treasures which their abbots had bestowed on them and the lands that had been granted to them by the kings of Northumbria.

The parallels with the *DA* are obvious. William explicitly proclaims that he will elicit the antiquity of the church *per successionum seriem* and then explains more fully that he intends to set out *abbatum seriem, et quid cuique, et a quo rege monasterio delegatum sit.*[27] So indeed he does, basing his history, as Bede did, on the list of abbots that he was able to disentangle from the charters available to him. He begins, like Bede, with the foundation of the monastery, proceeds to a eulogy of the sanctity and antiquity of the church (there is no equivalent in Bede who was writing, of course, within a generation of the foundations) and then comes to the *abbatum seriem*. Potted biographies of the early abbots, beginning with Patrick, lead on to those abbots whom William knew only through charter entries; and, if William confined himself principally to the lands that were granted to the monastery during their abbacies, this is surely because his sources largely limited him to these facts and not because he was not interested in relating their spiritual and material contributions as abbots; indeed when such information was available to him he incorporated it, noting, for instance, the books given by Aethelnoth and the treasures by Dunstan (as Bede recorded the gifts of Benedict Biscop) and speculating, on the basis of a picture, about the character of abbot Stihtheard.[28] Another parallel between the two works that ought to be noted concerns the place of miracles in each of them. Bede attributes no miracles to his abbots, in striking contrast to the importance of the miraculous in his *Ecclesiastical History*, and William follows him in this: although his *Vitae* of the Glastonbury saints contained many miracles, the *DA* lacks them entirely, with the exception of Patrick's journey to England on his altar and this, although presumably miraculous, is not described as such and is passed over in a few words.[29]

I do not want to press the analogy with Bede's work too far. Certainly the succession of abbots provides the basic structure of the *DA* but William allows himself flexibility within that framework so that if a king had been especially generous in his endowments to Glastonbury William focuses on him, not on the abbots who ruled during his reign, although he is always careful to note the names of the abbots.[30] More significantly, the different priorities of the twelfth century resulted in different emphases in William's work. His thoughtful attention to the foundation of the monastery, contrasting with Bede's more casual treatment, reflects the growing awareness of the importance of a venerable foundation, just as the embellishment of William's sober account by later interpolators is indicative of the even greater emphasis that was placed on a prestigious foundation later in the twelfth century.[31] Similarly, the care with which William details the relics to be found at Glastonbury shows him to be very much a man of his time; Bede does not ignore the relics that Benedict Biscop brought to England, but they were not as important in the eighth century as they became in the twelfth.[32] It might be argued that the differences are more fundamental, that Bede was writing biography and William local history. Such a distinction would not be invalid but it is to a certain extent a modern one and ignores the veneration in which William held Bede. As Bede's putative successor William would not have ignored the master's work: hence his organisation of material, as far as possible, around the series of abbots, hence his choice of what to say about these abbots.

Despite William's recognition of Bede as his master, the sources on which he was relying posed problems for him that could not be solved merely by a modified imitation of the *Historia Abbatum*. The core of his book was the collection of charters which he included or excerpted and on which he based his list of the monastery's abbots. His work was thus a more elaborate chronicle-cartulary, of which we will note other examples below.[33] Experiments in local histories which concerned themselves with the estates of their monastery had been made before William began to write, especially in the north where Bede's influence persisted strongly; but William does not seem to have been familiar with any of the results.[34] He did know some works whose authors drew on information contained in charters, but none of them had done so in a systematic way. Hermann the archdeacon, the eleventh century hagiographer of St Edmund with whose work William was familiar, had utilised charters in the compilation of his *Miracles*, but only to note the abbey's gains – as Bede had done – and not to provide any more general information.[35] His work is more interesting, as a precursor of the plethora of local histories produced in the twelfth century, in the range of issues on which it concentrates. Hermann reports a number of St Edmund's miracles concerned with preserving the lands of the monastery; he details at length an unsuccessful attempt by the bishop of Thetford to claim jurisdiction over the abbey; and he savours the grand occasion on which the saint's relics were translated to the new church.[36] There are obvious similarities with William's work but this is more a reflection of common monastic concerns than of direct inspiration.

More relevant to William's task of summarising the Glastonbury charters and extracting historical information from them was the work carried out at Worcester, especially that done at the instigation of bishop Wulfstan, who was particularly conscious of the importance of comprehensive records of the estates claimed by the monastery. William's well-documented contacts with Worcester suggest that he may have been aware of these developments. We know from his own translation of Colman's *Life of Wulfstan*, undertaken for the monks of Worcester, that he had visited them during the priorate of Nicholas (c.1113-1124) and had returned during the reign of his successor Warin (c.1124-1142) to prepare his translation.[37] Although it has not been possible to identify definitely books from the abbey library which William knew, it can be reasonably asserted that, following his usual practice, he would have searched the library for historical volumes.[38] William was also aware of the historical interest shown by Wulfstan and had probably met John of Worcester, although the connection between these two men has not yet been elucidated.[39] Certainly William's associations with Worcester are close enough to warrant an examination of two Worcester manuscripts whose authors were interested in charters and their historical value.

The first of these, 'Hemming's Cartulary', is well-known but it cannot be established that William was familiar with it, although his interest in Wulfstan, its instigator, and his pursuit of information on the English church enable us to surmise that he may have encountered it.[40] That section of the cartulary that was the work of Hemming, undertaken at the request of Wulfstan, reveals that the latter appreciated the importance of retaining records of the charters by which the monastery had gained possession of its lands (perhaps because, as the last of the Anglo-Saxon bishops, he knew too well the fragility of the monastic past).[41] Hemming states that he has composed his book 'so that it will be clear to our successors what and how many landed possessions came to this monastery as gifts . . . although we may no longer have them because they have been unjustly plundered either by force or by trickery'.[42] If this were all that Hemming achieved, he would have produced a bare cartulary which merely catalogued the estates claimed or possessed by Worcester. Such a straightforward compilation was clearly his main concern, and where he, like William, bolsters his work by quoting from or incorporating charters he does so to lament the estates plundered from Worcester or to describe estates obtained or regained by Ealdred and Wulfstan. This reveals that his purpose was much narrower than William's who was concerned not merely with the possessions of Glastonbury but with the whole of its past. But Hemming, in fact, went a little beyond his stated intentions. He did provide a certain amount of historical background to the fate of the church's estates. His account of those estates which had been alienated, drawn from both oral and written sources, contains, as well as a list of the properties, remarks on the general effects of the Danish invasions and a narrative of the dispute between Wulfstan and abbot Aethelwig of Evesham.[43] Moreover, some biographical data about Wulfstan enlarge that section of the cartulary dealing with his acquisitions.[44] In short, William might have learnt from Hemming the value of preserving charters and, more important, that they could be incorporated into a wider narrative. But the Worcester monk had revealed little of the variety of historical information that charters could yield or how they could be used to construct a continuous narrative.

It is William's organisation of his narrative around the succession of abbots, whose contributions to the landed possessions of the monastery are detailed, that leads on to the second Worcester document, because it evinces a similar method. This work, a short account of the history of Worcester, described as *De pontificali sede. Quomodo primitus statuta sit Wigorne et de possessionibus que a regibus, subregulis et a bone recordationis uiris date sunt Wigornensi ecclesie*, is extant on ff1-3v of CCC, Oxford, MS 157, a manuscript that contains the autograph of John of Worcester's *Chronicon*. As the rubric implies, an account is given of the foundation of the see and this is followed by a summary of various estates granted to Worcester, arranged chronologically in order of the bishops to whom they were given. This list of grants produces an account of the succession of the bishops of Worcester, ending with bishop Samson who died in 1112.[45] Presumably this brief history was written before Samson's death and would have been at Worcester when William visited the church but it is by no means certain that William saw it.[46] It is only a skeletal account as this typical entry reveals: *Uhtred Wicciorum subregulus, licencia regis Offari, Uuerabyrig, anno Dominice incarnacionis DCCLVI Milredo pontificante, ad uictum Wigornensis familie dedit et liberauit.*[47] But its principle of construction is the same as that adopted by William and it could have suggested to him that charter grants were valuable for providing information on the succession of abbots.

We can come closer to the method of the *DA* by examining the *Book of Llandaff*, an elaborate forgery composed in the environment in which William moved, at the same time as his *DA*.[48] The scribe responsible for the greater part of this tract, produced in the context of the great dispute between Llandaff and St David's, began with the *Lives* of three saints claimed by the church, to each of which was appended a series of charters, and then added a series of charters in chronological order with some notes on the succession of bishops.[49] The combination of saints' lives and the deduction of the succession of bishops from a collection of charters strongly parallels William's achievement in the *DA* – except of course that the Llandaff author greatly modified his material – and Brooke has gone as far as to suggest that the Llandaff author can best be understood if we imagine him to have seen William's work.[50] But recent research has uncovered a more definite link, between the scriptoria of Llandaff and Worcester. Specifically, the formulae that are used in the Llandaff charters seem to have been derived from those used at Worcester, and in particular those found in that section of 'Hemming's Cartulary' that was compiled in the second half of the eleventh century and that is associated with Wulfstan and Hemming himself. An explanation for this link is provided by the likelihood that bishop Urban of Llandaff (c.1107-1134) was a priest of Worcester before his promotion.[51]

It begins to look as though the monks of Worcester, with the encouragement of bishop Wulfstan, the Anglo-Saxon survivor in a Norman church, were in the forefront of an endeavour to preserve the charter records of the English church. Although the web of relationships is slender, we can nevertheless detect the impact of the research of Hemming and his fellow monks on the church of Llandaff; and there are reasons too, as we have seen, to suspect that William himself might have gained from them at least an appreciation of the importance of charters, if not an inkling of their wider value to the historian of the Anglo-Saxon church. Yet as we shall see in the next chapter, William's achievement was unique, especially in the use that he was able to make of the Glastonbury charters from which he drew conclusions about a wide range of historical problems. This will become even clearer if we examine similar historical work that was being carried out in other monasteries where there was an attempt to preserve records of the charters that had been granted to them.

At about the same time as William was writing their history for the monks of Glastonbury a monk of Abingdon was investigating the antiquity of his own church and attempting to fashion, from fragmentary materials, an account of its origins and early development.[52] He produced a chronicle-cartulary of a basic type in which he gathered together transcriptions of the monastery's charters in chronological order and connected them by a brief narrative outlining the circumstances of their issue. Although it is not easy to work from the printed text, whose editor conflated the early work with a later thirteenth century one, it is clear that the author was interested above all in preserving a record of the estates which the church had once owned, and that he had no pretensions to produce a thorough history of his house. As an example of the simple narrative by which the charters are introduced the remarks that precede the four charters of King Ine can be quoted: *Abeunte Ceadwalla Romam, Ine successit in regnum. Qui primo praedecessorum suorum donationes irritas facere decrevit; deinde facti poenitens, de suis etiam easdem longe uberius auxit.*[53] Yet it may be remarked that in the *DA* William often contents himself with as bare a summary of the events surrounding a donation, and that the Abingdon monk does not disdain to introduce a much fuller narrative, sometimes of events of national, as opposed to local relevance; he speaks sometimes of the abbots of his monastery in the same way as William does.[54] The real difference between William and the Abingdon monk is that the former attempts something quite new in the *DA*, a history of the monastery, its foundation, the saints associated with it, a list of its abbots and their contribution to its developments, whereas the latter is concerned principally with recording the charters with which the house had been enriched, although, in a quite unsystematic way, he makes occasional historical observations. The charters for William are a means by which he can learn more about the history of Glastonbury; for the Abingdon monk – as for Hemming – their preservation is the chief purpose of his work. Hence William merely summarises many of the Glastonbury charters, while deducing a variety of conclusions from them, but the Abingdon chronicler transcribes the charters complete and adds when possible the bounds of the estates.

If the Abingdon chronicle is the type of chronicle-cartularies – the *Textus Roffensis* is another which springs to mind – whose compilers were merely concerned with the record of grants, a historical work of a different kind, more substantial and more comparable to the *DA*, was undertaken at Ely in the several decades after William had completed his work for Glastonbury.[55] The *Liber Eliensis* is a thorough history of that monastery which draws on a wide range of sources to describe its fate from its foundation to the middle of the twelfth century. However, its author is severely limited by his sources for the years before its refoundation in the tenth century, relying on saints' lives and general histories. He did not have access to the charter evidence that William used so well nor was he able to make archaeological observations of the kind that were available to the historian of Glastonbury.[56] With the appearance of Aethelwold his account becomes much fuller, serving indeed as a sort of compendium of events relating to Ely, in which narrative sources and charter evidence are blended into a whole. Like William he was especially concerned with the monastery's abbots and gives detailed accounts of their rule, the lands they bought or were given and the ornaments for which they were responsible.[57] Nevertheless there are important differences, in particular in the awareness the men show of the usefulness of their sources. For Richard, the likely author of the *Liber Eliensis*, charters are records of landed possessions or of the rights of the monastery, not instruments that can lead to a fuller understanding of the past as they are for William: nor does Richard demonstrate William's keen eye for the physical remains of the past.

The only historical works of the time that can be compared with the *DA* in the range of sources on which they draw and the perceptive use which they make of charters are William's own larger histories and in particular his *GP*. I want to turn now, therefore, to a consideration of the place of the *DA* in the corpus of William's writings and to an examination of the historical skills which he developed in his earlier works and applied so fruitfully to the history of the church at Glastonbury.

3

The *De Antiquitate* and William's historical output

SOUTHERN has made clear that we can understand the prolific Anglo-Norman historians of the early twelfth century only if we imaginatively reconstruct the environment in which they wrote and the challenges which their way of life was undergoing.[1] These sprang from the Norman Conquest, an event which profoundly disturbed the ecclesiastical establishment of England and both stimulated the writing of history and determined the view of the past adopted by the historians. Their attitude to the conquerors was necessarily ambivalent, because although on the one hand the Normans were oppressors, and the churches often the main sufferers, on the other hand an ultimately providential conception of history necessitated seeing them as carrying out God's will.[2] This tension was exacerbated by the English historiographical tradition, which had interpreted the Anglo-Saxon defeat of the Britons as a victory for God's chosen people over a morally bankrupt race:[3] yet now these same chosen people had themselves been conquered. The most obvious way to interpret the event was to regard the Norman victory as a divinely inspired punishment of the Anglo-Saxons for themselves sinking into corruption. That William was inclined to reason in this manner seems clear from that notorious passage, worked up from a few hints thrown out by Eadmer, in which he denigrates the pre-Conquest church as lax and worldly.[4] We ought not be surprised, certainly not condemnatory, that William should have seized the opportunity to suggest an explanation for so cataclysmic an event.

Yet the forces urging a different view of the Anglo-Saxon church were even stronger. On a general level there was the conservative nature of monastic communities, 'a predisposition towards the traditional',[5] an approach that, on some views, manifested itself historiographically in the belief that all action was a disturbance of an ideal state and that stasis ought to be restored as soon as possible.[6] In the same context the influence of the 'golden age' topos must be borne in mind, an idea that had perhaps been important in Bede's wish for the church to regain a recently lost simplicity.[7] Leaving aside such considerations, there was much in their day-to-day lives that would lead the Anglo-Norman historians to take a more positive view of their pre-Conquest past. That past was all around them, in the books they read, the saints they venerated and the buildings they worshipped them in, and in the very language that many of them spoke; to reject these things would be to deny their whole way of life. Moreover, as William pointed out in the Prologue to his *GP*, it was from the fathers of the Anglo-Saxon church that his generation had learned the rudiments of the faith and had been instructed in Christian morality.[8] Whatever their view of the Norman kings it was impossible for the monk-historians of the early twelfth century to turn their backs on the past of their church.

Yet this is what they were expected to do. Malmesbury was not spared the threats to its cherished saints and its traditional estates that I have already outlined as characteristic of the problems of the post-Conquest church.[9] The first Norman abbot, Turold, was uncanonically appointed while Brihtric was still alive and was a disastrous head; he soon fell out with his monks because of his belligerent behaviour and he forced King William, who had appointed him as a reward for services rendered, to translate him to Peterborough where he would have someone to fight.[10] Warin, his successor, allowed the monastery to be despoiled by William II and alienated the monks further by his cavalier treatment of the relics of their saints, even professing doubts about Aldhelm himself until he was converted by a miracle. Then in 1118 the monastery fell into the clutches of Roger of Salisbury who retained control of it until his death in 1139.[11] William and his brothers, in other words, like so many of their fellow monks, were confronted by superiors who did not respect, or who even denied, the traditions that they lived by and who flouted the rights that they had accumulated over centuries and it was this behaviour that was the stimulus for the outburst of historical writing.

The historians hoped to recreate the glory of the Anglo-Saxon past by resurrecting its traditions for the new rulers of the Church, and to demonstrate that the continuity of English church life had not been dislocated by the events of 1066. The emphasis on continuity, especially important for the church, can be seen in William's remarks at the end of his secular history: even with that work the one achievement on which he congratulates himself is that of having put together the first continuous history of the *English* (*continuam Anglorum historiam*) since Bede.[12] We will find these two themes, the greatness of the Anglo-Saxon past and especially of its saints and the continuity of that past with the present, in all of William's historical works up to the *DA* which is in many ways the firmest articulation of them. It should be pointed out at once that one facet of this greatness is found in its very age, that the mere antiquity of an institution, particularly if it were associated with sanctity, was in itself laudable. William makes this clear in the Prologue to the *DA* in which he declares that it will be to the honour of the church if he establishes its beginnings and traces its history from its origins.[13] History is used to serve the present by establishing its ties with an ancient and glorious past. Let us follow this idea in William's works through to its culmination in the *DA*.

The *GR*, his first, was unique in being commissioned by a secular patron, Queen Matilda; yet she seems to have shared the view of history outlined above. Hearing that she was descended from the line of the West Saxon kings, she requested that a book be produced which would reflect the full history of her ancestors and so cover her with glory. Upon her death William abandoned the work, but was encouraged to break his silence by his friends and by his own feelings that such great men and deeds should not be lost to memory.[14] The preface to the work clearly expresses the intentions of the author: there was a gap in the record of history between the death of Bede and the era with which Eadmer began his work and William wanted to fill that gap, both because of his love for his homeland (*propter patriae caritatem*) and because of the authority of those who were encouraging him.[15] The letters prefixed to the Troyes MS which beg the assistance of King David of Scotland and the Empress Matilda in detaching the monastery from the control of Roger suggest that those who were encouraging him may have been his own brethren and also illuminate the problems of the monks as outlined above.[16] William's intentions are reinforced in the preface to the second book, in which he records his labours to extract from foreign chronicles anything memorable about his own people, and his desire to bring to light events that were hidden in the heap of antiquity.[17] Of course, patriotic zeal to recover his country's antiquity is not the only motivation that the preface records – inevitably, history as *exemplum* figures largely, good deeds to be emulated, bad one eschewed[18] – nor do the contents of the *GR* reflect such single-mindedness. But it is revealing that when William does trespass beyond England he attempts to justify the digression and is aware that it is not part of the plan for his work.[19] We might note too a certain selectivity in his coverage of the Anglo-Saxon kingdoms: he passes quickly over the East Angles and the East Saxons, the least powerful – and therefore the least glorious – of the early kingdoms, with the comment that they are unworthy of his labour or the regard of posterity.[20]

This purpose, to honour the Anglo-Saxon past by recreating its glory, came even more to the fore in the *GP*, a work that William was already contemplating while he was in the throes of composing the *GR.*[21] Unlike his first work, the *GP* was apparently not commissioned, but was a labour of love in which the historian reminded his contemporaries of the debt they owed to the Anglo-Saxon church. There were two main themes in the work: one was to eulogise the famous saints of the country, disgracefully neglected by other writers, and to express his love for them;[22] and the other was to establish the continuity of episcopal succession, recording, if that were all he knew (as it often was) at least the names of Anglo-Saxon bishops.[23] These two facets of the English church, its sanctity and its long, continuous existence, were what its defenders emphasised – as William did in his work at Glastonbury – and so Southern is able to assert that the *GP* extended 'to the whole kingdom the corporate aims of each monastic researcher of his day.'[24]

This concern for his native saints found further expression in his subsequent writings, the *VW* and the Glastonbury commissions. Because of Wulfstan's special place in the history of the Anglo-Saxon church, as the last of its bishops and because of his own dedication to the task of preserving the past of the church, William's translation of his *Life* fulfilled his own plans as well as satisfying the wishes of the prior and convent of Worcester. As the *VW* is a translation of the English Life by Coleman it is worth taking note here of William's attitude to fellow workers in the field of hagiography. Although he sometimes made specific criticisms of their work,[25] on the whole he was grateful to anyone who helped to celebrate the virtues and miracles of the English saints: Coleman's work received the highest praise in William's resolve to make few changes to it in his translation[26] and the prolific hagiographer Goscelin of St Bertin was extravagantly lauded in the *GR* for his work in restoring knowledge of those ancients whose memories had been lost.[27]

It should now be obvious how William's writings for the monks of Glastonbury continue the themes of his earlier works. He arrived at their church as an historian and hagiographer whose talents had been employed, either on his own behalf or for others, in the recovery and recreation of the glory of the Anglo-Saxon past and its great saints and in the demonstration of the continuity of the English church. He found there material with which to celebrate the lives of four more saints, including one of England's most illustrious, St Dunstan, and evidence that the monastery had a large collection of saints' relics. He found too, evidence, mainly in charters but also in the physical remains of the past, that the church had a long history; even more significantly he discovered that he could trace the continuous succession of the abbots of the monastery for most of its history. As a result he was able to uphold the glory of the oldest church in England against some recent sceptics and to reaffirm the antiquity and sanctity of the whole English church in this one example.[28] If the long continuity that he was able to demonstrate at Glastonbury – comparable only to the history of his own abbey that filled the last book of the *GP* – was in many ways the culmination of the work that he had been doing on the Anglo-Saxon church, it was certainly methodologically dependent on the experience that he had gained in the earlier work. It is to a consideration of William's methodology that I want to turn now.

A striking feature of the *DA* is the wide range of sources on which William drew to complete his picture, particularly the information that he was able to extract from charters and from archaeological remains, and he had demonstrated a similar facility in his earlier works. In the *GR* he incorporated a very wide range of written sources – from earlier histories to letters, from hagiographies to a topographical description of Rome – and included a fair number of documents, as had Eusebius and Bede before him, but charters were relatively unimportant. The synthesis that he produced from his multitudinous sources was masterly and measured; even Stubbs, who was more interested in William's independent contributions, admitted that: 'In the first two books, certainly, he has brought together all that he could find, and, where he was able to balance conflicting accounts of the same event, has shown discrimination in doing so.'[29] This is certainly not the place to undertake a full study of William's use of sources in the *GR*: all that I want to do is to consider briefly the use that he makes of charters. Such a consideration reveals that even in his first historical work William demonstrated an appreciation of the uses to which an historian could put charters.

It seems that William incorporated a number of Malmesbury charters into the *GR* chiefly to compensate for the inadequacy of other sources of information. Thus, neither Bede nor the *ASC* could provide him with very much about bishop Leuthere, who had patronised William's own monastery, and so to remedy the deficiency William transcribed part of the bishop's charter to Malmesbury.[30] Similarly, more light is thrown on the character of King Athelstan by selective quotation from a charter which reveals his wisdom and piety.[31] More adventurous was William's use of a charter of King Edgar from which he quoted in order to substantiate a generalisation about the monastic revival of that king's time. He introduced it thus: 'At that time the monastic order, which had been depressed for a long time, raised up its head; whereby it happened that even our monastery regained its former liberty, which perhaps can be made known more conveniently in the words of the king himself.'[32] This insight into historical method is matched by the skill with which William employed charter evidence to build up a picture of King Aethelbald of Mercia.

It is worth investigating William's treatment of King Aethelbald in a little more detail in order to show that even in his earliest work he was able to construct a coherent picture of events from a few disparate sources. William knew a charter of this king freeing all monasteries and churches from their main public burdens and he knew what the *ASC* could tell him: which was that the king ruled for 41 years, had been harshly rebuked by Boniface and had, with Cuthbert (also a victim of Boniface's wrath) convoked the Council of Clovesho, whose acts were known to William.[33] William managed to construct a plausible and convincing picture of the king out of these sources, reasoning that he had been converted from his viciousness by Boniface who had inspired him to convoke the Council and that the charter which William knew was a product of that Council and the newly inspired king. These inferences represented received opinion until Haddan and Stubbs demonstrated that it was more likely that Boniface's rebuke of Cuthbert post-dated the Council and that Aethelbald's charter was issued in 749, two years after Clovesho.[34] That William was wrong is not as important as that he endeavoured to fit all his information together intelligently and to locate it in an historical context. In this endeavour the king's charter was an important component.

In the *GP* William continued to draw on charters to fill gaps left by his other sources. In particular, they were important for his task of tracing the fortunes (especially the material fortunes) of his own monastery. He extracted from them the names of abbots and included not only the grants made to those abbots, but any other details he could discover about them.[35] William therefore knew the historical value of charters before he arrived at Glastonbury and so must have realised what a treasure was available to him in the *Liber Terrarum*. Initially he had to grapple with the doubts inevitably occasioned by the *incredibilem numerum ac quantitatem terrarum* that the monastery laid claim to. William himself did not doubt that all these estates, as well as others about which he was more uncertain, had been granted to the monastery, and he foresaw the objection that some manors had been granted by a number of different donors. There were, he suggested, a number of possible explanations of this phenomenon: different manors may bear the same name; some may have been conferred, then alienated and finally restored by a later donor; or portions of the one manor may have been the gifts of various donors to each of whom the whole manor was ascribed.[36] Once he had thoughtfully resolved some of the difficulties presented by the charters, he could begin to use them to help him unravel the antiquity of Glastonbury. They were of most use in the task of constructing a list of abbots, but concentration on this did not distract William from reading them with a keen eye for other information. He deduced, from the oldest charter to which he referred, that the unnamed king who issued it must have been British because he gave the island of Glastonbury its British name Yniswitrin and he added, in the *GR*, that this grant confirmed the antiquity of the church which, even then, was described as *uetustus*.[37] Nor was he unaware of the historical context of the charters, as is revealed by his note that at the time when King Caedwalla confirmed a grant with the sign of the cross he was not yet a Christian, and by his speculations about the identity of the recipient of a grant from King Cenwulf.[38]

The important innovation and achievement of the *DA* was William's attempt to substantiate a continuous Christian presence at Glastonbury and an unbroken succession of abbots since at least 601 by reference to the abbey's charters. He thoroughly examined all the charters available to him, not ignoring the witness lists, and was able to draw up a list of abbots from Beorhtwald, the first abbot whose name he could locate on a charter, to Henry of Blois, while filling in the years before then, as much as he could, with the help of local traditions. He also calculated the lengths of the abbacies of some, although he did so by assuming erroneously that the first charter-mention of an abbot represented the date of his appointment.[39] There is no need to investigate the accuracy of William's computations because this has already been done by Robinson, who concluded that for the centuries prior to 900 – after which there are few charters anyway – William is on the whole very reliable, and has submitted the charters to 'patient investigation' although he may at times have been misled by faulty or unreliable charters.[40] The recent editors of *Heads of Religious Houses* admire William's research while dismissing the independent value of his results,[41] but even modern scholars with more resources and sophisticated techniques are uncertain with the pre-Conquest period; the easier task of making up lists of bishops cannot yet be done with finality.[42] I think that we can conclude that William had realised the historical potential of charters when he perused those from his own monastery for the composition of his early books; and so, when he came to Glastonbury, he saw that he could use its charters for the important task of establishing the long and continuous succession of its abbots.

The thoughtful examination of charters is one aspect of William's awareness that any scrap of evidence is vital to the historian trying to conjure up a coherent vision of the past; another facet is his extraction of historical details from the physical remains of the past. This ability was hardly necessary to him in writing the *GR* because the written sources for it were so abundant; but the *GP* was a different project, as William himself announced in the preface where he lamented the poverty of available sources and recognised that he was entering the dense shades of ignorance without the lamp of history to guide him.[43] Perhaps it was this shortage of conventional sources that encouraged him to record whatever he thought might cast a glimmer of light in the darkness. Hence his famous topographical descriptions and, of more interest to us, his use of archaeological evidence. He derives straightforward information from the memorials of the past as when he notes the date on an ancient inscribed stone at Shaftesbury which records the founding of the town by King Alfred in 880.[44] On a different level, he substantiates his account of the translation of the remains of Aldhelm to Malmesbury, organised and recorded by St Ecgwine, by pointing out that the crosses that were erected along the route can still be seen and are known to the local inhabitants as *biscepstane.*[45] The third example worth recording is his quotation of the inscriptions that Cuthbert ordered at Hereford; he wants to show the reader an aspect of Cuthbert's character, that he held his predecessors in great honour.[46]

In this area too, the techniques that William had developed while he was writing his earlier books were invaluable to him at Glastonbury. In fact, the abundance of physical remains there enabled him to extend his facility in interpreting such evidence. The most striking of the remains were the two old 'pyramids' which stood a few feet from the church bordering on the monk's cemetery and these William described very carefully and exactly, recording their precise sizes and the inscriptions on them. He admitted to ignorance of the contents but speculated that contained therein were the bones of those whose names were written on the outside. More than that: he linked the names of some with the names of some of the local districts and could identify others as abbots because he had seen their names elsewhere.[47] It is interesting that Ralph of Coggeshall wrote an account of the discovery of Arthur's tomb about 1195 and described it as between two pyramids 'on which some letters were inscribed, but on account of their great uncouthness and deformation they could not be read.'[48] Either William was more capable than Ralph or the inscriptions had suffered severely in the intervening 60 years.

Apart from this general interest in the monuments of the past, William made use of archaeological observations to obtain information that was otherwise unavailable. There was no charter evidence relating to the years between 601 and 670 but a picture that William had seen near the altar enabled him to record at least the names of three of the intervening abbots and to deduce from their names that they must have been British.[49] Again, a picture of abbot Stihtheard about whom nothing else is known, permits William to suggest that his name did not belie his character as he is shown with a whip.[50] Similarly the scant details available about Benignus are supplemented by recording his sepulchral inscription, a practice that William habitually observed.[51] I think that we can conclude that just as the skills that William had developed in the interpretation of charters were brought to bear on the *Liber Terrarum* of Glastonbury, so was what he had learnt about the historical value of the physical remains of the past. Indeed, the *DA* best exhibits his techniques because so much of it had to be written without access to conventional written sources and so forced him to utilise all that he had learnt about historical research. No available evidence could be ignored under the stimulus of such a project.

This is the place to make some remarks about a very important source of information for William, and indeed for all medieval historians: oral testimony. The first fact to be remarked is that the testimony of an eye-witness was considered impeccable; inevitably so in a society in which written records were just beginning to supplant oral testimony and important reports were still entrusted to messengers rather than to writing.[52] Besides, the historian of the Anglo-Saxon church often had only oral tradition to assist him. If there were any doubts about the validity of such reports – and we shall see that William had some – they could be eased by reference to the authority of Bede, who explicitly spelt out his debt to oral reports, or even to Gregory the Great or Luke the Evangelist.[53] This is not to say that William believed and recorded whatever he was told; indeed he twice rejects *opiniones volaticae*, contrasting them on the one hand with chronicle evidence and on the other with visible proof or an historical record.[54] It is by no means clear what the contrasts are that William has in mind here and only a study of specific instances will enable us to be sure. I do not intend a thorough examination of William's use of oral tradition nor do I want to award him marks or demerits for critical acumen, but rather to refer to some of his experiences with such sources prior to his exposure to the rich tradition of Glastonbury.

Certain stories are granted unquestioning belief, especially tales of visions and miracles, not only because of the long hagiographic tradition that William was heir to, with his master Bede an irreproachable model, but because scepticism would have undermined one of the bases of religion. As William himself put it in reporting a vision of Wulfstan's presence with the saints in glory, 'anyone who does not believe their words offends against religion.'[55] He made a similar point, with a slightly different emphasis, when he protested that his reluctance to record the names of the saints buried at Thorney was not due to disbelief, because he had no authority to call into dispute what had been consecrated by holy antiquity.[56] Similarly, tales of marvels or legends are recorded without contradiction: the belief in an active and malevolent demonic presence was unquestioned and stories of natural phenomena, such as the outlandish mice stories,[57] were quite within the bounds of reason for someone whose knowledge of natural phenomena came from bestiaries. All this is just to say that William was a man of his time and saw no reason to question what was generally believed.

Yet most of these stories in the *GR* are peripheral to William's stated historical purpose and it will be more revealing to study his reliance on oral testimony in regard to matters that pertain directly to the deeds of the English kings. The sections on King Athelstan are filled out with some material from popular ballads but William cautions that it is not as trustworthy as his earlier details and that he cannot vouch for its veracity but has included it so as not to deprive the reader of knowledge.[58] The legend concerning the assassination of William, Duke of Normandy is firmly labelled as such and is followed by an account of *veraciores litterae.*[59] The common report, the work of rumour-mongers, *rumigeruli*, that Godwin had been responsible for the death of Aethelred's son Alfred is included but once again William does not vouch for it, on this occasion because it is not in the *ASC.*[60] We might finally note his warning that he has not included all of the deeds of Baldwin in the Holy Land, but only those he found in writing, because an historian ought not believe every flattering report and so deceive the good faith of his listeners.[61]

I think that we can conclude that William was circumspect in his reliance on oral tradition in the *GR* and was certainly aware that it ought at least be distinguished from written evidence – his attitude was perforce different when he had only oral testimony to rely upon as in his account of the Norman kings. This same hesitant approach is revealed in an important section of the *GP*, where William is introducing the miracles of Aldhelm, a subject of great importance to him and one which should have given him few qualms. He begins by admitting that he lacks written testimony for the miracles and justifies his reliance on the traditions of the monastery by assuring his readers that they have the approbation of all, that they have been handed down through succeeding generations by continuous succession and so must have some basis and that God had implanted them in the minds of men lest they disappear from memory. Besides, if he is to be condemned, then so are Saints Luke and Gregory, who wrote of much greater things on the basis of oral tradition. He rounds off a lengthy defence with the remark that the miracles do not lack visible proof anyway, because they are inscribed on a silver reliquary.[62] The point to note is the need William felt to justify his dependence on local tradition for these miracles, as though he were aware that the miracles might be questioned on that account, and that an earlier written source would have been more acceptable. Perhaps he was aware too that his own ties to the monastery would render the account even more suspicious.

In any assessment of William's attitude to oral tradition, the Glastonbury works and particularly the *DA* are crucial because they rely so heavily on local legends. Certainly his knowledge of the Celtic saints depends largely on oral accounts but in most cases there was no reason for William to doubt these. He knew from the lives of Dunstan by 'B' and Osbern that notable Irishmen had come to Glastonbury because of its associations with Patrick;[63] and that Benignus was one of these was proved by the monument erected to him, and by the words of the *vita tertia* that Patrick had baptised a Benignus who was to become his successor.[64] For the others there was no reason not to accept that Indract and Bridget had been among the disciples, although William does express doubt that the latter was buried there despite the memorials she had left behind.[65] He accepts the account of the vision that appeared to St David when he came to consecrate the church at Glastonbury but professes himself unsure where that saint was buried, despite the fact that local tradition, as expressed in a later interpolation, held that it had been proved that he was not buried in his own church.[66] William's version of the life of St Patrick is the only occasion on which his account is at odds with the written sources that he knew. That the saint was buried at Glastonbury was affirmed by two of Dunstan's biographers and by the version of the *vita tertia* that William was using, but none of them suggest that he had become abbot there or even spent any time there. The account of his arrival in Britain and of his subsequent life at Glastonbury can only be based on the traditions of the monastery. I think that one can argue that the clear evidence of Patrick's interment at Glastonbury and the strength of the local tradition bolstered by a vision convinced William that the lives he had seen were accurate for the saint's missionary activity in Ireland but could not adequately explain his connection with his burial place and that the stories he was told rectified this deficiency.[67]

On the whole, then, for William, as for his contemporaries, the word of reliable men, *traditio maiorum* or *traditio patrum*, was as reliable a basis for a historian to found his work on as was a written record, although this did not preclude warning the reader that some uncertainty attached to some such propositions.[68] It therefore needs to be explained why William rejected two of the local Glastonbury legends. The first of these, already mentioned, was William's refusal to believe that the monks had translated the body of St Dunstan to their church in the eleventh century, although the monks had been putting that story around since at least the early 1120s. The interpolation of a lengthy account of that event into the *DA* indicates that it must have been close to the heart of the Glastonbury community and so William must have had to resist considerable pressure to adopt it. William's association with Canterbury and his support of that church must have persuaded him that the Glastonbury monks were wrong and that, moreover, the Canterbury community would be deeply offended if he were to betray their interest (Eadmer's letter reveals the depths of their feelings), but the affair must have placed William in an awkward position in relation to his hosts.[69] Less easy to account for is William's treatment of Gildas, about whom he merely says that he was attracted by the sanctity of Glastonbury and spent many years there. A later interpolater added that Gildas had died at Glastonbury and was buried before the altar, but the fully developed legend was much richer, and to find it we need to examine the *Life of Gildas* by William's contemporary Caradoc of Llancarvan. This work portrays Gildas as coming to Glastonbury in the time of King Melvas, writing his history while there and also mediating in a dispute between that king and king Arthur. As a result of this successful mediation the kings gave many territories to the church, promised to obey Gildas faithfully and swore never to violate that most sacred place again.[70] It is impossible not to believe that some version of this legend was circulating at Glastonbury while William was there, and yet his work shows no sign of it.[71] It can hardly be asserted that the story affronted William's credibility, since it is intrinsically no more unlikely than the Patrick legends that he reported. His scepticism is obviously linked with his suspicion of other 'idle ravings' about king Arthur and his wish for more 'reliable facts' about him. I can only suggest, very hesitantly, that the political climate persuaded William that he should be very circumspect in the support which he gave to Arthurian legends and that this attitude influenced his presentation of Gildas.[72]

I think that I have succeeded in showing thus far the extent to which the task which William undertook in the *DA* forced him to draw on all the technical skills that he knew; the shortage of conventional written sources impelled William to pore over the Glastonbury charters with his already practised eye, to examine the physical remains of the past with an awareness of what they could tell him and to give a ready ear to those local legends which could fill in gaps in the past without offending the sensibilities of the present. Technically, the *DA* is the culmination of William's historical training. More than that, however, William brought to the *DA* the historical awareness that he had acquired in writing his earlier works. In particular, he was able to fit local events into their historical framework. The simplest example is the introductory remarks to the charter of King Cnut which make plain the circumstances of the grant, by reference to King Edmund's early death, his burial at Glastonbury and Cnut's decision to honour him because of the fraternal treaty which they had agreed upon. Most of it was based on his own work in the *GR* and provides an example of the way in which William could use his knowledge of English history to make his account of a charter grant both fuller and more convincing.[73]

Another instance of William's supplying a skeleton context for a charter is his introduction to the grants of Pope Leo and King Cenwulf in which he enumerates the kings who were ruling at the time and refers the reader who wants more details to the *GR*. The importance of this introduction will become clear from an examination of the problems associated with the two grants and William's analysis of them.[74] The Pope granted the abbey of Glastonbury to *Cynhelm rex* and King Cenwulf confirmed the grant. The difficulty concerns the identity of the grantee, whom William thought ought to be Cynehelm the son of Cenwulf; but he was familiar with a *Passio Kenelmi* which portrayed Cynehelm as succeeding his father in 819 as a seven year old boy and being murdered a few months later at the instigation of his sister. Given that Cenwulf had confirmed the charter in 797 William could do no more than provide the reader with as much relevant information as possible and confess that he himself was unable to identify the Cynehelm to whom the grant had been made. The grants present no problem today because the apocryphal nature of much of the *Passio Kenelmi* is recognised, as is the contemporary custom of referring to members of the royal family who have been given some share of authority as *rex*,[75] but this does not detract from William's achievement in seeing a need to identify the personages about whom he was writing, drawing on his knowledge of English history to attempt to do that and recognising that the most likely identification was not justified by his sources.

William's knowledge and understanding of English history enabled him to see single events in their total context and grasp their significance for the direction in which the whole flowed. Isolated occurrences suddenly assumed prominence because of their relationship with analogous or contemporary events. The alleged request by King Lucius to Pope Eleutherius for Christian missionaries was well known because it was reported both by Bede and the *ASC*[76] but no details were known about this most important event which heralded the first encounter between Christianity and Britain. Despite these deficiencies in his sources, William was able to call on his historical understanding in order to highlight the significance of the request. Firstly, he set the king's request in its historical context, pointing out that his contemporaries had all been persecuting the faith and that Lucius himself had only hearsay knowledge of it. At once Lucius' action seems more striking to the reader and its historical significance becomes clearer. Then William drew an analogy between Lucius' behaviour and the reception of the Gregorian missionaries by Aethelberht centuries later. This comparison with a later event of undoubted importance tellingly illuminated Lucius' deed in a way that not even Bede had attempted.[77]

A similar demonstration of William's imaginative grasp of the past is found in his discussion of the claim that the church at Glastonbury had been built by the disciples of Christ. Because he was able to situate this claim in its appropriate historical context William could point out that the historian Freculph had recorded that St Philip had preached to the Gauls and that therefore it was possible that the saint had also cast the seeds of truth across the Channel. This plausible hypothesis was recognised for what it was by William who concluded the reasoning with the remark that he had better return to the narration of solid truth.[78] What is striking here is not merely the attempt to collect evidence for an hypothesis from appropriate sources, but the realisation that such evidence was still purely speculative and ought to be distinguished from the evidence on which other conclusions were based. Both of these examples illustrate William's historical perspective and demonstrate his ability to grasp the essence of an historical event. They reveal his ability to seize on and explicate other events that will help the reader to understand and evaluate the first. In his attempt to recreate the total past of the church of Glastonbury William was forced to call on all the skills that he had developed in his earlier historical writings.

In fine, the *DA* occupies an important place in the corpus of William's historical writings. It was the last work that he wrote in which he upheld the Anglo-Saxon past and defended the English church from the attacks of Norman critics. Glastonbury provided him with an unparalleled opportunity to establish the sanctity of the English church and its continued existence throughout the centuries preceding the Conquest despite external threats to its survival. Moreover, the Glastonbury commission inspired him to utilise all the skills that he had acquired and all the insights that he had gained in his years of studying the past of his country. Yet for all William's skill and his success in establishing the antiquity of Glastonbury and the aura of sanctity that had always pervaded it the monks soon found that it was no longer adequate for their needs. They found themselves in a new world, facing different challenges that could not be parried by boasting of the great age of their monastery or celebrating the glorious Celtic saints who had made pilgrimages to it. In the great age of forgery the *DA* needed to be embellished, and it is to that process that I will now turn.

4

Forgery and the interpolations in the *De Antiquitate*

THE main task that had confronted William's generation of historians had been to save some of the traditions and honour of the Anglo-Saxon church in the face of the wholesale importation of Norman churchmen. The Benedictines of the late twelfth and early thirteenth centuries had to confront even more serious threats to their position and influence in society, which was being challenged by the prestige of the Cistercians and the striking popularity of the friars and undermined by the state which no longer relied on monks as advisers and administrators. One of the results of this was that many monasteries rewrote their histories in order to exaggerate the antiquity of their foundations and add to the aura of sanctity that surrounded them in the hope that they would succeed in the competition for pilgrims.[1] The situation of the Glastonbury monks was more serious than most because their problems had been exacerbated by a fire which had destroyed the monastery in 1184 and by the struggle that they waged for their independence against the bishop of Bath.[2] In their desperate need for funds they indulged in a number of propaganda exercises, of which one was the revision of the *DA*, in order to make their church more attractive to pilgrims. Rather than trace the legendary accretions to William's work, a task already performed by Gransden,[3] I want to set them in the context of similar endeavours by other monasteries in the hope of demonstrating that the notoriety of Glastonbury is undeserved.

The prestige of a monastery was greatly increased if it could establish an ancient foundation and a saintly founder.[4] William had served Glastonbury well on this score by identifying the builders of the church as the missionaries who had been sent by Pope Eleutherius to King Lucius; but, in a confessedly speculative aside, he raised the even more appealing possibility that the church had been founded by the disciples themselves.[5] This hint was taken up by the monks who boldly expanded William's sober and guarded account. They gave names to the missionaries, who had been unknown to William, and invented a document in which Phagan and Deruvian recounted the story of the foundation of Glastonbury by the disciples of St Philip.[6] The truth of these new assertions was guaranteed by the fantastic charter of St Patrick, a concoction of these legends, some unlikely papal indulgences and some fanciful stories about Patrick himself, which was probably put together about 1220.[7] An even later embellishment of the foundation story brought Joseph of Arimathea to Glastonbury as the leader of the missionaries sent by St Philip and thenceforth his integral connection with the monastery was reaffirmed and elaborated.[8]

Myth-making of this kind was not confined to Glastonbury and there is a striking parallel in the writings of the Abingdon monks, who developed a plethora of foundation legends. Like the Glastonbury monks they too set about rewriting a fairly simple chronicle, which had been produced about 1130 and had attributed the foundation of the monastery to the west Saxon king Cissa and its consolidation to his successors Caedwalla and Ine. By the late thirteenth century the story had been completely revised and actually began – a tribute perhaps to the success of the Glastonbury propaganda – with the mission of 'Fagn' and 'Divian' to King Lucius. These two, however, were not credited with the building of the church, an honour that belonged to the Irish monk Abennus, a contemporary of Diocletian to whom the British kings gave a large part of the province of Berkshire. To the monastery which Abennus founded he attracted some 300 monks who lived under the Rule of St Benedict and maintained the faith until the coming of the English.[9] The similarities between these inventions and the Glastonbury interpolations, going well beyond the adoption of the Lucius legend, need hardly be stressed. Both situate their foundations in an early age of special sanctity (the era of the apostles and of the persecutions of Diocletian), and both associate the early years of their monastery with an Irish holy man (Patrick, Abennus), as though to benefit from the reputation for sanctity that Bede had given the Irish hermits. Needless to say, both emphasise the generosity that the British kings had shown to their house.[10]

While Abingdon provides the best other example of a wholesale rewriting of the early history of a monastery, many other houses made extravagant claims about their foundations. Westminster propounded the view that its consecration in the seventh century was attended by an appearance of St Peter who assured a simple fisherman that he had already consecrated the church to himself – analogous to the Glastonbury claim that Christ had consecrated the church there in honour of himself and his mother.[11] This legend however had already been formulated by the end of the eleventh century and we have to look elsewhere to find monks tampering with the received history of their monastery's foundation. The antiquity of Ely was securely established on the magisterial authority of Bede, who had recorded its foundation by Aethelthryth in about 660 but this was no longer satisfactory in the twelfth century. The monks began to propagate the view that Aethelthryth had in fact rebuilt a church originally constructed by St Augustine and subsequently destroyed by Penda. Moreover, the account of the refoundation by St Aethelwold in the tenth century was modified to give the impression that there had been clerics living on the site before the saint's arrival.[12] The monks of Bury too, it can be noted, continually elaborated the stories concerning the beginning of church life in the borough and tried to lengthen the monastic tradition on which the house could draw.[13] These examples demonstrate that Glastonbury was not unique in manipulating its history in order to be able to claim an early foundation and associate its origins with a well-known saint.

If an ancient and venerable foundation was an important means of securing a monastery's prestige and attracting pilgrims, an even greater boon was the possession of the relics of a powerful saint.[14] Although the saints' lives that William wrote and the catalogue of relics that he included in the *DA* must have contributed to the monastery's reputation, the monks were not at all satisfied with his work, especially, as we have seen, with his treatment of St Dunstan.[15] Their dissatisfaction must have become more pressing after the canonisations of King Edward, whose remains were at Westminster, and Becket, whose martyrdom at once made Canterbury the most popular destination of pilgrims.[16] The fire of 1184 which made their need for funds even more urgent, because it destroyed many of their treasures and damaged their relic collection, was not without its compensations.[17] It reminded the monks of the local legend about the burial of St Dunstan, whose remains the monks did indeed claim to have found after a diligent search. It must have been soon after the fire that they incorporated into the *DA* a lengthy account of the translation of the saint's remains and the subsequent happy discovery of them after the fire in circumstances that permitted no possibility of doubt.[18] Yet the possession of the relics of Dunstan, like those of Patrick, did not go unchallenged and the monks' claim that they possessed the remains of Gildas and David, asserted in their interpolations in the *DA*, could hardly have been felt to be adequate compensation.[19]

The monks desperately needed an unimpeachable attraction for pilgrims, relics whose possession would be unchallenged and whose appeal would be widespread. The purported discovery of the bones of king Arthur fitted the bill exactly. It is not certain whether the inspiration for this invention came from Henry II, as asserted by Gerald of Wales, or from the monks themselves, stimulated by the association with Arthur that had already been adumbrated by Caradoc;[20] but, once concocted, Arthur's links with Glastonbury became an important element in the local legends. Curiously, an account of the discovery of his remains is not to be found in the *DA*, although other facets of the legend are incorporated, including an adventure of the king's with the young prince Ider, which is used to justify the monastery's possession of certain lands, and a far-fetched story which explains that Avalon is an alternative name for Glastonbury.[21] The boldness of the monks was not content with the spectacular exhumation of Arthur's bones. They seem to have endeavoured, with no little success, to ensure that the story would become widely known, by inviting Gerald of Wales along as a spectator and reporter and by circulating an account of the occasion to other monasteries.[22]

Once again we find that other monasteries tried to bolster their reputations by similarly elaborating stories about the saints whose relics they possessed. The thirteenth-century Abingdon history mentioned above added to the earlier account of local history the detail that St Helen had lived on the site of the monastery and that a miraculous black cross found there in the tenth century was associated with her or her son Constantine.[23] Incidentally it ought to be noted here that the Glastonbury interpolators did not fail to insert descriptions of certain holy objects, analogous to the black cross of Abingdon, into the *DA*, again with the intention, no doubt, of adding to the monastery's appeal to pilgrims.[24] Although the Abingdon monks were untiring in the propagation of their monastery's glory the best parallel to the vigour with which the Glastonbury monks advertised the fame of their relics is to be found at Westminster. We have already remarked upon the local belief that St Peter had consecrated the church, but during the twelfth century the monks began to search for a more exclusive and proximate patron, probably because they, like the monks of Glastonbury, were under attack from their local bishop.[25] They began to promote the sanctity of King Edward the Confessor whose body lay in their church. It is no surprise to find that the campaign was led by that indefatigable hagiographer Osbert of Clare whose spirited defence of the rights of his own monastery led to his being twice banished from it. It was he who wrote a *Life* of the king and led the mission to Rome that offered that *Life* in an endeavour to win his canonisation. Our main interest is in Osbert's *Life* and especially in the modifications which he made to the earlier *Life* that was the main source for his own work.[26] These related mainly to the miracles of the king and to his chaste relationship with his wife, because Osbert's problem was not to establish Westminster's possession of the king's body but rather to prove that he had been a saint. Unfortunately the harvest of miracles was meagre and Osbert could only introduce five that had been performed between 1066 and 1134, although he was able to recount a promising translation that took place in 1102.[27] More revealing than these outright additions are the revisions that Osbert made. Edward is made to be younger than his brother Alfred so that God's reservation of the crown for him can be seen as a miracle; the king of the Danes is said to have refrained from recognising Edward and is therefore miraculously chastised; and the last words of Edward to his wife are altered in order to emphasise the chasteness of their relationship.[28] In short, Osbert changed his source so as to glorify the king and bring about the canonisation that would bring so much prestige to his monastery. In fact his labours bore no fruit in his own day, but within a generation the king's sanctity was recognised and Osbert's *Life* served as the basis for the official *Life* written by Ailred of Rievaulx. Ailred too changed his source to make his *Life* more suitable for the needs of the day. He introduced anti-Wessex propaganda, incorporated some miracles that occurred during Osbert's priorate and laid particular stress on the sanctity of the church through its connection with St Peter whose support, he affirmed, would be invaluable in the next life.[29] Moreover, in a more specific parallel with the Glastonbury legends, the links between Westminster and St Denis, both closely aligned with royalty, were emphasised by the Westminster forgers, just as the Glastonbury monk who visited St Denis was said to have been assured that the two monasteries had an equal status, except perhaps that Glastonbury, by virtue of being a second Rome, was greater.[30]

Further evidence could also be adduced to demonstrate the importance that was placed on the possession of a saint whose holiness and ability to perform miracles were generally acknowledged and could be expected to attract pilgrims to pay homage – and offerings. The monks of Bury had to keep producing evidence of the miracles performed at the shrine of St Edmund, just as the Canterbury monks maintained a record of the miracles of St Thomas.[31] The monks of Ely revised the legends about Saints Seaxburg and Eormenhild, so as to establish that their bodies had been translated thither, and engaged in a dispute with the monks of St Alban's over the whereabouts of the martyr's remains which they claimed to have come into their possession at the time of the Conquest.[32] This latter affair, reminiscent of the quarrel between Glastonbury and Canterbury over St Dunstan, reminds us that the Glastonbury monks may have been more imaginative than most other communities in manipulating the story of their past to suit their present needs, but that they were not engaged in an activity of a different kind. No monastic communities were averse to modifying the writings they possessed if these no longer served their current requirements.

Is there any evidence about the use to which the legends of a house were put by its monks? In most cases, local histories had no circulation outside the community concerned and the monks seem to have relied on word of mouth to have their claims known abroad. There is nice evidence that this was not considered ineffective in Eadmer's concern that the Glastonbury monks should be telling their story of the translation to their church of the remains of St Dunstan.[33] But the monks of Glastonbury did not rely on word of mouth only. I have already mentioned the care they took to have the exhumation of Arthur bruited abroad, and written publicity of a different kind served to remind pilgrims that Glastonbury deserved their support. I refer to Oxford, Bodl. MS Lat. Hist. a.2., a large manuscript which was affixed to boards attached to a wooden frame in such a way that the whole would unfold and could be read as though it were a book. This was apparently nailed to a prominent wall of the monastery where it would be easily accessible to pilgrims. As one might expect 'it told in full the stories of Joseph of Arimathea and of King Arthur, of St Patrick and his charter, of the translation of the body of St Dunstan, and much besides.'[34]

A monastery's reputation for antiquity and sanctity was not only useful in attracting pilgrims. It also fortified the monks in their struggles to preserve their rights and possessions. Yet strangely Glastonbury did not make much of its history in its long dispute with the bishop of Bath. In none of the documents cited by Adam of Domerham are there any specific references to the circumstances of the monastery's foundation or to its saintly relics. The monks refer to the age and wealth of their church in a letter to King John protesting the loss of their seal and in a lengthy list of articles of complaint against bishop Jocelin of Bath they affirm that their church is the oldest in England and that the memory is preserved of all their abbots.[35] On the other hand the dispute does bring forth a substantial number of letters, from noblemen as well as other monastic communities, which lament the fate that Glastonbury has suffered and demand a restoration of its rights. Although this might seem to suggest the success of the Glastonbury propaganda exercise it has to be noticed that the letters refer principally to the monastery's previous reputation for hospitality and only in general terms to the suffering of the pilgrims.[36] It is difficult to assess, therefore, the extent to which the ultimate success of Glastonbury in that dispute was due to the prestige which its legends had enabled it to acquire. It is perhaps more likely that the whole affair convinced the monks that they needed to do more propaganda work and that the real work of embellishing their history began after its conclusion.

In the contentious area of the relationship between a monastery and its diocesan bishop there was little that the monks needed to add to William's work. He had incorporated in the *DA*, and also in the later recension of the *GR*, three forged Anglo-Saxon charters which pretended to establish Glastonbury's independence.[37] These provided the monks with extensive rights and privileges, especially against their local bishop who in fact in Edgar's charter is specifically said to have no rights over Glastonbury or any of its parish churches.[38] To the rights underlined in these charters the monks made only one bold addition. This was the charter of St Patrick which asserted that a certain Wellias had been one of the saint's disciples, an obvious attempt to challenge the authority of the bishop of Bath and Wells by portraying the eponymous founder of his see as subordinate to the first abbot of Glastonbury.[39]

Claims of immunity from episcopal control inspired forgery in other monasteries too, as we might expect. The monks of Ely were in a difficult situation in the twelfth century because their abbey had become the seat of a bishopric in 1109 and they had to try to impose limitations on their own bishops. To achieve this they doctored many of their documents. They claimed that the church had been bestowed on Aethelthryth *pro dotalico iure* and concluded from this that they ought to be free from royal interference and free to call on any bishop they wished.[40] Like the monks of Glastonbury their ambitions led them to amend charters.[41] Nor, of course, was Westminster backward in this area and Osbert took care to include in his *Life of Edward* some forged royal privileges which emphasise the independence of the monastery and its freedom from all episcopal exactions.[42] The monastery that had the most success in its claims of exemption was Bury whose rights were recognised by both the king and the pope in the eleventh century. Even so a number of spurious royal grants were manufactured to substantiate the community's privileges against the local bishop.[43] Besides these forgeries, the additions made by the monks to their manuscript of the chronicle of John of Worcester are very revealing. They inserted some questionable charters and an account of the journey to Rome by bishop Herbert of Norwich, based on the narrative of Eadmer but modified to present a more unfavourable impression of Herbert's motives and his reception by the pope – changes that can be understood only in the context of the monks' attempts to resist the aggression of the bishops of Norwich.[44] So again we find that the activities of the Glastonbury monks are in accord with those of many other Benedictine communities.

I have referred above to some of the many reasons why monastic communities rewrote the record of their past, but I have not yet mentioned the most common of all motives. Surely most of the energies of monastic forgers were directed towards laying claim to estates and other possessions, claims which might often be justified but for which the evidence might have disappeared or become illegible.[45] Very often Anglo-Saxon charters are not what they purport to be, but often too the transactions which they record embody genuine materials from the past. Thus most of the original charters to which William refers in the *DA* have been lost, and many of those which he does preserve are obvious forgeries, but, as a comparison between the claims of the monastery and its holdings at the time of Domesday reveal, many must also record genuine gifts to Glastonbury.[46] So comprehensive was the *Liber Terrarum* that the monks had little cause to be dissatisfied with the land to which William laid claim in the *DA* for them – indeed the possibility is not to be discounted that William himself concocted for them three of their most grandiose forged charters[47] – and the later interpolations refer to estates only *en passant*, as a by-product of the important business of associating a famous name with the monastery.[48] It hardly needs to be emphasised that the other monasteries with which I have from time to time compared Glastonbury themselves indulged in the forging of charters and I reserve only Westminster for special mention because it forged royal and papal charters for itself and also served as a centre of forgery for neighbouring monastic houses.[49]

The conclusion to which this chapter leads is that the concerns of the monks of Glastonbury were no different from those of other houses; they had to maintain their places in a world that was increasingly unsympathetic to the black monks, who had previously worked hand-in-hand with the crown in the administration of the church and the state. The influence that had once been exerted unchallenged, and almost effortlessly, had now to be struggled for; the monks had to prove that their churches were ancient and venerable foundations, that they boasted the remains of influential saints and that their privileges and possessions had been freely granted by devout kings in the Anglo-Saxon past. Among those who had to be convinced were themselves – it was important to maintain morale as their numbers shrank[50] – and this was the context in which so many monastic communities set about rewriting their own history, reconstructing the past as they believed it had been, or ought to have been. The monks of Glastonbury were fortunate that they had had a powerful and influential abbot for vital years in the middle of the twelfth century and that they had been able to enlist the services of one of the most dedicated and skilled investigators of the Anglo-Saxon past to record their history. When their fortunes changed towards the end of the twelfth century they began to build on William's work, adding to it and altering it to conform to their new needs, just as many of their contemporaries did. Glastonbury, however, was more audacious than most and so the revisions of the monks have continued to attract attention to this day.

5

The Manuscripts of the *De Antiquitate*

IT is well known that the *DA* does not survive in the form in which William wrote it and that our knowledge of the work depends upon a mid-thirteenth century MS whose version incorporates a number of later interpolations. Before describing that MS I want to try to unravel the threads of which it is composed, to determine whether it is possible to establish the recensions through which the original work passed before it attained the form in which we now find it.

It is possible to ascertain a date *post quem* for most of the additions to the original text. Certain incidents which refer to the abbacy of Henry of Blois as in the past must have been added after his death in 1171.[1] Another series of interpolations, including the lengthy account of the rediscovery of the remains of St Dunstan, post-date the fire that devastated the abbey in 1184.[2] Finally we can be sure that all references to king Arthur must have been written after the purported discovery of his remains buried between the two pyramids in 1190-1, as must those chapters that seek to identify Avalon with Glastonbury because such an identification only became necessary and meaningful, after, and as further evidence for, the claim that Arthur had been buried at Glastonbury.[3]

Can we identify a *terminus ante quem* for these additions? An examination of the spectacular legends about the early history of Glastonbury provides a clue. The most notorious of all the Glastonbury forgeries is the charter of St Patrick, which includes details (which ostensibly derive from a document left behind by the Saints Phagan and Deruvian) about the foundation of the old church. This document was obviously concocted later than the visit of William, who lamented that he was ignorant of the names of the preachers sent to King Lucius by Pope Eleutherius. The extravagant indulgences claimed in it indicate a date in the thirteenth century, as Robinson argued many years ago. Such a date is also suggested by the invention of a companion for St Patrick named Wellias, clearly a brazen manoeuvre in the monastery's struggle for independence from the bishop of Bath and Wells in the last decade of the twelfth and the first decade of the thirteenth century. However, the conspicuous absence of the name of Joseph of Arimathea, later to become the most prestigious luminary claimed by the monastery, shows that the charter was composed before his name became associated with Glastonbury.[4]

The charter of St Patrick had amplified the hints that William threw out about St Philip's connections with Glastonbury and had asserted that the monastery had been founded by twelve disciples sent to England by St Philip and St James. This version of the early history of the monastery, underlining its crucial role in the conversion of England, was undermined by the appearance about 1230 of the *History of the Holy Grail*. This work emphasised the centrality of Joseph of

Arimathea as a convert of St Philip and as the apostle of Britain. The Glastonbury monks were forced to take account of his presence and did so by making him the leader of the disciples sent by Saints Philip and James, an obvious step especially since the *History of the Holy Grail* had associated Joseph with Arthur who had already been claimed by them. From the mid-thirteenth century Joseph begins to play a more and more prominent role in the Glastonbury legends, as marginal additions in the Trinity MS and later accounts of the abbey's history reveal.[5] The omission of Joseph from the charter of St Patrick, therefore, allows it to be asserted confidently that the charter must have been concocted before about 1230. A close analysis of the charter and chapters one and two which contain the references to Joseph confirms that they proceeded from a different pen. In particular, the simplistic grammatical structure of the two Joseph chapters, which are dominated by present participles and gerunds and lack subordinate clauses almost entirely, distinguishes them from the other interpolations. Moreover, there are factual differences between the charter and those chapters, despite the fact that they are basically merely expansions of the charter aimed at finding a place for Joseph of Arimathea.[6]

Can a *terminus ante quem* be established for the other interpolations? No date can be proven but the most plausible explanation is that the difficulties that beset the monastery at the end of the twelfth century, the death of Henry of Blois, the destruction of the monastery by fire and the encroachments of the bishop of Bath, forced the monks into action. The well-publicised exhumation of Arthur's bones was one response[7] and the historical propaganda campaign embodied in the additions to William's work was another. It is possible that William's manuscript was annotated at different times by various monks but at some time a substantial rearrangement of the work must have been undertaken to synthesise these additions into a coherent whole. The poor latinity of the second reviser, the monk responsible for the Joseph additions, makes me reluctant to ascribe this revision to him. However, an obvious candidate emerges from an examination of the later history of the monastery, attributed by Hearne to Adam of Domerham. In fact, it can be discerned easily that at least two different monks were involved. It is the first of these, who carried the history of the monastery down to 1230, to whom it is plausible to attribute the revision of William's work and the incorporation into it of the marginal additions which had accumulated since William wrote.[8] It was the work of this monk which the scribe of the Trinity MS copied and modified to the extent of adding chapter one and revising chapter two.[9]

Let me briefly summarise what seems to me to have been the fate of William's *DA*. The monks of Glastonbury were never completely satisfied with his interpretation of their past, but its inadequacies were not important while Henry of Blois was alive. When his death was followed by the fire that devastated their church and the threats to their independence from their local bishop, they began to look around for means of recovering lost finances and prestige. They began to publicise an audacious claim that the bones of king Arthur had been discovered buried near their monastery and started to alter William's history to suit their requirements. Among these alterations the most substantial were the claim to possess the relics of St Dunstan and the bold fabrication of the charter of St Patrick. About 1230

William's work was completely refashioned to incorporate these additions and the history of the monastery was continued to provide an account of its dispute with bishop Savaric and his successors. The appearance of the *History of the Holy Grail* made another revision imperative and so in 1247 the reworked version of the *DA* was itself copied and the scribe introduced Joseph into the monastery's history by dint of adding chapter one and rewriting chapter two. The manuscript for which he was responsible is the one that now survives as the earliest copy of the *DA*.

This is T, Cambridge, Trinity College, MS R.5.33 (724), a Glastonbury manuscript containing miscellaneous material relating to the monastery, and it is fully described in James' catalogue.[10] The *DA* occupies folios 1-18v and is written in the same small neat hand of the mid-thirteenth century which is also responsible for the continuation of the history of the monastery down to about 1230 (attributed to Adam of Domerham) and for a catalogue of the contents of its library. It is this last item that enables us to establish an approximate date for the scribe because he has dated the catalogue 1247 and another monk revised his work in the following year, noting additions to and losses from the library and altering the date to 1248.[11] The obvious conclusion, that this copy of the *DA* was written by about 1247, conforms to the speculations above as to the effect of discovering a translation of the *History of the Holy Grail*. Because the embellishment and improvement of their history was a matter of continuing concern to the monks of Glastonbury there are numerous marginal glosses in T in various hands of the thirteenth, fourteenth and fifteenth centuries. Most of these can only be dated very approximately, unless they were copied into M (see below), and so I have been satisfied to transcribe them, assign them to the century in which they were added and, where possible, identify entries by the same hand.

Although T contains the earliest surviving copy of the *DA* and must form the basis of an edition, there is a slightly later manuscript which might also be important. This is Oxford, Bodleian Library, MS Laud.Misc.750, (L), a small Glastonbury volume written in the second half of the thirteenth century in a neat, attractive hand. It does not survive entire but its remnants are pasted onto paper pages and make up 16 folios, each of which has 4 pages of vellum on each side.[12] With the help of a fifteenth-century copy (C, see below), one can establish with tolerable certainty what it must have contained. The volume begins with a series of historical notes about England, of which the first refers to the arrival of the Anglo-Saxons and the defeat of the Britons. These are followed by annals which begin with the Creation (although in L the earliest to survive is for 1223) and end in 1264 – obviously near to the date of composition – while the date 1265 is entered but nothing is recorded; their content is an unexceptional combination of local news, English ecclesiastical and political affairs and the occasional continental event. Then comes material on the antiquity and possessions of Glastonbury, adapted from an interpolated version of William's work from which the author has chosen those sections which interest him. In L, these extracts begin halfway through a sentence from chapter 72, but if C is to be trusted they began originally with a modified version of chapter one, followed by adaptations of chapters two, four and five. L concludes with a short arithmetical treatise, a genealogy from Adam to Noah, the story of Noah and a table of the measurements of the ark. The Glastonbury extracts in CL are not a mere copy from the recension in T; the material has been thoroughly reworked and rearranged and although T was almost certainly his source, it is just possible that CL's author had access to an earlier recension of the *DA*.

These are the facts. There are considerable similarities between T and CL, with many slabs of the texts identical, other places where only the order of the material differs and other sentences whose structure is identical but whose vocabulary varies, without distorting their sense. On the other hand, some chapters in CL have been comprehensively reworked, and contain material not found in T. Most of these differences are not significant; but some may be. There is an account in L (fol. 7v) of the saints buried at Glastonbury which is based on material from a number of different chapters of the *DA* but which differs from T in omitting Paulinus. This is consistent with what was apparently William's view.[13] L agrees with the William of the *GR* over T in two other instances as well. These are two pre-Conquest charters, the second of which is followed by an account of its confirmation by the Pope which is in the *GR* but not in T.[14] These readings suggest the possibility that the author of L had access to an earlier recension of the *DA*, possibly to William's original MS, but in fact this does not seem likely. In the first place, even if this were so, he must also have used T because he is aware of the purported connection between Glastonbury and Joseph of Arimathea and even uses the phrase *nobilis decurio* to describe him, a phrase found not in the body of T but in an early marginal addition.[15] Besides it is more likely, given William's methods of work, that he gave different versions of the same charter in the *GR* and the *DA* than that the scribe of T, elsewhere so faithful to William's text, should have altered the texts of the charters, especially as the changes are not significant.[16] The conclusion that this suggests, that the author of L drew on the *GR* when he was preparing that MS, is confirmed by what else we know of his technique. He was not a mere transcriber but an historian who created an original synthesis out of a number of different sources, including the *Vita Gildae* of Caradoc of Llancarvan and a *Vita Indracti*, probably William's.[17] Since there was a copy of the *GR* in the Glastonbury library the similarities between it and L are almost certainly explained by the use made of it by the author of L. Yet because of the slight possibility that he did have access to an earlier draft of the *DA* than that in T, I have noted the variants of CL for those chapters that are not obviously later interpolations.

The next surviving manuscript, British Library, MS Additional 22934, (M), a Glastonbury volume written about 1313, contains the *DA*, the text known as Adam of Domerham which has been continued down to 1313, and copies of documents relating to Glastonbury dating from the second half of the thirteenth century. The *DA*, written in one hand of the early fourteenth century, was copied from T, as is clear from the incorporation of some of the latter's marginalia into its text and its perpetuation of the few errors found in T.[18] Yet the matter is complicated by the appearance in M of some sentences found in CL but not in T. This cannot be explained by postulating an intermediate manuscript between T and CL/M because there are a few crucial instances where T has been corrected, evidently between the writing of CL and M, and CL preserves the original reading and M the corrected one.[19] The explanation is rather that the scribe of M had access to L as well as T, as is borne out by a glimpse we gain of his method of working. Chapter one contains a topographical description of Glastonbury taken from the earliest life of Dunstan which is introduced in T by a reference to the location of the source, *Quorum unus Britonum historiographus, prout apud sanctum Edmundum itemque apud sanctum Augustinum Anglorum apostolum uidimus, ita exorsus*. Before this M has inserted, from CL, *Et enim unus ex antiquis Britonum nobilis historiographus, prout in codicibus suis apud gloriosis simul regem et martirem Edmundum, item apud sanctum Augustinum apostolum et in aliis pluribus locis reperitur, ita exorsus*, but this has been crossed out. Although one cannot demonstrate that it was crossed out by the scribe, the similarity of the two sentences surely prompts the conclusion that he transcribed the sentence from L but immediately realised that it produced a pointless repetition and so excised it. If this explanation is correct – and it certainly seems the most satisfactory one – one is left to wonder why the scribe of M incorporated so little from L, some of whose additions to T would have made the text of M much fuller. I can only speculate that the authority of William inhibited him from tampering grossly with the text.

I have already commented on the importance of C, British Library, Cotton Cleopatra C.x., fos 72v-100r, a fifteenth century copy of L which is bound, in a later make-up, with a miscellaneous group of historical and theological works. There seems to be no doubt that it was copied from L because it includes the historical notes on England, the annals and the Glastonbury material that are found in that manuscript, agreeing with its readings where it differs from T and its descendents.[20] It is, however, not a complete copy of L as it omits that volume's account of the burial of Dunstan's remains at Glastonbury and its list of the possessions of the monastery. It also excludes the arithmetical treatise with which L finishes, concluding with some verses on Joseph of Arimathea. Despite this, it seems to be legitimate to use C to complete L where that volume is deficient.

There are a number of other manuscripts which contain extracts from the *DA* but they cast no light on the darkness surrounding William's original text because later writers were invariably interested in the more sensational events connected with the history of the monastery, notably its connections with king Arthur and Joseph of Arimathea, and so chose their extracts from the most heavily interpolated sections of the text.[21] One manuscript in particular ought to be mentioned because it reveals clearly the use that was made of the legends for propaganda purposes. This is Oxford, Bodleian Library, MS Lat.Hist.a.2. (B), which consists of six large folio pages of the fifteenth century pasted onto the boards of a show case which must have been screwed onto a wall of the monastery where all the visitors could read it. The first folio is concerned with stories about Joseph and Arthur, and then follow selected chapters from the *DA*, with either T or M as exemplar, which highlight the saints connected with the monastery.[22] A stemma will clarify the history of the text.

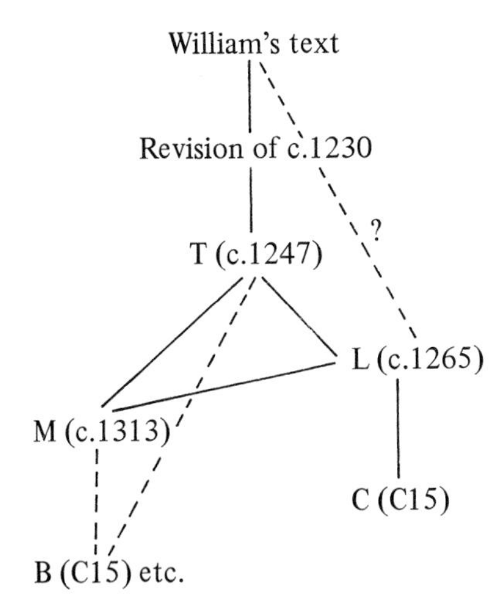

In short, the text here edited is based on T, with the variants in CL noted if it seems that they might throw any light on an earlier stage in the revision of William's text. T itself has been heavily annotated by readers of the thirteenth, fourteenth and fifteenth centuries. I have included in the body of the text those marginal and interlinear additions which were made before the end of the thirteenth century and incorporated in M, but the later additions have been consigned to the footnotes. The justification for incorporating thirteenth century additions in the body of the text is that they contain some interesting material on Joseph of Arimathea and king Arthur, and that they therefore provide evidence of the way in which the Glastonbury legends were elaborated. The text of c.1247 (unannotated T) is so different from William's original work that nothing would be gained by accepting it as the basis of the edition. Variants from Hearne's edition,[23] H, are noted, but not from Gale's strikingly inaccurate edition.[24] I have reproduced the orthography of T except where it would have been confusing to do so, in which cases I have noted T's reading in a note. The punctuation of the text is my own and is simply intended to help the reader. The chapter headings are in T. In undertaking a translation of the text I have learnt from the earlier translation by Frank Lomax, although his was incomplete and misleading in places, particularly in its confrontation with William's difficult Latin.[25]

Prologus Willelmi Malmesburiensis De Antiquitate Glastoniensis Ecclesie

Domino in Christi uisceribus multum amplectendo et honorando Henrico Wintoniensi episcopo,[1] Willelmus, uestre dignitatis filius, quicquid optari potest beacius. Si quicquam est quod in hac uita hominem teneat et inter aduersa et turbines mundi equo animo manere persuadeat, id esse in primis, reor, meditacionem sanctarum scripturarum. Et quidem scripta gentilium hactenus utilitatem sui pretendunt, ut uerborum splendore legentis et palpent ingenium et liment eloquium. At uero librorum celitus inspiratorum longe fructus preponderat, quia, et hic iocunde dulcedinis pastum animo infundunt, et alias eterne beatitudinis emolumentum adquirunt. Multa porro, et ut mea fert opinio innumera, sunt in scripturis sanctis quibus diuina dignacio mentes moralium ad bone uite cultum informat, tum precepta, tum exempla. Illis qualiter uiuendum sit instruimur; istis innuitur quam sint, Deo iuuante, factu facilia que iubentur. Natura sane hunc quibusdam ingenerauit animum ut, quamuis utraque sciant necessaria, magis tamen exemplorum quam adhortacionum eos prolectet auditus. Et alienigenarum quidem gestis pro[a] sanctitatis assurgunt reuerencia, set alacriori capiuntur dulcedine, si alicuius sancti, qui compatriota fuerit, uita producatur in medium, in qua sicut e speculo conspicentur, ut ita dictum sit uiuum religionis simulacrum. Accedit enim iocunde relacioni propinquitas, ne aliquis desperet a se per Dei gratiam fieri posse, quod audit ab alio de proximo factum fuisse.[2]

Unde sicut estimo non contempnende stilum dedi opere, qui beati Dunstani prius Glastoniensis abbatis, deinde archiepiscopi Cantuariensis uitam labore meo eterne mandaui memorie duosque libros de hoc uolentibus Glastonie fratribus, filiis uestris, dominis et sociis meis, dudum integra rerum ueritate absolui.[3] Uerumtamen, ne quid sedulitatis mee desit officio, eiusdem ecclesie uestre rudimentum et processum in huius libri auspicio repetens ab origine pandam.[4] Nec hoc[b] multum a proposito alienum putari debet, cum honor ecclesie in Dunstanum et laus Dunstani ad ecclesiam redundet. Nam et illa Dunstanum materno gremio in uirum confouit, et ipse matri plurimum splendoris adiecit. Quapropter in spem non nichil animus meus accrescit hoc scriptum fortasse sanctum procurasse, ut alumpni occasione digeratur dignitas nutricule. Illos ergo libellos set et uitam beati Patricii, miracula uenerabilis Benigni, passionem martiris Indracti,[5] que simili cura procuderam, iam pridem in eorum permisi uersari manibus, ut si quid citra racionem dictum esset corrigeretur pro tempore. Illi uero propensiori consilio diu scripta trutinantes omni me liberauerunt culparum neuo, nichil contuitu religionis aut dantes offense aut deferentes gracie.

[a] *prae* H.
[b] *haec* H.

William of Malmesbury's Preface to his History of the Church of Glastonbury

To his lord, Henry, bishop of Winchester, who deserves to be cherished and honoured in the deep embrace of Christ, William, a son of your church, sends whatever joy you might wish for. If there be any one thing which may sustain a man in this life and persuade him to endure tranquilly the reverses and disturbances of the world, it is, I think, above all, contemplation of the Holy Scriptures. Even the writings of the pagans can claim to be useful insofar as the brilliance of their language inspires the reader's talents and refines his speech. But truly the harvest of those books inspired by heaven is far richer, for on one hand they pour sustenance of delightful sweetness into the soul, and on the other hand they secure the reward of eternal bliss. Moreover there are many, nay to my mind innumerable, truths in the Holy Scriptures, both precepts and examples, by which divine grace instructs the minds of mortals in right living. Precepts teach us how we ought to live, examples demonstrate how easy it is, with God's help, to carry out His commands. Yet nature has so fashioned the minds of some men that, although they know that both are necessary, they are incited more by hearing examples than exhortations. Similarly they respect the deeds of foreigners out of reverence for their sanctity but are seized by a keener joy if the life of any saint who was their countryman is set forth, in which, as it were, they may perceive as in a mirror a living image of religion. For the affinity adds to the pleasure of the report and no-one despairs of being able to do himself, through the grace of God, what he hears has been done by another from his part of the world.

Wherefore I have employed my pen on that work, which I judge to be of no small value, in which I laboured to commit to eternal memory the life of the blessed Dunstan, abbot of Glastonbury and later archbishop of Canterbury, and have now completed, with scrupulous regard for the truth, the two books about him for which the brethren at Glastonbury, your sons and my masters and companions, had asked. However, lest I seem to have lacked zeal in the performance of my duty, I will begin this book by going back to the origins of your church and will unfold its progress since those earliest beginnings. Nor ought this be considered very different from the original plan, since the honour of the church redounds to Dunstan and praise of him to the church. For she fostered Dunstan at her maternal breast until manhood and he added greatly to his mother's splendour. Therefore a small hope has begun to grow in my heart that this holy work may cause the dignity of the nurse to be highlighted by the example of her nursling. Some time ago I allowed those small books, the *Life of the Blessed Patrick*, and *Miracles of the Venerable Benignus* and the *Passion of the Martyr Indract*, which I had fashioned with like care, to be examined by the monks so that if anything unreasonable had been said it could be properly corrected. After assessing my writings at length and deliberating favourably they left me free of any blemish of blame because nothing in them gave offence to religious eyes or lacked graciousness.

Hoc igitur qualecumque opusculum uestre deuoueo examinandum prudencie, domine uenerabilis et merito amabilis pater. Facti mei racio est in promptu, ut noscat excellentia uestra, qui et quanti uiri fundauerunt et prouexerunt ecclesiam, que uestre potissimum sub Deo et sanctis eius modo tutele innititur. Sciatis eciam uos priscorum heroum imitatum, et pene dico supergressum, facta priusquam audissetis uocabula. Nam ut cum obtrectatore, si quis forte fuerit audacius, conferam pedem. In quo prisci possessores uobis possunt preferri? In ampliandis patrimoniis? At uos et dudum eliminata reducitis et habita industria sollerti cumulatis. In extruendis edificiis? Atqui quantum in ea re omnibus predecessoribus emineatis, melius monstrabit mirantis digitus quam laudantis titulus. In pace incolarum tuenda? Sed uos nominis uestri umbone omnes predones deicitis, uultus splendore nebulas mesticie propulsatis, sermonis prudencia calumpnias litigatorum enodatis. In religione monachorum? Que cum semper tum ita Deo propicio uestris temporibus floret, ut infelix liuor aliquid sinistrum de ipsa erubescat confingere. Accedit publicus amor ipsorum pectori uestro quia[c] nullo eos exterretis roncho,[6] sed uenientes, iocunde admittitis, affabiliter tractatis, abeuntibus paterne ualefactitis. Nec enim profecto de uobis dicitur quod de quibusdam potentibus a poeta usurpatum non inmerito cantatur: 'Late sibi submouet omne uulgus, et in uacuis regnat basiliscus harenis.'[7] Est igitur infra meritum uestrum omnis eloquencia, laudes uestre ita excellunt ut nichil supra. Que cum ita sint, accipite, queso, deuotionis mee munus, sedulitatis pignus, et agite ne fructu laboris excidam. Adestote igitur, si animo[d] placet, et attendite, dum per successionum seriem antiquitatem ecclesie temptabo suspicionibus eruere quantum ex strue monimentorum uestrorum potui corradere.[8]

1. Incipit quomodo duodecim discipuli sanctorum Philippi et Jacobi apostolorum primo ecclesiam Glastoniensis fundauerunt.

Post Dominice resurrectionis gloriam ascensionisque triumphum ac spiritus paracleti[e] de supernis missionem, qui discipulorum corda temporalis poene[f] adhuc formidine trepidancia repleuit, scienciam omnium linguarum tribuendo, erant omnes credentes simul cum mulieribus et Maria matre Jesu, ut Lucas narrat euuangelista;[9] et uerbum Dei disseminabatur crescebatque numerus credencium cotidie; eratque omnibus cor unum et anima una.

Inuidie ergo fascibus accensi, sacerdotes Judeorum cum Phariseis et scribis concitauerunt persecucionem in ecclesia interficiendo prothomartirem Stephanum et fere a finibus suis omnes procul pellentes. Hac igitur persecucionis procella seuiente dispersi credentes pecierunt diuersa regna terrarum a Domino sibi delegata uerbum salutis gentibus propinando. Sanctus autem Philippus, ut testatur Freculfus libro

[c] *quod* H.
[d] *omnino* H.
[e] *paracliti* H.
[f] *pene* T.

So, venerable master and deservedly beloved father, I offer this little work, whatever its worth, for your careful perusal. The motive for my action is clear: that your excellency should know the number and identity of the men who founded and exalted the church which, under God and His saints, now relies chiefly on your protection. Know, however, that you had imitated – I almost said surpassed – the deeds of these ancient heroes before you heard their names. As for detractors, if perchance anyone should be so bold, I shall oppose them vigorously for in what way can earlier guardians be preferred to you? In extending the patrimony? But you both recover holdings earlier lost and by your able skills amass new ones. In constructing buildings? But an admiring guide will reveal more effectively than my words of praise the extent to which you surpass all your predecessors in this regard. In protecting the peace of the inhabitants? But you drive out all plunderers before the shield of your name, you banish clouds of dejection by the splendour of your countenance and you expose the chicanery of litigants by the good sense of your words. In the piety of your monks? But, as always, with God's beneficence religion so flourishes in your time that miserable envy is ashamed to fabricate any falsehood about it. The monks openly offer their love to your heart because you do not terrify them with a sneer but receive them joyfully when they come, treat them kindly and, like a father, wish them well when they leave. These words which the poet used, not unjustly, of certain powerful men certainly do not apply to you: 'He compels all the inferior serpents to keep their distance, and lords it over the empty desert.' In short any eloquence falls short of your worth and your praise is valued more highly than anything else. Since this is so, accept, I beg you, this tribute of my devotion and pledge of my zeal and do not deprive me of the fruit of my labour. So attend, if it please your heart, and give heed while I try to rescue from suspicion the antiquity of your church, arranged according to the succession of its prelates, in so far as I have been able to scrape them together from the heap of your muniments.

1. The account of how the twelve disciples of the apostles St Philip and St James first founded the church of Glastonbury begins here.

After the glory of the Lord's resurrection and the triumph of His ascension and the sending from heaven of the comforting Spirit to fortify the disciples' hearts, still trembling with dread of temporal punishment, by bestowing on them a knowledge of all tongues, all the believers were together including the women and Mary, the mother of Jesus, as Luke the evangelist narrates; and the word of God was being disseminated and the number of believers increased daily and 'they were all of one heart and one soul'.

As a result the priests of the Jews, with the pharisees and scribes, inflamed by envy's torch, instigated a persecution of the Church, killing Stephen, the first martyr, and driving most of the rest far from their homes. The believers who were dispersed by the raging hurricane of this persecution sought out the various kingdoms of the world assigned to them by the Lord in order to refresh their inhabitants with the word of salvation. St Philip, as Freculph attests in the fourth chapter of his

secundo, capitulo IIII°,[10] regionem Francorum adiens gracia predicandi plures ad fidem conuertit et baptizauit. Uolens igitur uerbum Christi dilatari, duodecim ex suis discipulis[g] ad euuangelizandum uerbum uite misit in Britanniam.[h] Quibus, ut ferunt, karrissimum amicum suum Joseph ab Arimathia, qui et Dominum sepeleuit, prefecit. Uenientes igitur in Britanniam anno ab incarnacione Domini LXIII, ab assumpcione beate Marie XV, fidem Christi fiducialiter predicabant. Rex autem barbarus cum sua gente tam noua audiens et inconsueta omnino predicacioni eorum consentire renuebat, nec paternas tradiciones commutare uolebat; quia tamen de longe uenerant uiteque eorum exigebat modestia[i],[11] quandam insulam siluis, rubis atque paludibus circumdatam, ab incolis Ynsuuitrim nuncupatam, in lateribus sue regionis ad habitandum concessit. Postea eciam alii duo reges, licet pagani, comperta eorum uite sanctimonia, successiue unicuique eorum unam porcionem[j] terre concesserunt ac[k] confirmauerunt. Unde et XII hide per eos adhuc, ut creditur, nomen sorciuntur. Predicti itaque sancti in eodem deserto conuersantes, post pusillum temporis uisione archangeli Gabrielis admoniti sunt ecclesiam in honore sancte Dei genetricis et uirginis Marie in loco celitus eis demonstrato construere. Qui diuinis preceptis non segniter obedientes, secundum quod eis fuerat ostensum quamdam capellam, inferius per circuitum uirgis torquatis muros perficientes, consummauerunt in[l] anno post passionem Domini XXXI, post assumpcionem gloriose uirginis XV, ex deformi quidem scemate sed Dei multipliciter adornatam uirtute. Et cum hec in hac regione prima fuerit, ampliori eam dignitate Dei filius insigniuit, ipsam uidelicet in honore sue matris dedicando. Duodecim igitur sancti sepius memorati in eodem loco Deo et beate uirgini deuota exhibentes obsequia, uigiliis, ieiuniis et oracionibus uacantes, eiusdem uirginis auxilio ac uisione, ut credi pium est, in omnibus necessitatibus refocillabantur.

Hec autem ita se habere tum ex carta beati Patricii, tum ex scriptis seniorum cognoscimus[12].[m] Quorum unus Britonum historiographus, prout apud sanctum

[g] A later hand has added above the line at this point *elegit et* in M.

[h] A marginal note, both at the bottom and the top of the folio, in hands of the fourteenth and fifteenth centuries reads: *et ad predicandum incarnacionem Jesu Christi et super singulos manum dexteram deuotissime extendit.* M reads: *(in Britanniam) et ad predicandum incarnacionem Jesu Christi et super singulos eorum dextram manum deuotissime extendit eisque (quibus, ut ferunt . . .).* CL (C fol. 85r) reads: *(in Britanniam) ad predicandum incarnacionem Christi eisque (carissimum . . .)*, which is the explanation of the garbled *eisque quibus* in M.

[i] *ad peticionem eorum* added in margin about 1300. In M, CL.

[j] *unam hidam* added interlinearly about 1300. In CL.

[k] *ad peticionem ipsorum secundum morem gentilium omnes XII porciones* added in margin about 1300. M reads: *ad peticionem ipsorum secundum morem gentilium dictas XII hidas eisdem XII confirmauerunt* and L: *ad peticionem ipsorum duodecim ipsorum secundum morem gentilium duodecim hidas in principio confirmauerunt.*

[l] *in* om. H.

[m] As noted in chapter 5, M, copying from L, inserts here after *cognoscimus*: *Et enim unus ex antiquis Britonum nobilis historiographus, prout in codicibus suis*

second book, came to the land of the Franks where he converted many to the faith by his preaching and baptised them. Desiring to spread the word of Christ further he sent twelve of his disciples into Britain to teach the word of life. It is said that he appointed as their leader his very dear friend, Joseph of Arimathea, who had buried the Lord. They came to Britain in 63 AD, the fifteenth year after the assumption of the blessed Mary, and confidently began to preach the faith of Christ. The barbarian king and his people, hearing this new and unfamiliar preaching, refused absolutely to agree with it and would not alter the teachings of their forefathers; yet because they had come from afar, and because the sobriety of their life demanded it of him, the king granted them a certain island on the outskirts of his territory on which they could live, a place surrounded by woods, bramble bushes and marshes and called by its inhabitants Yniswitrin. Later two other kings, who, though themselves pagan, had learnt of the sanctity of their lives, successively granted and confirmed to each of them a portion of land. From these saints, it is believed, the 'twelve hides' derive the name by which they are still known. After living in that wilderness for a short time the saints were incited by a vision of the archangel Gabriel to build a church in honour of the Virgin Mary, the holy mother of God, in a place that was pointed out to them from heaven. They were not slow to obey this divine command and in the thirty-first year after the passion of the Lord, the fifteenth after the assumption of the glorious Virgin, they completed a chapel as they had been instructed, making the lower part of all its walls of twisted wattle, an unsightly construction no doubt but one adorned by God with many miracles. Since it was the first one in that territory the son of God dignified it with a greater honour by dedicating it in honour of his mother. The twelve saints of whom we have been speaking offered faithful obedience to God and the blessed Virgin in that place, devoting themselves to vigils, fasting and prayers, and were supplied with all necessities by the Virgin's aid and, as the pious believe, by a vision of her.

These things we learn both from the charter of St Patrick and the writings of the elders. In the church of St Edmund and also in the church of St Augustine, the

Edmundum itemque apud sanctum Augustinum Anglorum apostolum uidimus, ita f2 exorsus est./ 'Est in confinio occidentalis Britannie quedam regalis insula, antiquo uocabulo Glastonia nuncupata, latis locorum dimensa sinibus,[n] piscosis aquis stagneisque circumdata fluminibus, et plurimis humane indigencie apta usibus atque sacris, quod maximum est, dedicata muneribus. In ea siquidem Anglorum primi catholice legis neophite antiquam Deo dictante reppererunt ecclesiam, nulla hominum arte, ut ferunt, constructam, immo humane saluti a Deo paratam; quam postmodum ipse celorum fabricator multis miraculorum gestis multisque uirtutum misteriis sibi sancteque Dei genitrici Marie se consecrasse demonstrauit.'[13] Set de hiis postea; nunc ad incepta redeamus.

Sancti igitur memorati in eadem heremo sic degentes, effluentibus multis annorum curriculis, carnis ergastulo sunt educti idemque locus cepit esse ferarum latibulum, qui prius fuerat habitacio sanctorum, donec placuit beate uirgini suum oratorium redire ad memoriam fidelium. Quod quomodo euenerit iam prosequamur.[14]

([o]Joseph ab Arimathia nobilem decurionem cum filio suo Iosephes dicto et aliis pluribus in maiorem Britanniam, que nunc Anglia dicta est, uenisse et ibidem uitam finisse testatur liber de gestis incliti regis Arturi. In inquisicione scilicet cuiusdam illustris militis dicti Lanceloth de Lac facta per socios rotunde tabule, uidelicet ubi quidam heremita exponit Walwano misterium cuiusdam fontis, saporem et colorem crebro mutantis; ubi et scribebatur quod miraculum illud non terminaretur donec ueniret magnus leo qui et collum magnis uinculis haberet constrictum. Item in sequentibus in inquisicione uasis quod ibi uocant sanctum graal idem refertur fere in principio ubi albus miles exponit Galaat, filio Lancelot, misterium cuiusdam mirabilis scuti quod eidem deferendum commisit quod nemo alius sine graui dispendio ne una quidem die poterat portare.[15])

2. *Quomodo sancti Phaganus et Deruuianus Britannos ad fidem conuerterunt et in insulam Auallonie uenerunt.*

Tradunt bone credulitatis annales,[16] quod Lucius rex Britannorum ad Eleutherium, XIII loco post beatum Petrum[p] miserit, oratum[q] ut Britannie tenebras luce Christiane predicacionis illustraret. Mactus animi[r] rex, magne prorsus laudis factum adorsus, ut fidem, quam tunc temporis pene omnes reges et populi persequerentur exibitam, ipse ultro appeteret uix auditam. De qua re ut aliquid extrinsecus dicam,

apud gloriosissimum regem et martirem Edmundum, item apud sanctum Augustinum, Anglorum apostolum et eciam in aliis pluribus locis reperitur ita exorsus est.

[n] *finibus* H.

[o] At the foot of the page in a late C13 hand; also in M where it follows Ch. 1.

[p] *papam* is added interlinearly in C13 hand. In M.

[q] *orans* is added interlinearly in C13 hand. In M.

[r] *Magnanimus* added interlinearly in C13 hand. Not in M.

apostle of the English, we have seen a work by one of the latter, an historian of the Britons, which begins thus: 'There is on the western border of Britain a certain royal island, called by its ancient name of Glastonia, spacious and undulating, surrounded by sluggish rivers whose waters are well-stocked with fish, fit to serve many human needs and, best of all, consecrated to sacred offices. It was there that the first English converts to the Christian religion discovered, with God's guidance, an ancient church, not built, they say, by human skill but prepared by God himself for human salvation. Later the Maker of Heaven proved by many miracles and sacred mysteries that he had consecrated it to himself and to Mary, the holy mother of God.' But more of this later; now let us return to what we had begun.

After the lapse of many years, those same saints, who had been living as we described in that wilderness, were led out of the prison of their flesh and the place itself, which had earlier been the habitation of saints, began to serve as a lair for wild beasts, until it pleased the Virgin that her oratory should again become a memorial for the faithful. We will now describe how this came about.

(The book of the deeds of the famous King Arthur bears witness that the high-born decurion Joseph of Arimathea, together with his son named Joseph and very many others, came into greater Britain, now called England, and ended his life there. Also recorded is the search of a certain famous knight, named Lancelot of the Lake, with the help of his comrades of the round table, after a certain hermit had set forth to Walwan the mystery of a particular fountain, the water from which continually changed its taste and colour, a miracle, it was written, that would not cease until the coming of a great lion whose neck was fettered with thick chains. Again in a later part of the book, about the search for a vessel that is called there the holy grail, almost the same thing is recorded where a white knight explains to Galahad, son of Lancelot, the mystery of a certain miraculous shieid which he entrusts to him to bear because no-one else could carry it, even for a day, except at great cost.)

2. *How the saints Phagan and Deruvian converted the Britons to the faith and came to the island of Avalon.*

Reliable annals record that Lucius, king of the Britons, sent a plea to Eleutherius, the thirteenth in line from the blessed Peter, that he should illuminate the darkness of Britain with the light of Christian preaching. This great-souled king undertook a truly praiseworthy task in voluntarily seeking out a faith of which he had scarcely heard, at the very time when almost all kings and peoples were persecuting it when it was revealed to them. To throw light on this matter from another source,

in eiusdem meriti laudem concurrit Ethelbirtus, multis annis post Lucium rex Cancie, qui predicatores ad se de Roma missos non turbido abegit responso, sed benigno excepit hospicio. Accessit benignitati sollers uerborum festiuitas, quod, etsi nollet uerbis eorum preproperum[s] assensum apponere, tamen quia de longe uenerant ut que optima credebant ei communicarent, absurdum uideri posset si eis quicquam inferret molestie. Sunt ergo hii uiri amplissima recordacione digni, quorum alter Christianitatem prudenter inuitauit, alter libenter excepit.[17]

Uenerunt ergo, Eleutherio mittente, predicatores Brittanniam duo uiri sanctissimi, Phaganus uidelicet atque Deruuianus, prout carta sancti Patricii gestaque Britannorum testantur.[18] Hii igitur uerbum uite euuangelizantes, regem cum suo populo sacro fonte abluerunt anno Domini CLX sexto. Hinc predicando et baptizando Britannie partes peragrantes, in insulam Auallonie, more Moysy legislatoris interiora deserti penetrantes, sunt ingressi, ubi antiquam Deo dictante reppererunt ecclesiam manibus discipulorum Christi constructam[t] et humane saluti a Deo paratam; quam postmodum ipse celorum fabricator multis miraculorum gestis multisque uirtutum misteriis sibi sancteque Dei genetrici Marie se consecrasse demonstrauit[19].[u] Fluxerant autem ab aduentu discipulorum sancti Philippi in Britanniam usque ad aduentum sanctorum memoratorum CIII anni. Igitur predicti sancti Phaganus et Deruuianus, oratorio illo sic reperto, ineffabili sunt referti[v] gaudio, ibidem in Dei laudibus moram protrahentes diuturnam, per nouem uidelicet annos. Locum eciam diligenter perscrutantes, figuram nostre redempcionis aliaque signa manifesta reppererunt, quibus bene cognouerunt quod Christiani prius locum inhabitauerant; postea celesti perpendentes oraculo quod Dominus ipsum locum pre ceteris Britannie specialiter elegerit ad nomen gloriose genitricis sue ibidem inuocandum.[w]

Omnem eciam narracionem in antiquis scriptis inuenerunt, qualiter, sanctis apostolis per uniuersum orbem dispersis, sanctus Philippus apostolus cum multitudine discipulorum in Franciam ueniens duodecim ex ipsis in Britanniam misit ad predicandum. Qui predictam capellam angelica docti reuelatione construxerunt; quam postmodum filius altissimi in honorem sue matris dedicauit; ipsisque XII tres reges, licet pagani, XII porciones terre dederunt ad eorum sustentacionem. Insuper gesta eorum scripta inuenerunt. Ideoque locum ipsum pre ceteris dilexerunt, qui eciam in memoriam primorum XII ex suis sociis[x] XII elegerunt et in prefata insula rege Lucio consenciente habitare fecerunt. Qui postea in diuersis locis sicut anachorite manserunt ibidem, in eisdem uidelicet locis in quibus primi duodecim primitus

[s] *proprium* H.

[t] A marginal gloss in a later hand of about 1300 which is incorporated in M after *constructam* reads *ut ferunt*.

[u] After *demonstrauit* M inserts the following sentence, taken from L: *Et hoc factum est tempore predicti regis Lucii qui primus Britannie regis catholice fidei et sancti baptismatis sacramenta simul cum sua gente suscepit anno Dominice incarnacionis CLXVI*[to].

[v] *referti* om. H.

[w] After *inuocandum* M inserts, from L, *et auxilium de eadem uirgine pre cunctis necessitatibus impetrandum.*

[x] *sociis* om. H.

Aethelberht, king of Kent many years after Lucius, can claim praise for a similar good deed because he did not reject and drive away the preachers sent to him from Rome but received them with generous hospitality. The wit and humour of his speech added to his kindness, for, although he refused to pledge a speedy assent to their words, it seemed to him absurd to harm them since they had come from afar to tell him those things that they considered so important. Both of these men then, one of whom wisely invited Christianity and the other of whom willingly received it, are worthy of the fullest remembrance.

At the bidding of Eleutherius, therefore, two very holy men, the preachers Phagan and Deruvian, came to Britain, as the charter of St Patrick and the Deeds of the Britons attest. Proclaiming the word of life, they cleansed the king and his people at the sacred font in 166 AD. Then they travelled through the realm of Britain preaching and baptising until, penetrating like Moses the lawgiver into the very heart of the wilderness, they came to the island of Avalon where, with God's guidance, they found an old church built by the hands of the disciples of Christ and prepared by God for man's salvation; later the Architect of Heaven showed by many miracles and sacred mysteries that He had consecrated it to Himself and Mary, the holy mother of God. One hundred and three years had passed between the arrival in Britain of the disciples of St Philip and the coming of these two saints. So when Saints Phagan and Deruvian discovered that oratory, as mentioned, they were filled with ineffable joy and, giving praise to God, prolonged their stay there for a long time, namely for nine years. Carefully examining the place, they came across a figure of our Redeemer and other manifest signs by means of which they clearly knew that Christians had inhabited the spot earlier; later, they inferred from a heavenly oracle that the Lord had especially chosen that place before all others in Britain to invoke the name of his glorious mother.

They also found in some old documents a complete account of how, when the holy apostles were scattered all over the world, St Philip the apostle, who had come into France with a crowd of disciples, sent twelve of them into Britain to preach. Following instructions revealed to them by angels they constructed the chapel of which we have been speaking and which later the son of the Highest dedicated to His mother. Three pagan kings had given to those twelve twelve portions of land for their sustenance. Moreover they found their deeds written down. Therefore they loved that place before all others and, in memory of the first twelve, chose twelve of their own companions whom, with the consent of King Lucius, they established on that island. These twelve stayed there in separate dwellings, like anchorites, in the very places which the first twelve had originally inhabited. Yet they used to

habitauerant. In uetustam tamen ecclesiam, ad diuina obsequia deuocius complenda, crebro[y] conuenerunt. Et sicut tres reges pagani dictam insulam cum adiacenciis suis XII primis Christi discipulis dudum concesserant; ita predicti Phaganus et Deruuianus, istis XII sociis et aliis in posterum secuturis, ab eodem rege Lucio eamdem[z] confirmari impetrabant. Sic autem multi aliis succedentes, semper tamen in numero duodenario, per multa annorum curricula usque ad aduentum sancti Patricii Hyberniensium apostoli in memorata insula permanserunt. Huic eciam ecclesie sic reperte aliud addiderunt sancti neophite opere lapideo oratorium, quod Christo sanctisque apostolis Petro et Paulo dedicauerunt.

Horum ergo restaurata fuit opera uetusta sancte Marie in Glastonia ecclesia, sicut fidelis per succidua secula non tacuit antiquitas. Sunt et ille non exigue fidei litere apud sanctum Edmundum reperte ad hanc sentenciam: Ecclesiam Glastonie non fecerunt aliorum hominum manus, sed ipsi discipuli Christi eam edificauerunt, mittente scilicet sancto Philippo apostolo. Nec abhorret a uero, ut premissum est, quia si Philippus apostolus Gallis predicauit, sicut Freculfus libro secundo capitulo quarto dicit, potest credi quod eciam trans occeanum sermonis semina iecit.[20]

3. Quomodo monachus quidam de sancto Dionisio de Glastonie referebat.

Ad comprobandam eciam[a] antiquitatem ecclesie de qua prefati sumus paululum digrediamur. Monachus quidam Glastonie, Godefridus nomine, de cuius epistola et hoc et quod subiungemus capitulum assumpsimus, tempore Henrici Blesensis, abbatis Glastonie,[21] cum in pago Parisiacensi apud sanctum Dionisium[b] moraretur, senior quidam ex monachis interogauit eum. 'Quo genus? Unde domo?' Respondit, 'Normannum, Britannie monasterio quod Glastingeia dicitur, monachum, pape.' Inquit, 'an adhuc stat illa perpetue uirginis et misericordie matris uetusta ecclesia?' 'Stat', inquid. Tum ille lepido attactu capud Godefridi Glastonie[c] demulcens, diu silencio suspensum tenuit ac sic demum ora resoluit. 'Hec gloriosissimi martiris Dionisii ecclesia et illa de qua te asseris eandem priuilegii dignitatem habent, ista in Gallia, illa in Britannia; uno eodem tempore exorte, a summo et magno pontifice consecrate. Uno tamen gradu illa supereminet: Roma etenim secunda uocatur.' Cumque ab ore uiri penderet, ille, cui prouincia suscipiendorum fratrum erat commissa, inuitos ab inuicem non reuisuros seperauit. Sed hoc[d] hactenus.

y Interlinear addition in a C13 hand, included in M but then crossed out, found in L reads: *cotidei*.

z Interlinear addition in the same hand responsible for *papam*, *orans* and *magnanimus* earlier in this chapter reads *liberam*. Not in M.

a *eciam* om. H.

b *Dionysium* H.

c *Glastoniensis* H.

d *haec* H.

gather together frequently in the old church in order to celebrate divine worship more devoutly. Just as the three pagan kings had formerly granted the island with its appurtenances to the first twelve disciples of Christ, so Phagan and Deruvian obtained confirmation of the same from King Lucius for their twelve companions and the others who should follow them in the future. Thus many successors, always in twelves, dwelt on that island throughout the course of many years until the arrival of St Patrick, the apostle of the Irish. To the church that they found there these holy neophytes added another oratory made of stone, which they dedicated to Christ and the holy apostles Peter and Paul.

So it was by the work of these men that the old church of St Mary at Glastonbury was restored, as trustworthy history has continued to repeat throughout the succeeding ages. There are also letters worthy of belief to be found at St Edmund's to this effect: 'the hands of other men did not make the church at Glastonbury, but the very disciples of Christ, namely those sent by St Philip the apostle, built it'. Nor is this inconsistent with the truth, as was set down before, because if the apostle Philip preached to the Gauls, as Freculph says in chapter four of his second book, it can be believed that he also cast the seeds of the Word across the ocean.

3. How a certain monk of St Denis spoke of Glastonbury.

Let us digress a little in order to further establish the antiquity of this church. When a certain monk of Glastonbury named Godfrey, from whose letter we have taken both this chapter and the next, was staying at St Denis in the district of Paris in the time of Henry of Blois, abbot of Glastonbury, one of the older monks asked him, 'Where do your people come from? Where do you live?' He replied, 'I am a Norman monk, father, from the monastery in Britain that is called Glastonbury.' 'Is that ancient church of the perpetual Virgin and compassionate mother still standing?', he asked. 'It is', the monk said. At this the elder, who was gently stroking Godfrey's head, remained wrapt in silence for a long time and at length spoke thus. 'This church of the most glorious martyr Denis and that which you claim as yours share the same honour and privilege the one in France, the other in Britain; they both arose at the same time and each was consecrated by the highest and greatest priest. Yet in one degree yours is superior, for it is called a second Rome.' While he was hanging on that man's words, the guest-master separated them from each other, despite their reluctance, and they never saw each other again. But no more of this.

4. Quomodo multitudo popularis primitus Glastoniam inhabitauerit.

Descriptis fundacione, dedicacione, ac postea inuencione huius oratorii, restat apponere qualiter hec insula a multitudine fuerit inhabitata. Legitur in antiquis Britonum gestis,[22] quod a boreali Britannie parte uenerunt in occidentem XII fratres et tenuerunt plurimas regiones, Uenedociam, Demeciam, Guther, Kedweli, quas proauus eorum Cuneda tenuerat. Nomina eorum fratrum interius annotantur: Ludnerth, Morgen, Catgur, Cathmor, Merguid, Moruined, Morehel, Morcant, Boten, Morgent,[e] Mortineil, Glasteing, Hic[f] est ille Glasteing, qui per mediterraneos Anglos secus uillam que dicitur Escebtiorne[23] scrofam suam, usque ad Wellis, et a Wellis per inuiam et aquosam uiam que sugewege, id est scrofe uia, dicitur, sequens, porcellos suos iuxta ecclesiam, de qua nobis sermo est, lactentem sub malo inuenit. Unde usque ad nos emanauit, quod mala mali illius ealdecyrcenas epple, id est[g] ueteris ecclesie poma, uocantur. Sus quoque ealdecyrce suge idcirco nominabatur. Que cum cetere sues IIIIor pedes habeant, mirum dictu, ista habuit octo. Hic[h] igitur Glasteing, postquam insulam illam ingressus eam multimodis bonis uidit affluentem, cum omni familia sua in ea uenit habitare cursumque uite sue ibidem peregit. Ex cuius progenie et familia ei succedente locus ille primitus dicitur populatus. Hec de antiquis Britonum libris sunt./[24]

f3 *5. De diuersis nominibus eiusdem insule*

Hec itaque insula primo Ynswytrin[25] a Britonibus dicta, demum ab Anglis terram sibi subiugantibus, interpretato priore uocabulo, dicta est sua lingua Glastinbiry, uel de Glasteing, de quo premisimus; eciam insula Auallonie celebriter nominatur. Cuius uocabuli hec fuit origo. Supradictum est quod Glasteing scrofam suam sub arbore pomifera iuxta uetustam ecclesiam inuenit. Ubi quia primum adueniens poma in partibus illis rarissima repperit, insulam, Auallonie sua lingua, id est insulam pomorum, nominauit; aualla enim britonice, poma interpretatur latine. Uel cognominatur de quodam Aualloc qui ibidem cum suis filiabus propter loci secretum fertur inhabitasse.

6. Quanta deuocione diuersi sancti illuc aduenerint

Ecclesia de qua sane loquimur, que pro antiquitate sui celebriter ab Anglis, 'uetusta', dicitur,[26] primo uirgea, nescio quid diuine sanctitatis iam inde a principio redoluit spirauitque in omnem patriam quamuis ex deformi grandis reuerencia cultu.

[e] *t* added to *Morgen* later; *Morgen* M.
[f] *hinc* T; *hinc* M.
[g] *id est* om. H.
[h] *hinc* T; *hinc* M.

4. How a great number of people first began to live at Glastonbury.

Having described the foundation, dedication and later rediscovery of this oratory it remains for me to describe how this island came to be inhabited by a large number of people. We read in the *Deeds of the Ancient Britons* that twelve brothers from the northern parts of Britain came into the west where they held several territories, namely Gwynedd, Dyfed, Gower and Kidwelly, which their ancestor Cuneda had possessed. The names of the brothers are noted below: Ludnerth, Morgen, Catgur, Cathmor, Merguid, Morvined, Morehel, Morcant, Boten, Morgent, Mortineil and Glasteing. It was this Glasteing who, following his sow through the kingdom of the inland Angles from near the town called *Escebtiorne* up to Wells and from Wells along an inaccessible and watery track called *Sugewege*, that is 'the Sow's Way', found her suckling her piglets under an apple tree near the church of which we have been speaking. From this it has been passed down to us that the apples from that tree are known as *Ealde Cyrcenas epple*, that is Old Church apples. Similarly the sow was called the *Ealde Cyrce suge*. While all other sows have four feet, this one had eight, remarkable though that may sound. As soon as Glasteing reached that island he saw that it abounded with many good things and so came to live on it with all his family and spent the rest of his life there. That place is said to have first been populated by his offspring and the household that succeeded him. These things have been taken from the ancient books of the Britons.

5. On the various names of that island.

This island was at first called Yniswitrin by the Britons but at length was named by the English, who had brought the land under their yoke, Glastinbiry, either a translation into their language of its previous name, or after the Glasteing of whom we spoke above. It is also frequently called the island of Avalon, a name of which this is the origin. It was mentioned above that Glasteing found his sow under an apple tree near the church. Because he discovered on his arrival that apples were very rare in that region he named the island *Avallonie* in his own language, that is Apple Island, for *avalla* in British is the same as *poma* in Latin. Or it was named after a certain Avalloc who is said to have lived there with his daughters because of the solitude of the spot.

6. With what great devotion various saints came thither.

The church of which we are speaking, frequently called by the English 'the Old Church' because of its antiquity, was at first made of brushwood. Yet from the very beginning it possessed a mysterious fragrance of divine sanctity, so that, despite its mean appearance, great reverence for it wafted throughout the whole country.

Hinc confluencium illuc populorum totis callibus unde, hinc opulentorum deposita pompa conuentus, hinc religiosorum et litteratorum frequens perendinacio.

7. De sancto Gilda.

Nam, sicut a maioribus accepimus, Gildas, neque insulsus neque infacetus historicus, cui Britanni debent si quid noticie inter ceteras gentes habent, multum annorum ibi exegit loci sanctitudine captus. Ibique anno domini DXII° de medio factus, in uetusta ecclesia ante altare est sepultus.[27]

8. De sancto Patricio.

Quo fere tempore antea tamen Anglis Britannorum infestantibus pacem et Pelagianis eorum expugnantibus fidem, sanctus Germanus Autisiodorensis, ut alibi legitur,[28] contra utrosque suppecias[i] tulit. Illos enim[j] alleluiatico cantu fudit, et istos euuangelicis et apostolicis tonitribus fulminauit. Inde in patriam meditatus reditum, Patricium ad familiare contubernium asciuit, eundemque post aliquot annos Hyberniensibus, iubente Celestino papa, predicatorem misit. Ille munus iniunctum gnauiter executus, extremis diebus Britanniam remeans, priorem celsitudinem salutacionesque in foro respuens, super altare suum Cornubiam appulit; quod usque hodie apud incolas magne ueneracioni est, tum propter sanctitudinem et utilitatem, tum propter infirmorum salutem. Inde Glastoniam ueniens, XII fratres anachoritice uiuentes ibidem repperiens, congregauit abbatisque suscipiens officium eosdem agere uitam docuit cenobialem, sicut sequens scriptum, quod idem tempore suo conscripsit, manifestius declarat.[29]

9. Carta sancti Patricii episcopi.[30]

In nomine Domini nostri Iesu Christi, ego Patricius, humilis seruunculus Dei, anno incarnacionis eiusdem CCCCXXX[k] in Hyberniam a sanctissimo papa Celestino legatus, Dei gracia Ybernicos ad uiam ueritatis conuerti; et cum eos in fide catholica solidassem, tandem in Britanniam sum reuersus ac, ut credo, duce Deo qui uita est

[i] *suppeticias* T.

[j] *uero* H.

[k] In the margin the date 425 is written, a date that was probably originally in the text because the final X of CCCCXXX is written over an erasure, and the following note, in a late C13 hand, has been added: *et eodem anno uel precedente misit idem papa ad predicandum ibidem uirum nomine Palladium, Britannicum genere. Sed idem cito repatriauit sine ullo effectu*. Not in M.

Hence the streams of people flowing along all the roads that led there; hence the assemblies of the wealthy divested of their pomp; hence the constant succession of men of religion and letters.

7. On St Gildas.

For, as we have heard from our forefathers, Gildas, neither an unlearned nor an inelegant historian, to whom the Britons are indebted for any fame they have among other peoples, passed many years there, captivated by the holiness of the spot. There too he died in 512 AD and was buried before the altar in the old church.

8. On St Patrick.

A little before this time, when the Angles were threatening the peace of the Britons and the Pelagians were assaulting their faith, St Germanus of Auxerre provided help against both, as can be read elsewhere. For he scattered the former with an Alleluia chant and blasted the latter with the thunder of the evangelists and apostles. Then, when he was considering a return to his own country, he received Patrick into his immediate company before sending him some years later, at the command of Pope Celestine, to preach to the Irish. After he had diligently carried out the duty enjoined on him Patrick returned to Britain in his old age, rejecting his former dignity and popular acclaim. He landed in Cornwall on his altar, which is still held in great veneration by the inhabitants, both on account of its sanctity and usefulness and on account of its deliverance of the sick. Then, coming to Glastonbury and finding twelve brothers living there as hermits, he gathered them together and, assuming the office of abbot, taught them to live a communal life, as he quite clearly declares in the following document that he wrote at the time.

9. The charter of St Patrick, bishop.

In the name of our Lord Jesus Christ. I, Patrick, the most humble and least of God's servants was dispatched in 430 AD to Ireland by the most holy Pope Celestine to convert the Irish to the way of truth by the grace of God. After I had established them in the catholic faith I at length returned to Britain where, as I believe by the

et uia, incidi in insulam Ynsgytrin.[31] In qua inueni locum sanctum ac uetustum a Deo electum et sanctificatum in honore intemerate uirginis Dei genitricis Marie, ibique quosdam fratres rudimentis catholice fidei inbutos et pie conuersacionis qui successerunt discipulis sanctorum Phagani et Deruuiani, quorum nomina pro uite meritis ueraciter credo scripta in celis. Et quia 'in memoria eterna erunt iusti', cum eosdem fratres tenere dilexissem, eorum nomina scripto meo redigere uolui. Que sunt Brumbam,[l] Hyregaan, Brenwal, Wencreth, Bamtonmeweng, Adelwlred, Lothor, Wellias, Breden Swelwes, Hin Loernius, et alius Hin.[32] Hii cum essent nobilibus orti natalibus, nobilitatem suam fidei operibus ornare cupientes heremeticam uitam ducere elegerunt. Et quoniam inueni eos humiles ac quietos, elegi pocius cum illis 'abiectus esse magis quam in regalibus curiis habitare'. Sed quia omnium nostrum erat cor unum et anima una, elegimus simul omnes habitare, comedere et bibere pariter et in eadem domo dormire. Sicque me licet inuitum sibi pretulerunt. Non enim dignus eram soluere corrigias calciamentorum eorum.[33] Et cum uitam monasticam ita duceremus iuxta normam probabilium patrum, ostenderunt mihi prefati fratres scripta sanctorum Phagani et Deruuiani, in quibus continebatur quod XII discipuli sanctorum[m] Philippi et Iacobi ipsam uetustam ecclesiam construxerant in honore prelibate aduocatricis nostre per doctrinamentum beati archangeli Gabrielis. Insuper et quod Dominus eamdem ecclesiam celitus in honore sue matris dedicauerat, et quod tres reges pagani ipsis XII ad eorum sustenementum XII porciones terre dederunt. Nec non et in scriptis recencioribus inueni quod sancti Phaganus et Deruuianus perquisierant ab Eleutherio papa, qui eos miserat decem annos indulgencie. Et ego frater Patricius a pie memorie Celestino papa duodecim annos tempore meo adquisiui.

Post multum uero temporis, assumpto mecum Wellia, confratre meo, per condensitatem silue cum magna difficultate conscendimus[n] cacumen montis qui eminet in eadem insula. Quo cum peruenissemus, apparuit[o] oratorium unum uetustum et fere dirutum,[p] habile tamen deuocioni Christiane, et, pro ut mihi uidebatur, a Deo electum. Quod cum ingressi essemus tanta odoris suauitate replebamur, uti in paradisi amenitate positos nos crederemus.[q] Egredientes igitur et reingredientes locumque diligencius perscrutantes, inuenimus uolumen unum, in quo scripti (actus)[r] erant apostolorum pariter cum actis et gestis sanctorum Phagani et Deruuiani, ex magna parte consumptum. In cuius tamen fine uoluminis invenimus scripturam que dicebat, quod predicti sancti Phaganus et Deruuianus per reuelacionem (Domini nostri)[r] Ihesu Christi idem oratorium edificarunt in honore sancti Michaelis archangeli,

l *Brumban* H.

m A later hand has crudely altered the *sanctorum* to *sancti* and erased the name *Jacobi*; a C15 hand has restored the original in the margin and M reads *sanctorum Philippi et Jacobi*.

n *concendimus* T and H.

o *apperuit* H.

p *dirrutum* T.

q *credrermus* T.

r A contemporary hand, probably the scribe's, has inserted these additions, which can be found in M, above the line and indicated their position by a caret sign.

guidance of God who is the life and the way, I came to the island of Yniswitrin on which I discovered a holy and ancient place chosen by God and consecrated in honour of the undefiled Virgin Mary, the mother of God. There too I encountered some brothers, instructed in the rudiments of the catholic faith and pious in their lives, who had succeeded the disciples of the saints Phagan and Deruvian and whose names I truly believe to be inscribed in heaven for the merit of their lives. Because 'the righteous shall be held in eternal remembrance' and since I loved those brothers dearly I propose to record their names in this document. They are: Brumbam, Hyregaan, Brenwal, Wencreth, Bamtonmeweng, Adelwlrd, Lothor, Wellias, Breden, Swelwes, Hin Loernius and another Hin. Since they were born to noble families and wanted to crown their nobility with works of faith they chose to live the lives of hermits. Since I found them humble and tranquil I preferred 'to be cast out with them than to live in the courts of kings'. Because we were 'all of one heart and one soul' we elected to all live together, sharing our food and drink and sleeping in the same house. And although I was unwilling, for 'I was not worthy to unloose the latchets of their shoes', they set me at their head. After we had been leading the monastic life in this way, following what we believed to be the rules of the fathers, the brothers showed me writings by saints Phagan and Deruvian which asserted that twelve disciples of saints Philip and James had built that old church in honour of our patroness, instructed by the blessed archangel Gabriel; and that moreover the Lord of Heaven had consecrated that church in honour of his mother, while three pagan kings had given twelve portions of land to those twelve for their sustenance. In addition I discovered in a more recent document that saints Phagan and Deruvian had petitioned Pope Eleutherius who had granted them an indulgence of ten years. I too, brother Patrick, acquired in my own time an indulgence of twelve years from Pope Celestine of pious memory.

Much later, taking brother Wellias with me, I climbed with great difficulty through a dense wood to the peak of a hill which rises on that island. When we reached it we saw an old oratory, almost destroyed yet suitable for Christian devotion and, so it seemed to me, chosen by God. As soon as we entered it we were engulfed by so sweet an odour that we believed ourselves to be amid the delights of paradise, whereupon, examining that place very carefully inside and out, we found a single volume, the great part of which was destroyed, in which had been written the acts of the apostles together with the acts and deeds of saints Phagan and Deruvian. At the end of the volume we found writing to the effect that saints Phagan and Deruvian had built the oratory at the inspiration of our Lord Jesus Christ in honour of St Michael the archangel so that he who would lead men to

quatinus ibi ab hominibus haberet honorem, qui homines in perpetuos honores iubente Deo est introducturus. At cum delectaret nos illa scriptura, nitebamur eam ad finem legere. Dicebat (et)[s] enim eadem scriptura, quod uenerandi Phaganus et Deruuianus moram ibi fecerunt per nouem annos, et quod ipsi eciam perquisierant triginta annorum indulgenciam omnibus Christicolis locum ipsum ob honorem beati Michaelis propria[t] uoluntate uisitantibus.[u]

Inuento ergo tanto diuine bonitatis thesauro, ego et frater Wellias tribus mensibus ieiunauimus, oracionibus uacantes et uigiliis demonibusque et beluis multiformiter apparentibus imperantes. Quadam autem nocte cum me sopori dedissem, apparuit mihi dominus Ihesus in uisu dicens: 'Patrici, serue meus, scias me elegisse locum istum ad honorem nominis mei et ut hic honoranter inuocent adiutorium archangeli mei Michaelis; et hoc tibi signum et fratribus tuis, quatinus et ipsi credant; brachium tuum sinistrum arescet donec, que uidisti, annunciaueris fratribus,[v] qui in cella sunt inferiori, et denuo huc redieris.' Et factum est ita. Ab illo die statuimus[w] duos fratres in perpetuum ibi, nisi pastores futuri ob iustam causam aliter decreuerint. Arnulfo autem et Ogmar,[34] Ybernicis fratribus qui mecum uenerant de Ybernia, pro eo quod ad exhortacionem meam apud dictum humiliter oratorium manere ceperunt, presentem paginam commisi, aliam similem in archa sancte Marie retinens in monimentum posteris. Et ego Patricius per consilium fratrum meorum, omnibus qui siluam ex omni (parte)[x] prefati montis in securi et ascia pia intencione deiecerint, ut facilior paretur aditus Christianis ecclesiam beate perpetueque uirginis pie uisitaturis et oratorium predictum, centum dies uenie concedo.

Hec autem ita ueraciter se habere, testimonio scripture uetustissime simul cum relacionibus seniorum comprobauimus. Hic itaque sanctus supramemoratus, qui est Yberniensium apostolus et in insula Auallonie abbas primus, postquam predictos fratres regularibus disciplinis conuenienter informauerat et eundem locum terris (et)[y] possessionibus de dono regum ac aliorum principum competenter ditauerat, post aliquot[z] annos decursos nature cessit et sepulturam, angelo demonstrante flammaque ingenti de eodem loco cunctis uidentibus qui aderant erumpente, in uetusta ecclesia a dextra altaris promeruit.[35]

[s] A contemporary hand, probably the scribe's, has inserted this addition, which can be found in M, above the line and indicated its position by a caret sign.

[t] *pia* H.

[u] *uisitatis* T.

[v] *tuis* inserted after *fratribus* in H.

[w] *statumus* T.

[x] A contemporary hand, probably the scribe's, has added this above the line and indicated its position by a caret sign. In M.

[y] *et* om. T.

[z] *aliquos* H.

eternal honour at God's command would there be honoured by men. Since that writing delighted us we struggled to read it to the end. It went on to say that the venerable Phagan and Deruvian remained there for nine years and acquired an indulgence of thirty years for all Christians who voluntarily visited that place in honour of the blessed Michael.

After we had discovered such a treasure of divine goodness brother Wellias and I fasted for three months, devoting ourselves to prayers and vigils and gaining control over the demons and beasts that appeared before us in many forms. Then on a certain night when I had given myself to sleep the Lord Jesus appeared to me in a vision and said, 'Patrick, my servant, know that I have chosen this place to honour My name and that here men may invoke the aid of My archangel Michael; and as a sign to you and to your brethren, that they might believe too, your left arm shall wither until you have made known what you have seen to the brethren in the cell below and then returned here.' And so it happened. From that day we decided that there should always be two brothers in that place, unless in the future church leaders should determine otherwise for some proper reason. To my Irish brothers, Arnulf and Ogmar, who had come with me from Ireland, I entrusted this document because they began to abide humbly in this oratory at my request and I kept another copy in St Mary's chest as a monument for posterity. And I Patrick, on the advice of my brethren, grant one hundred days of indulgence to all who shall hew with axe or mattock the wood that covers this hill with the pious intention of facilitating the approach of pious Christians who visit the church of the blessed and perpetual Virgin and the aforesaid oratory.

That these things truly occurred we have confirmed in the testimony of a very ancient document as well as by the traditions of our elders. After this the saint who was the apostle of the Irish and the first abbot on the island of Avalon suitably instructed the brethren in the disciplinary rules and appropriately enriched the place with lands and possessions, the gifts of kings and other leaders. Some years passed by and at length he yielded up to nature and earned burial in the old church to the right of the altar, a place, indicated by an angel, from which a huge flame, visible to all who were present, burst forth.

10. De excessu sancti Patricii.

Excessit ergo Patricius anno etatis sue CXI, incarnacionis uero Domini CCCCLXXII, qui fuit annus ex quo in Yberniam missus est XLVII. Si quidem anno Domini CCCLXI in lucem uenit et anno Domini CCCCXXV a Celestino papa in Hyberniam missus fuit, hic fuit annus etatis sue LXIIII et anno Domini CCCCXXXIII Ybernicos ad fidem Christi conuertit. Demum Britanniam reuersus in optima conuersacione XXXIX annos in insula Auallonie permansit. Requieuit autem in f4 uetusta / ecclesia a dextro latere altaris per multorum annorum curricula, uidelicet DCC et decem annos, usque ad combustionem eiusdem ecclesie. Corpus uero suum in piramide saxea fuit collocatum iuxta altare uersus austrum quam, pro ueneracione eiusdem sancti, auro et argento postea nobiliter uestiuit domesticorum diligencia.[36]

11. Uisio de sancto Patricio.

Cum autem longe post obitum beati Patricii frequens questio utrum ibi monachus et abbas fuerit, omnem scrupulum absoluit uisio cuiusdam fratris, qui post obitum beati uiri, nutante memoria utrum ibi monachus et abbas fuerit, cum de hoc frequens uerteretur questio, tali confirmatus est oraculo. Resolutus enim in soporem, uisus audire quendam legentem post multa eius miracula, hec uerba. 'Hic igitur metropolitani pallii decoratus est sanctitate; postmodum uero hic monachus et abbas factus est.' Adiecit eciam ut non integre credenti litteris aureis quod dixerat scriptum ostenderet.[37]

12. De sancto Indracto et de sancta Brigida.

Hinc Yberniensibus mos inolitus ad exosculandas patroni reliquias locum frequentare. Unde et sanctum Indractum et beatam Brigidam illius terre non obscuros incolas illuc olim commeasse celeberrimus sermo est. Brigidam quidem, que anno Domini CCCCLXXXVIII illuc uenerat post aliquantulam moram quam in insula que dicitur Beokery fecerat, domum reuersam, relictis ibidem quibusdam insigniis suis, uidelicet pera, monili, nola et textrilibus armis, que ibidem ad eius memoriam reseruantur.[38] Indractum uero cum sociis ibidem martirizatum et sepultum, sicut alias stilus noster non tacuit. Postea per Ynam regem de loco martirii in Glastoniensem translatum ecclesiam[39].[a]

[a] I record here remarks found in L about Indract as they may be taken from William's missing *Life. Ibidem etiam requiescit sanctus Indractus martir cum vii sociis suis commartiribus. Hii uero sancti ex regali Hiberniensium progenie Romam tum peregrinacionis euntes et per Glastoniam ad patriam suam redeuntes, beato Patricio tunc ibidem existente abbate, ut eiusdem salubriter fruerentur colloquio, in quadam uilla iuxta Glastoniam, Shapewick nominata, hospitati,*

10. On the death of St Patrick.

Patrick died at the age of 111 in 472 AD, which was the 47th year after he had been sent into Ireland. If he was indeed born in 361 and was sent into Ireland in 425 this took place when he was 64; and he converted the Irish to the faith of Christ in 433. When he eventually returned to Britain he remained on the island of Avalon for 39 years leading the best possible life. Then he rested at the right hand side of the altar in the old church for many years, 710 in fact, until the fire in that church, whereupon his body was placed in a stone pyramid near the altar to the south and the diligence of the inmates of the house later ensured that this was nobly covered in gold and silver out of reverence for the saint.

11. A vision of St Patrick.

Long after the death of the blessed Patrick, when the question often arose whether he had been a monk and abbot there, all doubt was eliminated by the vision of a certain brother whose memory had grown shaky after the blessed man's death so that he continually asked himself whether it had been so or not. It was confirmed by the following oracle. When he had sunk into sleep he seemed to hear someone who was reciting the saint's miracles add these words: 'Therefore this man was distinguished with the holiness of a metropolitan pall; and later he became a monk and abbot.' He added too that he would show what he had said written down in letters of gold for anyone who did not completely believe it.

12. On St Indract and St Bridget.

Hence the custom developed among the Irish of visiting that place to kiss the relics of their patron. Whence the well-known story that St Indract and the blessed Bridget, prominent citizens of that land, once frequented the place. They say that after St Bridget, who had come there in 488 AD, had tarried for some time on the island called Beckery, she returned home but left behind certain of her ornaments, namely a bag, a necklace, a small bell and weaving implements, which are still preserved there in memory of her. As our pen has recorded elsewhere, Indract and his companions were martyred and buried there. Later he was translated by King Ine from his place of martyrdom into the church of Glastonbury.

13. De sancto Benigno.

Anno Domini CCCCLX sanctus Benignus uenit Glastoniam. Hic discipulus sancti Patricii et successor in episcopatu eius tertius in Ybernia fuit, quemadmodum eorum gesta testantur. Hic igitur, angelo monente, patriam pontificiique dignitatem ex uoto deserens, uoluntaria peregrinacione suscepta, Glastoniam, Deo duce, peruenit, ubi et sanctum Patricium inuenit. Quante autem apud Deum gracie fuerit, multis patet uirtutum indiciis; hoc eciam testantur eius insignia apud Fernigemere, data eius precibus aqua largissima et ex eius baculo arido ingens arbor uirens et frondifera. Hic itaque post inmensos agones in dicta insula beato fine quieuit ac post multorum curricula annorum, id est anno Domini M^o nonagesimo primo,[b] Glastoniam honorifice translatus est[40].[c]

14. De sancto Columkilla.

Anno Domini DIIII sanctus Kolumkilla uenit Glastoniam. Quidam affirmant hunc sanctum uite sue cursum ibidem consummasse, sed utrum sic, aut inde repatriauerit, non diffinio.[41]

15. De sancto Dauid archiepiscopo.

Iam uero quanti eum locum[d] penderit magnus ille Dauid Meneuensium archiepiscopus celebrius est quam ut nostro indigeat illustrari relatu. Is antiquitatem

noctis silentio in lectulis suis dormientes ab infelicibus satellitibus martirizati sunt. Qualiter uero corpora postmodo sanctissimo Ine regi Westsaxonum Dei prouidentia fuerunt reuelata et per eundem Glastoniam translata, in libris de gestis eorum apud Glastoniam plenius habetur. fol. 8r.

b *nongentesimo primo* T, M.

c I record here L's very similar remarks about Benignus: *Anno Dominice incarnacionis CCCCLX^O sanctus Benignus uenit Glastoniam. Hic discipulus sancti Patricii et successor in episcopatu eius tertius in Hibernia fuit, sicut in gestis eorum scriptum est. Hic, angelo admonente, patriam pontificiique dignitatem ex uoto deseruit. Uoluntaria igitur pereg(r)inacione pro dileccione Dei suscepta, ob amorem sancti Patricii Glastoniam usque peruenit. Hic quante apud Deum gracie fuerit ostendit Deus crebro multis uirtutum indiciis mirabilis in sanctis suis. Hoc testantur eius insignia apud Ferlingemere, data eius precibus aqua latissima et ex eius baculo arido ingens arbor uirens et frondifera. Hic uero sanctus multorum aliorum patrator miraculorum post immensos agones in eadem insula anno ab incarnacione Domini CCCC(LX)IIII in Domino requieuit qui post multos annos, scilicet anno gracie M^O nonagesimo primo, Glastoniam honorifice translatus est.*

d For *eum locum* L reads *Glastoniam.*

13. On St Benignus.

In 460 AD St Benignus came to Glastonbury. He was a disciple of St Patrick and the third to succeed him in his Irish see, as their *Acts* attest. Admonished by an angel, he forsook his homeland and the dignity of his episcopate in accordance with a vow and undertook a voluntary pilgrimage which led him, under God's guidance, to Glastonbury where he found St Patrick. How much favour he found with God is revealed by many signs and miracles; witness the marks of his presence still at Meare, the broad expanse of water granted at his prayers and the huge leafy tree that flourished from his withered staff. After endless struggles on the island he came to a blessed end and, after many years had passed, in 1091 AD, he was translated to Glastonbury with honour.

14. On St Columba.

In 504 AD St Columba came to Glastonbury. Some men say that this saint completed the course of his life there, but whether this is so or whether he returned to his own country I cannot determine.

15. On St David the archbishop.

How highly St David, the great archbishop of Menevia, esteemed that place is too well-known to need illustration by our account. He verified the antiquity and

et sanctitudinem ecclesie[e] diuino comprobauit oraculo. Dedicacioni enim (eius)[f] intendens, cum episcopis septem, quorum primas erat, ad locum uenit. Paratis autem omnibus que officii usus exposceret, nocte precessura, ut putabat, festiuitatem, sompno indulsit. Omnes ergo sensus in quietem solutus, uidit Dominum (Ihesum)[f] assistere causam aduentus blande sciscitantem. Quam cum ille incunctanter[g] aperuisset, reuocauit eum a sentencia Dominus hoc dicto. Dedicatam a se dudum[h] ecclesiam in honore[i] sue matris, iteracione humana sacramentum temerari non oportere. Simulque cum dicto, uolam digito terebrare uisus, hec subiecit: Hoc haberet signum repeti non debere quod ipse anticipasset facere, set quia intencionis illius non tam fuerit audacia quam deuocio, penam non prolongandam. Denique mane futuro cum in missa, 'per ipsum et cum ipso et in ipso', dicturus esset, plenum ei salutis uigorem refundendum. Hiis terroribus antistes sompno excussus, sicut tunc sanie ulcerosa impalluit, sic postea prophetie ueritati applausit. Sed ne nichil uideretur egisse, aliam ecclesiam citato fecit et dedicauit opere[j].[42]

16. De reliquiis sancti Dauid.

Excessit autem hic sanctus Deo dignus anno domini DXLVI. Quidam sane affirmant reliquias de hoc sancto et incomparabili uiro cum beato Patricio in uetusta ecclesia fuisse collocatas, et Walenses oracionum frequentacione et multiplici sermone id proculdubio astruunt et corroborant, illud in medium proferentes, Bernardum episcopum Rosine Uallis ibidem semel et secundo reliquias predicti sancti quesisse, et multis reclamantibus non inuenisse. Set qualiter de Rosina Ualle usque ad Glastoniam dicte reliquie translate fuerint, subiungemus. Quedam matrona, nomine Aelswiza, tempore Edgari regis, predictas reliquias adquisiuit per quemdam cognatum suum, qui tunc temporis fuit episcopus apud Rosinam Uallem, quando tota terra illa ita uastata erat, ut uix aliquis homo illic inueniretur, nisi pauce femine, et eciam in raris locis, et eas Glastonie contulit.[43]

17. De reliquiis a Guallia Glastoniam translatis.

Testes sunt Walenses, religiosi terre illius, qui ea tempestate plurima corpora sanctorum et reliquias, Romam ituri, secum Glastoniam detulerunt et, itinerando

[e] L inserts *illi* before *diuino*.
[f] Interlinear additions in the same, or a contemporary, hand; part of the text of M.
[g] *incunctatus* H.
[h] L inserts *illam* before *ecclesiam*.
[i] *honorem* in L.
[j] L adds after *opere, quam a domesticis seinte Marie la petite nominabatur. Locus reuera terribilis ac metuendus est quem Deus sanctificauit et tabernaculum suum fecit.*

sanctity of the church through a divine oracle, for he came thither with seven bishops, of whom he was the chief, in order to dedicate it. But after everything that the service customarily required had been prepared he was indulging himself in sleep on what he thought would be the night preceding the ceremony. He had submerged all his senses in slumber when he saw the Lord Jesus standing beside him, gently asking him why he had come. Upon his instantly disclosing the reason the Lord restrained him from his purpose by saying that He Himself had long ago dedicated the church in honour of His mother and that it would not be seemly to profane the sacrament with a human repetition. As He was speaking He seemed to pierce the saint's palm with His finger and added that he should take it as a sign that he ought not repeat what the Lord had done beforehand; but because he had been motivated by devotion, not impudence, his punishment would not be prolonged, so that, when he was about to say the words 'through Him and with Him and in Him' in the mass on the following morning, the full vigour of his health would be restored to him. The priest was shaken out of his sleep by these terrors and, just as at the time he grew pale at the ulcerous sore, so later he applauded the truth of the prophecy. But so that he might not seem to have done nothing he quickly built another church and dedicated it as his own work.

16. On the relics of St David.

This worthy saint of God died in 546 AD. Moreover certain men assert that the relics of this saintly and incomparable man have been placed with those of the blessed Patrick in the old church, a claim supported and confirmed as beyond doubt by the frequent prayers of the Welsh and many of their stories, in which they openly disclose that Bernard, bishop of the Ross Valley, has more than once looked for the relics of the saint there despite the opposition of many but has not found them. We will append an account of how his relics were translated from the Ross Valley to Glastonbury. In the time of King Edgar a certain lady named Aelswitha acquired them through a kinsman of hers, who was bishop of the Ross Valley at that time when all the districts had been so devastated that scarcely anyone was to be found there, except a few women and these in scattered places. And she bore the relics to Glastonbury.

17. On the relics translated from Wales to Glastonbury.

Certain religious men from Wales bear witness that, intending a journey to Rome in those days, they brought with them to Glastonbury many bodies of saints and

proficiscentes, dimiserunt ibidem. Facta est hec translacio anno post mortem eiusdem CCCCXX, incarnacionis Dominice nongentesimo LXII.[44]

18. De sanctitate et dignitate Glastoniensis ecclesie.

Est ergo Glastoniensis ecclesia omnium quas quidem nouerim antiquissima in Anglia, indeque cognomen sortita. In ea, preter beatum Patricium et alios de quibus superius dixi, multorum sanctorum corporales seruantur exuuie, nec a beatorum cineribus uacat ullus fani ambitus. Adeo pauimentum lapide constratum, adeo altaris latera, ipsumque altare supra et infra, reliquiis confertissimis aggerantur.[k] Merito ergo dicitur celeste in terris sanctuarium tot sanctorum reconditorium. Quam felices, Deus bone, habitatores, quos ipsa loci reuerencia ad morum composicionem inuitat. Nullum de hiis crediderim deperire celo, quos corporibus egressos tantorum patronorum excipit laus uel excusacio. Ubi autem notare licet in pauimento, uel per triangulum, uel per quadratum, lapides altrinsecus ex industria positos, ex plumbo sigillatos, sub quibus quiddam archani sacri contineri si credo, iniuriam religioni non facio. Antiquitas et sanctorum congeries exciuit reverenciam loco, ut uix ibi quis noctu presumat excubias agere, uix interdiu excrescens flegma proicere; illusorie feditatis conscius toto cohorreat corpore. Nullus inter contiguum cimiterium uel auem uenatoriam aduexit, uel quadrupedes induxit, qui sui uel rei possesse indempnis abierit. Ferro uel aqua examinandi si oracionem ibi deposuerunt, omnes quos presens memoria complectitur, uno excepto, de salute sua tripudiarunt. Si quis e uicino aliquod edificium locandum putasset, quod obumbracione sua lucem inuideret ecclesie, patuit ruine. Satisque constat homines illius prouincie nullum sanctius uel crebrius iuramentum habere, quam per ueterem ecclesiam, nichil magis uitantes, metu celeris uindicte, quam periurare. Labantem ueritatem dictorum que proposuimus plurimorum ueracissimorum hominum pro successu annorum fulciunt testimonia[l].[45]

19. De sancto Paulino episcopo.

Set ut ad propositum redeam, sancti Patricii natiuitas, que anno Dominice incarnacionis CCCLXI fuit, aduentum beati Augustini in Britanniam ducentis triginta sex annis precessit. Cuius predicacionis commilitonem, Paulinum, ex archiepiscopo Eboracensi, Rofensem episcopum, asserit patrum tradicio, ecclesie contextum dudum, ut diximus, uirgee ligneo tabulatu induisse et plumbo a summo usque deorsum cooperuisse. Egit nimirum predicabilis uiri sollercia, ut nichil decederet sanctitati, et plurimum accederet ornatui. Et certe solet ecclesiarum cultus

[k] *aggeruntur* T.
[l] *testimonio* H.

relics which they left behind there when they set out on their journey. This translation occurred in 962 AD, the 420th year after the death of St David.

18. On the sanctity and dignity of the church of Glastonbury.

The church of Glastonbury, therefore, is the oldest of all those that I know of in England and hence the epithet applied to it. In it are preserved the bodily remains of many saints, besides Patrick and the others of whom I spoke above, and there is no part of the church that is without the ashes of the blessed. The stone-paved floor, the sides of the altar, the very altar itself, above and within, are filled with relics close-packed. Deservedly indeed is the repository of so many saints said to be a heavenly shirine on earth. How fortunate, good Lord, are those inhabitants who have been summoned to an upright life by reverence for that place. I cannot believe that any of these can fail of heaven, for their deaths are accompanied by the recommendation and advocacy of such great patrons. There one can observe all over the floor stones, artfully interlaced in the forms of triangles or squares and sealed with lead; I do no harm to religion if I believe some sacred mystery is contained beneath them. Its age and its multitude of saints have called forth such reverence for the place that at night scarcely anyone presumes to keep watch there, nor during the day to spit there; let anyone aware of displaying such foul contempt quake with bodily fear. No one has brought a hunting bird within the neighbouring cemetery or led a horse thither and left again without himself or his possessions being harmed. Within living memory everyone undergoing ordeal by iron or water who has offered a prayer there has, with one exception, rejoiced in his salvation. If anyone thought to place any building nearby which by its shade interfered with the light of the church that building became a ruin. It is quite clear that to the men of that province no oath was holier or more oft repeated than that 'by the old church', upon which they did anything rather than perjure themselves, out of fear of sudden retribution. The testimony of many absolutely truthful men throughout the ages upholds the truth, if it be doubtful, of the words we have set down.

19. On St Paulinus the bishop.

To return to my theme, the birth of St Patrick in 361 AD preceded the arrival in Britain of the blessed Augustine by 236 years. The traditions of our fathers maintain that the latter's comrade in preaching, Paulinus, bishop of Rochester and earlier archbishop of York, had strengthened the structure of the church, previously made of wattle as we said, with a layer of boards and had covered it from the top down with lead. It was managed with such skill by this celebrated man that the church lost none of its sanctity and its beauty was much increased. And certainly the more

augustior[m] quamlibet brutas mentes ad orandum illicere, quamlibet ceruicositatem ad supplicandum inflectere.[46]

20. De translacione Indracti ac sociorum eius.

Aliquantis autem annis elapsis, per Ynam, regem Westsaxonum, diuine uisionis compotem, martiris Indracti et sociorum eius corpora de loco martirii translata et in eadem ecclesia tumulata sunt. Ipsius quidem in lapidea piramide ad sinistrum altaris, ceterorum in pauimento, pro ut uel casus tulit uel industria locauit.[47]

21. De reliquiis a terra Northambimbrorum[n] usque Glastoniam translatis.

f5 /Item multo post tempore infestantibus Danis Northanimbriam, Tica, earum parcium abbas, sub optentu pacis a borea in occidentem commigrans, Glastoniam concessit eamdemque ecclesiam abbatis iure anno Dominice incarnacionis septingentesimo LIIII rexit. Multis enim annis aquilonalis regio piratarum patuit prede, cum interim alie partes Anglie nichil sustulerunt[o] hostile.[p] Attulit sane secum locupletes incolatus sui obsides, reliquias scilicet Aidani Lindisfarnesis episcopi,[48] corpora sanctorum Ceolfridi,[49] Benedicti,[50] Estrepini, Hetberti, Selfridi,[q] Wiorensium abbatum,[51] Bede presbiteri,[52] Hebbe, Bege, Borsili.[53] Item corpus Hilde abbatisse monasterii quod quondam Strenesheal h nunc Wyteby nuncupatur.[54] Hee igitur super[r] altare locate reliquie non parum reuerencie loco adiecere. Idem[s] porro Tica, cum ualefecisset uite, in dextro angulo maioris ecclesie iuxta introitum uetuste notabilem accepit sepulturam. Ea est et mole structure et arte celature non ignobilis.[55]

[m] *angustior* T.

[n] *Norhtamhimbrorum* H.

[o] *susspirarent* T.

[p] A siglum above *attulit* directs the reader to the following marginal note in a hand of the late C13 which is found in M after *hostile*: *Hoc forte factum fuit procurante rege Edmundo seniore, sicut in Gestis Pontificum* (i.e. p.198) *legitur. Multos sanctos Glastoniam rex Edmundus in expedicione aquilonali compertos et de terra leuatos misit. Inter quos Hildam, Celfridum abbatem et Aidanum fecit illuc deportari.*

[q] *Sigfridi* originally but *Sel* interlined; *Seifridi* M.

[r] *supra* H.

[s] *Isdem* T.

grandly constructed a church is the more likely it is to entice the dullest minds to prayer and to bend the most stubborn to supplication.

20. On the translation of Indract and his comrades.

Some years later the bodies of the martyr Indract and his comrades were translated from their place of martyrdom and buried in that church by Ine, King of the West Saxons, who had received a divine vision. Indract's body was put in a stone pyramid to the left of the altar, the others were put under the floor in places either carefully chosen or dictated by chance.

21. On the relics translated from Northumbria to Glastonbury.

Some time later when the Danes were attacking Northumbria, Tyccea, an abbot from those parts, migrating from the north to the west under cover of peace, retired to Glastonbury where, in his capacity of abbot, he assumed the rule of the church in 754 AD. For many years the north of the country was exposed to the plunder of these pirates while the rest of England suffered no attacks. Naturally Tyccea brought with him rich sureties from his homeland, namely the relics of Aidan, bishop of Lindisfarne, the bodies of the saints Ceolfrith, Benedict, Eosterwine, Hwaetberht and Selfrith, abbots of Wearmouth, Bede the presbyter, Hebba, Begu and Boisil, together with the body of Hilda, abbess of the monastery once known as Streoneshalh but now called Whitby. These relics were placed above the altar and added greatly to reverence for the place. Moreover when Tyccea himself bid farewell to life he received a distinguished burial in the right hand corner of the greater church near the entrance to the old one. His sepulcre is notable both for its size and for its artistic engraving.

22. De diuersis reliquiis Glastonie repositis.

Et quoniam Glastonie insula multorum insignitur sanctorum cineribus preter supra enumeratos, libet paucorum ex multis annotare nomina,[t] quorum corporales exuuias pro maiori parte ibidem requiescere non dubitamus. Nam particulares reliquias sanctorum illuc a regibus et magnatibus collatas enumerare, in immensum esset uolumen extendere; et in textis euuangeliorum annotantur. Pretermissis igitur supramemoratis, uidelicet XII discipulis sancti Philippi, Phagano et Deruuiano et eorum multis discipulis, Patricio, Benigno, Indracto cum suis sociis, Gilda sapiente, sancto Dauid Meneuense et aliis quos uenerabilis Tica refertur illuc portasse. Sciendum quod illic ueraciter dicuntur requiescere sanctus Paulinus, Northanimbrorum archiepiscopus,[56] duo Innocentes a pio rege Edgaro de Bethleem illuc translati, sanctus Dunstanus, pater magnificus cuius translacionem a Cantuaria ad Glastoniam subiungemus. Item sanctus Idanus episcopus et sanctus Ultanus episcopus, frater beati Fursei, cuius gesta miranda leguntur. Illic et sanctus Iltuit, inter Walenses famosissimus, et sanctus Besilius, in etate tenera martirizatus. Item reliquie sancti Urbani pape et martiris, ossa sancti Anastasii martiris,[57] ossa sancti Cesarii martiris, ossa sancti Benigni martiris, ossa sancti Melani episcopi et martiris. Ibi eciam requiescit sancta Ealfleda[u] regina, et sancta Aelswitha[v] uirgo tota integra in carne et osse, sicut testantur qui eam uiderunt, cum cilicio et sacro uelamine non putrefactis. Illic eciam sunt ossa sancte Batildis[w] regine et ossa sancte Mamille uirginis. Insuper corpora sanctarum[x] Ursule, Darie,[58] Crisante, Udilie, Marie, Marthe, Lucie, Lucei, Waleburge,[y] Geretrude[z] et Cecilie. Et preter sanctos enumeratos,[a] ibidem sunt sanctorum reliquie[b] innumerabiles de dono regum, principum, pontificum et aliorum nobilium, quorum quedam nomina[c] in antiquis[d] ecclesie libris annotantur. Multe eciam reliquie de terra Northanimbrorum tempore guerre eis a Danis[e] illate, de Guallia[f] insuper tempore sue persecucionis ad Glastoniam, quasi ad sanctorum reconditorium, sunt delate, et quamuis apud nos non sit eorum plena cognicio, cognicione tamen diuina et contemplacione plenius perfruuntur.[59]

t L inserts *infinita* after *nomina.*

u *Aelfleda* L.

v In the margin in a fourteenth century hand is: *nota: de uirgine integra.*

w *Baltildis* L.

x L inserts *uirginum* after *sanctarum.*

y *Waleburge* L, but *Waleburbe* T.

z *Geretrudis* L.

a *supramemoratos* L.

b L inserts *particulares* before *innumerabiles.*

c L inserts *infinita* after *nomina.*

d L inserts *Glastonie* before *ecclesie.*

e *a Danis eis* L.

f *Wallia* L.

22. On the various relics deposited at Glastonbury.

Since the island of Glastonbury is remarkable in containing the ashes of so many saints besides those mentioned above it is a pleasure to record the names of a few out of the many whose bodily remains, we do not doubt, for the most part rest there. For to recount in detail the relics of saints collected there by kings and magnates would be to extend this volume immeasurably; besides, they are recorded in the Gospel-Books. I will pass over the ones mentioned before, namely the twelve disciples of St Philip, Phagan and Deruvian and their many disciples, Patrick, Benignus, Indract and his comrades, Gildas the wise, St David of Menevia and those whom the venerable Tyccea is said to have brought thither. Know that it is reliably said that resting there are St Paulinus, archbishop of Northumbria, two Innocents translated thither from Bethlehem by pious King Edgar, St Dunstan, our magnificent father an account of whose translation from Canterbury to Glastonbury we subjoin, as well as the bishops St Aidan and St Ultan, the brother of the blessed Fursey of whose wonderful deeds we read. There too are St Iltuit, so celebrated among the Welsh, and St Besilius, martyred at a tender age; also the relics of St Urban, pope and martyr, the bones of the martyrs St Anastasius, St Cesarius, St Benignus and St Melanus the bishop. There also rest St Aelflaed the queen and St Aelswitha, the virgin whose flesh and bones are still whole, as those who have seen them attest, and whose hair shirt and holy robe have not rotted. There too are the bones of the queen St Balthild and the virgin St Mamilla as well as the bodies of the saints Ursula, Daria, Crisanta, Udilia, Mary, Martha, Lucy, Luceus, Waleburga, Gertrude and Cecilia. In addition to the saints just mentioned there are innumerable relics of saints, the gifts of kings, princes, bishops and other noblemen, some of whose names are recorded in the old books of the church. Many relics too, carried from the kingdom of Northumbria at the time the Danes were waging war there. Others were brought from Wales, when it was being persecuted, to Glastonbury, as though to a storehouse of saints. And although we do not have complete knowledge of them, they themselves rejoice in their full knowledge and contemplation of God.

23. De translacione sancti Dunstani a Cantuaria ad Glastoniam.

Iam quia de aliis sanctis mencionem fecimus, modum translacionis sancti Dunstani subiungemus. Anno ab incarnacione Domini MXII, regnante illustri rege Eadmundo,[g] patria lingua Yreneside numcupato, aduenientes Dani in orientales Anglie plagas tocius Cancie fines in suam redigebant potestatem, a quibus multi propria dignitate priuati, multi a patria eliminati, multi crudelissima sunt morte trucidati. Sicque usque ad ciuitatem Londoniensem, non gradui, non etati, uel sexui parcentes, homicidiis, rapinis, incendiis, diuina eque ut humana exterminabant. Hinc, ut de aliis taceam, uenerandus archipresul Elfegus,[h] proprie dignitatis est sede propulsus, predia deuastantur, possessiones diripiuntur.[i] Cetera sine fletu quis referat? Proh dolor! ingressi sunt sceleratissimi metropolitanam Anglorum ecclesiam, in religiosos famulos Christi irruentes et, quod dictu horrendum est, a domo Dei singulos eliminantes omniaque incendio consumentes.[60]

Contigit isdem temporibus prefatum regem Edmundum Glastoniam aduentare; commoratusque illic aliquamdiu, Brithredo abbati et fratribus eiusdem loci tante captiuitatis ex ordine retulit historiam, memorans eisdem Cantuariensem ecclesiam incensam et habitatoribus ac religione penitus uiduatam. Quibus auditis abbas totaque congregacio ita sunt contristati, ac si singulorum animas gladius pertransiret. Inter cetera eciam eximii patris sui Dunstani uirtutes precelsas recitabant, qui, dum uiueret amplis possessionibus donis, libertatibusque magnificis et, quod pluris est, regularibus institutis Glastoniam mirifice insigniuit. De hiis silere preter religionem existimantes, precibus uberrimis opem consiliumque regis simul implorant, quatinus reliquias gloriosi uiri ad loca transferrent religiosa ubi quondam religionis lacte nutritus ad tantas uirtutes excreuerat, ut non solum gregem Glastonie sed et tocius Anglie prouincias sua posset illustrare doctrina.

Quibus auditis, rex eorum desideriis pio occurrens affectu, quod pecierant celeri decreuit effectui mancipari. Nec mora; memoratus abbas, uoti iam compos, quatuor ex commilitonibus huius legacionis iniungit officium hoc modo, ut, uidelicet, adiunctis sibi sociorum auxiliis, Cantuariam properantes ad Glastoniam ossa

[g] A marginal note in a contemporary hand which locates it after *Eadmundo* reads: *siue Ethelredo patre suo cui per aliquod tempus idem Edmundus conregnauit propter patris inpotenciam, immo, ut uerum fateamur, ignauiam*. It is not found in M.

[h] The same contemporary hand indicates that the following note is to be read here: *Legitur in Uita eiusdem sancti Elfegi martiris quod, tota ciuitate Cantuarensi simul cum ecclesia principali Domini saluatoris per incendium in cineres redacta, clerus et populus sunt crudeliter trucidati, ita quod ex omni numero qui ad octo milia hominum protendebatur quatuor solummodo monastice professionis octingentos autem inferioris ordinis uiros remansisse accepimus, quos primum beneficii gracia pro decimis computatos, deinde uerberibus acriter exaratos aut pecuniaria redempcione dignos iudicauerunt aut seruilibus mancipandos operibus secum abduxerunt. Postremo quia ipsum sanctum Elfegum post squalores carceris diuturnos ac multiplicia genera tormentorum morte crudelissima dampnauerunt*. This marginal note is not found in M.

[i] *dirripiuntur* T.

23. On the translation of St Dunstan from Canterbury to Glastonbury.

Since we have been talking about other saints we will append an account of how St Dunstan was translated. In 1012 AD during the reign of the famous King Edmund, called Ironside in his native tongue, the Danes landed on the eastern shores of England and brought all of the territory of Kent under their control. There they deprived many of their proper rank, banished many from their homeland and subjected many to a very cruel death. In this way, by slaughter, rapine and burning, they destroyed divine things as much as human ones all the way to the city of London, sparing neither rank nor age nor sex. As a result the venerable Archbishop Aelfheah, not to mention any others, was driven from his seat of high office, had his estates devastated and his possessions seized. Who could tell of the rest without weeping? Alas, the sorrow of it! The wicked villains entered the metropolitan church of the English people, attacked the religious servants of God – it is horrible to tell of it – and drove all of them from the house of God and destroyed everything by fire.

It came to pass that at that time King Edmund came to Glastonbury. There he spent some time during which he related the complete story of that terrible captivity to Abbot Beorhtred and the brethren of the house, telling them that the church of Canterbury had been burnt and entirely bereft of inhabitants and religion. The abbot and the whole congregation were saddened at hearing this, as if a sword had pierced the heart of each of them. Among other things they began to recite the lofty virtues of their distinguished father Dunstan who had, throughout his life wonderfully honoured Glastonbury by gifts of ample estates and magnificent liberties and, above all, by instituting there the regular life. Deciding to be silent about all except religious matters they at once fervently entreat the king and beseech his help and advice, that they might transfer the relics of that glorious man to the religious place where, nourished once on the milk of religion, he had attained such great virtues that he had been able to illuminate not only the flock at Glastonbury but all the provinces of England.

Hearing this the king met their desire with pious goodwill and determined that what they asked of him should be speedily effected. There was no delay; with his wish now granted the abbot enjoined the undertaking of this mission on four of his fellow monks, specifying that, with the help of some friends, they should hasten to Canterbury and should transfer the bones of the most holy Dunstan to Glastonbury.

sanctissimi transferrent Dunstani. Iussionem patris suscipiunt filii deuotissime, paratisque tanto itineri neccessariis ac benedictione suscepta, iniuncta sibi uoluntate prosecuntur alata, de misericordia Dei simulque ope dicti sancti plurimum confisi. Idem autem monachi beato Dunstano in carne degenti dudum adheserant, capelle sue complentes officium, qui eciam corpus eius, anima in quietas sedes translata, sepulture tradiderunt, postea eciam cum successore suo, sancto uidelicet Aelfego archiepiscopo, usque ad eiusdem commanentes martirium. Complacuit namque prefatis pontificibus de cetu monachili Glastonie[j] collaterales indiuiduos habere, tum propter prerogatiuam caritatis qua nutriculam amplectebantur precipue, tum ut, eorum familiari contubernio exemplariter inflammati, a priori uita quam cum eis agere solebant in[k] cenobio non deuiarent. Fratrum autem ipsorum nomina hec fuerunt, Sebrithtus,[l] Ethelbrithtus,[m] Bursius, Adelwordus cognomento Quadrans. Igitur memorati fratres Cantuariam uenientes, locum, sicut a rege audierant, omni habitatore nudatum inueniunt. Et continuo sepulcrum sanctissimi uiri adeunt a se optime recognitum, utpote qui eumdem in mausoleo locauerant. Quo aperto, ossa sancti Dunstani super aurum et topacium preciosa reperiunt, carne tam diuturni temporis spacio resoluta, repertaque, reuerencia qua decebat, nec sine lacrimis recolligunt. Anulum eciam digito sancti, cum sepulture traderetur, inpositum, quem et ipse etate teneriori fecisse dicitur, recognoscunt. Patratis ergo omnibus pro quibus uenerant, prosperatori itineris sui gracias rependentes inmensas, Glastoniam reuertuntur cum gaudio preciosissimas reliquias secum deportantes. Quibus reuersis, cum quanta omnium leticia, precipue monachorum, fuerint recepti, apcius perpendit legentis caritas quam scribentis euoluat facultas. Facta est autem hec translacio anno Domini MXII secundo uidelicet anno post interfectionem sancti Elfegi archiepiscopi, XXIIII anno post dormicionem sancti Dunstani.

24. Qualiter reliquie sancti Dunstani sub terra recondebantur.

Hiis ita patratis, inmensis Dei beneficiis fratres refocillati, crebris insistebant collocucionibus, tractantes qualiter memoratum thesaurum tuciori custodie mandarent, non inmerito formidantes ne, hostili rabie sedata Cantuariensique ecclesia in pristinum statum reformata, archiepiscopus,[n] auctoritate potenciaque preminens, easdem sibi albatas reuocaret reliquias, et sic, quanto beaciores fuerant ipsarum adquisicione, tanto miseriores fierent posteriori priuacione. Communicato[o] demum consilio, decreuerunt ut duo ex fratribus senioribus, in commisis sibi archanis fideliores,[p] loco secreciori ossa sanctissima absconderent nullique, quoad uiuerent,

[j] *Glastoniensis* H.
[k] *in* om. H.
[l] *Sebrichtus* H.
[m] *Ethelbrichtus* H.
[n] *archiepiscopi* H.
[o] *comunicato* T, H.
[p] *fedeliores* T.

His sons received their father's orders most dutifully and, when they had made all the preparations for their great journey and had been blessed, they flew forth to obey their orders enthusiastically, trusting in the mercy of God and, especially, in the power of the saint himself. For these monks had formerly clung to the blessed Dunstan while he was alive by performing services in his chapel and had also committed his body to its burial place after his soul had been translated to peaceful rest; they had then remained by the side of his successor St Aelfheah until his martyrdom. For it pleased both these archbishops to have as assistants individuals from the monastic community of Glastonbury, both on account of the unsurpassed love and affection in which they especially held their nursemaid and so that, spurred on by the examples of their immediate attendants, they would not deviate from the life which they had previously been accustomed to live with them in the monastery. The names of those brothers were Sebrithtus, Ethelbrithtus, Bursius and Adelwordus, surnamed Quadrans. When these brothers came to Canterbury they found the place bereft of all its inhabitants, just as they had heard from the king. They went at once to the tomb of that most holy man, which was easily recognised by them because they themselves had placed him in his sepulcre. When they opened it they found the bones of St Dunstan, more precious than gold or topaz – for his flesh had been destroyed over the long period of time – and gathered them up with fitting reverence, and not without tears. They also recognised the ring that had been placed on the saint's finger when he had been committed to burial, the one that he was said to have made himself when he was a young man. When they had accomplished everything for which they had come they gave boundless thanks to the One who had made their journey prosperous and returned to Glastonbury, joyfully bringing back with them the most precious relics. With how much delight their return was received by everyone, especially the monks, can be more easily inferred by a sympathetic reader than it can be disclosed by this writer's skill. This translation was effected in 1012 AD, the second year after the murder of the archbishop St Aelfheah and the twenty-fourth year after St Dunstan's final sleep.

24. How the relics of St Dunstan were hidden under the ground.

When this had been accomplished the brethren, refreshed by God's bounteous kindness, began a series of discussions to consider how they could commit their treasure to a safer place of confinement, for they feared, with some justification, that when the enemy's fury had been appeased and the church of Canterbury restored to its original state the archbishop, who was pre-eminent in authority and power, would demand back the relics that had been taken from him, whereupon the happiness that the monks had felt at their acquisition would be equalled by their misery at their subsequent loss. The conclusion of their deliberations was a decision that two of the senior brethren, who were more reliable in keeping secrets, should conceal the most holy bones in an undisclosed place and acquaint no-one with the knowledge of the secret as long as they lived. Only when faced with

tanti secreti cognicionem participarent. Set tantum in extremis laborantes, locum f6 alicui fratrum maturiori et sapienciori designarent, qui similiter in / mortis articulo alicui, sicut et sibi fiebat, rem patefaceret. Ita ut, currente tempore, propter uarios euentus locus idem permaneret omnibus incognitus, uno dumtaxat conscio ueritatis, quousque placeret altissimo ut lux non lateret sub modio set super candelabrum posita luceret omnibus in domo Dei existentibus. Consilium igitur sic initum, duo fratres ad hoc electi ducunt ad effectum. Locellum namque ligneum, ad hoc satis decenter compositum, interius depingunt ac in dextro latere locelli, S̄, cum titulo, in sinistro uero, D̄, cum titulo, inscribunt, quibus litteris nomen sancti Dunstani innuere uolebant. Inferentes igitur prefatas reliquias in locellum, sub lapide ad hoc exciso recondunt in maiori[q] ecclesia secus aquam benedictam in dextra parte introitus monachorum, omnibus aliis locum penitus ignorantibus. Ibidem igitur centum et LXXII annis latebat absconditus, unius tantum cognicioni successiue modo prescripto commissus.

25. Qualiter eedem reliquie iterum inueniebantur.

Procedente uero tempore cum adhuc idem sanctus in loco lateret subterraneo, erat ibidem monachus quidem, Iohannes Canan nomine, euo maturus, animo sagacissimus, antiqua monasterii statuta habens notissima cuius eciam noticie non falsa fratrum opinio huius archani scienciam testabatur, successiua relacione fuisse commissam. Huius custodie deputatus erat frater quidam, Iohannes de Watelege dictus, tam etate quam conuersione tener, quam ob bone indolis florem senior nimio mentis amplectebatur affectu. Is a sociis suis incitatus, magistrum suum, licet diucius renitentem, precibus uberimis, blandiciis quoque intersertis, sollicitabat ut locum tanti thesauri conscium sibi demonstraret. Demum crebris precum blandimentis emollitus, quadam die puero more solito sciscitante, senior in hec uerba linguam resoluit. 'Fili mi dilectissime, non ingredieris ecclesiam aqua benedicta te aspersurus, quin lapidem uestibus tuis contingas sub quo reconduntur que requiris. Set de hoc amplius nil[r] me pulses, set audita, mente tacita sagacique pertracta.' Puero igitur hec dicta obliuionis uelo nequaquam obducente, senior post dies suos expletos in fata concessit.

Post cuius obitum, que dicebantur ab eo in tenebris, predicabantur super tecta et in communem deuenerunt cognicionem. Omnibus tamen de sermonis ambiguitate titubantibus torporeque nimio frigescentibus, nullus experiencie manum apposuit, qua tante dubietatis nodum absolueret. Post modici temporis curriculum, Glastonie cenobium inuasit incendium,[61] quod non solum ecclesiam ceteraque edificia, set eiusdem ornamenta, thesauros, et quod pluris est, reliquias, pro magna parte, consumpsit. Ceterum dolores incendio tali causatos non est nostrum hic describere, quia nec circa hec nostra uersatur intencio. Monachi tamen suo merori solacium

[q] *uel uetusta* interlined above; not in M.

[r] *nichil* H.

imminent death should they point out the place to one of the older and wiser brethren, who would similarly disclose it to someone at the moment of his death, just as had happened to him. In this way it would happen that as time passed and event followed event the place would remain unknown to all, except for one person who would know the truth, until it should please the Most High that this light should not be hid under a bushel but should be placed on a candlestick to give light to all in the house of God. Once the plan had been so conceived the two brothers chosen for the purpose put it into effect. For they did a painting on the inside of a small wooden receptacle, properly prepared for this end, and wrote on the right hand side S, with an inscription, and on the left D, with an inscription, wishing to signify by these letters the name of St Dunstan. They put his remains in the receptacle and concealed it in the larger church beneath a stone cut out for the purpose beside the holy water on the right hand side of the monks' entrance, a place of which all the others were quite ignorant. There he lay hidden for 172 years, knowledge of his resting-place being entrusted to one man only at a time in the prescribed fashion.

25. How those relics were rediscovered.

Time passed and the saint still lay hidden underground until there was a certain monk there named John Canan, mature in years and most wise in mind, who was very well informed about the ancient regulations of the monastery and into whose keeping knowledge of this secret had, in turn, been committed, according to the reliable testimony of the brothers. This monk had been assigned guardianship of a certain brother named John of Whatley who was youthful in years and in the monastic life and whom the elder loved with exceeding fondness for his sunny nature. Urged by his fellows, the young monk used to exhort his master, despite constant rejection, entreating him urgently and sometimes flattering him, to point out to him the spot which contained so great a treasure. Finally the elder was softened by these repeated flattering requests and so one day, when the boy was questioning him in the usual way, he gave vent to these words: 'My most beloved son, you cannot enter the church and sprinkle yourself with holy water without your clothes touching the stone under which that which you seek lies hidden. But do not press me any more about this; rather consider wisely and in silence what you have heard.' The youth certainly did not cover what he had heard with a curtain of oblivion, while the elder in due course yielded to fate.

After his death what he had said in secret was proclaimed from the rooftops and became common knowledge. Yet although all were perplexed by the ambiguity of his words they languished in complete inactivity and no-one applied his hand to a test by which the knot of so great a doubt could have been untied. Some time later the monastery of Glastonbury was assailed by a fire which consumed not only the church and other buildings but its ornaments, treasures and, what is more, the greater part of its relics. It is not our task to describe here the sorrows caused by the fire because it is not our intention to occupy ourselves with these matters. The monks, seeking some solace for their grief, gathered together those few things that

querentes, pauca, que flamma reliquid,[s] maxime de reliquiis recolligebant. Tandem de sancto Dunstano solliciti, ea que de eo Iohannes Canan et postea Iohannes de Watelege, ut prenotauimus, protulerant, ad memoriam reducta proferunt in commune. Paucis itaque diebus emensis, duo fratres, in hoc ceteris animosiores, Ricardus uidelicet de Tantone[t] et Radulfus Toc, ad locum per Iohannem dudum presignatum pari gradiuntur affectu. Quem diligencius indagantes, lapidem prout dudum audierant reperiunt. Quem reuoluentes, locellum ligneum, ferrea compagine undique consolidatum, subtus aspiciunt. Conuocatis igitur priore totalique conuentu, thecam aperientes, sacratissima beati Dunstani ossa reperiunt simulque anulum suum super quoddam os digiti sui. Et ad omnem ambiguitatis nodum absoluendum, picturam uident intrinsecus, et S, cum titulo, in dextra parte locelli, D, cum titulo, in sinistra, nomen sancti Dunstani ibidem locati exprimencia. Ueritate igitur relacionis Iohannis Canan manifeste comprobata, monachi de inuencione reliquiarum desideratissimarum post priorem refocillati miseriam, easdem leti suscipiunt ac in scrinio auro et argento decenter uestito reponunt ea reuerencia et deuocione quibus decebat, associantes eisdem humerum cum brachio sancti Oswaldi regis et martiris. Gaudeat ergo Glastonie ecclesia tanti munita patroni presencia, per cuius intercessiones et merita Deus ibidem sua non cessat operari magnalia, mortuis uitam, infirmis omnimodis sanitatem, creberrime restituendo, frequenter eciam brutis in plurimis periculis subueniendo.[62]

26. De uenerabili cruce que quondam locuta est.

In ecclesia Glastonie est quedam crux merito uenerabilis, auro et argento cooperta, que quondam locuta est – immo uerius, Spiritus Sanctus in ea – cum quodam monacho illius loci, Aylsi nomine, hoc modo. Cum idem monachus per eandem crucem, sicut et per altaria, transiens, nequaquam debita se reuerencia inclinaret secundum regularem disciplinam, tandem quadam uice per eam transitum faciens, inclinauit. Crux igitur in uocem quasi debitis organis formatam erumpens, sic ait: 'Nu to late, Aylsi. Nu to late, Aylsi.' Qui diuina uoce percussus statim corruens exspirauit.

27. De alia cruce de qua cecidit diadema.

Est eciam ibidem alia crux antiquissima que olim in refectorio stare consueuit. De hac ferunt quod cum die quadam Edgarus rex et Dunstanus archiepiscopus ad mensam sederent in refectorio, cogitacionibus diuine uoluntati contrariis in cor regis ascendentibus, mirum dictu, ymago dominica, ligno crucis affixa, toto se corpore excessit ita ut, motus impetu, diadema eius inter regem et archiepiscopum

[s] *sic* in T.
[t] *Cantone* H.

the flames had spared, especially the relics. Then, troubled about St Dunstan, they recalled what John Canan and after him John of Whately had said about him, which we related above, and they discussed it among themselves. After a few days had passed two of the brethren, Richard of Taunton and Ralph Toc, who were bolder than the rest in this matter, went with like mind to the place indicated earlier by John. They investigated it thoroughly and discovered the stone of which they had heard. Turning it over they beheld beneath it a wooden receptacle strengthened on all sides by iron bands. Calling the prior and the whole congregation together they opened it and found therein the most sacred bones of the blessed Dunstan, with his ring on the bone of one of his fingers. And to remove every shred of doubt they saw a painting of him on the inside and S, with an inscription, on the right of the receptacle and D, with an inscription, on the left, representing the name of St Dunstan who had been placed therein. John Canan's story was thereby confirmed and the monks, cheered by the discovery of these most desirable relics after their earlier distress, took them up joyfully and placed them with fitting reverence and devotion in a shrine suitably covered with gold and silver where they joined the shoulder and arm of St Oswald, king and martyr. The church of Glastonbury may therefore rejoice that it is fortified by the presence of so great a patron, thanks to whose intercessions and merits God continues to perform his great works there, repeatedly restoring life to the dead and health to those with all kinds of illnesses and frequently bringing aid to the foolish in all their perils.

26. On a venerable cross which once spoke.

In the church of Glastonbury there is a certain cross, worthy of veneration and covered in gold and silver, which once spoke – or rather, the Holy Spirit spoke through it – to a monk of that place named Aylsi, in this fashion. When the monk passed by the cross – and it was as though it was by an altar – he did not incline his head with due reverence as the discipline of the Rule required, although eventually on a certain occasion he did so bow when passing it. At this the cross burst into speech, as if it had the appropriate organs, saying, 'Now too late, Aylsi. Now too late, Aylsi.' Shocked by the divine voice he fell immediately to the ground and died.

27. On another cross from which a crown fell.

There is also in that place another very ancient cross which once used to stand in the refectory. Of this it is said that when one day King Edgar and Archbishop Dunstan were sitting at the table in the refectory thoughts contrary to the divine will arose in the king's heart, at which, marvellous to relate, an image of the Lord attached to the beam of the cross shook its whole body, so that the force of this motion caused its crown to fall between the king and the archbishop. The king's

caderet. Quid hoc portenderet, confessio regis manifestauit. Inquisitus enim rex a sancto Dunstano quid tunc cogitaret aut quid se acturum fore disponeret,[u] fatebatur quod eadem hora cogitauit ut, monachis ad alium locum translatis, illic moniales aggregaret. Increpatus igitur reuerenter ab archiepiscopo, dicente hoc diuine uoluntati contrarium, rex tale propositum reuocauit in irritum.

28. De cruce uulnerata.

Est ibidem tercia crux, ceteris minor, populo tamen celebrior, ab antiquo auro argentoque uestita, de qua olim ex percussione sagitte sanguis plurimus uirtute diuina profluxit; quod qualiter euenerit alias scriptum non tacebit.

29. De quadam ymagine beate Marie.

Est eciam ibi ymago beate Marie quam, cum ignis ingens olim circumdans pallas et omnia altaris ornamenta consumeret, ipsam non tetigit, nec eciam peplum capiti eius appensum. In facie tamen ipsius pro uapore ignis uesice, quasi in homine uiuente, surgentes, diuinam testabantur uirtutem, et per multum temporis intuentibus apparebant.[63]

30. De altari sancti Dauid quod dicitur uulgo saphirus.

Legitur in uita sancti Dauid Meneuensis archiepiscopi,[64] quod cum idem sanctus in Rosina Ualle monasterio, quod ipse construxerat, multis fratribus in abbatis officio ministraret, nocte quadam angelus ei affuit dicens: 'Crastina die precingens et calcians te Ierusalem usque proficiscere. Sed et duos tibi familiares et probitate notos, uidelicet Eliud et Paternum, itineris huius comites habebis, qui ad condictum, quod tibi modo ostendo, crastino conuenient.' Sanctus autem nichil moratus, dispositis cellule utilitatibus, accepta fratrum benedictione, primo mane iter aggrediens peruenit ad condictum, promissos fratres repperit. Igitur pariter intrant uiam, non fastu circumdati satellitum, sed unitate locupletes animorum, quilibet eorum dominus, quilibet et minister. Uenientibus autem eisdem in externas prouincias, sanctus Dauid ita linguarum gracia ditatus est ne inter barbaros interprete egerent. Appropinquantibus demum ad locum optatum, nocte precedenti eorum aduentum patriarche Ierusalemitano angelus apparuit dicens: 'Tres ab occidentis finibus uiri catholici adueniunt, quos cum gaudio et hospitalitatis gracia suscipiens, mihi in episcopos consecrabis.' Patriarcha uero diuine uisionis compos, aduenientibus sanctis imperata letus exsequebatur. Quibus consecratis, ait patriarchia. 'Iudeorum

[u] *rex* once preceded *fatebatur* but has been erased; it is not found in M.

confession made clear what this portended. For when asked by St Dunstan what he had been thinking or what he had been considering doing, the king acknowledged that at that very moment he had been considering transfering the monks to another place and bringing nuns thither. The king was on this account reverently rebuked by the archbishop, who pointed out that it was contrary to the divine will, and so he withdrew the proposition as an error.

28. On a wounded cross.

There is a third cross, smaller than the others yet more renowned among the people, which has of old been covered with gold and silver. By a divine miracle a great volume of blood once flowed from this when it was struck by an arrow; how this came about I will not fail to recount elsewhere.

29. On a certain image of the blessed Mary.

Also to be found there is an image of the blessed Mary which was not touched – not even the veil that hung from its head – by the great fire that surrounded the altar and consumed the cloth and all the ornaments on it. Yet because of the fire's heat blisters, like those on a living man, arose on its face and remained visible for a long time to all who looked, testifying to a divine miracle.

30. On the altar of St David, commonly called 'the sapphire'.

We read in the *Life of St David*, archbishop of Menevia, that while he was ministering, in his office of abbot, to many of the brethren in the monastery of the Ross Valley that he himself had built, an angel appeared to him one night saying: 'Tomorrow morning you must gird yourself, put on your shoes, and set out for Jerusalem. But you will have companions on your journey, two men from your household well-known for their uprightness, Teilo and Padarn, who will meet you tomorrow at an agreed place which I will now show you.' Without delay the saint disposed of the useful articles from his small cell, received the benediction from his brethren and, setting out on his journey early in the morning, reached the agreed place where he found the brothers as promised. So they began their journey together, not surrounded proudly with escorts but rich in the unity of their souls, none of them the lord, none the servant. As they approached foreign lands St David was enriched with the gift of tongues so that they would not need an interpreter among the strangers. At last they drew near to the desired place and on the night before their arrival an angel appeared to the patriarch of Jerusalem and said: 'Three catholic men are approaching from the far west whom you are to receive with joy and courteous hospitality, and consecrate as my bishops.' As a result of this divine vision the patriarch gladly carried out the orders concerning the approaching saints. After he had consecrated them he said to them: 'The power of the Jews prevails

potestas inualescit in Christianos nosque commouentes fidem repellunt. Parete[v] itaque et ad predicacionem singulis diebus procedite ut eorum uiolencia confutata quiescat, noscens fidem Christianam occidentis finibus diuulgatam ac ultimis terre extremitatibus decantatam.' Obediunt imperio, predicacioni insistentes, acceptataque[w] sua predicacione infideles conuertunt, infirmos roborant, perfectisque omnibus repatriare disponunt. Tunc patriarcha uenerabilem patrem Dewy IIII
f7 muneribus ditauit, altari scilicet consecrato, in / quo Dominicum corpus sacrabat quod et innumeris pollet uirtutibus, insgni eciam nola, baculo et tunica ex auro texta, que omnia gloriosis predicantur[x] corusca miraculis. 'Sed quia,' inquit patriarcha, 'hec itinerantibus uobis esset onerosa, cum ad uestra ueneritis ea uobis transmittam.' Ualedicto igitur patriarcha, ad sua demum perueniunt sancti uiri, promissum expectantes. Accipiunt tandem munera per angelos sibi destinata, Dewy in monasterio quod dicitur Langemelech, Paternus et Eliud in suis monasteriis. Inde ea uulgus uocat e celo ueniencia. Sanctus autem Dauid cum tam preciosi thesauri post se custodem gestiret habere dignissimum, eumdem lapidem ecclesie Glastonie adhuc uiuens delegauit, quam, ob loci uenerandam antiquitatem et sancti Patricii precipue aliorumque sanctorum reliquias ibidem reconditas, miro amplectebatur affectu, ut gesta sua a legentibus multis claret argumentis. Ostenditur autem adhuc memoratum altare in Glastoniensi ecclesia in memoriam dicti sancti, non humana reseruatum industria, sed diuina prouidencia, que, inter innumeros rerum turbines, inter regum regnorumque permutaciones, inter grauissimas guerrarum procellas, omnibus aliis pene sublatis, ab eiusdem surrepcione auidas hostium manus iugiter contraxit. Cassula autem, in qua eumdem lapidem suscepit beatus Dauid, adhuc in episcopali sede eiusdem condigno reseruatur honore. Cum uere sepe dictus lapis olim metu guerre multo tempore latuisset absconditus, omnibus loci nesciis, pie recordacionis[65] Henricus Wintoniensis episcopus et abbas Glastonie eumdem in quodam hostio ecclesie beate Marie repperit ac auro et argento et lapidibus preciosis, sicut adhuc apparet, magnifice decorauit.

31. De nobilibus Glastonie sepultis.

Quantum autem Glastonie ecclesia fuerit eciam primatibus patrie uenerabilis et ad sepulturam desiderabilis, ut ibi potissimum sub protectione Dei genitricis opperirentur[y] diem resurrectionis,[z] multa sunt indicio quibus pro cautela fastidii abstineo.[66] Pretermitto de Arturo, inclito rege Britonum, in cimiterio monachorum inter duas piramides cum sua coniuge tumulato,[67] de multis eciam Britonum principibus;[a] pretermitto eciam de Kenwino in una piramide locato.[68] Insuper

[v] *petite* H.
[w] *acceptaque* H.
[x] *predicatur* H.
[y] *operirentur* T.
[z] *resurectionis* T.
[a] A marginal note in a C13 hand reads: *Idem Arturus anno incarnacionis Dominice*

over Christians and by confuting us they drive out the faith. Appear before them therefore and preach to them constantly every day so that their vehemence will be checked and will abate when they come to know that the Christian faith has spread to the far west and that its praises are sung at the ends of the earth.' In obedience to his command they devote themselves to preaching and by its success convert the infidels and strengthen the weak. After completing all their tasks they arrange to return home. Thereupon the patriarch enriched the venerable father David with four gifts, namely a consecrated altar on which he used to offer the body of our Lord and which was valued for its innumerable miracles, a remarkable bell, a staff, and a tunic of woven gold, all of which are vaunted for the brilliance of their glorious miracles. 'But,' said the patriarch, 'because these would be burdensome to you on your journey I will send them to you when you have arrived home.' The holy men bid farewell to the patriarch and at length reached their homeland where they awaited the fulfillment of his promise. Eventually they received their gifts, brought to them by angels, David in the monastery called *Langemelech* and Padarn and Teilo in their own monasteries. Hence it is commonly said that those gifts came from heaven.

Since St David wished so precious a treasure to have a most worthy guardian after his death he presented that stone to the church of Glastonbury while he was still alive because he cherished that church with fond love on account of its venerable antiquity and especially on account of the relics of St Patrick and the other saints preserved there, as will most clearly be proven to anyone reading his deeds. Moreover that altar is still displayed in the church of Glastonbury in memory of the saint, preserved not by human diligence but by divine providence which, amid constant storms of change with kings and kingdoms rising and falling, the fierce hurricanes of war raging and almost everything else being destroyed, continued to check the greedy hands of those who would have stolen it. The cover in which the blessed David received that stone is still preserved and appropriately honoured in his episcopal see. After this famous stone, hidden in the past for fear of war, had lain concealed for a long time, its whereabouts known to no-one, Henry of blessed memory, bishop of Winchester and abbot of Glastonbury, located it in a doorway of the church of the blessed Mary and adorned it sumptuously with gold, silver and precious stones, as can be seen today.

31. On the nobles buried at Glastonbury.

There is much proof of how venerated the church of Glastonbury was even by the nobles of our country and how desirable for burial, that there especially under the protection of the mother of God they might await the day of resurrection, but I omit it from fear of being tedious. I pass over Arthur, famous King of the Britons, buried with his wife in the monks' cemetery between two pyramids, and many other leaders of the Britons, as well as Centwine who lies in one of the pyramids.

tumulos regum, Edmundi senioris in turri ad dexteram,[69] Edmundi minoris ante magnum altare,[70] Edgari, prius in capitulo ante introitum ecclesie, modo in scrinio quod eciam de martire superbit Uincencio.[71] De quibus, si se locus dederit, non me ista frustra suscepisse causabitur posteritas. Taceo et episcoporum sepulcra Brithuuii et Brithuuoldi, que porticum aquilonarem ad sanctus Iohannem baptistam uberem insigniunt,[72] Liuingi eciam et Seifridi episcoporum,[73] Alfari, Aedthelstani, Aetheluuini, Aelnoti ducum, quorum uidelicet ducum quilibet centum libratas terre cum multis aliis bonis contulit Glastonie.[74]

32. De duabus piramidibus.

Illud quod clam pene omnibus est libenter predicarem, si ueritatem exculpere possem, quid ille[b] piramides sibi uelint, que, aliquantis pedibus ab ecclesia uetusta posite, cimiterium monachorum pretexunt. Procerior sane et propinquior ecclesie habet quinque tabulatus, et altitudinem XXVI pedum. Hec, pre nimia uetustate etsi ruinam minetur, habet tamen antiquitatis non nulla spectacula, que plane possunt legi, licet non plene possint intelligi. In superiori enim tabulatu est ymago pontificali scemate facta. In secundo, ymago regiam pretendens pompam, et littere: Her, Sexi, et Blisyer. In tercio, nichilominus nomina, Wemcrest, Bantomp, Winethegn. In quarto, Hate, Wulfred et Eanfled. In quinto, qui et inferior est, ymago et hec scriptura: Logwor, Weslicas et Bregden, Syelwes, Hwingendes, Bern. Altera uero piramis habet XVIII pedes et IIII tabulatus, in quibus hec leguntur: Hedde episcopus, Bregored, et Beoruuard. Quid hec significent non temere diffinio, sed ex suspicione colligo eorum interius in cauatis lapidibus contineri ossa, quorum exterius leguntur nomina. Certe Logwor is pro certo asseritur esse, du cuius nomine Logweresbeorh dicebatur, qui nunc Mons Acutus dicitur; Bregden, a quo Brentacnolle, qui nunc Brentamirse dicitur: Beorwald nichilominus abbas post Hemgiselum; de quibus et de ceteris qui occurrere poterunt, ex hinc liberiori campo exultabit oratio. Iam enim[c] abbatum seriem, et quid cuique, et a quo rege ad usus monasterii delegatum sit, sermo explicare contendet.[75]

DXLII in Cornubia iuxta fluuium Cambam a Modredo letaliter uulneratus est, qui inde ad sananda uulnera sua in insulam Auallonis est euectus in ibidem defunctus in estate circa Pentachosten, fere centenarius, aut circiter. Also in M. It is based on the account in *HRB*, p.261.

[b] A marginal note in a late (?C16) hand reads: *Primi monachi hic uenerunt ex Egypto*. Not in M.

[c] *uero* H.

Also there are the tombs of the kings Edmund the Elder, in the tower to the right, Edmund the Younger, before the high altar, and Edgar, previously in a column before the entrance to the church but now in a shrine which also boasts the remains of the martyr Vincent. If space be available posterity will not complain that I was told such things in vain. I pass over in silence too the tombs of the bishops Brihtwig and Brihtwold, which richly adorn the northern portico of St John the Baptist, and those of the bishops Lyfing and Sigfrid and the ealdormen Aelfheah, Athelstan, Aethelwine and Aethelnoth, each of whom granted 100 pounds worth of land and many other goods to Glastonbury.

32. On the two pyramids.

If I could elicit the truth I would gladly explain the significance of those pyramids which are a mystery to almost everyone. They are located a few feet from the old church and border on the monks' cemetery. The taller one, which is nearer to the church, has five storeys and is 26 feet high. Although it is almost in ruins due to its great age it still preserves some memorials of antiquity which can be clearly read, even if not fully understood. For on the highest storey is an image fashioned in the likeness of a bishop and on the second an image displaying regal ostentation and the words *Her, Sexi* and *Blisyer*; on the third the names *Wemcrest, Bantomp* and *Winethegn*; on the fourth *Hate, Wulfred* and *Eanfled*; and on the fifth and lowest storey an image and this writing *Logwor, Weslicas* and *Bregden, Swelwes, Hwingendes, Bern*. The other pyramid of 18 feet has four storeys, on which may be read Bishop *Hedde, Bregored* and *Beoruuard*. I will not rashly certify what these mean but hesitantly suggest that within those hollow stones are contained the bones of those whose names can be read on the outside. It can certainly be maintained that *Logwor* is he after whom Ludgersbury, now Montacute, is named, that *Bregden* gave his name to Brent Knoll, now Brent Marsh, and that Beorhtwald was abbot after Haemgils. Concerning these and others who may come up I will speak at greater length later. For now I will proceed to set down the series of abbots, what was given to each for the use of the monastery, and by which king.

33. De regibus, abbatibus, et aliis fundatoribus Glastonie[d] *ecclesie seriatim expressis.*

In primis memorandum, quod duodecim discipulis sanctorum Philippi et Iacobi anno Dominice incarnacionis LXIII in Britanniam uenientibus, tres reges, licet pagani, XII porciones terre contulerunt, unde adhuc nomen XII hidarum perseuerat. Deinde sancti Phaganus et Deruuianus in Britanniam uenientes et eam fidei gracia illustrantes, a rege Lucio, per eosdem in Christo renato, insulam Auallonie cum suis adiacenciis confirmari optinuerunt XII fratribus ibidem institutis ac aliis post eos instituendis. Successit post multum tempus beatus Patricius, qui adhuc fratres XII, quasi heremeticam uitam agentes, reperiens, eosdem uita cenobiali informauit et multis possessionibus, licet nobis incognitis, ut credi fas est, ditauit. Successit sanctus Benignus. Quis autem hic fuerit, et quomodo patria lingua dictus, non infacete exprimunt uersus qui in epitaphio sepulcri eius apud Ferremere scripti sunt.

Hoc patris in lapide Beonne sunt ossa locata.
Qui pater extiterat monachorum hic tempore prisco.
Hunc fore Patricii dudum fortasse ministrum
Fantur Hybernigene, et Beonnam de nomine dicunt.

Successerunt ibidem plures de nacione Britonum abbates, quorum tam nomina quam gesta et memoriam obliuionis nubilo obducens deleuit antiquitas. Ipsam tamen ecclesiam apud magnates Britonum in maxima fuisse ueneracione ostendunt eorum exuuie ibidem requiescentes. Trium tantum horum abbatum nomina, rerum preteritarum[e] recordatrix, manifestat pictura, que sunt Worgret, Lademund, Bregored. Sed de hiis postea[f].[76]

34. De illustri Arturo.

Legitur in gestis illustrissimi regis Arturi, quod cum in quadam festiuitate Natalis Domini apud Karliun strenuissimum adolescentem, filium scilicet regis Nuth, dictum Ider, insigniis militaribus decorasset, et eumdem experiendi causa in montem Ranarum, nunc dictum Brentecnol, ubi tres gigantes malefactis famosissimos esse didicerat, contra eosdem dimicaturum duxisset, idem tiro Arturum et suos comites ignorantes precedens, dictos gigantes fortiter aggressus mira cede

d *Glastoniensis* H.

e *preceritarum* T.

f Adjacent to ch.33 in a C14 hand, but not in M, is the following: *Huic erat unicus filius nomen eius Lucius, primus Christianus rex Britannie. Huius tempore uenerunt Britannie sanctus Faganus et Diriuianus, a quibus accepit idem rex Christianitatem, ut habetur in fine quarti libri Bruti.*

An arrow points from the *Huic* to: *Reges pagani* { *Aruiragus*, *Marius*, *Coillus* }

33. *On the kings, abbots and other founders of the church of Glastonbury, arranged chronologically.*

It ought first be mentioned that three pagan kings gave twelve portions of land to the twelve disciples of Saints Philip and James who came to Britain in 63 AD, whence the name 'the twelve hides' still persists. Then Saints Phagan and Deruvian, who came to Britain and illuminated it with the gift of faith, obtained from King Lucius, who was reborn in Christ through their efforts, confirmation of the island of Avalon and its appurtenances for the twelve brethren established there and the others who should follow them. Their successor after many years was the blessed Patrick who, finding twelve brothers still there leading a sort of eremetic life, instructed them in the communal life and enriched them with many possessions, as we can well believe even if they are unknown to us. His successor was St Benignus. Who he was and what his name was in the native tongue is expressed not inelegantly by the verses which are written as an epitaph on his tomb at Meare.

> The bones of father Beonna are disposed within this stone.
> He was in ancient times the father of the monks here.
> And formerly Patrick's servant too, perhaps.
> So say the Irish who call him *Beonna.*

He was succeeded there by many abbots of the British nation, whose names and deeds, veiled in a cloud of oblivion, have been lost to memory over time. Yet their remains which still rest there reveal that the church was held in the highest veneration by the great men of the British. A painting commemorating events of the past exhibits the names of three only of those abbots, namely Worgret, Lademund and Bregored, about whom I will have more to say later.

34. *On the illustrious Arthur.*

We read in the deeds of the most illustrious King Arthur that at Caerleon one Christmas he distinguished with military honours a most vigorous youth named Ider, the son of King Nuth, and, in order to try him, led him to Frog Mountain, now called Brent Knoll, to do battle with three giants notorious for their wickedness who he had learnt were there. This young soldier had gone on ahead of Arthur and his companions without their knowing it and had boldly attacked the giants

trucidauit. Quibus peremptis, Arturus adueniens dictum Ider nimio labore deficientem et sui omnino inpotem in exstasi collapsum inueniens, eumdem quasi defunctum cum suis lamentabatur. Rediens ergo ad sua cum ineffabili tristicia, corpus quod exanime existimabat, ibidem reliquit, donec uehiculum ad illud reportandum illuc destinasset. Sese eciam necis eius causam reputans, quia tardius ad auxilium eius uenerat, cum demum Glastoniam aduenirett, ibidem quater uiginti monachos pro anima eiusdem instituit, possessiones et territoria ad eorum sustenacionem,[g] aurum et argentum, calices et alia ornamenta ecclesiastica largiens abundanter[77].[h]

35. De terra Ynswitrin data Glastonie tempore Anglorum ad fidem conuersorum.

Anno Dominice incarnacionis sexcentesimo primo rex Domnonie terram, que appellatur Inesuuitrin,[i] ad ecclesiam uetustam concessit[j] ob peticionem Worgret abbatis in quinque cassatis.[k] Ego Mauuron episcopus hanc cartam scripsi. Ego Worgret eiusdem loci abbas subscripsi. Quis iste rex fuerit scedule uetustas negat scire, uerumptamen quod Britannus fuerit hinc presumi potest, quod Glastoniam[l] lingua sua Yneswitrin appellauit,[m] sic enim eam Britannice uocari apud eos constat. Worgret autem abbati, cuius nomen Britannicam barbariem redolet, successit
f8 Lademund et ei Bregoretd. / Prelacionis eorum tempora sunt in obscuro set nomina illorum et dignitates in maiori ecclesia prodente secus altare pictura sunt in propatulo. Bregoredo successit Berthwald.[78] (Magis creditur hunc de Anglis fuisse, tum quia tempore Britonum semper monarchi fuerunt non reges prouinciales, sicuti tempore Anglorum, tum quia, ut patet ex precedentibus, eadem terra et multa alia tempore Britonum collata sunt Glastonie, sed Angli, Britonibus expulsis, que ab ipsis /
f8 ecclesie collata sunt, auferentes ut pagani, ablata cum multis aliis, demum ad fidem conuersi, restituerunt.[n])[79]

[g] An asterisk refers to the following marginal note, in a C14 hand, not found in M: *scilicet Brent, sic liberatam, et Poldone cum terris uicinis.*

[h] *Pro Arturo nota bene IX^m librum Bruti, de gestis suis et de coronatione sua, et X^m et XI^m. Pro prophetiis Merlini nota VII librum eiusdem. Et qualiter generabatur, reperies in fine sexti libri eiusdem.* In the margin adjacent to ch. 34 but lacking in M, in the same C14 hand as the reference to the *Brut* which immediately precedes this chapter.

[i] *Yneswitrin* H.

[j] A marginal note in the same hand adds *que ibi sita est*; it is in M.

[k] Above in a similar hand is *id est hidis*. M reads *quinque id est hydis cassatis.*

[l] *Glastonia* H.

[m] *apellauit* in T and H but corrected in M.

[n] *Magis . . . restituerunt*, certainly a later comment, is written parallel to the rest of the chapter by the same scribe with the column divided in two by a line for that purpose. In M it is located as here.

whom he killed in a terrible slaughter. After he had done so Arthur arrived and finding Ider weak from excessive exertion and helplessly lying in a trance where he had fallen, he and his companions began to lament that the youth was almost dead. So he returned home unutterably sad, leaving behind the body that he thought was lifeless, until he could send a conveyance there to bring it back. He considered himself responsible for the young man's death because he had come to his aid too late and so when he returned to Glastonbury he established 80 monks there for his soul, generously granting them lands and territories for their sustenance, as well as gold, silver, chalices and other ecclesiastical ornaments.

35. On the estate of Yniswitrin, given to Glastonbury at the time the English were converted to the faith.

In 601 AD the King of Devon granted 5 cassates on the estate called Yniswitrin to the old church on the petition of Abbot Worgret. I, Bishop Mawron wrote this charter. I, Worgret, abbot of that place, have subscribed. The age of the document prevents us knowing who that king was, yet it can be presumed that he was British because he referred to Glastonbury in his own tongue as Yniswitrin which, as we know, was the British name. But Abbot Worgret, whose name smacks of British barbarism, was succeeded by Lademund and he by Bregored. The dates of their rule are obscure but their names and ranks can be clearly seen in a painting to be found near the altar in the greater church. Beorhtwald succeeded Bregored. (It ought rather be believed that this king was an Englishman because in the time of the Britons there were no provincial kings, as in the time of the English, but only absolute monarchs and also because although that estate and many others were granted to Glastonbury in the time of the Britons, as is plain from the preceding, yet when the English drove out the Britons they, being pagans, seized the lands that had been granted to churches before finally restoring the stolen lands and many others at the time of their conversion to the Faith.)

36. De Kenewalchio rege et Berthwaldo abbate.

Anno Dominice incarnacionis sexcentesimo septuagesimo Cenwald, qui et Keneuualchius,[o] qui a Cerdicio septimus apud Westsaxones et per beatum Birinum in Christum credidit anno regni sui XXIX, Berthwaldo abbate, interueniente Theodoro archiepiscopo, dedit Ferramere II hidas. Ego Theodorus subscripsi. Dedit eciam idem rex Beokerie, Godenie, Martinesye[p] et Andreyesie. Iste Bertuuald,[q] transactis X annis in regimine Glastonie, Cantuariensis archiepiscopus fuit. Quod autem Glastonie regimini, renitente rege et illius diocesis episcopo, renunciauerit, in sequentibus palam erit.[80]

37. De Kenwino rege qui Glastoniam libertate donauit.

Berthuualdo successit Hemgisel qui XXV annis Glastonie prefuit. Huic anno ab incarnacione Domini DCLXXVIII Kentuuinus rex Glastingai liberas[r] ab omni seruicio concessit vi hidas. Quem, pro sua fideli conuersacione et episcopi Hedde et monachorum peticione, abbatem ibi constituit ea tamen condicione, quatinus fratres eiusdem loci habeant ius eligendi et constituendi rectorem iuxta regulam sancti Benedicti.[81] 'Et iuxta siluam,' inquit, 'que uocatur Cantucdun, xxiii hidas, in Caric xx hidas et in Crucan iii hidas, ad supplementum[s] uite regularis in monasterio Glastingabiri, sub diuini timoris instinctu humiliter largitus sum,' et cetera. Huius regis exuuie in cimiterio monachorum in piramide quondam nobiliter exculpta requiescunt.[82]

38. De Baldredo rege qui dedit Pennard et Muntagu.

Anno Dominice incarnacionis DCLXXXI Baldred rex Penger[t] vi hidas, Logworesbeorh xvi hidas, et capturam piscium in Pedride Hemgislo abbati, ad supplementum[u] honorabilis ecclesie beate Marie et beati Patricii que sita est in Glastingaburi, cum consensu et licencia pontificis nostri Hedde, Kenewino eciam consenciente, dedit. Et post aliquanta: Ego Hedde episcopus hanc cartulam conscripsi. Ego Aldelmus abbas consensi et subscripsi.[83]

[o] *Kenuualchius* H.

[p] *Martynesye* H.

[q] Originally *Beoruuald* with dots under the *or* and *rt* written above. M has *Bertwald*.

[r] *liberam* in T and M.

[s] *suplementum* in T, H and M.

[t] A similar hand has added above, *id est Pennard*. M reads: '*rex id est Pennard Penger VI . . .*'

[u] *suplementum* in T, H and M.

36. On king Cenwalh and abbot Brihtwold.

In 670 AD Cenwalh, also called Kenewalch, the seventh West Saxon king after Cerdic, who in the 29th year of his reign believed in Christ because of the blessed Birinus, gave 2 hides at Meare to Abbot Brihtwold, at the request of Archbishop Theodore. I, Theodore, have subscribed. The same king also gave Beckery, Godney, Marchey and Nyland. Brihtwold himself became archbishop of Canterbury after ruling Glastonbury for 10 years. That he renounced the rule of Glastonbury against the will of the king and of his diocesan bishop will become clear from what follows.

37. On king Centwine who endowed Glastonbury with a liberty.

Brihtwold was succeeded by Haemgils who ruled Glastonbury for 25 years. In 678 AD King Centwine gave him 6 hides at Glastonbury free from all servitude. At the request of Bishop Haeddi and the monks and because of his constant observance of the faith, the king appointed him abbot there, on the condition that the brethren of the place should have the right of electing and constituting their head according to the Rule of St Benedict. 'Impelled by my fear of the divine,' he said, 'I have granted 23 hides near Quantock Wood, 20 hides at Cary and 3 hides at Creech St Michael for the assistance of those leading the regular life in the monastery of Glastonbury, etc.' The remains of this king rest in a pyramid in the monks' cemetery that was once nobly carved.

38. On king Baldred who gave Pennard and Montacute.

In 681 AD King Baldred gave 6 hides at Pennard, 16 hides at Ludgersbury and fishing rights on the Parrett to Abbot Haemgils for the assistance of the honourable church of the blessed Mary and the blessed Patrick situated at Glastonbury, with the consent and authorisation of our bishop Haeddi and with the approval of Centwine. And after other matters: I, Bishop Haeddi, have drawn up this charter. I, Abbot Aldhelm, have consented and subscribed.

De Leghe.

Eodem anno Hedde episcopus Lantocay vi hidas, Kentuino eciam et Baldredo consencientibus, dedit Glastonie; quam donacionem Cedualla confirmauit et propria manu, licet paganus, signum crucis expressit.[84]

39. De glorioso rege Ina qui Glastoniam tam in donis quam priuilegiis multipliciter honorauit.

Nunc quia, serie annorum ducente, ad Inam regem Westsaxonum uenimus, libet terras particulatim exprimere quas idem eximius uir uetuste ecclesie in Glastonia pia contulit liberalitate.

De Brente data per Ynam.

Anno ab incarnacione Domini DCXC Ina dedit Hemgislo abbati Brente x hidas; quam terram Berhwald abbas sponte propria deseruit, et sine nostra uiolencia et sine expulsione locum proprii cenobii dimisit, et contra interdictum et uoluntatem pontificis nostri discessit.[v] Idem rex eidem abbati in hec uerba priuilegium concessit.[85]

40. Primum priuilegium Ine.

In nomine Domini nostri Ihesu Christi ego Ina rex, decreto et consilio presulis nostri Aldelmi simulque cunctorum Dei sacerdotum suggestione et monachorum peticione, qui in parochia Westsaxonum conuersantur, hanc libertatem monachis, qui in ecclesia beate Dei genitricis Marie et beati Patricii omnipotenti[w] Deo sub abbate Hemgislo famulantur in pristina urbe que dicitur Glastingai, impendo et hanc priuilegii dignitatem super altare pono, ut sine impedimento rerum secularium et absque tributo fiscalium negociorum liberis mentibus soli Deo seruiant et monasticam disciplinam, Christo suffragium largiente, regulariter exerceant et pro statu et prosperitate regni nostri et indulgencia commissorum criminum ante conspectum diuine maiestatis[x] preces fundere dignentur;[y] et infra. Pro ampliori

[v] *dicessit* T; in a later hand (C15?) is the marginal note, *Factus est abbas Racuylf postea archiepiscopus Cantuarie.* It is not found in M.

[w] *omnipocenti* T.

[x] *magestatis* T; *maiestatis* M.

[y] A marginal passage, apparently taken from *GP*, p.381 where it follows *dignentur*, is to be read here according to a later but C13 hand but is not in M: *et orationum officia frequentantes in ecclesiis pro nostra fragilitate interpellare nitantur. Si quis uero contra huius decreti singrapham uenire temptauerit, sciat se coram*

On Leigh-in-Street.

In the same year Bishop Haeddi gave 6 hides at Leigh-in-Street to Glastonbury, with the consent of Centwine and Baldred, and this donation was confirmed by Caedwalla who inscribed the sign of the cross with his own hand, although he was a pagan.

39. On glorious king Ine who honoured Glastonbury in various ways, both by gifts and privileges.

Now that our chronological survey has brought us to Ine, King of the West Saxons, it will be best to describe one by one the estates which that distinguished man bestowed with pious generosity upon the old church at Glastonbury.

On Brent given by Ine.

In 690 AD Ine gave Abbot Haemgils 10 hides at Brent, an estate which Abbot Brihtwold gave up of his own free will. He abandoned his own monastery without any violence from us or without being expelled and went away against the command and wish of our bishop. The said king granted a privilege to Abbot Haemgils in these words.

40. The first privilege of king Ine.

In the name of our Lord Jesus Christ, I, King Ine, by the decision and advice of our bishop Aldhelm and at the suggestion also of all the priests of God and as a result of a request from the monks who dwell in the province of the West Saxons do confer this liberty on the monks in the ancient town called Glastonbury who serve the omnipotent God under Abbot Haemgils in the church of the blessed Mother of God Mary and the blessed Patrick and do place this lofty privilege upon the altar, so that with untroubled minds they might serve God alone without the hindrance of worldly affairs and without the need to pay financial dues; and so that they might practise, with the help that Christ shall offer, the monastic discipline according to the Rule; and so that they might deign to pour out prayers for the peace and prosperity of our kingdom and for the forgiveness of offences committed in the sight of the Divine Majesty; and so on. To strengthen the validity of this

firmitatis testamento principes et senatores, iudices et patricios subscribere fecimus. Actum publice confirmatum in lignea basilica anno ab incarnacione Domini DCCIIII. Ego Aldelmus subscripsi; et cetera.[86]

Hic Hemgislus fato perfunctus in uetusta ecclesia pausam corporis suscepit. Successit Berwaldus. Anno ab incarnacione Domini DCCV Ina Berwaldo abbati dedit xx hidas iuxta Tamer[z] et xx hidas in loco qui dicitur Bouelt, Soei xii hidas, Corregs v[a] hidas, Escford dimidiam hidam cum captura piscium, Dulting xx hidas. Ego Aldelmus hanc scedulam scripsi. Dedit eciam[b] Ina rex Pilton' xx hidas.[87] Eidem abbati dedit Wilfridus episcopus insulam de Wethmor lxx hidas, a rege Kenwino sibi datas, et uillam de Cliwere i hidam. Illi successit Albert anno incarnacionis Domini DCCXII cui Forthere episcopus, successor sancti Aldelmi dedit Bledahit i hidam. Successit Echfrid cui anno incarnacionis Domini DCCXIX dedit Ina unam hidam, cum[c] captura piscium, Axe. Eidem Bugu abbatissa dedit Ora iii hidas.[88]

Fundauit insuper Ina maiorem ecclesiam de apostolis Petro et Paulo et, quia plures ibidem basilice fuerunt, libet de situ diuersarum ecclesiarum Glastonie et fundatoribus earum ueritatem interserere. Primam igitur et uetustissimam fecerunt XII discipuli apostolorum Philippi et Iacobi, ut prescriptum est, et[d] hec sita fuit in occidentali parte aliarum. Secundam fecit sanctus Dauid Meneuensis episcopus in orientali parte antiquioris ecclesie in honorem beate Marie, quando uetustam ecclesiam dedicare disposuit ac a Domino prohibitus est eo quod ipse eamdem dedicauerat. Terciam fecerunt XII uiri a boreali parte Britannie uenientes, scilicet Morgen, Catgur, Cadmor et ceteri superius memorati, et hec similiter erat sita in orientali parte uetuste ecclesie. Quartam et maiorem construxit Ina rex in honore Domini saluatoris et apostolorum Petri et Pauli in orientali parte aliarum pro anima fratris sui Mules, quem Cantuarite infra Cantuariam incenderant. In cuius supremo ordine hos uersus fecit describi.[89]

Siderei montes, speciosa cacumina Syon,
A Libano, gemine, flore comante, cedri,
Celorum porte, lati duo lumina mundi,
Ore tonat Paulus, fulgurat arce Petrus.
Inter apostolicas radianti luce coronas,
celsior ille gradu, doctior hic monitis.
Corda per hunc hominum reserantur, et astra per illum.
Quos docet iste stilo, suscipit ille polo.

Christo IXque angelorum ordinibus in tremendo examine racionem redditurum. Pro amp . . .

z Interlined above in a similar hand is *scilicet Linis*. M reads *iuxta scilicet Linis Tamer . . .*

a Interlined above in a similar hand is *uel I*. M: *Corrego VI hidas.*

b *et* H.

c Interlined above in a contemporary hand is *scilicet Scipelade*; M reads *Ina scilicet Scipelade unam hidam.*

d *et* om. H.

charter we have caused it to be subscribed by princes and ealdormen, doomsmen and nobles. This deed was publicly confirmed in the wooden church in 704 AD. I, Aldhelm, have subscribed; etc.

When this Haemgils had fulfilled his fate his body obtained a resting-place in the old church. Beorhtwald succeeded him. In 705 AD Ine gave Abbot Beorhtwald 20 hides near the Tone, 20 hides at the place called Polden Hill, 12 hides at Zoy, 5 hides at Croscombe, ½ hide and fishing rights at *Escford*, and 20 hides at Doulting. I, Aldhelm, wrote this document. King Ine also gave 20 hides at Pilton. Bishop Wilfrid gave the same abbot 70 hides on the island of Wedmore, which had been given to him by King Centwine, and 1 hide in the village of Clewer.

Ealdberht succeeded him in 712 AD and was given 1 hide at Bleadney by Bishop Forthhere, the successor to St Aldhelm.

He was succeeded by Ecgfrith, to whom Ine gave 1 hide with fishing rights on the Axe in 719 AD. The Abbess Bugu gave 3 hides at *Ora* to the same abbot.

Ine also founded the greater church of the Apostles Peter and Paul and because there were many churches there I wish to insert here the facts about the location of the different churches at Glastonbury and their founders. The first and oldest was built, as noted before, by the twelve disciples of the apostles Philip and James and was situated to the west of the others. The second, to the east of the older church, was built by St David, Bishop of Menevia, in honour of the blessed Mary, after he had arranged to dedicate the old church but had been prevented by the Lord because He Himself had already dedicated it. The third was built by the twelve men who came from the north of Britain, namely Morgen, Catgur, Cadmor and the others mentioned above, and this too was situated to the east of the old church. The fourth and largest was constructed to the east of the others by King Ine in honour of the Lord our Saviour and of the apostles Peter and Paul for the soul of his brother Mul, whom the Kentish people had burnt to death in Kent. At the very top of it he had the following verses inscribed.

> O starry mounts, ye splendid peaks of Syon,
> Lebanon's twin cedars, wreathed in bloom,
> O gates of heaven, twin lights of this wide world,
> Paul thundering forth, Peter glittering from above,
> Of all the apostolic crowns aglow,
> None more great or none more wise.
> Men's hearts the one, the other stars unlocks.
> Who cons the words of one shares heaven with the other.

Pandit iter celi hic dogmate, clauibus alter.
Est uia cui Paulus, ianua fida Petrus.
Hic petra firma manens, ille architectus[e] habetur.
Surgit in hiis templum quo placet ara Deo.
Anglia plaude libens, mittit tibi Roma salutem.
Fulgor apostolicus Glastoniam irradiat.
A facie hostili duo propugnacula surgunt,
Quos fidei turres urbs, capud orbis, habet.
Hec pius egregio rex Ina refertus amore
Dona[f] suo populo non moritura dedit.
Totus in affectu diue pietatis inherens,
Ecclesie iuges amplificauit opes.
Melchisedec noster, merito rex et sacerdos,
Conpleuit uere religionis opus.
Publica iura regens et celsa palacia seruans,
Unica pontificum gloria norma fuit.
Hinc abiens, illic meritorum uiuet honore.
Hic quoque gestorum laude perennis[g] erit.

41. De capella argentea quam ibidem fecit rex Ina cum suis uasis.

Fecit eciam idem rex construere quandam capellam[h] ex auro et argento cum ornamentis et uasis, similiter aureis et argenteis,[i] ac infra maiorem collocauit. Ad capellam itaque construendam[i] duo milia[j] et sexcenta et quadraginta libras argenti donauit. Et altare ex ducentis et sexaginta quatuor libris auri erat,[k] calix cum patena de X libris auri,[l] incensarium de viii libris[m] et xx mankis auri, candelabra ex xii libris[m] et dimidia argenti, coopertoria librorum euuangelii de xx libris[m] et lx mankis auri, uasa aquaria[n] et alia uasa altaris ex xvii libris auri, pelues de viii libris auri, uas ad aquam benedictam ex xx libris[m] argenti, ymago Domini et beate[o] Marie et duodecim apostolorum ex centum et lxxv libris argenti et xxviii[p] libris[m] auri, palla

[e] *achitectus* T.
[f] *Bona* H.
[g] *perhennis* T and M.
[h] L inserts *in Glastonia* after *capellam*.
[i] L reads *argenteis. Ad quam construendam . . .*
[j] *millia* H.
[k] *fabricare fecit* L.
[l] L inserts *erat* after *auri*.
[m] In all cases T reads *librarum*; M reads *librarum* for the last two, *libris* for the others.
[n] *aquatica* L.
[o] *sancte* L.
[p] *xxxviii* H.

Paul's teaching opens heaven's gate and Peter's keys prevail.
Paul points the way to Peter's trusty door.
Firm stable rock the one, on which the other builds.
They raise a temple whose altar pleaseth God.
England's joyous praise saluteth thee, O Rome.
Your apostolic light illumines Glastonbury.
Two ramparts rise against the foeman's frown,
Towers of faith sprung from all-conquering Rome.
Pious King Ine, filled with generous love,
Gives all his people gifts that will not die.
Full in his love, a pious child of God,
His wealth increased the riches of the church.
Our Melchisedech, truly king and priest,
Completed true religion's work.
Just public rule and heaven's mighty service,
His bishops' glory was his only rule.
Departing hence he shall thrive in heaven,
Here too his deeds win everlasting praise.

41. On the silver chapel that king Ine built there and its vessels.

The same king also had a certain chapel built out of gold and silver, with ornaments and vases likewise of gold and silver, and sited it below the greater church. He donated 2,640 pounds of silver for the construction of the chapel. The altar was composed of 264 pounds of gold, the chalice and paten of 10 pounds of gold, the censer of 8 pounds and 20 mancusses of gold, the candlesticks of 12½ pounds of silver, covers for the Gospel Books of 20 pounds and 60 mancusses of gold, water vessels and other altar vessels of 17 pounds of gold, basins of 8 pounds of gold, the stoup for holy water of 20 pounds of silver, an image of the Lord, the blessed Mary and the twelve apostles of 175 pounds of silver and 28 pounds of gold, and the altar

f9 altaris et ornamenta sacerdotalia undique auro et la / pidibus preciosis subtiliter contexta.[q] Hunc ergo thesaurum, ob amorem sancte Dei genitricis et uirginis Marie, monasterio Glastonie dictus rex contulit deuotissime. Insuper scripto regio terras, possessiones et libertates eiusdem ecclesie confirmauit in hec uerba.[90]

42. Magnum priuilegium regis Ine.

Adiuua nos, Deus salutaris noster! Quecumque secundum decreta canonum atque ecclesiastica instituta salubri consilio diffiniuntur, quamquam sermo tantum absque textu sufficeret, tamen quoniam plerumque nostris temporibus tempestates et turbines (secularium)[r] rerum eciam portas ecclesie pulsant, idcirco opere precium censuimus ob cautelam futurorum ea, que diffinita sunt paginis scripturarum, annectere, ne in posterum obliuioni tradita ignorentur. Quapropter ego Ina regali fretus dignitate a Domino, cum consilio Sexburge regine et licencia Beorthwaldi, Dorobernensis ecclesie pontificis, et omnium suffraganeorum suorum, necnon eciam hortatu Baltredi et Athelardi subregulorum, ecclesie uetuste que est in loco qui dicitur Glasteie, quam magnus sacerdos et pontifex summus angelorum obsequio sibi ac perpetue uirgini Marie, beato Dauid, multis et inauditis miraculis olim se sanctificasse innotuit, ex hiis que paterna hereditate possideo, et in dominium peculiare teneo, locis continuis et congruentibus, concedo[s] ad supplementum[t] uite regularis et ad usum monachorum, Brente decem hidas, Sowi duodecim hidas, Pilton' uiginti hidas,[u] Dulting decem hidas, Bledeni unam hidam, cum hiis omnibus que antecessores mei eidem ecclesie contulerunt, Kenewalchius qui, sancto Theodoro archiepiscopo interueniente, Ferlingmere, Beokerie, Godenie, Martinesie, Edredesie;[u] Kenwinus rex qui Glastoningeie matrem sanctorum uocare solitus fuerat et eam ab omni seculari et ecclesiastico obsequio immunem statuit et hanc priuilegii dignitatem concessit, ut habeant fratres eiusdem loci potestatem eligendi et constituendi sibi rectorem iuxta regulam sancti Benedicti; Hedde episcopus qui, Cedwalla annuente et propria manu licet paganus confirmante, Lantokay; Baltdrec qui Pennard vi hidas; Adthelard qui Poeld' lx hidas, me[v] annuente et confirmante, dederunt.[91] Quorum ego deuocioni et benigne peticioni assentio, et contra malignancium hominum et oblacrancium canum insidias regalium munimine inuigilo litterarum, quatinus ecclesia Domini nostri Ihesu Christi et perpetue uirginis Marie, sicut in regno Britannie est prima et fons et origo tocius religionis, ita et in ipsa supereminentem priuilegii obtineat dignitatem, nec ulli omnino hominum ancillare obsequium faciat in terris,

[q] L finishes with . . . *subtiliter contexta.*

[r] This has been written above by the same or a contemporary hand with a caret to indicate its position; in the text in M.

[s] *getedo* T, *concedo* M.

[t] *Suplementum* T, M.

[u] *Dulting . . . Edredesie* is bracketed in T with this marginal note in a C15 hand beside it: *hoc non dicitur supra*, om. M.

[v] *Ine* M.

cloth and sacerdotal ornaments were subtly interwoven all over with gold and precious stones. This king most devoutly gave all this treasure to the monastery of Glastonbury out of his love for the Virgin Mary, the holy mother of God. Moreover in a royal document he confirmed the estates, possessions and liberties of that church in these words.

42. The great privilege of king Ine.

Help us, o God of our salvation. Although our word alone ought to suffice for whatever is decided after sound advice and is in accord with canonical decretals and ecclesiastical ordinances, without its needing to be written down, yet, since in our times the storms and tempests of secular affairs beat even on the doors of the church, our prayers have led us to propose that those things we have decided on should be bound up in the pages of the Scriptures, for the security of future generations, lest they be consigned to oblivion and unknown to posterity. Wherefore, I, Ine, given my royal dignity by the Lord, with the advice of Queen Seaxburg and the approval of Brihtwold, Archbishop of Canterbury, and all his suffragans, and also with the encouragement of the sub-kings Baldred and Aethelheard, to the old church in the place called Glastonbury – the church which the great priest and highest bishop with the help of angels had once dedicated with many unheard-of miracles to Himself and the perpetual Virgin Mary, as He revealed to the blessed David – do grant out of those places that I possess by paternal inheritance and hold in my own demesne, they being adjacent and suitable, for the maintenance of the regular life and the use of the monks, 10 hides at Brent, 12 hides at Zoy, 20 hides at Pilton, 10 hides at Doulting and 1 hide at Bleadney, together with everything that my predecessors bestowed on the church, namely Cenwalh, who granted Meare, Beckery, Godney, Marchey and Nyland, at the instance of Archbishop Theodore, King Centwine, who was accustomed to call Glastonbury the mother of saints and granted it immunity from all secular and ecclesiastical services and conceded it the lofty privilege that the brothers there should have the power of choosing and appointing their own ruler in accordance with the Rule of St Benedict, Bishop Haeddi, who gave Leigh with the approval of Caedwalla who confirmed it with his own hand although he was a pagan, Baldred, who gave 6 hides at Pennard, and Aethelheard, who gave 60 hides at Polden Wood, with my agreement and confirmation. To the piety and bounteous entreaty of those men I assent and do guard against the plots of wicked men and barking hounds with the rampart of my royal words so that the church of our Lord Jesus Christ and the perpetual Virgin Mary, as it is the first in the kingdom of Britain and the fount and origin of all religion, may obtain for that reason a privilege of surpassing dignity and so that She who rules over choirs of angels in heaven will not yield servile obedience to any man on

que super choros angelorum dominatur in celis. Igitur, summo pontifice Gregorio annuente, et ut matrem Domini sui in sinum et procectionem sancte Romane ecclesie me, licet indignum, cum ipsa suscipiente, consencientibus eciam omnibus Britannie regibus, archiepiscopis, (episcopis)[w] ducibus atque abbatibus, statuo ego atque confirmo quatinus omnes terre et loca et possessiones beate Marie Glasteie sint quieta et ab omnibus regiis exactionibus et operibus que indici solent, uidelicet expedicione et pontis arcisue constructione, et ab omnium archiepiscoporum et (episcoporum)[w] promulgacionibus et perturbacionibus, sicut in antiquis eiusdem ecclesie cartis ratum esse inuenitur et a predecessoribus meis, Kenewalchio, Kenwino, Cedwalla, Baldredo confirmatum esse dinoscitur, inconcussa et illibata permaneant. Et quecumque emerserint[x] cause, in homicidiis, sacrilegiis, ueneficiis, furtis, rapinis, in disposicione ecclesiarum et descripcione, in ordinacione clericorum, in conuenticulis sinodalibus et in omnibus iudicariis examinacionibus, absque ullius hominis preiudicio, abbatis et conuentus disposicione diffiniantur. Sed et omnibus regni mei regibus, archiepiscopis, episcopis, ducibus et principibus super honorem suum et amorem meum precipio, et omnibus tam meis quam eorum ministris super salutem corporis sui precipio, ne ullus eorum in insulam Domini nostri Ihesu Christi et perpetue uirginis Marie Glasteie, nec eiusdem ecclesie possessiones, causa placitandi, perscrutandi, rapiendi, precipiendi, interdicendi, uel aliquid faciendi quod ibidem Deo famulantibus possit esse in scandalum audeat intrare. Illud autem omnipotentis Dei et perpetue uirginis Marie et beatorum apostolorum Petri et Pauli et omnium intercessione sanctorum interdictione interdico, ne in ipsa Glastonie ecclesia nec in ecclesiis sibi subditis, uidelicet, Sowy, Brente, Merlinge, Sapewic, Stret, Budecaleth, Pilton', nec in earum capellis, sed nec in insulis, aliqua interueniente occasione, episcopus cathedram sibi episcopalem statuere, nec missas solempnes celebrare, nec altaria consecrare, nec ecclesias dedicare, nec ordines facere, nec aliquid omnino disponere presumat, nisi ab abbate uel a fratribus inuitatus fuerit. Quod si ad hec inuitatus fuerit, nichil de rebus ecclesie sed nec de ipsis oblacionibus ipse sibi aliquid usurpet. Duobus in locis ex ipsius ecclesie possessionibus duas ei delegamus mansiones, unam in Poelt,[y] alteram in uilla que Piltona dicitur, ut habeat ubi adueniens hospitetur uel inde ueniens sese recipiat. Neque enim eum ibi, nisi inportunitate temporis aut molestia corporis detentus fuerit aut ab abbate uel a fratribus rogatus fuerit, nec amplius quam cum tribus aut cum[z] quatuor clericis pernoctare licet. Hoc eciam prouideat idem episcopus ut singulis annis cum clericis suis qui Fontanetum sunt ipsam matrem suam Glastoniensem uidelicet ecclesiam, feria secunda post ascensionem Domini, cum letania recognoscat.[a] Quod si, superbia inflatus, eam distulerit, et que superius dicta et confirmata sunt preuaricauerit, mansiones sibi superius delegatas amittat. Abbas uel monachi a quocumque uoluerint, qui pascha canonicum celebret, ecclesiastica sacramenta in

[w] These have been written above by the same or a contemporary hand with a caret to indicate their position; in the text in M.

[x] *immerserint* T; *GR* reads *emerserint*.

[y] A marginal note in a C13 hand adds *id est Grenton*, om. M.

[z] *cum* om. H.

[a] *recongnoscat* T, M.

earth. And so with the assent of the chief pontiff Gregory, who has received Glastonbury into the bosom and protection of the Holy Roman Church, as the mother of his Lord, and me with it, although I am unworthy, and with the consent too of all the kings, archbishops, bishops, ealdormen and abbots of Britain I do determine and confirm that all the estates, places and possessions of the blessed Mary at Glastonbury be quit of all royal charges and customary services, namely military service and the building of bridges and forts, and be undisturbed and unharmed by the edicts and interference of all archbishops and bishops, as is found to have been established in the ancient charters of the church and is known to have been confirmed by my predecessors, Cenwalh, Centwine, Caedwalla and Baldred. And whatever suits shall arise, whether of homicide, sacrilege, poisoning, theft or rapine, or concerning the disposal and boundaries of churches or the ordination of clerks, or in any ecclesiastical synod or judicial inquiry, shall be decided by the direction of the abbot and convent without the interference of any other man. Moreover I do enjoin all the kings, archbishops, bishops, ealdormen and governors of my kingdom, for the sake of their own honour and their love of me, and all my dependents and theirs, for the sake of their personal safety, not to dare enter the island of our Lord Jesus Christ and the perpetual Virgin Mary at Glastonbury nor any of the possessions of that church with the intention of hearing pleas, making inquiries, plundering, commanding, laying under interdict, or doing anything which could offend those serving God there. Moreover I especially do prohibit and forbid, calling on the intercession of Almighty God, the perpetual Virgin Mary, the blessed apostles Peter and Paul and all the saints, any bishop to presume, on any pretext at all, to establish his episcopal seat, or to celebrate solemn mass, or to consecrate altars, or to dedicate churches, or to confer holy orders, or to do anything at all in the church of Glastonbury itself, or in any of the churches subject to it, namely Middle Zoy, East Brent, Moorlinch, Shapwick, Street, Butleigh and Pilton, or in any of their chapels or islands, unless he be invited by the abbot or brethren. If he be so invited he shall take nothing to himself of the things of the church nor of the offerings. We appoint two estates for the invited bishop in two places that the church possesses, one in Greinton and the other in the village called Pilton, so that, when coming or going, he will have a place of refreshment and entertainment. But he shall not be permitted to spend the night there unless detained by unsuitable weather or bodily illness or invited by the abbot or brethren, and even then with not more than three or four clerks. Moreover let such a bishop make provision for this, that every year he, and his clerks that are at Wells, should acknowledge his mother church of Glastonbury with litanies on the second day after the Lord's ascension. But if, in his swollen pride, he should defer that or should transgress against the commands recited and confirmed above he shall forfeit the mansions made over to him above. The abbots and monks shall receive the holy sacrament in

Glastoniensi ecclesia aut in ecclesiis sibi subiectis aut in earum capellis percipiant.[b] Quisquis autem huius mee munificencie et libertatis[c] testamentum, quouis deinceps tempore, aliqua occasione, cuiuslibet eciam dignitatis uel professionis uel gradus peruertere uel in irritum deducere temptauerit, sciat se cum Iuda proditore eterna confusione edacibus ineffabilium tormentorum periturum flammis. Scripta est autem huius donacionis et priuilegii pagina anno Dominice incarnacionis DCCXXV, indictione iiii[a], sub presencia Ine regis et Beorthwald Dorobernensis[d] pontificis uenerandorumque antistitum Danielis atque Fordredis et aliorum quorum nomina inferius annotantur. Ego Ina rex proprie manus subscripcione hanc donacionem et libertatem sub sigillo sancte crucis ratam fieri decerno. Ego Aedelburga regina consensi. Ego Baldredus rex confirmaui. Ego Adelard frater regine consensi. Ego Beorthwaldus[e] Dorobernensis ecclesie archiepiscopus Ine regis donacionem et libertatem sub sigillo sancte crucis corroboraui et magnates quamplures alii.[92]

43. De fine regis Ine.

Dehinc predictus rex Yna (litteras)[f] regali signaculo signatas summo pontifici direxit, in quibus omnia predicta continebantur, simul cum quodam cipho aureo ac aliis donis regalibus supplicans ut Glastoniensem ecclesiam cum pertinenciis et libertatibus suis in proteccionem sancte Romane ecclesie susciperet et ipsam auctoritate apostolica in perpetuum confirmaret. Eodem autem anno quo idem rex Romam personaliter adiit priuilegium apostolico signaculo corroboratum in redeundo Glastoniam apportauit. Et postea iterum cum Ethelburga regina sua instinctu uidelicet eiusdem Romam abiit. Ibi, ne conuersionis sue pompam faceret, ut solius Dei placeret oculis, amictu plebeio tectus clam consenuit demum uiam uniuerse carnis ingressus non sine magnis, ut accepimus, miraculis.[93]

44. De Cengisle[g] abbate.

Eethfrido abbati successit Cengisle. Anno Dominice incarnacionis DCCXXIX Edelard successor Ine concessit familie, que in monasterio Glastingebirie omnipotenti Deo sub religioso abbate Cengislo famulantur, in stabilem possessionem lx hidas in f10 Pothonholt / et in Torric x.

Eiusque uxor Fridogitha[h] Brunantun v hidas.[94]

[b] *percipiat* M.
[c] *liberalitatis* H.
[d] *Dorobernersis* M.
[e] *Borthwaldus* H.
[f] The same or a contemporary hand, adds this above the line, with a caret as indication of position, in the text of M.
[g] *Cengille* H.
[h] *Fredogitha* H.

the church of Glastonbury or in the churches subject to it or in their chapels from whomever they wish to have celebrate the Easter mass. Whoever shall try hereafter on any occasion whatever, regardless of his dignity, profession or rank, to pervert or nullify this my grant of gifts and liberty, let him know that, to his eternal confounding, he will perish with the traitor Judas in the devouring flames of unspeakable torment. This document of donation and privilege was written in 725 AD in the fourth indiction in the presence of King Ine, Brihtwold, Archbishop of Canterbury, the venerable bishops Daniel and Forthhere, and the others whose names are noted below. I, King Ine, decree that this donation and liberty is established under the seal of the holy cross by my own subscription. I, Queen Aethelberg, have consented. I, King Baldred, have confirmed it. I, Aethelheard, the queen's brother, have consented. I, Brihtwold, Archbishop of Canterbury, have corroborated this donation and liberty of King Ine with the seal of the holy cross. Very many other magnates too.

43. King Ine's end.

Afterwards King Ine sent to the highest pontiff letters, signed with the royal seal, in which all the aforementioned was contained, together with a golden bowl and other regal gifts, with the request that the pope receive the church of Glastonbury with its appurtenances and liberties into the protection of the Holy Roman church and confirm the same by his apostolic authority. Moreover in that same year the king went to Rome in person and brought back to Glastonbury that charter corroborated by the apostolic seal. Later, at her instigation, he went again to Rome with Queen Aethelberg. There, lest he make a display of his conversion and in order to be pleasing in the eyes of God alone, he grew old in obscurity wearing common clothes and eventually went the way of all flesh, not, as we have heard, without great miracles.

44. On Abbot Coengils.

Coengils succeeded Abbot Ecgfrith. In 729 AD Ine's successor Aethelheard conceded to the community which serves Almighty God under the pious abbot Coengils in the monastery of Glastonbury enduring possession of 60 hides in Polden Wood and 10 hides in the valley of the river Torridge. His wife Frithugyth granted 5 hides at Brompton.

45. Priuilegium Cuthredi regis.

Anno Dominice incarnacionis DCCXLIIII Cuthred rex Westsaxonum dedit huiuscemodi priuilegium Glastonie. In nomine Domini nostri Ihesu Christi ego Cuthredus rex Westsaxonum, uniuersa regum priorum suppeticia, Kentwines, Baldredes, Cedwallan, Ines, Ethelardes, Aethelbaldes regis Merciorum, in uillis et in uicis et in agris ac in prediis mansisque maioribus, ut est pristina urbs Glastonie corroborata, sicque proprie manus subscripcione crucisque signo confirmatum hoc donatiuum stabili iure gratum et ratum regum predictorum decerno durare, quamdiu uertigo poli terras atque equora circa ethera siderum iusso moderamine uoluet. Si quis autem huius mee donacionis testamentum nisus fuerit confringere, uel gressum pedis nobis hengissingum traditum uberemque glebam extra terminos prefixos uel definitos limites seu constitutos fines adimere, ipse acrius mulctatus sit infernalis ergastuli in pena demersus uiolencieque sue presumpcionem luat in euum. Amen. Ego Cuthredus rex Westsaxonum proprie manus subscripcione sancte crucis designaui effigiem ut nemo, qui se regeneratum in Christo nouerit, presumat mutare hanc donacionem. Ego Herewaldus episcopus subscripsi et confirmaui. Signum manus Cumbran prefecti regis et aliorum multorum nobilium. Exemplar huius largicionis et priuilegii promulgatum est anno incarnacionis Domini DCCXLIIII in predicto cenobio sub presencia regis Cuthredi, quod proprie manus munificencia, uotiua uero deuocione, altario sacro commendauit in lignea basilica et honorabili, qua fratres beate memorie Hemgisli sarcophagum sorciuntur. Ego Daniel subscripsi.[95]

46. De Ure et Baltenesbeorghe.

Anno sequente, id est incarnacionis Dominice DCCXLV, idem Cuthred dedit Tumberto abbati Ure iii hidas; Lulle Baltenesbeorthe et Scrobbamurht[i] x hidas. Sequente uero, id est incarnacionis Domini DCCXLVI anno, ego Aethelbald, pro redempcione anime mee, Tumberto, IX annos presidenti, et familie que in monasterio Glastingabirie[j] fideli Deo famulantur obsequio largitus sum, precio cccc solidorum, iiii hidas, duobus in locis, Jecesig[k] et Bradanleghe.[96]

47. De Tican abbate.

Anno DCCLIIII Sigebertus, precio l solidorum auri, concessit Tican abbati et monachis in urbe Glastingensium degentibus xxii hidas in Poholt. Idem eciam Tican vi hidas que in occidentali parte illius remanserant precio regio, scilicet l solidorum auri, ab eodem rege conparauit ut eterna esset hereditas monasterii

[i] Interlined above in T and also in the margin is *uel Sabewrche*; om. M.
[j] *Glastingabiry* H.
[k] Interlined above in T is *uel Gassig*; M reads *locis et Gassig, Jecessig et . . .*

45. *King Cuthred's privilege.*

In 744 AD Cuthred, King of the West Saxons, granted the following privilege to Glastonbury:

In the name of our Lord Jesus Christ, I, Cuthred, King of the West Saxons, do decree that, as the ancient city of Glastonbury has been confirmed with its villages, hamlets, fields, farms and greater manors, at the universal request of former kings, Centwine, Baldred, Caedwalla, Ine, Aethelheard and Aethelbald, King of the Mercians, this donation, settled by right to the satisfaction of those kings and confirmed by the subscription of my own hand and with the sign of the cross, endure as long as the whirling of heaven carries the land and sea around the starry sky in regular motion. But if anyone endeavour to violate this charter of donation or to take away the foot-merchet or hanging fine that we have made over or the rich land outside the fixed boundaries and established borders let him be punished most fiercely, immersed in the suffering of the infernal dungeon, and atone eternally for the presumption of his violence. Amen.

I, Cuthred, King of the West Saxons, inscribed this image of the holy cross with my own hand so that no-one who believes himself regenerated in Christ will presume to alter this donation. I, Bishop Hereweald, have subscribed and confirmed it. Signatures in the hands of Cumbran, the king's *prefectus* and many other nobles. A copy of this donation and privilege was promulgated in 744 AD in the aforesaid monastery in the presence of King Cuthred who, with true devotion, generously placed it himself on the holy altar in the honourable wooden church, where the brethren had chosen to locate the coffin of Haemgils of blessed memory. I, Daniel, have subscribed.

46. *On* Ure *and Baltonsborough.*

In the following year, that is 745 AD, the same Cuthred gave 3 hides at *Ure* to Abbot Tunberht and Lulla gave 10 hides at Baltonsborough and *Scrobbamurht*. In the following year, that is 746 AD, I, Aethelbald, for the redemption of my soul, have granted to Tunberht, who has been abbot for 9 years, and to the community which serves God in faithful obedience in the monastery of Glastonbury 4 hides in two places, *Jecesig* and *Bradanleghe*, for 400 shillings.

47. *On abbot Tyccea.*

In the year 754 Sigeberht granted to Abbot Tyccea and the monks living in the town of Glastonbury 22 hides in the Polden Hills for 50 gold *solidi*. The same Tyccea also obtained from that king, at the royal price of 50 gold *solidi*, 6 remaining hides to the west of there to be a possession of the monastery of Glastonbury

Glastonie. De hoc qui et VI annis Glastonie prefuit superius preoccupaui dicere, quas scilicet reliquias ecclesie attulerit. Ubi sepulturam cum sociis acceperit testatur hoc epitaphium quod legere non neglexi:

> Tumba hec mirifico fulget fabricata decore.
> Desuper exsculptum condit sub culmine Tican.

De quo sepulcro per succidua secula istud narratur miraculum, quod cum illud quidam agressus esset diruere, statim cecitate mulctatus cognouit culpam. Nescio si promeruit ueniam.[97]

48. De Guban abbate sub Cinewlfo rege.

Anno DCCLX Cinewlfus rex dedit Guban abbati, qui et Glastonie II annis prefuit, Wudeton' v hidas, Huneresberg in orientali ripa Petride. Ethelard minister eius iii hidas in Cedern.[l] Sulca Christi ancilla dedit Culum xi hidas, Cumbe iii hidas. Anno DCCLXII Cinewlf dedit Walduno abbati Cumtun v hidas. Hic prefuit Glastonie XXXII annis. Anno DCCXCIIII Offa rex Merciorum dedit Beadeuulfo abbati ad supplementum[m] uenerabilis ecclesie in Eswirht x hidas. Hic prefuit VI annis. Ethelmund assensu regis Offe dedit Hunespulle i hidam.[98]

49. De libertate data Kinelmo in ecclesia Glastonie.

Anno DCCXCVI[n] Leo, tercius eius nominis, papa factus est. Quo tempore Karolus magnus regnabat in Francia, Brihtricus erat rex[o] Westsaxonum, Kenwulfus, post Egfridum, qui patri Offe uix quatuor mensibus successerat, rex Merciorum in Anglia. Sed de papa isto et regibus, si quis dignabitur legere, in Gestis Regum Anglorum, libro primo, poterit inuenire.[99] Nunc eorum nomina tetigisse sufficiat, quoniam ad rem quam explicare conamur multum attinet. Leo enim papa confirmauit Kinhelmo libertatem donacionis monasterii Glastoniensis in octingentis hidis, ipsi et successoribus eius in perpetuum, ita tamen ut monasterium in sua religione et stabilitate in omnia secula perseueraret. Data est autem libertas Kinelmo annitente et confirmante Kenuulfo rege Merciorum. Et fortasse, sicut ex consequentibus conici[p] potest, mutato ut fit regnorum statu, quamuis Glastonia sit in Westsaxonia, Merciorum reges uel eam pro amore defensitabant uel ei pro iure imperitabant. Priuilegia sane pape et regis quia nusquam, nisi anglice, scripta repperi, meo labore transfundam in latinum, quantum intelligo ex sensu sensum.[100]

[l] Interlined above is *id est Elenbeorge*; in the text in M.
[m] *suplementum* T, M.
[n] *DCCXXVI* H.
[o] *rex* om. H.
[p] *connici* T, M.

for ever. I referred above to this abbot who ruled Glastonbury, mentioning the relics that he brought to the church. The following epitaph, which I have been careful to read, testifies to where he and his comrades were buried:

> This shining tomb was built with marvellous skill.
> Carved above, Tyccea lies interred beneath its roof.

Through the succeeding centuries this miracle has been related about his sepulcre, that when a certain man set about destroying it he learnt at once that he had sinned because he was struck blind. I do not know if he obtained pardon.

48. On abbot Guba under king Cynewulf.

In the year 760 AD King Cynewulf gave 5 hides at Wootton and Houndsborough on the eastern bank of the Parret to Abbot Guba, who ruled Glastonbury for 2 years. His thane Aethelheard gave 3 hides at Elborough. Sulca, a handmaiden of Christ, gave 11 hides at Culmstock and 3 hides at Culm Davy. In the year 762 Cynewulf gave 5 hides at *Cumtun* to Abbot Wealdhun who ruled at Glastonbury for 32 years. In the year 794 Offa, King of the Mercians, gave 10 hides at *Eswirht* to Abbot Beaduwulf for the maintenance of his venerable church. The latter was abbot for 6 years. Aethelmund gave 1 hide at Huntspill, with the consent of King Offa.

49. On the liberty given to Cynehelm in the church of Glastonbury.

In the year 796 Leo was made pope, the third of that name. At that time Charlemagne was ruling in Francia and in England Beorhtric was King of the West Saxons and Cenwulf was King of the Mercians, after Ecgfrith who had succeeded his father Offa for scarcely four months. If anyone care to read about that pope or those kings he can find an account of them in book one of *The Deeds of the Kings of England*. For the moment it is enough to have mentioned their names since they are important for what we are trying to explain. For Pope Leo confirmed to Cynehelm the liberty of the gift of the monastery of Glastonbury, consisting of 800 hides, for him and his successors forever, so that the monastery should presevere undisturbed in its religion for all time. This liberty was given to Cynehelm with the support and confirmation of Cenwulf, King of the Mercians. Probably, as can be inferred from what follows, this was done because of a change in the state of the kingdoms for, although Glastonbury is in Wessex, the kings of Mercia were either protecting it out of love or governing it by right. Because I have not found the privileges of the pope and the king recorded, other than in English, I will labour to translate into Latin as much of their meaning as I understand.

50. Priuilegium Leonis pape.

Leo apostolice sedis papa, seruus seruorum Dei, Kinelmo regi et eius ministris et cognatis et successoribus eius optat et mittit pacem et salutem perpetuam. Bone uoluntatis et laudabilis operacionis cogitacio cum apostolicis scriptis est confirmanda et corroboranda, ut, quod bene fuerit factum et per racionabilia exempla confirmatum, nulla deinceps possit corrupcione uel turbari uel frangi, immo pocius inuiolabili rectitudine et diuina auctoritate debeat inconcussum permanere; et ideo egregie apostolica sentencia precipitur, (et incunctanter confirmari debeat) quod recte inchoatum fuisse constat. Quapropter quia notum est quod tua illustris fides petiit a nobis ut tibi scripto confirmaremus monasterium Domini Ihesu Christi in Glastonia Westsaxonum regni in quo monasterio seruorum Dei congregacio est cuius terre ad octingentas hidas numerantur in multis prouinciis et locis posite, sicut Egfridus rex omnem illam terram descripsit cum iudicio et licencia Brihtrici regis et cum licencia et testimonio Merciorum episcoporum et principum et sicut postea Kenulfo regi Merciorum omnes ille terre scripto confirmate sunt, ideo concessionem illam regum et episcoporum et principum cum corroboracione regis Merciorum Kenulfi cum apostolico robore et auctoritate confirmamus tibi Kenelme et successoribus tuis, monasterium scilicet libere in perpetuum habendi cum omnibus uillis et agris in multis regionibus diuisis, cum omnibus rebus ad hoc pertinentibus, siluis et pratis et pascuis et piscium capturis, hac condicione, ut frequententur ibi luminaria coram Deo et spirituales cantus et psalmi et misse cantentur et concordia sine simulacione. Hinc enim scriptum est in euuangelio: Domus mea domus oracionis uocabitur.[101] Quocirca serui Dei, qui in hac uita laborant, debent diatim cum timore diuino totum spirituale officium implere ut possint Domino nostro Ihesu Christo placere. Preterea constituimus cum apostolico precepto et sub timore diuini iudicii et sub excommunicacionis interminacione ne ullus rex aut archiepiscopus aut episcopus aut princeps aut alicuius potestatis homo exaltatus, siue in maiori ordine siue in minori, ista nostra apostolica decreta uiolenter infringat aut minuat. Sed magis decernimus ut prefatum monasterium firmum et stabile in omnia tempora perseueret. Quod si quilibet, quod non optamus, ista precepta nostra debilitauerit, sciat se ipsum per auctoritatem Domini Petri apostolorum principis excommunicacionis uinculis irretitum et a regno Dei extorrem. Quicumque uero tenuerit et seruauerit ista nostra apostolica decreta, sciat se promeruisse benedictionem apostolicam et eternam uitam a misericordi[q] creatore nostro. Data per manus Eustachii, primicerii nocariorum, mense marcio, indictione tertia, octaua die marcii. Confirmata per manus Paschalis senioris et consilarii apostolice sedis, regnante Domino nostro Ihesu Christo cum Deo patre per infinita secula, tertio anno per misericordiam Dei papatus Domini nostri Leonis in sancta et apostolica sede sancti Petri et eciam per licenciam Domini Karoli Francorum regis et Longobardorum et patricii Romanorum anno regni eius XXV.

q *misericorde* H.

50. The privilege of pope Leo.

Leo, Pope of the apostolic see, servant of the servants of God, sends his wish for peace and eternal salvation to King Cynehelm, his thanes, kinsmen and successors. Resolutions of good will and praiseworthy charity ought to be confirmed and corroborated by apostolic writ so that what has been well propounded and confirmed in reasonable cases cannot later be disturbed or violated by any act of corruption but, rather, will remain unshaken by virtue of its inviolable rightness and divine authority, and therefore what is known to have been correctly initiated is here properly enjoined by apostolic pronouncement and ought to be confirmed without delay. Wherefore, because we know that your manifest faith has asked us to confirm for you in writing the monastery of our Lord Jesus Christ in Glastonbury in the kingdom of the West Saxons – in which monastery there is a congregation of God's servants whose lands, located in many provinces and regions, total 800 hides, as recorded by King Ecgfrith in accord with the decision and permission of King Beorhtric and with the approval and attestation of the bishops and chief men of the Mercians and as subsequently confirmed in writing for Cenwulf, King of the Mercians – we do confirm by our apostolic power and authority to you, Cynehelm, and your successors that concession granted by kings, bishops and princes with the corroboration of Cenwulf, King of the Mercians, namely the right of holding that monastery forever without hindrance, together with all its villages and fields distributed thoughout many regions, and all its appurtenances, woods and meadows, pasture lands and fishing rights, on the condition that candles be constantly maintained there before God, that spiritual chants, psalms and masses be sung and that genuine concord be preserved. For it is written in the Gospel. 'My house shall be called a house of prayer.' Wherefore God's servants who labour in this life ought daily complete the whole spiritual office in the fear of God so that they might please our Lord Jesus Christ. We affirm besides, by apostolic command invoking the fear of divine judgement and an eternity of excommunication, that no king or archbishop or bishop or prince or man raised to any position of power, whether of a greater or a lesser order, should by force violate or restrict these our apostolic decrees. On the contrary we decree that the aforesaid monastery should persist, stable and enduring, throughout all time. But if anyone undermine these our commands, which we wish not to happen, let him know that by the authority of Peter, the chief of the apostles of the Lord, he will be bound by the chains of excommunication and will be banished from the kingdom of God. Let whoever maintain and preserve these our apostolic decrees know that he has deserved apostolic benediction and eternal life from our merciful Creator. Given on the 8th day of March in the third indiction by the hand of Eustace, our chief notary. Confirmed, with our Lord Jesus Christ ruling with God his Father through the infinite centuries, by the hand of Paschal, elder and counsellor of the apostolic see, in the third year, by the mercy of God, of the papacy of our Lord Leo, in the holy and apostolic see of St Peter and with the permission of our Lord Charles, King of the Franks and Lombards and Patrician of the Romans, in the 25th year of his reign.

51. Priuilegium Cenwlfi[r] *regis.*

f11 Regnante in perpetuum Domino Ihesu Christo, omnium regnorum / Domino, ego Cenuulf rex Merciorum, postquam electus sum in regem per Deum omnipotentem qui est omnium bonorum largitor et retributor, hanc suprascriptam[s] libertatem a domino Leone apostolico papa adquisiui Kinelmo et successoribus suis. Et sicut eamdem libertatem Egfridus rex antecessor meus ei firmiter condonauit, ita quoque ego ei scripto confirmo cum consilio et licencia terrenorum principum, quorum inferius nomina scripta sunt, et ei sine ullo mendacio aut dolo largior firmiter habendam. Hec confirmacio Cenuulfi et episcoporum eius et principum fuit constituta (et scripta in uenerabili)[t] loco qui dicitur Glastingebir' anno DCCXCVII incarnacionis Domini, secundo anno regni mei quod mihi Deus concessit.

Ego Kinedrith abbatissa cum carissimis cognatis meis Ethelburh et Celfled hanc libertatem hic ascriptam, Kinelmo concedendo, subscribo, hac racione, ut si eciam post tempus contigerit quod uenerabilis loci Glastoniensis possessionem et potestatem alterius progeniei homo suscipiat, tamen Kinelmus et eius successores stabiliter sine ulla perturbacione et fiducialiter permaneant in sua libertate et perpetua pace. Ad confirmandam uero hanc libertatis potestatem ego Cenwulf rex signum sancte crucis impressi. Subscripserunt Ethelardus Cantuarie et Higbertus Eboraci archiepiscopi et IX episcopi et XIII abbates, inter quos Beadulf abbas eiusdem loci, et sex principes.

Quis Kenelmus iste fuerit cui rex Cenuulf tantam libertatem indulsit ambigo. Nam quamuis filius eius Kenelmus dictus sit, qui uix septennis post patris obitum interemptus est dolo sororis, non putandus est esse iste, presertim cum secundo anno regni Kenulfi[u] hec libertas data fuerit et ipse XXIIII annis regnauerit.[102] Sed nos, hiis dimissis, cepta prosequamur.

52. De Cuman abbate et Egberto rege.

Anno DCCC successit Cuman abbas qui et Glastonie prefuit XXII[v] annis. Anno incarnacionis DCCCII Egbertus rex Westsaxonum ad ecclesiam Glastonie et ad usum monachorum dedit v manencium possessionem secus flumen quod dicitur Toric ob peticionem Mucan abbatis. Aedgisilius dedit Budecleg xx hidas assensu regis Egberti. Anno incarnacionis DCCCXXIIII Cuthlac abbas dedit Eanulfo unius cassati porcionem in Brunham precio quingentorum solidorum, ducentorum abbati, ccc[or] monachis.[103]

[r] Original erased, added in hand about 1300; also in M.

[s] *subscriptam* H.

[t] A contemporary hand adds this in the margin with an asterisk to indicate its location; in M.

[u] *Kenwlfi* H.

[v] *II* in H. T originally read *xxii* but the *xx* has been rudely erased. M reads *XXII.*

51. The privilege of king Cenwulf.

With our Lord Jesus Christ, the Lord of all kingdoms ruling forever, I Cenwulf, King of the Mercians, after my election to the kingship by Almighty God, the bestower and requiter of all good things, acquired from our lord Leo, apostolic Pope, the liberty recorded above for Cynehelm and his successors. And just as my predecessor King Ecgfrith conceded the same liberty to him to last forever so I, too, confirm it for him in writing, with the advice and permission of the earthly leaders whose names are written below, and bestow it on him without deceit or trickery to be held forever. This confirmation by Cenwulf and his bishops and chief men was agreed upon and written down in the venerable place called Glastonbury in 797 AD, the second year of the rule which God had allowed me.

I, Abbess Cynethryth, with my dearest kin, Aethelburh and Ceolflaed, subscribe the liberty here written with its concession to Cynehelm for this reason, that even if it should happen in the future that a man from another clan should obtain possession of and power over that venerable place Glastonbury, yet Cynehelm and his successors will remain steadfast and faithful, undisturbed in their liberty and perpetual peace. I, King Cenwulf, have imprinted the sign of the holy cross in order to confirm the power of this liberty. Subscribed by Aethelheard, Archbishop of Canterbury, Hygeberht, Archbishop of York, 9 bishops, 13 abbots, including Beaduwulf, abbot of that very place, and 6 princes.

I am unsure who that Cynehelm was to whom King Cenwulf granted so great a liberty. For although his son was called Cynehelm, he was killed by his sister's deceit after his father's death when scarcely seven years old, and so cannot be considered to be the one, especially since this liberty was granted in the second year of the reign of Cenwulf, who ruled for 24 years. But let us put aside these matters and proceed with our undertaking.

52. On abbot Cuma and king Egbert.

In the year 800 Cuma succeeded as abbot and ruled at Glastonbury for 22 years. In 802 AD Egbert, King of the West Saxons, at the request of Abbot Muca gave to the church of Glastonbury, for the use of the monks, the possession of 5 manors near the river called the Torridge. Eadgils gave 20 hides at Butleigh with the agreement of King Egbert. In 824 AD Abbot Guthlac gave part of one *cassatum* in *Brunham* to Eanulf, with a value of 500 *solidi*, 200 for the abbot and 300 for the monks.

53. *De Elmund abbate et Aethelwlfo rege qui decimam partem terrarum suarum dedit ecclesiis.*

Anno DCCCLI Elmund abbas, Aetheluulfo rege annuente, Dulting in ius monasteriale transtulit; cui eciam rex prefatus, Alhstano episcopo consenciente, xx hidas addidit ad supplementum[w] uite regularis.[104] Idem rex decimam terrarum suarum ecclesiis sui regni legitur pie contulisse. Quo tempore monasterio Glastonie dedit Offaculum xxiiii hidas, Bocland v hidas, Pennard ix hidas, Occenefeld, Scearamton' vi hidas, Sowy x hidas, Pirinton', Logderesbeorgu', Occemund et Bedul, Branuc, Duneafd.[105] Ethelstanus comes dedit Clutton' x hidas assensu eiusdem Aetheluulfi regis. Cartulam hanc prefate hereditatis prefatus comes cum corpore suo commendauit ad monasterium Glastonie obsecrans in nomine Iesu Christi ut fratres illius monasterii nunquam ipsam linquant. Aenulfus comes dedit Dicheswite et Lottesham xxx hidas assensu regis Aetheluulfi, et Hornblawerton'[x] et Beangean-hangran. Ethelredus rex filius Aetheluulfi dedit Winterburn' xxv hidas Wlfere comiti quas ipse postea Glastonie contulit. Anno DCCCLXVII Aethelbald filius Atheluulfi[y] regis dedit Herefertho abbati XIIII annis presidenti Branucmunster x hidas ad capturam isiciorum, ad ecclesiam uetustam beate Dei genitricis Marie et ad usum monachorum in Glestingensi[z] monasterio.[106] Quo tempore rex Alfredus, frater Athelbaldi filius Atheluulfi, dedit Glastonie lignum Domini quod ei papa Martinus[107] dedit.[a]

54. *De Ethelstano rege.*

Anno DCCCCXXVI Ethelstan rex dedit Merkesbur' Athelmo duci x hidas, quas ipse postea contulit Glastonie. Wlhelm archiepiscopus dedit Deuerel xx hidas assensu eiusdem regis. Offricus dedit Werdeuerel, hoc est Munecaton', x hidas. Aelfleda regina Eduuardi regis dedit Winterburne[b] x hidas. Ethelstanus dux dedit Wrington' xx hidas a rege Ethelstano sibi collatas; quam possessionem idem dux conuersus et factus monachus ad monasterium Glastonie secum optulit. Idem insuper dedit Weston', que nunc Foxcote dicitur, v scilicet hidas; dedit eciam Lim vi hidas. Uffa uidua dedit Stoka v hidas.[108] Prefuit autem Glastonie tunc temporis Elfricus abbas

[w] *suplementum* T, M.

[x] *Honblawertone* H.

[y] *Aetheluulfi* H.

[z] *Sic* in M; *Glastingensi* H.

[a] There are two marginal notes adjacent to the end of this chapter, one in a later C14 hand N reads: *nota hic de ligno Domini*; the other, which Hearne suggests is in Gale's hand, reads: *V. Hoved. et hunc Malm. hoc ipsum lignum intra biennium hoc in manu cuiusdam sacerdotis R. deprehensum fuit. Regique delatum Carolo ipse cuidam ex. Conn. ss. n. Portsmouth dedit anno D. 1680.* Both are omitted in M.

[b] *Wintburne* H.

53. *On abbot Ealmund and king Aethelwulf, who gave a tenth part of his lands to the church.*

In the year 851 Abbot Ealmund, with the agreement of King Aethelwulf, transfered Doulting to the jurisdiction of the monastery and to it, the king, with the consent of Bishop Aelfstan, added 20 hides for the maintenance of the regular life. We read that this king piously bestowed a tenth of his lands on the churches of his kingdom. At that time he gave to the monastery of Glastonbury 24 hides at Culmstock, 5 hides at Buckland Newton, 9 hides at Pennard, *Occenefeld*, 6 hides at Crowcombe, 10 hides at Zoy, Puriton, Montacute, Monk Okehampton, *Bedul*, Braunton and Downhead. His thane, Athelstan, gave 10 hides at Clutton with the king's approval. This thane commended that charter of inheritance to the monastery of Glastonbury along with his body, beseeching the brethren of the monastery in the name of Jesus Christ never to relinquish it. The thane Eanwulf gave 30 hides at Ditcheat and Lottisham, with the assent of King Aethelwulf, and also Hornblotton and Binegar. King Aethelred, the son of King Aethelwulf, gave to his thane Wulfhere 25 hides at Winterbourne, which the latter subsequently granted to Glastonbury. In the year 867 Aethelbald, the son of King Aethelwulf, gave 10 hides at Braunton with fishing rights to Abbot Hereferth, who presided there for 14 years, for the old church of the blessed mother of God Mary and for the use of the monks in the monastery of Glastonbury. At this time Alfred, the brother of Aethelbald and the son of Aethelwulf, gave to Glastonbury a piece of the Lord's cross which Pope Martin had given him.

54. *On king Athelstan.*

In the year 926 king Athelstan gave to the ealdorman Aethelhelm 10 hides at Marksbury, which the latter subsequently granted to Glastonbury. Archbishop Wulfhelm gave 20 hides at Deverill, with the assent of the same king. Osfrith gave 10 hides at Over (alias Monkton) Deverill. Aelfflaed, king Edward's queen, gave 10 hides at Winterbourne. The ealdorman Athelstan gave 20 hides at Wrington which had been granted to him by king Athelstan; this possession the ealdorman brought with him to the monastery of Glastonbury when he was 'converted' and became a monk. The same man also gave 5 hides at *Weston*, now called Forscote, and 6 hides at Lyme Regis. The widow Uffa gave 5 hides at *Stoka*. This was during the abbacy

XIIII annis. Predicta igitur omnia per ministros regis Ethelstani Glastonie collata eiusdem regis ascribuntur munificencie et pium eius in Glastoniam affectum famulorum loquitur liberalitas, quorum deuocio frequenter inclinatur quo dominorum animum uiderint inardescere. Que idem rex uetuste ecclesie in Glastonia deuote confirmans,[c] scilicet lxxxvi hidas, multaque adiciens precellentes innumerasque reliquias, prout in texto sancti Dunstani annotatum est, Glastonie conferebat. Anno DCCCCLXXXI[d] successit Stitherd, huius mores a nomine non dissedisse picture testantur, semper eum in omni ymagine sua cum flagello uel scope representantes. Anno Dominice incarnacionis DCCCCXCII[e] Edwardus reddidit Aldhuno abbati Cumton'[f].[109]

55. De sancto Dunstano abbate.

Puto palam esse quantum a ueritate ille longe fuit, qui beatum Dunstanum primum abbatem Glastonia fuisse delirauit.[110] Sed quia ex antiquitatis gurgite rerum noticiam eliquauimus et, quasi ex ignorancie tenebris, in lucidiora tempora euasimus, nunc liberiore ocio in hiis spaciabimur que tempore beati uiri, qui Glastoniam XXII annis regebat, monasterio collata noscuntur. Primam itaque diebus eius liberalitatis palmam preripuit Edmundus frater Ethelstani qui eciam, ut ante dictum est,[111] diuine mentis consilio eum ibidem abbatem constituerat. Is anno Dominice incarnacionis DCCCCXL dedit Dunstano Cristemuleford xx hidas, Kingestan viii hidas, Wudetun' v hidas, Watelea iiii[g] hidas, reddidit Wrington' xxi[h] hidas. Dedit eciam Pukelescircean xxx hidas, Escford cum captura piscium dimidiam hidam.[i] Eius uxor Ethelfled eius iussu Domerham cum Merton' et Pendrington'[j] c hidas. Dedit eciam Stane viii hidas. 'Hec,' inquit, 'pro abstersione piaculorum meorum et Aelfredi, aui mei, et Edwardi, patris mei, confero ad ecclesiam uetustam beate Dei genitricis in monte Glestingensi.' Aelfleda, uidua Edwardi regina, dedit Acford, Bocland et Plis xxvii hidas, Hamedune xv hidas assensu regis Edmundi. Wilfridus, minister dicti regis, assensu eiusdem dedit Kington' xxx hidas et Girdlingeton' x hidas et ad Turnanwrthe v hidas. Idem Wilfridus dedit post obitum coniugis sue Gretelington' xxx hidas et Netelington'[k] xx hidas, quod tamen successor eius Aelwinus datis cartulis, assumpto habitu regulari, compleuit. Item prefatus rex Edmundus dederat eidem Wilfrico Tintanhulla v hidas, quas idem Wilfricus postea cum corpore suo Glastonie commendauit. Aelsy dedit Badecumbe xx hidas assensu

c *inclinans* H.
d *DCCCCLXXXXI* H.
e *DCCCCXXII* H.
f A marginal comment in the C14 hand N reads: *Nota Cumpton restit*; om. M.
g *iv* H; *x* T with *iiii* interlined above, *x* in ch.69; *iv* M.
h *xx* H, and in ch.69; *xxi* M.
i *dim. hid.* H.
j *Pendrigtone* H.
k *Netelington* H.

of Aelfric who presided at Glastonbury for 14 years. All the aforesaid grants to Glastonbury by king Athelstan's thanes are ascribed to the munificence of the king himself, and the generosity of his household testifies to his pious affection for Glastonbury, for their devotion is frequently offered to the place which they see their master's heart burning for. The king devoutly confirmed these gifts, that is 86 hides, and added many others, besides bestowing on Glastonbury innumerable outstanding relics, as is noted in St Dunstan's Gospel Book.

In the year 891 Stihtheard succeeded and pictures of him bear witness that his habits did not differ from his name, for in all portrayals he is shown with a scourge or a birch.

In 922 Edward returned Compton to Abbot Aldhun.

55. *On St Dunstan, abbot.*

I think that it is well known how far from the truth that man was who raved about the blessed Dunstan being the first abbot of Glastonbury. Because we have salvaged some knowledge of the facts from the whirlpool of the past and have now escaped, as it were, from the shadows of ignorance into brighter times we will expatiate at greater leisure on those things we know were granted to the monastery in the time of that blessed man, who ruled Glastonbury for 22 years. In his time Edmund, the brother of Athelstan, first carried off the palm for generosity, he who, as I reported before, established him as abbot there on the advice of the divine mind. In 940 AD he gave to Dunstan 20 hides at Christian Malford, 8 hides at Kingston, 5 hides at North Wootton, 4 hides at Whatley and returned to him 21 hides at Wrington. He also gave 30 hides at Pucklechurch and ½ hide with fishing rights at *Escford*. At his command his wife Aethelflaed gave 100 hides at Damerham, Martin and Pentridge. She also gave 8 hides at *Stane*. 'These lands,' he said, 'I do confer on the old church of the blessed mother of God on the hill of Glastonbury to wipe away my sins and those of my grandfather Alfred and my father Edward.' Queen Aelfflaed, Edward's widow, gave 27 hides at Okeford Fitzpaine, Buckland and Plush and 15 hides at Hannington, with King Edmund's approval. Wilfrid, one of the king's thanes, gave, with his approval, 30 hides at Kingston, 10 hides at Yarlington and 5 hides at Turnworth. The same Wilfrid after the death of his wife gave 30 hides at Grittleton and 20 hides at Nettleton, a promise fulfilled by his successor Aethelwine who granted them by charter when he donned the monastic habit. King Edmund had also given to this Wilfrid 5 hides at Tintinhull, which the latter later commended to Glastonbury with his body. Aelfswith gave 20 hides at

regis Edmundi. Idem rex dederat Ethelstano comiti Melnes xx hidas quas idem comes Glastonie contulit. Sigewlfus dedit Abbedesbur' v hidas assensu regis Edmundi. Wlfeh dedit Langeford ii hidas.[112] He[l] omnes terre, uidelicet ccclxviii et dimidium hide,[m] ab Edmundo rege et suis ministris collate, eiusdem regis et suorum in Glastonie monasterium et protectorem eius, Dunstanum gloriosissimum, miram testantur deuocionem. Idem eciam rex, quo dictum locum donis insigneret maioribus, multas reliquias, quas per terram Norhanimbrorum aut eciam in partibus transmarinis perquisierat, Glastonie pia contulit liberalitate, quas in ueteribus libris annotatas reperies; cui eciam corpus proprium post decessum suum, loci alectus sanctitudine, deuouit, ubi et requiescit usque in hodiernum diem. Dedit et huiusmodi priuilegium.[113]

56. Priuilegium Edmundi regis senioris.

In nomine Domini nostri Ihesu Christi ego Edmundus, rex Anglorum cete / f12 rarumque in circuitu gencium persistencium gubernator et rector, cum consilio et consensu optimatum meorum pro eterne retribucionis spe et relaxacione peccaminum meorum concedo ecclesie sancte[n] Dei genetricis Marie Glastonie et uenerabili uiro Dunstano, quem ibidem abbatem constitui, libertatem et potestatem, iura et consuetudines et omnes forisfacturas omnium terrarum suarum,[o] burgebrice, hundredsocna, athas, ordelas, infangenetheofas, hamsocne, frithbrice, foresteall et toll et team,[114] in omni[p] regno meo, et sint terre sue[q] libere et solute ab omni calumpnia, sicut mee mihi habentur. Sed precipue ipsa uilla Glastonie, in qua celeberrima uetusta ecclesia[r] sita est, pre ceteris sit liberior cum terminis suis. Abbati tantum eiusdem loci[s] tantummodo potestas sit, tam in notis causis quam in ignotis, in modicis et in magnis, et in hiis eciam queque super[t] et subtus terram, in aridis et[u] in riuis, in siluis et[v] planis, et eandem auctoritatem puniendi aut[w] dimittendi delinquencium in ea commissa habeat quam mea curia, quemadmodum mei antecessores concesserunt et statuendo firmauerunt,[x] uidelicet Edwardus pater

l *Hee* H, T, M.
m *dim' hid* H.
n *sancte* om. L.
o L inserts *id est* after *suarum*.
p L reads *burgerihte and hundredes setene, othas and hordeles and infangenethef, hamsocne and frithbriche and forstal, tol and theam in omni . . .*
q L inserts *sibi* after *sue*.
r L inserts *sancte Dei genitricis* after *ecclesia*.
s L omits *tantum* and *loci*.
t L reads *et que sunt super . . .*
u *et* om. L.
v L inserts *in* before *planis*.
w *et* L.
x *confirmauerunt* L.

Batcombe with King Edmund's approval. That king had given to his companion Athelstan 20 hides at Mells which the latter granted to Glastonbury. Sigewulf gave 5 hides at Abbotsbury with King Edmund's assent. Wulfheah gave 2 hides at Langford. All these lands, to wit 368½ hides, granted by king Edmund and his thanes, testify to the marvellous devotion of the king and his followers towards the monastery of Glastonbury and its protector, the most glorious Dunstan. Moreover, in order to distinguish the place with greater gifts, the king, with pious generosity, conferred upon Glastonbury many relics which he had sought throughout Northumbria and even in regions across the sea and which you will find recorded in the old books. Attracted by the sanctity of the place he even vowed his own body to it after his death – and it remains there to this very day. He also gave the following privilege.

56. Privilege of king Edmund the Elder.

In the name of our Lord Jesus Christ I, Edmund, king of the English and governor and ruler of the other peoples living round about, with the advice and consent of my magnates and in the hope of an eternal reward and the remission of my sins, do grant to the church of the holy mother of God Mary at Glastonbury and to the venerable Dunstan, whom I established as abbot there, franchise and dominion, rights and customs, and all forfeitures in all their lands in whatever part of my kingdom namely burgbryce, hundred-socn, athes, ordel, infangenetheof, ham-socn, frithbraec, forsteal, toll and team, and let their lands be free and released from all exactions, as mine are. Let the town of Glastonbury especially, in which that most famous old church is situated, together with its bounds, be freer than the rest. Let the abbot of that place alone have the only power in specified as well as unspecified causes, in small ones and in great ones, also in those above and below the earth, in dry land and in streams, in forests and in plains and let him have the same authority in punishing or discharging the transgressions of delinquents in that town as my court has, as has been granted and confirmed in charters by my predecessors, namely my father Edward, his father Alfred and Centwine, Ine, Cuthred,

meus et Elfredus[y] pater eius et Centuuines,[z] Ines, Cuthredus et alii quamplures qui locum illum honorantes gloriosum habuerunt et apostolica auctoritate roborauerunt, quibus cum omni alacritate consencio.[a] Et ne quisquam mortalium, seu episcopus aut dux, uel quislibet minister eorum,[b] audeat eam temere[c] intrare causa placitandi uel rapiendi uel[d] quippiam faciendi quod contrarium possit esse[e] inibi Deo seruientibus Dei interdictione prohibeo. Quisquis igitur[f] beniuola mente meam donacionem ampliare et priuilegii dignitatem seruare satagerit,[g] in hoc presenti seculo uita illius prospera sit et[h] longiturne uite gaudia (teneat).[i] Si quis autem propria temeritate uiolenter inuadere temptauerit,[j] sciat se proculdubio ante tribunal districti iudicis titubantem tremebundumque racionem redditurum, nisi prius digna satisfactione emendare maluerit. Acta est autem huius priuilegii pagina anno Dominice incarnacionis nongentesimo quadragesimo quarto, indictione secunda, scriptaque est litteris aureis in libro[115] euuangeliorum,[k] quem eidem ecclesie[l] optulit, opere satis eleganti composito.[116]

Hactenus de Edmundo qui, sicut plusquam semel in hoc opusculo dixi, iacet Glastonie ad sinistram in turri maioris ecclesie.[117]

57. De Edredo rege Anglorum.

Anno nongentesimo LIIII dedit Edredus rex, frater Edmundi, Dunstano precio quinquaginta solidorum auri Baddebiri xxvi hidas, et iuxta opidum Twinam, id est Cristescirce, ii[m] hidas et capturam piscium. Dedit eciam Ternuc et Staplewill', et partem de Nuni et de Elenberwe. Reddidit insuper Pukelescirce et Dulting, pridem alienatas aut aliqua tirannide seu incuria prelatorum. Idem eciam dedit Wilfrico ministro suo Horton' x hidas quas ipse consensu domini sui post obitum suum Glastonie delegauit. Sed Aelwinus, successor in hereditate, ibidem regulari suscepto habitu, alterius uotum duxit ad effectum. Aelfred dedit Camelarton v hidas assensu regis Edredi.[118]

[y] *Alfredus* L.
[z] *Kentwines* L.
[a] L omits *et apostolica . . . consencio.*
[b] L reads *seu dux, aut princeps, aut quilibet ministrorum meorum.*
[c] L inserts *omnino* after *temere.*
[d] *aut* L.
[e] *fore possit* L.
[f] *ergo* L.
[g] L reads *amplificare satagerit.*
[h] *feliciter* for *sit et* in L.
[i] This is interlined above in the same or a contemporary hand with a caret to indicate its position; in M, which agrees with T against L.
[j] *presumpserit* L.
[k] *euuangel'* H.
[l] L finishes *optulit predictus rex eleganti satis opere compositum.*
[m] Originally *i* T with *ii* interlined above; *ii hidas* M; *i hid'* H.

and many others who honoured and glorified that place and strengthened it with apostolic authority, to all of which I unhesitatingly consent. And lest any mortal, whether bishop or ealdorman, or any servant of theirs, should rashly dare to enter that town in order to hold pleas or plunder or do anything which could be in opposition to those serving God there, I forbid it by God's prohibition. Whoever shall take the trouble to augment my donation benevolently and to preserve the dignity of my charter, may his life prosper in this present world and may he gain the joys of eternal life. But if any rash person endeavour violently to transgress against it let him know that he will have to render account, quivering and shaking, before the tribunal of the Last Judgement, unless he choose to atone beforehand with an appropriate penance.

The deed of the privilege was enacted in 944 AD, in the second indiction, and was inscribed in golden letters in the elegantly adorned Gospel Book which the king presented to the church. So much for Edmund who, as I have said more than once in this small book, lies at Glastonbury in the tower of the larger church, to the left.

57. On Eadred, king of the English.

In the year 954 king Eadred, the brother of Edmund, gave Dunstan 26 hides at Badbury, for 50 golden *solidi*, and 2 hides with fishing rights near the town of Twynham, that is Christchurch. He also gave Tarnock, Stawell, part of Nunney and Elborough. Moreover he returned Pucklechurch and Doulting, which had been alienated in the past, either through the actions of some tyrant or by the carelessness of the abbots. The same king also gave his thane Wilfric 10 hides at Horton, which the latter, with his lord's consent, bequeathed to Glastonbury after his death. It was Aethelwine, succeeding to the inheritance, who put the other's vow into effect after he had donned the monastic habit there. Alfred gave 5 hides at Camerton with the assent of king Eadred.

58. De Edwio rege.

Anno DCCCCLVI Edwi, filius Edmundi, acto in exilium patre Dunstano, pseudo-abbati Elsio quem Glastonie intruserat dedit Pagenebeorh ii[n] hidas ab omni seruicio liberas[119].[o] Idem dedit Blakeford iii hidas. (Elfegus minister eiusdem assensu suo dedit Cranemere[p] xii hidas.)[q] Ezericus assensu eiusdem regis dedit Widecumbe vi hidas. Aelwinus miles dedit unam partem de Sturton', Brihtricus Gisselton v hidas assensu eiusdem regis. Cartulam hanc prefate hereditatis Brihtricus cum corpore suo ad monasterium Glastonie commendauit, obsecrans in nomine Domini nostri Ihesu Christi ut fratres illius monasterii nunquam illam linquant. Brithcere dedit Widangete assensu Edwii[r] regis domini sui.[120]

59. De Edgaro rege.

Post enumeracionem anteriorum abbatum et largiciones regum, tandem ad felicissima[s] Edgari tempora uenimus. Que ideo felicissima dixerim quia et angelorum nunciante tripudio et beati patris Dunstani in archiepiscopum sullimacione perindeque omnis boni copia floruere. Quod paulo lacius prosequamur. De ipso beatus Dunstanus, in[t] ecclesia beate Marie Glastonie celestibus studiis inuigilans, in hora natiuitatis eiusdem uocem celitus intonantem audiuit. 'Pax Anglorum ecclesie, exorti nunc pueri et Dunstani nostri tempore.' Cuius oraculi ueritatem, ut alibi digestum est, rerum exitus comprobauit. Idem, regni suscepto regimine, Dunstanum per Edwium exilio dampnatum cum gloria reuocauit et magna optimatum ambicione, primo in episcopum Wigornie, secundo in episcopum Lundonie, tercio in primatem Cantuarie promouit. Regni quidem curas rex optime administrans ecclesie pacem non negligebat. Nullus enim umquam regum Anglorum poterit certare laudibus Edgari quorum ipse omnium et pace quiecior et diuiciis exuberancior et pietate in Deum pronior fuit. Non autem quiete temporum abutebatur ut quidam qui pacis indulte rapientes in suos usus occasione uel supinantur[u] illecebris uel montes auri congerentes incumbunt diuiciis. Quin pocius frequentibus doctoris sui et patroni stimulatus monitis, quasi emulo deuocionis officio, Dei respondebat gracie, tum per se, tum per suos monasteriorum utilitatibus prospiciens, quorum Glastoniense maximo pre ceteris dignatus amore optimatum patrie consilio tali honorauit priuilegio

n *i* T with *ii* interlined above. *ii hid'* H; *ii* M.

o *liberam* T, M.

p *Cranmere* H.

q Added in the margin in the same hand; an asterisk to indicate its position. In the text of M.

r *Edwi* H.

s *feliscissima* T; corrected in M.

t A marginal note in a C14 hand N reads: *nota in ecclesia beate Marie Glastonie*; om. M.

u *suppinantur* T, H.

58. On king Eadwig.

In the year 956, after he had driven father Dunstan into exile, Eadwig, the son of Edmund, gave to the pseudo-abbot Aelsige, whom he had thrust upon Glastonbury, 2 hides at Panborough free from all servitude. He also gave 3 hides at Blackford. (His thane Aelfheah gave 12 hides at Cranmore with his assent.) Aethelric gave 6 hides at *Widecumbe* with the king's assent. The soldier Aelfwine gave a part of Stourton and Brihtric gave 5 hides at Yeovilton with the king's assent. Brihtric commended the charter of his bequest to the monastery of Glastonbury along with his body, beseeching the brethren of that monastery in the name of our Lord Jesus Christ never to relinquish it. Brihthere gave Woodyates with the assent of his lord king Eadwig.

59. On king Edgar.

After enumerating the earlier abbots and gifts of the kings we come at length to the most happy times of Edgar. I have called them most happy because, after a jubilant announcement by angels and the elevation of the blessed father Dunstan to the archbishopric, everything flourished rich in goodness. Let me expand a little on this. It refers to the fact that while the blessed Dunstan was attending to his divine studies in the church of the blessed Mary at Glastonbury he heard, at the very hour of the king's birth, a voice thunder from heaven: 'There will be peace for the English church in the days of the boy child just born and our Dunstan.' The outcome of events proved the truth of this oracle, as has been shown elsewhere. As soon as he took up the reins of government the king recalled Dunstan in glory from the exile to which Eadwig had condemned him and, at the continual canvassing of the magnates, promoted him first to the bishopric of Worcester, then to the bishopric of London and finally to the primacy of Canterbury. While the king was administering the concerns of the kingdom excellently he did not neglect the peace of the church. Not one of the English kings could compete with Edgar in renown for he was, of all of them, the most peace-loving, the most generous with his wealth and the most inclined in piety towards God. Nor did he abuse the quietness of the times like those who, seizing the opportunity of a peaceful age to seek plunder for their own use, either are destroyed by temptations or wallow luxuriously in the mountains of gold they have collected. Rather, spurred on by the constant counsel of his teacher and patron, as if rivalling him in devotion, he repaid God's grace by looking after the interests of the monasteries, either personally or through his servants, and especially Glastonbury which he deemed most worthy of his great love and which, with the advice of the magnates of the kingdom, he honoured with the following privilege.

ut numquam ibi abbas, nisi eiusdem loci monachus, esset si ullo modo aptus uel eciam congregacionis infimus inueniri posset. Sin uero extrema indigenarum penuria alterius monachum loci postularet, is promoueretur in quo Glastoniensis congregacionis unanimitas conueniret. Porro abbas et ipse a quolibet episcopo, benedictionem susciperet et monachos clericosue suos benedici iuberet, et suorum seruiencium commissa sine preiudicio episcopi uel ministrorum regis incunctanter coherceret. Nec ullus omnino insulam natiuitatis sue consciam, siue episcopus, siue dux, aut princeps, aut cuiuscumque ordinis alius intraret causa placitandi uel quippiam faciendi, et infra, sicut et predecessores sui sanxerunt, scilicet Kenwines, Ines, Athelardus, Cuthredus, Aelfredus, Edwardus, Ethelstanus et Edmundus. Hoc donum ne instabile uel inglorium esset lituo eburneo,[v] quem linibus auri pretexebat, super altare dato confirmauit. Lituum sane se presente per medium sectum fide asseruari iussit custodie ut, et testimonio in posterum proficeret, et cupiditatem raptorum incisionis dampno frenaret. Dedit eciam aliud priuilegium in hec uerba.[121]

60. Priuilegium Edgari regis.

In nomine Domini nostri Ihesu Christi.[w] Quamuis decreta pontificum et uerba sacerdotum, uelud fundamenta moncium, inconuulsis ligaminibus fixa sint, tamen plerumque tempestatibus et turbinibus secularium rerum religio sancte ecclesie maculis reproborum dissipatur ac rumpitur. Iccirco profuturum succedentibus posteris esse decreuimus, ut ea, que salubri consilio et communi assensu diffiniuntur, nostris litteris roborata firmentur. Quapropter dignum uidetur ut ecclesia beatissime Dei genitricis semperque uirginis Marie Glastonie, sicut ex antiquo principalem in regno meo[x] optinet dignitatem, ita speciali quadam et singulari priuilegii libertate per nos honoretur. Hoc itaque Dunstano Dorobernensi atque Osuualdo Eboracensi archiepiscopis adhortantibus, consenciente eciam et annuente Brictellino Fontanensi episcopo, ceterisque episcopis, (abbatibus)[y] et primatibus,[z] ego Aedgar,[a] diuina disposicione rex Anglorum, ceterarumque gencium in circuitu persistencium gubernator et rector, in nomine alme trinitatis pro anima patris mei qui ibi[b] requiescit, et antecessorum meorum presenti priuilegio decerno, statuo, confirmo, ut predictum monasterium omnisque possessio eius ab omni tributo fiscalium negociorum nunc et in perpetuum libera et quieta permaneant[c] et habeant socam et sacam on stronde[d] et on streame et on uude et on felde, on grithbrice, on burbrice,

[v] In the margin N adds *nota de ligno uel cornu eburneo regis Edgari*; not in M.
[w] L omits *quamuis . . . primatibus.*
[x] *meo* om. H.
[y] Interlinear in same hand; caret in M.
[z] L omits *quamuis . . . primatibus.*
[a] *Edgar* H.
[b] *in Glastonia* L.
[c] *maneant* L.
[d] L reads *on stronde, on streme, on wode, on felde, on grithbrice, on burghbrice, hundredes setene, mordres, othes an hordelas, alle hordes buuen eorthen and*

That there should never be an abbot there who was not a monk of that place, as long as one could be found who was in some way suitable, even if he were the meanest of the congregation. But if the extreme need of the locals demanded a monk from another place, he would be promoted upon whom the congregation of of Glastonbury unanimously agreed. Moreover the abbot himself should receive the blessing from, and order his monks and clerics to be blessed by, whatever bishop he chose and should correct the transgressions of his servants forthwith, without the prior judgement of the bishop or the king's thanes. Nor should anyone, be he bishop, ealdorman, prince, or someone of any other rank, enter that island, where his birth had been prophesied, in order to hold pleas or do anything, etc. as his predecessors have affirmed, namely Centwine, Ine, Aethelheard, Cuthred, Alfred, Edward, Athelstan and Edmund. That this gift might prove permanent and glorious he confirmed it with the gift of an ivory staff, decorated with patterns of gold lines, which he laid upon the altar. Then he ordered that the staff should be cut down the middle in his presence and guarded faithfully so that it would contribute its testimony forever and restrain, by virtue of that cut, the greed of plunderers. He also gave another privilege in these words.

60. King Edgar's privilege.

In the name of our Lord Jesus Christ. Although the decrees of bishops and the words of priests, like the foundations of mountains, ought to be fixed by unshakable bonds, yet in the storms and upheavals of secular affairs reverence for the holy church is very often routed and shattered by the sins of reprobates. Therefore we have decided that it would be advantageous to succeeding generations for us to strengthen and confirm in writing those things that have been determined by sound counsel and common consent. Wherefore it seems fitting that the church of the most blessed mother of God and eternal Virgin Mary at Glastonbury, as it long ago attained the highest dignity in my kingdom, should be honoured by us with a special and singular liberty and privilege. And so, at the urging of Dunstan and Oswald, Archbishops of Canterbury and York, and with the agreement and approval of Beorhthelm, Bishop of Wells, and other bishops, abbots and magnates, I, Edgar, by divine disposition King of the English and governor and ruler of the other peoples living round about, do determine, constitute and confirm by this present charter, in the name of the Holy Trinity and for the sake of the soul of my father who rests there and of my other ancestors, that that monastery and all its possessions should remain now and forever free from and quit of all payments of fiscal burdens and should have *socn* and *sacu* on *strand* and *stream*, on *wudo* and *feld*, on *grithbrice*,

hundred-setena, adas et ordelas, ealle hordas bufan eorderam et beneoderam, infangenetheof et utfangenetheof[e] et flemeneferdere, hamsocne, friderbrice,[f] forsteal, toll et team,[122] ita libere[d] et quiete, sicut ego habeo in toto[g] regno meo. Eamdem quoque libertatem et potestatem quam ego in curia mea habeo, tam in dimittendo quam in puniendo et in quibuslibet omnino negociis, abbas et[h] monachi prefati monasterii[h] in sua curia habeant. Si autem abbas uel quilibet monachus[i] loci illius latronem, qui ad suspendium uel ad quodlibet mortis periculum ducitur, in itinere obuium habuerit, potestatem habeant[j] eripiendi eum ab imminenti[k] periculo in toto regno meo. Confirmo eciam et corroboro ut, quod hactenus ab omnibus f13 nostris antecessoribus[l] diligenter obseruatum est, Fontanen / sis episcopus uel eius ministri super hoc monasterium uel super parochiales[m] eiusdem ecclesias, uidelicet Stret',[n] Mirieling, Budeclega, Sapeuik,[o] Sowi,[p] aut super earum capellas, nec eciam super eas que in insulis continentur, scilicet Bekeria, que parua Ybernia dicitur, Godeneia,[q] Marteneseia, Ferramere, Patheneberga et Adredeseia, nullam potestatem omnino habeant,[r] nisi tantum cum ab abbate causa dedicandi uel ordinandi aduocati fuerint, nec eorum presbyteros[s] ad sinodum suam uel[t] capitulum uel ad quodlibet placitum conuocent, nec ab officio diuino suspendant et omnino nullum ius in eos excercere presumant; monachos suos et predictarum ecclesiarum clericos, secundum antiquam ecclesie[u] Glastonie[v] consuetudinem et apostolicam auctoritatem archipresulis Dunstani et omnium episcoporum regni mei assensu, abbas a quocumque conprouinciali episcopo uoluerit ordinari faciat. Dedicaciones uero ecclesiarum,[w] si ab abbate rogatus fuerit, Fontanensi episcopo permittimus. In pascha quoque crisma sanctificacionis et oleum a Fontanensi episcopo ex more accipiat et per prefatas ecclesias suas distribuat. Hoc super omnia[x] Dei interdictione et nostra

binethe eorthen, infangenethef and utfangenethef and flemeneferde, hamsocne, frithbriche, forstal, tol and team, ita libere . . .

e *unfangenetheof* H.
f *fridbrice* H.
g *toto* om. L.
h L reads *conuentus Glastonie.*
i *monachus quilibet* L.
j L reads *ducitur obuium habuerit, in itinere habeant potestatem.*
k *iminenti* T, M.
l *antecessoribus nostris* L.
m *perochiales* H.
n *Merelinch, Budekel', Sapwik, Sowy* L.
o *Sapeuice* H.
p *Sowy* H.
q *Bekerie . . . Hibernia . . . Godenie* L.
r L reads *Martinesie, Patheneberge, Andredesie, Ferlingemere, nullam omnino potestatem habeant.*
s *presbiteros* L.
t L inserts *ad* before *capitulum.*
u *Glastonie ecclesie* L.
v *Glastoniensis* H.
w L reads *dedicaciones earum.*
x L substitutes *uero precipue* for *super omnia.*

on *burgbryce, hundred-socn, athes* and *ordel, eall hord bufan eorthan* and *beneodan, infangenetheof* and *utfangenetheof* and *flemene ferdede, ham-socn, frithbraec, forsteal, toll* and *team*, as freely and with the same immunity as I have throughout my kingdom. Moreover the abbot and monks of the monastery should have in their court the same freedom and power as I have in my court, in both forgiving and punishing in any matter at all. If the abbot or any monk of that place on a journey should meet a thief being led to the gallows or any other form of capital punishment, he shall have the power throughout my whole kingdom of snatching him away from the impending danger. I also confirm and corroborate, what has hitherto been scrupulously observed by all my ancestors, that neither the Bishop of Wells nor his servants shall have any power at all over this monastery or its parochial churches, namely Street, Moorlinch, Butleigh, Shapwick and Zoy, or over their chapels, or even over those located on the islands, namely Beckery, which is called Little Ireland, Godney, Marchey, Meare, Panborough and Nyland, except when they have been summoned by the abbot for dedications or ordinations; nor shall they summon any of their priests to a synod or chapter or any assembly, nor suspend them from holy office, nor presume to exercise any rights over them at all. The abbot shall have his monks and the clerks of those churches ordained by whatever bishop of the province he wish, in accord with the ancient custom of that church of Glastonbury and with the apostolic authority of Archbishop Dunstan and the approval of all the bishops of my kingdom. But the dedications of its churches we consign to the Bishop of Wells, if he be asked by the abbot. At Easter the latter shall receive the chrism of sanctification and holy oil from the Bishop of Wells, as is the custom, and distribute them to his churches. This above all I forbid, saving only

auctoritate,[y] salua tamen sancte Romane ecclesie et Dorobernensis dignitate, prohibeo, ne persona cuiuscumque potestatis, siue rex, siue episcopus, siue dux aut princeps, uel quilibet ministrorum eorum[z] Glastonie terminos uel supradictarum parochiarum[a] perscrutandi, rapiendi, placitandi gracia uel quicquam[b] aliud faciendi quod contrarium possit[c] esse ibidem Deo seruientibus intrare presumant.[d] Abbati tantummodo et conuentui potestas sit, tam in notis causis quam in ignotis, in modicis et in magnis, et in omnibus omnino negociis, sicut supra memorauimus. Quisquis autem huius priuilegii mei[e] dignitatem qualibet occasione, cuiuscumque dignitatis, cuiuscumque ordinis, cuiuscumque professionis,[f] peruertere uel in irritum deducere sacrilega presumpcione amodo temptauerit, sciat se proculdubio ante districtum iudicem titubantem tremebundumque racionem redditurum, nisi prius digna satisfactione emendare studuerit.[g] Acta est huius[h] pruiulegii pagina et confirmata apud Londoniam communi consilio omnium primatum meorum anno ab incarnacione Domini nostri Ihesu Christi DCCCCLXXI, indictione XIIII. Huius doni constipulatores fuerunt quorum nomina inferius carraxari uidentur. Ego Edgar rex tocius Britannie prefatam libertatem cum sigillo sancte crucis confirmaui. Ego Aeilfgiua eiusdem regis mater cum gaudio consensi. Ego Edward clito patris mei donum cum triumpho sancte crucis inpressi. Ego Kinadius rex Albanie adquieui. Ego Mascusius archipirata confortaui. Ego[i] Dunstanus Dorobernensis archiepiscopus, Oswal Eboracensis primas, Athelwol Wintonie episcopus, Brihtelin Fontanensis episcopus, hii et multi alii, quorum nomina alibi annotantur, consencientes et confirmantes signum crucis inpresserunt.

Ad supplementum uero securitatis, ne tanta liberalitas nutaret, Iohanne tunc temporis octauo eius nominis papa persuaso, donum suum apostolico suffulsit edicto, cuius hec est series.[123]

y *authoritate* H.

z *eorum ministrorum* L.

a *perochiarum* H.

b *aliquid* L.

c *posset* L.

d *presumat* L.

e *mei* om. L.

f L reads *cuiuscumque professionis, cuiuscumque ordinis.*

g L reads: *Acta est huius priuilegii pagina et confirmata anno Dominice incarnacionis DCCCCLXXI, presentibus et consencientibus beato Dunstano archiepiscopo Cantuariensi et Oswaldo Eboracensi et Athelwoldo Wintonensi et Brihtelin Fontanesi et regina Edgiua et inclitis aliis ducibus et principibus et aliis innumeris. Hanc priuilegii paginam predictus rex Edgarus XII anno regni sui sacro scripto apud Lundoniam communi consilio optimatum suorum confirmauit. Eodemque anno, qui fuit DCCCCLXXI Dominice incarnacionis, indictione XIIII[a], Papa Iohannis hanc ipsam paginam Rome in generali sinodo auctorizauit cunctosque potioris dignitatis uiros qui prefuerunt eidem concilio confirmare fecit, ad instantiam predicti regis Edgari et beati Dunstani et aliorum nobilium prescriptorum. Prescripta uero priuilegia ab illo tempore usque in presens confirmata sunt ab omnibus regibus Anglie, tam Anglicis quam Normannis.*

h *haec* H.

i *Item* originally with dots beneath and *ego* above the line in a contemporary hand;

the dignity of the holy churches of Rome and Canterbury, by God's prohibition and by my own authority, that any person of any position, be he king or bishop, ealdorman or prince, or any servants of theirs, should presume to enter the bounds of Glastonbury or any of its churches to search, seize, hold court or do anything which could be to the prejudice of those serving God there. The abbot and convent alone shall have power in specified as well as unspecified causes, in small ones and in great ones and in all those matters to which we referred above. Whoever henceforth shall attempt on any occasion, whatever his dignity, order or profession, to pervert or nullify with sacrilegious presumption the dignity of this my privilege, let him know that he will indubitably render account for it, shaking and trembling, at the Last Judgement, unless he take pains to make amends before then by a proper satisfaction. The document of this privilege was enacted and confirmed in London in 971 AD in the 14th indiction on the common advice of all my magnates. The names of those who stipulated this gift may be seen written below.

I, Edgar, king of the whole of Britain, have confirmed this liberty with the sign of the holy cross. I, Aelfgifu, the king's mother, have consented with joy. I, Prince Edward, have marked my father's gift with the triumph of the holy cross. I, Cyneheard, King of *Albania*, have agreed. I, Admiral Mascusius, have corroborated it. Dunstan, Archbishop of Canterbury, Oswald, Primate of York, Aethelwold, Bishop of Winchester, Beorhthelm, Bishop of Wells, and many others whose names are noted elsewhere have consented and confirmed it by impressing the sign of the cross.

To supplement its safeguards and lest so much generosity go for nought the then pope, John, the eighth of that name, was persuaded to support the king's gift with an apostolic edict, of which this was the content.

61. Priuilegium Iohannis pape.

Nouerit cunctorum noticia fidelium quod ego Iohannes, pii conditoris clemencia sancte Romane sedis existens indignus papa, gloriosi Anglorum regis Edgari necnon et sancte Dorobernensis ecclesie archipresulis Dunstani summisso rogatus sum pulsatu pro monasterio sancte Marie Glastingebiry, quod ipsi, acti amore superni[j] regis, in melius restaurarunt et, monachorum ibi maiorem numerum aggregantes normamque arciorem instituentes, precepto regali firmauerant, ut et ipse idem facere non differam. Quorum assenciens benigne peticioni, in sinu Romane ecclesie et beatorum apostolorum protectione[k] eumdem locum suscipio et priuilegiis astruo et corroboro, quo fine tenus in eo quo nunc pollet permaneat monachili ordine ipsique monachi de suis sibi adhibeant pastorem et se suosque, quos idoneos iudicauerint, quocumque in Dorobernensi diocesi placuerit ad ordinandum dirigant. Decernimus eciam ut nulli omnino hominum eamdem insulam placitandi causa uel aliquid aliud ibi perscrutandi aut corrigendi intrare liceat. Si quis autem huic rei molitus fuerit contraire, aut possessiones eiusdem ecclesie auferre, retinere, minuere, uel temerariis uexacionibus fatigare, ex auctoritate Patris et Filii et Spiritus Sancti sancteque Dei genitricis Marie sanctique Petri apostoli omniumque sanctorum, perpetue sit addictus[l] maledictioni, nisi resipuerit. Omnibus autem eidem loco iusta seruantibus sit pax Domini nostri Ihesu Christi. Nostra autem astipulacio inconuulsa permaneat. Actum tempore Egeluuardi, eiusdem monasterii abbatis. Hoc apostolicum decretum anno incarnacionis Domini nongentesimo LXV° idem papa in generali concilio Rome promulgans ratum fecit regique sua itidem auctoritate communiendum direxit. Applausit pontificali facto regalis assensus et frequenti in Londonia curia anno regni sui XII° omnium optimatum consensu rem eterne stabilitati magna deuotacione transgressorum mancipauit; itaque quoad uixit uoti se ipse compotem fecit et, uestigia paterna auitaque insecutus, decori eorum et glorie sue non defuit et alios ad idem animauit, sicut progrediens sermo propalabit.[124]

62. De rebus collatis Glastonie per Edgarum.

Anno incarnacionis Domini DCCCCLXIII ego Edgarus, sola misericordi clemencia Dei roboratus rex, ob remuneracionem maioris premii ad ecclesiam beate et intemerate uirginis Marie in loco celebri nuncupato Glastingabiry, ad usum monachorum regulariter Deo seruiencium sub abbate Egeluuardo, dedi Sture xxx hidas, Merkesbir' reddidi x hidas, Midelton' dedi ii hidas, Lucum ii hidas, Blakeford vi hidas. Anno DCCCCLXV ego Edgarus Sigegaro abbati iure perpetuo ad ecclesiam uetustam honorabilem pro remedio anime mee et pro anima patris mei confero Hamme xvii hidas, Dundene v hidas, Wetehulle iii hidas. Eius eciam tempore dedit

M reads *ego*, agreeing with T against L.

j *supremi* H.

k *protectionem* T.

l *adictus* T, M.

61. Pope John's privilege.

Let all the faithful know that I, John, unworthy pope through the clemency of the pious founder of the Holy Roman See, have been humbly besought by Edgar, glorious King of the English, and Dunstan, Archbishop of the holy church of Canterbury, on behalf of the monastery of St Mary at Glastonbury. They have been impelled by their love of the heavenly King to restore it for the better, augmenting the number of monks there and instituting a stricter rule, and to strengthen it with a royal decree, and they have asked me to hasten to do likewise. In compliance with their courteous request I receive that place into the bosom of the Roman church and the protection of the blessed apostles and I affirm and augment its privileges so that it will always remain in that monastic order in which it now flourishes and so that its monks can appoint their pastor from among themselves and can arrange for themselves, and any clerks they consider suitable, to be ordained by whomsoever they please in the diocese of Canterbury. We decree too that no person at all be allowed to enter that island to hold pleas or to examine anything else there or to administer correction. But if anyone strive to oppose this privilege or to steal, retain or diminish the possessions of that church or to disturb it with bold interference, let him be subject to an eternal curse, unless he recover his senses, on the authority of the Father, Son and Holy Ghost and of the holy mother of God, Mary, and of St Peter the apostle and of all the saints. But let the peace of our Lord Jesus Christ be with all those who ensure justice for that place. Let our confirmation remain undisturbed. Enacted in the time of Aethelweard, abbot of that monastery.

The pope caused this apostolic decree to be promulgated and ratified in a general council at Rome in 965 AD and ordered that it be communicated by his authority to the king. The king gave the papal deed his approbation and, at his regular council in London in the twelfth year of his reign, with the consent of all his magnates, determined that it would be eternally unshakable, with potential offenders taking a solemn vow. As long as he lived he himself kept that vow and, following in the footsteps of his father and grandfather, did not neglect their honour and his own glory and he encouraged others to do the same, as the following words will make clear.

62. On the things granted to Glastonbury through Edgar's efforts.

In 963 AD I, Edgar, strengthened as king by God's compassionate mercy alone, in order to obtain a greater reward, have given to the church of the blessed and chaste Virgin Mary in the famous place called Glastonbury, for the use of the monks serving God there according to the Rule under abbot Aethelweard, 30 hides at Sturminster Newton, 2 hides at Podimore Milton, 2 hides at Luccombe and 6 hides at Blackford and have returned 10 hides at Marksbury. In the year 965 I, Edgar, for the relief of my soul and that of my father confer upon abbot Sigegar, as a perpetual right for the honourable old church, 17 hides at High Ham, 5 hides at Compton Dundon and 3 hides at Wheathill. In his time the ealdorman Aelfhere gave 40 hides

Alfara dux Westburi xl hidas et Othelee v hidas: Cartulam hanc prefate hereditatis ego Alfara dux pro remedio anime mee et Edgari regis commendaui ad monasterium Glastonie, obsecrans in nomine Ihesu Christi ut fratres illius monasterii numquam illam linquant. Aelwine dedit Gritelington' xxv hidas, Netelcumbe[m] xx hidas et sic compleuit uotum Wilfrici primi donatoris. Aelfare ealderman dedit Bantancumbe xx hidas. Ealdred dedit Clifan xi hidas: Hanc ruralem possessionem et predictam Clifan Ealdred commendauit ad ecclesiam beate Dei genitricis Marie et sancto Patricio sub testimonio regis Edgari optimatumque suorum. Aelfhelm dedit Diranbeorh[n] ii hidas, Aelfeah Cranemere x hidas, Aedelfleda Hanandon' xv hidas, Aelsuuith[o] regina Winescumbe xv hidas, Feimeston'[p] x, Strettun' vi, Tintanhulle v, Aetheredesie dimidiam hidam,[q] et ornamenta, stolam cum manipulo, casulam inconparabilem. Hedred dedit Mildenhele xv hidas, Essebur' xl hidas. Brinsige dedit Healtone v hidas.[125] Omnes has terras Edgarus uenerabili ecclesie in Glastingebury regia confirmauit auctoritate, scilicet ccxv hidas. Fecit preterea crucem super maius altare contextam undique auro et argento et maiora signa. Uestem eciam regalem in qua fuerat coronatus preciosissimam contulit ut altaris cederet ornamento. Scrinium eciam magnum, argento et auro coopertum, cum ymaginibus ex ebore decenter intersertis, continens reliquias sancti Uincencii et capud sancti Apolinaris dedit, in quo et ipse nunc requiescit. Multas insuper reliquias, quas per uniuersas terras a se peragratas adquisiuit, cum reliquiis duorum innocencium de Bethleem translatis, Glastonie[r] monasterio, cum quali decebat reuerencia, commendauit.[126]

Hactenus de temporibus Edgari, cuius merita nulla umquam tacebunt tempora, quippe qui uirtutibus famam uicerit et uix XXXII annis quibus uixit facta seculorum incluserit. Sepultus est, ut prediximus, in capitulo ad hostium ecclesie, sed qualiter inde translatus sit, in consequentibus liquebit.[127]

63. De Egelredo rege.

Eius filius Egelredus dedit Sigegaro abbati, qui annis XXVIII prefuit, Austanclif vi hidas, Siteberge i., Pukelescirce reddidit xxx; in Wiltone unam mansam emptam xl mancusis[s] auri anno DCCCCLXXXIIII°. Idem dedit Hanandune. Anno[t] M° incarnacionis dedit Egelred rex Berthredo abbati, qui et XVI annis prefuit, fiscwere; Wlfwin[u] Estun xx hidas.[128]

f14 Anno MXVII° Brithwius / abbas constitutus fecit tabulam ante altare, auro et argento et ebore polimitam, et crucem. Hic post decem annos suscepti regiminis in episcopum Wellensem est electus.[129]

m A marginal note in a C14 hand adds *secundum alicos Netelton'*; not in M.
n In the margin a C14 hand has written *Dureberge.*
o *Aelfuuith* H.
p Interlined above is *uel Ide*; om. M.
q *dim. hid.* H.
r *Glastoniense* H.
s *mansis* T.
t *ann.* H.
u *Wlfin* H.

at Westbury-on-Severn and 5 hides at Orchardleigh: I, the ealdorman Aelfhere, have granted this charter of inheritance to the monastery of Glastonbury for the relief of my soul and that of king Edgar, with a plea in the name of Jesus Christ that the brethren of that monastery should never abandon it. Aethelwine gave 25 hides at Grittleton and 20 hides at Nettleton, thereby fulfilling the vow of Wilfrid, the first donor. Ealdorman Aelfhere gave 20 hides at Batcombe. Ealdred gave 11 hides at Cleeve: this rural estate, Cleeve, Ealdred commended to the church of the blessed mother of God, Mary, and St Patrick, with king Edgar and his nobles as witnesses. Aelfhelm gave 2 hides at Durborough, Aelfheah 10 hides at Cranmore, Aethelflaed 15 hides at Hannington and queen Aelfthryth gave 15 hides at Winscombe, 10 hides at Idmiston, 6 hides at Stratton, 5 hides at Tintinhull and ½ hide at Nyland, as well as ornaments, a stole with maniple and an incomparable chasuble. Ealdred gave 15 hides at Mildenhall and 40 hides at *Esseburn*. Byrnsige gave 5 hides at Holton. Edgar confirmed all these lands, namely 215 hides, to the venerable church at Glastonbury by his royal authority. Moreover he had a cross made (to be put) above the greater altar which was woven throughout in gold and silver and also some impressive little bells. He also presented the most precious royal robe in which he had been crowned to serve as an ornament for the altar. He also gave a large shrine, covered with gold and silver and becomingly decorated with ivory images, which contained the relics of St Vincent and the head of St Apollinaris and in which he himself now rests. Moreover he commended to the monastery of Glastonbury with fitting reverence many relics acquired by him in all the lands he had traversed, including the remains of two of the Innocents, translated from Bethlehem. So much for the times of Edgar about whose merits no age will ever be silent, who won fame by his virtues and who included the deeds of centuries in the mere 32 years he lived. He is buried, as I said before, in the chapter near the entrance to the church, but how he was translated thence will become clear from what follows.

63. On king Aethelred.

To Abbot Sigegar, who was in charge there for 28 years, his son Aethelred gave 6 hides at Aust Cliff and 1 hide at *Siteberge* and returned 30 hides at Pucklechurch; in 984 he gave 1 manse at Wilton that had been bought for 40 mancuses of gold. He also gave Hannington. In 1000 AD king Aethelred gave a fishery to Abbot Beorhtred who ruled for 16 years; Wulfwyn gave 20 hides at *Estun*.

When Brihtwig was made abbot in 1017 he had a frontal made, inlaid with gold, silver and ivory, to put before the altar, and a cross. He was elected Bishop of Wells after he had guided Glastonbury for 10 years.

64. De Cnutone.

Eodem fere tempore Cnuto rex Danorum Angliam hostiliter peruagabatur. Quem licet Edmundus filius Egelredi aliquantis bellis contudisset, postremo tamen icto federe, fraterna inter eos pax conuenit, uidelicet ut Cnutoni Mercia, Edmundo Westsaxonia remaneret. At uero non multo post Edmundus, letali tactus incommodo, ad extrema deuenit et, Glastoniensi monasterio Neweton' Kastel xvii hidas cum corpore suo in extremis delegans, ibidem ante maius altare sepulturam accepit. Quo cum Cnuto uie occasione in festo sancti Andree uenisset, pia querela fraternos manes honorans, super sepulcrum eius pallium misit, uersicoloribus pennis pauonum, ut uidetur, intextum. Contulit et priuilegium in hec uerba.[130]

65. Priuilegium Cnutonis.

Regnante in perpetuum Domino qui sua ineffabili potencia omnia disponit atque gubernat, uicesque temporum hominumque mirabiliter discernens terminumque incertum prout uult equanimiter inponens, et[v] de secretis nature misteriis misericorditer docet ut de fugitiuis et sine dubio transitoriis mansura regna Dei suffragio adipiscenda sunt. Quapropter ego Cnut, rex Anglorum ceterarumque gencium in circuitu persistencium gubernator et rector, cum consilio et decreto Aethelnoti simulque cunctorum Dei sacerdotum et consensu optimatum meorum, ob amorem celestis regni et peccaminum meorum remissionem et animam[w] fratris mei regis Edmundi, concedo ecclesie sancte Dei genetricis semperque uirginis Marie Glastonie iura et consuetudines in omni regno meo et omnes forisfacturas omnium terrarum suarum. Et sint terre eius sibi libere et solute ab omni calumpnia et inquietacione, sicut mee mihi habentur. Uerum illud precipue ex omnipotentis Patris et Filii et Spiritus Sancti auctoritate et perpetue uirginis interdictione prohibeo et uniuersis regni mei prepositis et primatibus super suam salutem precipio, ut nullus omnino illam insulam intrare audeat, cuiuscumque ordinis sit aut dignitatis, sed omnia, tam in ecclesiasticis quam in secularibus causis, tantummodo abbatis iudicium et conuentus expectent, sicuti predecessores mei sanxerunt et priuilegiis confirmauerunt, Kenuuines, Ines, Cuthredus, Elfredus, Eduuardus, Edmundus et incomparabilis Edgarus. Si quis autem quouis deinceps tempore sub aliqua occasione interrumpere aut irritum facere huius priuilegii testamentum[x] nisus fuerit, sit a consorcio piorum ultimi examinis uentilabro dispertitus. Si quis uero beniuola intencione hec facere, probare et defensare studuerit, beatissime Dei genitricis Marie et omnium sanctorum intercessione amplificet Deus porcionem eius in terra uiuencium. Scripta est huius priuilegii donacio et promulgata in lignea basilica sub presencia regis Cnutonis anno ab incarnacione Domini MXXXII°.[131]

[v] *etiam* H.
[w] *remissione et anima* T, M.
[x] *testimonium* H.

64. On Cnut.

At about the same time Cnut, king of the Danes, was rampaging through England. Although Aethelred's son Edmund crushed him in several battles a treaty was finally made and fraternal peace concluded between them, such that Mercia would remain with Cnut and Wessex with Edmund. But not long afterwards Edmund was stuck a fatal blow and died. On his death-bed he granted 17 hides at Sturminster Newton, along with his body, to the monastery of Glastonbury and so was buried there before the high altar. When Cnut came thither in the course of a journey on the Feast of St Andrew he did honour to the corpse as to a brother, with pious lamentations, and laid upon the sepulchre his cloak which, they say, was woven of many-coloured peacock feathers. He also granted a privilege in these words.

65. Cnut's privilege.

The Lord who rules forever, who arranges and governs everything by His ineffable power, miraculously determining the vicissitudes of time and mankind and calmly bringing them to an unpredictable conclusion according to His will, mercifully teaches us out of nature's unknown mysteries how with God's help a lasting kingdom is to be sought among fleeting and indubitably transitory affairs. Whereupon I, Cnut, king of the English and governor and ruler of the other adjoining nations round about, by the advice and decree of Aethelnoth together with all other priests of God and with the consent of my magnates, do grant, from love of the heavenly kingdom and for the remission of my sins and the soul of my brother king Edmund, to the church of the holy mother of God and perpetual Virgin Mary at Glastonbury its rights and customs throughout my whole kingdom and all forfeitures within its own lands. And let its lands be free from and undisturbed by any claim or disorder, just as mine are. And I especially forbid, on the authority of the omnipotent Father and the Son and the Holy Spirit and by the prohibition of the perpetual Virgin – and I enjoin obedience on all the nobles and magnates of my kingdom for their own salvation – anyone at all to dare to enter that island, regardless of his rank or dignity; rather, everything, in ecclesiastical as well as secular causes, should await the judgement of the abbot and the convent alone, as has been asserted and confirmed in privileges by my predecessors, Centwine, Ine, Cuthred, Alfred, Edward, Edmund and the incomparable Edgar. But if anyone at any time hereafter on any occasion try to infringe the terms of this privilege or make them void let him be separated from the fellowship of the pious by the winnowing-fan of the Last Judgement. However, if anyone take pains with good intentions to accomplish, recommend or defend these terms may God, through the intercession of the most blessed mother of God, Mary, and all the saints, increase his portion in the land of the living. This privilege of donation was written and promulgated in the wooden church in the presence of King Cnut in 1032 AD.

66. De Egelwardo abbate.

Anno MXXVII° Egelward successit XXVI annis Glastoniam occupans, cui Hardecnut dedit scrinium in quo nunc beati Benigni corpus requiescit.[y]

Anno MLIII° Egelnoth. Amborum regimen fuit perniciosum ecclesie, dum alter exterius terras proscripsit, alter interius ornamenta distraxit. Ex illo res Glastonie retro relabi et in peius fluere (ceperunt).[z] Denique creditum est non nullam loco imminuisse uindictam propter Egelwardi audaciam in regem Edgarum commissam. Nam cum bono fortasse mentis proposito (post XL annos obitus sui)[a] effodisset tumulum, inuenit corpus nullius labis conscium, sed solida integritate compactum. Quod cum eum ad reuerenciam debuisset inflectere, ad audaciam leuauit. Nam quia locellus quem parauerat difficilem pro magnitudine corporis minabatur ingressum regales exuuias ferro temerauit, ausus facinus auditu nedum, actu graue. Unde continuo sanguis undatim emicans astancium corda pauore concussit, uultus pallore[b] infecit. Ita regis ossa in scrinio super altare locata sunt cum capite sancti Apolinaris et reliquiis beati Uincencii martiris, que ille magno empta decori domus Dei adiecerat. Temeratorem porro sacri corporis animus reliquia nec multo post ecclesiam egressum fracta ceruice mors inuenit. In sepulcro autem regis positus est Egeluuardus qui beato Dunstano in regimine Glastonie primus successit. Nec in hiis hesit regie sanctitatis ostensio sed in ulteriora processit, sanatis ibi furioso et ceco.

Furiosus Teutonicus genere,[c] multis indiciis datis quod mente non constaret, ciuium in se armauerat manus, ut eum uincire ferro non dubitarent. Circumferebat miserandus sua ipse supplicia, penarum propriarum idem iudex et auctor. Nescias miserior(em) an miserabilior(em),[d] uel quod animo captiuus uel quod corpore grauatus erat. Ita multa(s)[e] pluribus annis prouincias emensus, frustra consumpsit tempora, nisi quod continuacio itineris erat accessus laboris. Tandem uero diuine miseracionis intuitu uisitatus, oraculum per noctem accepit ut Glastoniam pergeret, futurum ut meritis regis Edgari utroque leuaretur incommodo. Uenit ergo et conuenientem responso effectum sortitus est. Nam dum oraret in eadem quidem domo, sed longiuscule a sepulcro, omnis ferri nexus dissiluit et, quasi quodam turbine actus, super mausoleum cecidit. Cecus preterea prouincie notissimus, dum inportunas pro salute ad tumbam excubias pretendit, lucem repperit.[132]

[y] N adds in the margin: *nota scrinium beati Benigni.*

[z] Some such verb seems to be needed and this is supplied from John of Glastonbury.

[a] In the margin, with an asterisk, in a C13 hand, in M.

[b] *pauore* H.

[c] *genus* T, H, M.

[d] *miserior an miserabilior* T, H.

[e] *multa* T, H, M.

66. On abbot Aethelweard.

In 1027 Aethelweard succeeded and occupied the abbacy of Glastonbury for 26 years. Harthacnut gave him a reliquary, in which the body of the blessed Benignus now rests.

Aethelnoth succeeded in 1053. The government of both of these was destructive to the church, for the one confiscated lands outside the church and the other removed ornaments from within it. As a result the affairs of Glastonbury began to slide into decline and became worse and worse. Finally it came to be believed that because of Aethelweard's insolent behaviour towards king Edgar the security of the place was much diminished. For when he dug up the latter's grave 40 years after his death, perhaps with good intentions, he found the body quite unblemished, indeed whole and complete. Although this ought to have inclined him to reverence it only increased his audacity. Because the reliquary that he had prepared threatened to be too small for the size of the body, he profaned the royal remains with iron, perpetrating an outrage serious to hear of, let alone perform. Whereupon blood gushed out in streams, striking fear into the hearts of those standing by and turning his own countenance pale. Thus it is that the king's bones are to be found in a shrine above the altar, together with the head of St Apollinaris and the relics of the blessed martyr Vincent, the king's purchase of which had added to the great glory of God's house. But the desecrator of the holy body went out of his mind and not long afterwards met his death, breaking his neck as he left the church. In the king's sepulchre has been placed Aethelweard, who was Dunstan's immediate successor as Abbot of Glastonbury. Nor did the manifestations of royal sanctity cease with the above but continued on, with the healing there of a lunatic and a blind man.

The lunatic, a German by birth, had given many signs that his mind was not balanced so that an armed band of citizens came against him in order to bind him with iron chains. The pitiable man carried his own torment around with him, himself the judge and author of his own punishment. You could not know anyone unhappier or more miserable because his mind was captive and his body burdened. Although he had passed through many provinces over many years he had spent his time in vain, except that his continual journeying added to his suffering. But finally he was granted a glimpse of divine compassion when it was announced to him one night that he should proceed to Glastonbury where he would be relieved of both infirmities through the merits of king Edgar. So he came and obtained the result appropriate to the message. For while he was praying in that house, but a little way from the sepulchre, all his iron chains burst asunder and, as though carried by a whirlwind, fell upon the tomb. Meanwhile a blind man who was well known in the province recovered his sight while maintaining a diligent vigil at the tomb, hoping to be healed.

67. De archiepiscopis et episcopis de conuentu Glastonie electis.

Et quia iam ad tempora Normannorum uenimus et abbatum post illud tempus nota sunt et facta et nomina, hiis paulisper omissis, ponam illorum uocabula qui episcopi et archiepiscopi fuerunt[f] alias electi de illa ecclesia. Splendidum nimirum exemplum Glastonie et auctoritatis et gracie quod non solum sibi sed eciam aliis ecclesiis suffecerint tot illustres persone. Nec uero polliceor quod de omnibus possim episcopatuum loca expedire, nisi quantum in cronicis inueni quod ille uel ille episcopus obierit monachus huius loci. Adeo longiorum temporum fluxere curricula quam ut illa ullius hominis possit inuestigare memoria. Nunc de archiepiscopis:
Berhtuualdus, ex abbate quondam Glastonie, archiepiscopus Cantuarie, Adthelmus, prius Wellensis epicopus, deinde archiepiscopus Cantuarie fuit. Dunstanus, cuius industria refloruit ecclesia, hic fecit organa et signa duo precipua, pallium unum, campanam in refectorio ubi sunt hii uersus:

Hanc sibi campanam Dunstan perfundere iussit.
et cetera.

In urceolo altaris: 'Idriolam hanc fundi Dunstan mandauerat archipresul, cunctipotens quem saluet in euum'. Hic ex monacho et abbate Glastonie factus est episcopus Wigornie,[g] postea Londoniensis, postremo archiepiscopus Cantuarie. Egelgarus de monacho Glastonie factus est primus abbas noui monasterii Wintonie, scilicet de Hida, deinde episcopus Cicestrie, postremum[h] archiepiscopus Cantuarie. Sigericus ex monacho Glastonie fuit episcopus Wellensis, postea archiepiscopus Cantuarie, tercio loco post Dunstanum. Hic dedit VII pallia Glastonie cum albis leonibus, de quibus uetus ecclesia in anniuersario eius tota ornatur. Alphegus, ex monacho et priore Glastonie, Bathonie abbas, postea episcopus Wintonie,[i] postea archiepiscopus Cantuarie.[j] Elnotus ex monacho Glastonie factus est archiepiscopus Cantuarie de quo sermo precessit quod, cum a Dunstano baptizaretur, erectam manum tenuerit more episcopi benedicentis populum, unde Dunstanus eum, sicut ipsius diuinitatis conscius, archiepiscopum fore predixit. Fuit autem tempore Cnutonis archiepiscopus, cuius eciam solacio et iussu transtulit martirem Elphegum Canciam de loco quietis apud Londoniam. Hic dedit Rabanum, *De laude crucis*, et librum orationum auro pictum.[133]

Anno incarnacionis Domini DCCLXXXII° obiit Eanfridus episcopus, monachus Glastonie. Anno DCCLXXXII obiit Ethelwinus episcopus, monachus Glastonie. Anno DCCC obiit Wibertus episcopus, monachus Glastonie. Anno DCCCXXXVI obiit Wigthegu[k] episcopus, monachus Glastonie. Anno DCCCXLII obiit Alhstan episcopus, monachus Glastonie. Anno DCCCLXXVI obiit Tumbert episcopus,

[f] *fuerant* H.
[g] *Wigorniensis* H.
[h] *postremo* H.
[i] *Wintoniensis* H.
[j] *Cantuariensis* H.
[k] *Wigthegn* H.

67. On the archbishops and bishops chosen from the convent of Glastonbury.

I have now come to the times of the Normans, and as both the deeds and the names of the abbots after that time are well known I will put them aside for a little while and insert the names of those who were chosen from that church to be bishops and archbishops elsewhere. It is a splendid example of the authority and grace of Glastonbury that it has supplied so many distinguished individuals to other churches, not only for itself. However, I do not promise that I can identify the episcopal sees of all of them, but only where I have discovered in the chronicles, that this or that bishop who died had been a monk of that place. For a longer time has passed than the memory of any man can investigate. Now for the archbishops.

Brihtwold, once abbot of Glastonbury, archbishop of Canterbury.

Athelm was first bishop of Wells then archbishop of Canterbury.

Dunstan, through whose labour the church bloomed anew, made organs and two notable little bells here, an altar cloth and a bell in the refectory on which are these verses:

> Dunstan ordered this bell to be cast for himself.
> etc.

On the holy water vat on the altar can be read: 'Archbishop Dunstan ordered this stoup to be cast. May the Almighty grant him eternal salvation.' From being a monk and abbot of Glastonbury he became bishop of Worcester, then bishop of London and finally archbishop of Canterbury.

Aethelgar, a monk of Glastonbury, became abbot of the new monastery of Winchester, that is Hyde, then bishop of Chichester and finally archbishop of Canterbury.

Sigeric, monk of Glastonbury, was bishop of Wells then later archbishop of Canterbury, the third in that position after Dunstan. He gave to Glastonbury seven altar cloths ornamented with white lions and with these the old church is completely decorated on its anniversay.

Aelfheah, monk and prior of Glastonbury, was abbot of Bath, then bishop of Winchester and finally archbishop of Canterbury.

About Aethelnoth, a monk of Glastonbury who became archbishop of Canterbury, the story has spread that when he was being baptised by Dunstan he held his hand aloft, after the manner of a bishop blessing the people, whereupon Dunstan, as though aware of his excellence, prophesied that he would be an archbishop. He was indeed an archbishop in the time of Cnut, by whose assistance and decree he translated the martyr Aelfheah to Kent from his place of rest near London. He gave a copy of Rabanus' *In Praise of the Cross* and a prayer book illuminated in gold.

In 782 AD died bishop Eanfrith, a monk of Glastonbury. In the year 782 died bishop Aethelwine, a monk of Glastonbury. In the year 800 died bishop Wigbeorht, a monk of Glastonbury. In the year 836 died bishop Wigthegn, a monk of Glastonbury. In the year 842 died bishop Helmstan, a monk of Glastonbury. In the year 876 died bishop Tunbeorht, a monk of Glastonbury. In the year 956 on 8th October

monachus Glastonie. Anno DCCCCLVI obiit Daniel episcopus, monachus Glastonie, VIII idus Octobris. Anno DCCCCLXXXVIII obiit Elfricus episcopus, abbas Glastonie.[134]

Qui secuntur[l] fuerunt episcopi tempore Edgari regis in diuersis locis. Quarto Kalendas Iulii obiit Sigegarus Wellensis episcopus, abbas Glastonie – hic iacere fertur sub sancto Benigno. Idus Maii obiit Brihtelmus episcopus Wellensis, monachus Glastonie. Idus Februarii obiit Alfwoldus Cridiensis episcopus, monachus f15 Glastonie. Nonas Aprilis obiit Sigefridus Norwegen / sis episcopus, monachus Glastonie – hic misit iiii[or] cappas, ii cum leonibus et ii croceas. Kalendas Augusti obiit Athelwoldus episcopus Wintonie, monachus et prior Glastonie at abbas Abbendonie. Idus Ianuarii obiit Wilsinus episcopus, monachus Glastonie. Idus Februarii obiit Aelfstanus episcopus, monachus Glastonie. Octauo Idus Maii obiit Aegelricus episcopus, monachus Glastonie. Quarto Kalendas Iulii obiit Keneualdus episcopus, monachus Glastonie. Tercio Nonas Aprilis obiit Aelmer episcopus, monachus Glastonie.[m] Anno incarnacionis MXXXIIII[o] obiit Brihwius episcopus Wellensis, abbas Glastonie – de hoc superius aliqua libauimus; his iacet in aquilonari porticu ad sanctum Iohannem Baptistam.[135]

68. De Brithwoldo episcopo.

Anno M[o]XLV[o] obiit Brithwoldus episcopus Ramesberiensis[n] monachus Glastonie. Hic misit albam de serico preciosissimam, cappas eciam de palliis decem, auro et gemmis decenter ornatas. Misit eciam superhumerale, stolam, manipulum, casulam, calices duos, unum de xx marcis argenti et iiii[or] auri, alium minori pondere sed precio maiori, textus euuangeliorum ii[os], turribulum mire magnitudinis de auro et argento, altare precii xx marcarum, crucem ad processionem et alias xxv. Quas cum Aegelnotus abbas cum aliis ornamentis auro et argento nudasset, in duabus xxii auri marcas accepit. Potest ergo conici quanta uis pecunie fuerit in omnibus. Dedit eciam collectaneum auro illuminatum, pallium auro textum et alia ix, duo candelabra. Totam terram de Wiltesire redemit. Scrinia tria sanctorum Guhtlaci,[o] Georgii et Oswaldi in quo sunt hii uersus:

Exiguus presul Brihtwoldus onomate[p] dictus
Archonti Domino necnon matrique Marie
Confert exiguum deuoto pectore munus
Ecclesie ueteri transmittens Glastoniensi,
Dulcia perpetue capiat quo gaudia uite.

l *socuntur* T, M.

m A C13 hand adds here *XIIII Kalendas Aprilis obiit Liuingus episcopus, monachus Glastonie.* Not in M.

n *Salesbiriensis* T.

o *Guthlaci* H.

p *onamate* T.

died bishop Daniel, a monk of Glastonbury. In the year 988 died bishop Aelfric, an abbot of Glastonbury.

Those who follow were bishops in various places in the time of king Edgar. On 28th June died Sigegar, bishop of Wells, an abbot of Glastonbury. He is said to lie beneath St Benignus. On 15th May died Beorhthelm, bishop of Wells and a monk of Glastonbury. On 13th February died Aelfweald, bishop of Crediton and a monk of Glastonbury. On 5th April died Sigfrid, bishop of Norway and a monk of Glastonbury, who sent four copes, two with lions and two yellow ones. On 1st August died Aethelwold, bishop of Winchester, a monk and prior of Glastonbury and abbot of Abingdon. On 13th January died bishop Wulfsige, a monk of Glastonbury. On 13th February died bishop Aelfstan, a monk of Glastonbury. On 8th May died bishop Aethelric, a monk of Glastonbury. On 28th June died bishop Cyneward, a monk of Glastonbury. On 3rd April died bishop Aelfmaer, a monk of Glastonbury. In 1034 AD died Brihtwig, bishop of Wells and abbot of Glastonbury, of whom we learnt something above; he lies in the north transept near St John the Baptist.

68. On bishop Brihtwold.

In the year 1045 died Brihtwold, bishop of Ramsbury and a monk of Glastonbury. He sent a most precious alb of silk and 10 copes with palls, fittingly decorated with gold and gems. He also sent a superhumeral, a stole, a maniple, a chasuble, two chalices, one of 20 marks of silver and 4 of gold and the other of less weight but greater value, two Gospel-books, a wonderfully large censer of gold and silver, an altar worth 20 marks, a processional cross and 25 other crosses. When abbot Aethelnoth plundered these, along with other ornaments of gold and silver, he obtained 22 marks of gold for two of them – from which it can be concluded how much money they were worth all together. He also gave a Book of Collects illuminated in gold, a pall woven in gold, 9 other palls and two candlesticks. He also bought back all the monks' land in Wiltshire for them. (He gave) the three shrines of the saints Guthlac, George and Oswald, on which are the following verses.

The humble priest, Brihtwold by name,
To the Highest Lord and His mother Mary,
Grants this small gift with a devout heart,
Committing it to the old church of Glastonbury
So that he may win the sweet delights of eternal life.

Cappam cum albis auibus. Situs est cum Brihtwio in parte aquilonari, uir omni uita predicandus qui tanta contulit ecclesie, quanta nec adhuc predones potuerunt uellicare, quamuis sint aliqui qui crimen inferre moliantur eius glorie, dicentes quod res episcopatus dederit Glestonie.[q] Sed frustra in eum molares infigunt, qui nec curat laudes nec timet uituperaciones, presertim cum facta sanctorum ambigua in meliorem partem conuerti conueniat. Profecto enim, si delinquere se nosset, nunquam illa sanctus uir fecisset. Denique fama est non obscura omnes illas terras ab antiquo fuisse Glastonie sed tempore Danorum, cum inportabiles pensiones regnum grauarent, fisco regio uel alias pignori addictas, sed ab episcopo redemptas et redditas. Et sicut dicunt, cum de redemcione obolus deesset, uir magnificus, anulum suum creditoribus proiciens, deuocionem quam in Glastoniam habebat operis testabatur exhibicione.[136] (Uiderat[r] quondam sompnii reuelacione seculi illius felicitatem dictus uir, scilicet Brithwoldus Wiltonensis episcopus, uiderat et annunciauerat. Nam dum tempore regis Cnutonis celestibus apud Glastoniam lucubraret excubiis subissetque illum cogitacio, que frequenter angebat, de regia stirpe Anglorum pene deleta, hec meditanti sopor irrepsit. Et ecce in superna raptus, uidet apostolorum principem Petrum sanctum Edwardum, qui tunc in Normannia exulabat, in regem consecrare, celibe designata uita et certo XXIIII[or] annorum numero regni computato, eidemque conquerenti de posteritate respondere: Regnum Anglorum est Dei; post te prouidit regem ad placitum sui.)

69. De possessionibus Glastonie datis ab Anglis ad fidem conuersis.

Iam quia possessionum largitores manus contraxerunt, libet summatim inserere quid a quo Glastonie sit collatum aut regia confirmatum auctoritate.[137] In primis rex (Arturus[s] tempore Brytonum dedit Brentemareys, Poweldon', cum multis aliis terris in confinio sitis, pro anima Ider, ut supra tactum est; quas terras, per Anglos tunc paganos superuenientes ablatas, iterum post eorum conuersionem ad fidem restituerunt cum pluribus aliis.[138] Unde rex) Domnonie dedit terram apellatam Yneswitherim v hidas.[139] Kenewalchius, siue Cedwald, dedit Ferremere ii hidas, Beokeri, Godenie, Martenesye, Andrewesye.[140] Kenwinus rex dedit Munekaton' xxiii hidas et in Cary xx hidas et in Crucan iii hidas.[141] Baldredus rex dedit Pennard vi hidas, Loggaresbeorg, id est Muntagu, xvi hidas et Westwere cum captura piscium in Peret. Hedda episcopus dedit Lantokai, id est Lege, vi hidas, Cedwalla confirmante licet rege pagano.[142] Ina rex dedit Brentemareis[t] xx hidas,[143] Sowi xii hidas, Piltone xx hidas, Dulting xx hidas et iuxta Tamer, scilicet Lining, xx hidas et in Rouelt

[q] *Glastonia* H.

[r] *Uiderat . . . sui* is a marginal note, also found in M, where it is included in the text at this point.

[s] *Arturus . . . rex* is a marginal interpolation in a later C13 hand but it is also found in M in the text at this point. Probably the same hand as that of *Joseph ab Arimathia . . .* , p.46 above.

[t] *Brentmareis* H.

(He also gave) a cope with white birds. He was placed with Brihtwig in the northern transept, this man who preached with his whole life and gave so much to the church that thieves still have not been able to steal it, although there are some who try to mar his glory with the charge that he gave to Glastonbury the possessions of his diocese. But in vain do they fix their teeth in him since he neither cares for praise nor fears censure, especially since it is agreed that the ambiguous acts of saints ought to be construed in their best sense. For truly if he had known that he was doing wrong that saintly man would never have done those things. Finally it is well known that all those lands belonged to Glastonbury from of old, but that some, which had been yielded to the royal treasury as a mortgage in the time of the Danes, who burdened the kingdom with unpayable fines, were bought back and restored by the bishop. And, so they say, when a half-penny was missing for the repurchase that magnificent man flung his own ring to the creditors, testifying by such a surrender to the devotion in which he held Glastonbury.

(The said man, Brihtwold, bishop of Wilton, had once seen, revealed to him in his sleep, had seen and had announced, the happiness of that century. For while he was keeping a holy vigil one night at Glastonbury in the reign of king Cnut sleep crept up on him as he was meditating on the thought, which frequently distressed him, that the royal stock of England had been almost wiped out. And behold he was borne aloft to Heaven where he saw Peter, the chief of the apostles, consecrate as king St Edward, who was then in exile in Normandy, assign him the life of a celibate and fix the number of years of his reign at 24. To his lament for the future (St Peter) replied: 'The kingdom of England is God's; after you he will provide a king as it shall please him.')

69. On the possessions of Glastonbury given by English converts to the faith.

Because the bestowers of possessions have now withdrawn their hands I am disposed to incorporate a summary of what has been granted to Glastonbury and by whom or by whose royal authority it was confirmed.

Firstly King (Arthur in the time of the Britons gave Brent Marsh and *Poweldone*, with many other lands in the neighbourhood, for the soul of Ider, as has been mentioned above; these lands were fallen upon and taken away by the English when they were pagans but later restored, with many others, after their conversion to the faith.

Then the King) of Devon gave 5 hides of land known as Yniswitrin.

Cenwalh (or Cedwald) gave 2 hides at Meare, Beckery, Godney, Marchey and Nyland.

King Centwine gave 23 hides at West Monkton, 20 hides at Cary and 3 hides at Creech St Michael.

King Baldred gave 6 hides at Pennard, 16 hides at Ludgersbury, that is Montacute, and *Westwere* with fishing rights on the Parrett.

Bishop Haeddi gave 6 hides at Leigh and Caedwalla confirmed them although he was a pagan king.

King Ine gave 20 hides at Brent Knoll, 12 hides at Zoy, 20 hides at Pilton, 20 hides at Doulting, 20 hides near the river Tone at *Linig*, 20 hides at Polden Hill and

xx hidas et alibi cum piscaria unam hidam. Uuilfrid[u] episcopus Uethmor[v] lxx hidas, Cliwawere i hidam. Forthere episcopus Bledanhid i hidam. Buggu abbatissa Ora iii hidas, rege Ina consenciente et confirmante.[144] Adthelardus rex dedit Poholt lx hidas et in Torric x hidas. Bedeswitha eiusdem regina Brumanton' v hidas.[145]

Cuthredus rex dedit Ure iii hidas, domina Lulla Baltenesbeorge et Scrobanmurth, uel Sabewrtha x hidas. Athelbaldus[w] rex dedit Gassic[x] et Bradelegh iiii hidas.[146]

Sigebirtus[y] rex dedit in Poholt xxii hidas.[147]

Kineuulfus dedit et confirmauit Wodeton' v hidas, Cumpton' v hidas, Huneresburg; Adthelard eius minister iii hidas in Ceddren[z] et Cumbe iii hidas. Sulca Christi ancilla dedit Culum xi hidas. Offa rex dedit Ineswurth x hidas. Ethelmund dedit, Offa confirmante, Hunespulle[a] i hidam.[148]

Egbirtus rex dedit v hidas iuxta flumen Toric, Edgisilus, eo confirmante, Budeclege xx hidas.[149]

Adtheluulfus rex xxv hidas dedit et reddidit Dulting. Dedit eciam Offaculum xxiiii hidas, Bocland v hidas, Pennard ix hidas, Occenefeld,[b] Scearamton' vi hidas, Sowi x hidas, Pirinton', Legderesbeorgun, Occemund et Bedul, Branuc, Duneafd. Confirmauit eciam de dono Ethelstani Clutton' x hidas, de dono Aenulfi Dicheswite[c] et Lottesham xxx hidas, Horblawerton' et Beanganhangran. Edthelbald rex dedit Bramnucmunster x hidas, Aelfredus frater eius crucem de ligno Domini.[150]

Athelstanus rex concessit et confirmauit de dono Aethelmi ducis Merkesburi x hidas, de dono Wlfhelm Deuerel xx hidas, de dono Offrici Uuerdeuerel,[d] id est Munekaton', x hidas, de dono Aelflede regine Edwardi Winterburne x hidas, de dono Ethelstani[e] ducis Wrington' xx hidas, Weston', siue Foxcote, v hidas et Lim vi, de dono Uffe uidue Stoka v hidas.[151]

Edmundus rex dedit Cristemuleford xx hidas, Kingeston' viii hidas, Wodeton' v hidas, Watelegha x hidas, Pukeleschurice xxx hidas, Escford dimidiam hidam cum captura piscium, Domerham, Mertun' et Pendrith c hidas, Stane viii hidas. Confirmauit eciam de dono Aelflede, regine Edwardi, Acford, Bocland et Plis xxvii hidas, Hammedone xv hidas, de dono Wilfridi Kington' xxx[f] hidas, Girdlingeton' x hidas et ad Turnanwrthe v hidas et Tintanhulle v hidas, de dono Aelsy Batecumbe xx hidas, de dono Ethelstani comitis Melnes xx hidas, de dono Sigewlfi Abbedesburi v hidas, de dono Wlfec Langeford ii hidas. Reddidit eciam Wrington xx hidas.[152]

Eddredus rex dedit Baddeburi xxv hidas et in Cristeschurche ii hidas et Ternuc et Stapelwill', partem eciam de Nuni, scilicet ii hidas, et de Elenberwe i hidam et

u *Uuilfridus* H.
v *Wethmor* H.
w *Aethelbaldus* H.
x *uel Iecesig*, interlined above. M reads *dedit Gassic, Iesesig et . . .*
y *Sigebertus* H.
z *id est Eleanbearo*, interlined above; not in M.
a *iuxta*, interlined above; in the text in M.
b *uel Cecce*, interlined above; not in M.
c *Dichesyite* H.
d *Osfrici Werdeuerel* H.
e *Aethelstani* H.
f *xix* H.

1 hide with fishing rights elsewhere. Bishop Wilfrid gave 70 hides at Wedmore and 1 hide at Clewer. Bishop Forthhere gave 1 hide at Bleadney. Abbess Bugu gave 3 hides at *Ora* with the approval and confirmation of King Ine.

King Aethelheard gave 60 hides at Polden Wood and 10 hides in the valley of the river Torridge. His queen Frithugyth gave 5 hides at Brompton.

King Cuthred gave 3 hides at *Ure* and the lady Lulla 10 hides at Baltonsborough and *Scrobanmurth* or *Sabewrtha*.

King Aethelbald gave 4 hides at *Gassic* and *Bradelegh*.

King Sigeberht gave 22 hides in the Polden Hills.

Cynewulf gave and confirmed 5 hides at Wooton, 5 hides at *Cumpton'*, and Houndsborough. His thane Aethelheard gave 3 hides at Elborough and 3 hides at Culm Davy. Sulca, a handmaiden of Christ, gave 11 hides at Culmstock.

King Offa gave 10 hides at *Ineswurth*. Aethelmund gave 1 hide at Huntspill with the confirmation of King Offa.

King Egbert gave 5 hides near the river Torridge and confirmed 20 hides at Butleigh, the gift of Eadgils.

King Aethelwulf gave 25 hides and returned Doulting. He also gave 24 hides at Culmstock, 5 hides at Buckland Newton, 9 hides at Pennard, *Occenefeld*, 6 hides at Crowcombe, 10 hides at Zoy, Puriton, Montacute, Monk Okehampton, *Bedul*, Braunton and Downhead. He also confirmed Athelstan's gift of 10 hides at Clutton and Eanwulf's gift of 30 hides at Ditcheat and Lottisham as well as Hornblotten and Binegar.

King Aethelbald gave 10 hides at Braunton and his brother Alfred a cross made from the wood of the Lord's cross.

King Athelstan granted and confirmed 10 hides at Marksbury, the gift of the ealdorman Aethelhelm, 20 hides at Deverill, the gift of Wulfhelm, 10 hides at Monkton Deverill, the gift of Osfrith, 10 hides at Winterbourne, the gift of Aelfflaed, Edward's queen, 20 hides at Wrington, 5 hides at *Weston* (or Forscote) and 6 hides at Lyme Regis, the gifts of the ealdorman Athelstan and 5 hides at *Stoka*, the gift of the widow Uffa.

King Edmund gave 20 hides at Christian Malford, 8 hides at Kingston, 5 hides at Wooton, 10 hides at Whatley, 30 hides at Pucklechurch, ½ hide with fishing rights at *Escford*, 100 hides at Damerham, Martin and Pentridge and 8 hides at *Stane*. He also confirmed 27 hides at Okeford Fitzpaine, Buckland and Plush, the gift of Edward's queen Aelfflaed, 30 hides at Kingston, 10 hides at Yarlington, 5 hides at Turnworth and 5 hides at Tintinhull, the gifts of Wilfrid, 20 hides at Batcombe, the gift of Aelfswith, 20 hides at Mells, the gift of his thane Athelstan, 5 hides at Abbotsbury, the gift of Sigewulf, and 2 hides at Langford, the gift of Wulfheah. He also returned 20 hides at Wrington.

King Eadred gave 25 hides at Badbury, 2 hides at Christchurch, Tarnock, Stawell, part of Nunney (namely 2 hides) and 1 hide at Elborough and returned

reddidit Dulting. Aelfred dedit Camelarton' v hidas, Eddredo confirmante, et Aelfgitha sanctimonialis Pengeardmunster x hidas.[153]

Edwius rex dedit Padenebeorge[g] ii hidas, Blakeford vi hidas. Confirmauit de dono Aelphegi Cranemere xii hidas, de dono Ezerici Widecumbe vi hidas, de dono Aelwini unam partem de Sturton', scilicet viii hidas, de dono Brithrici Giffelton' v hidas, de dono Brihtere Widangate.[154]

Edgarus rex dedit Sture xxx hidas, Midelton' ii hidas, Lucum ii hidas, Blakeford v hidas, Hamme vii hidas, Dundene v hidas, Wetehulle iii hidas, et reddidit Merkesbur'. Confirmauit de dono Alfere[h] ducis Westburi xl hidas et Otherlee v hidas, de dono Aelwine Gritelingtone xxv hidas, Netelton' xx hidas, Horton' x hidas, de dono Aelfere aelderman Badecumbe xx hidas, de dono Ealdred Clifan xi hidas, de dono Aelfhelm Diranbeorg' ii hidas, de dono Aelfeah Cranemere x hidas, de dono Aedelfled Hanandon' xv hidas, de dono Aelswith regine Winescumbe xv hidas, Idemestone x, Strettone vi, Aedredesye dimidiam hidam, de dono Edred Middelhele[i] xv, Essebur' xl hidas, de dono Brinsige Healton' v hidas.[155]

Egelredus rex dedit Austanclif vi hidas, Siteberge i hidam et fiscwere et unam mansam in Wilton' et Hanandon'. Reddidit Pukeleschur'. Confirmauit de dono Wlfwini Esctun xx hidas.[156]

Edmundus Irenside dedit Niuueton' Kastel xvii hidas.[157]

70. Item de aliis datis Glastonie.

Memorandum de Aldamton' et aliis, Cinemeresforda, Leimucmere, Pillesdune, Portbrig, Litlanton', Eatumberg, Scippamhame, Brentfordlande, Pendescliue, Hubbanleghe.[j] Item de Elonsanige, Ocemund, Ceolanwirthe, Korstone, Camel, Ruthanbeorge, Peasucmere. Item de Lidenige, Lamageate, Hengesteshricge, Dilwisce, Orcirleage, Pidelan, Birhtulfintone[k] betocer, Huppauene, Easaetenacone.[l] Hec maneria a diuersis regibus collata suis familiaribus per eosdem ad Glastonie[m] ecclesiam deuenerunt, sicut per cartulas ueteres apparet. Et licet incredibilem numerum ac quantitatem terrarum uni loco spectancium hic posuerimus, omnes tamen has, et multo plures quas pro ambiguitate numerare nolumus, Glastonie monasterio datas fuisse non dubitamus. Nec est admirandum si quedam maneria, aut realiter aut nominetenus, a diuersis legantur collata, tum quia nomina equiuoca / f16 sunt, tum quia multa a prioribus data, deinde ablata, restituebantur, tum quia quidam partem manerii, alter partem eiusdem contulit et totum utrique fortassis ascribebatur.[158]

[g] *Pathenebeorge* H.
[h] After *Alfere* an asterisk points to the following note, not found in M, which has been added in a later C14 hand: *hic dedit iiii[or] minores pannos qui pendent ultra conuentum in choro estiuo tempore.*
[i] *Middelhale* H.
[j] *Hulbanleghe* H.
[k] *Buhtulfintone* H.
[l] *Easaetenatone* H.
[m] *Glastoniensem* H.

Doulting. Alfred gave 5 hides at Camerton with the confirmation of Eadred and the nun Aelfgyth gave 10 hides at Pennard Minster.

King Eadwig gave 2 hides at Panborough and 6 hides at Blackford. He also confirmed Aelfheah's gift of 12 hides at Cranmore, Aethelric's gift of 6 hides at *Widecumbe*, Aelfwine's gift of a part of Stourton (namely 8 hides), Brihtric's gift of 5 hides at Yeovilton and Brihthere's gift of Woodyates.

King Edgar gave 20 hides at Sturminster Newton, 2 hides at Podimore Milton, 2 hides at Luccombe, 5 hides at Blackford, 7 hides at High Ham, 5 hides at Compton Dundon and 3 hides at Wheathill and he returned Marksbury. He confirmed 40 hides at Westbury-on-Severn and 5 hides at Orchardleigh, the gifts of the ealdorman Aelfhere, 25 hides at Grittleton, 20 hides at Nettleton and 10 hides at Horton, the gifts of Aethelwine, 20 hides at Batcombe, the gift of the ealdorman Aelfhere, 11 hides at Cleeve, the gift of Ealdred, 2 hides at Durborough, the gift of Aelfhelm, 10 hides at Cranmore, the gift of Aelfheah, 15 hides at Hannington, the gift of Aethelflaed, 15 hides at Winscombe, 10 hides at Idmiston, 6 hides at Stratton and ½ hide at Nyland, the gifts of Queen Aelfthryth, 15 hides at Mildenhall and 40 hides at *Essebur'*, the gifts of Ealdred, and 5 hides at Holton, the gift of Byrnsige.

King Aethelred gave 6 hides at Aust Cliff, 1 hide at *Siteberge*, a fishery, 1 manse in Wilton and Hannington. He returned Pucklechurch and confirmed Wulfwyn's gift of 20 hides at *Esctun*.

Edmund Ironside gave 17 hides at Sturminister Newton.

70. On other estates also given to Glastonbury.

Also to be noted are Alhampton and these others: *Cinemeresforda, Leimucmere*, Pilsdon, Portsbury, *Litlantone, Eatumberg*, Shipham, Brampford Speke, *Pendesclive* and Ubley. Also *Elonsanige*, Monk Okehampton, Chelworth, Worston, Camel, Rowberrow and *Peasucmere*. Also Lydney, Lamyatt, Henstridge, Dulwich, Orchardleigh, Piddle, Burton near North Coker, Upavon and *Easaetencone*. These manors were granted by various kings to their followers, through whom they came to the church of Glastonbury, as may be seen in the old charters. Although we have included here an incredible number and quantity of estates as pertaining to one place yet we do not doubt that all these, and many more that we are unwilling to enumerate because of uncertainty, were given to the monastery of Glastonbury. Nor ought you to be astonished if you read that certain manors, either in reality or nominally, were granted by different people because some bear the same name or because many were given by our forefathers, then taken away, and finally restored or because one person granted part of a manor and someone else another part, with the whole perhaps being attributed to each.

[n] *71. Nomina abbatum Glastonie*[o] *ecclesie.*

	Hii de Britonibus[159]	
CCCCLX	Sanctus Patricius	
	Sanctus Benignus	
	Worgret	
	Lademund	
	Bregored	
Anni ordinacionis abbatum	*Hii de Anglis*	*anni regiminis*
DCLXX	Beorhwaldus	X annis
DCLXXX	Hemgisel	XXV
DCCV	Beorwaldus	VII
DCCXII	Aldbeorth	VII
DCCXIX	Aetfrith	X
DCCXXIX	Kemgisel	XVI
DCCXLIII	Cuban	II
DCCXLIIII	Ticcan	VI
DCCXLVI	Cuman	II
DCCLIIII	Walthun	XXXII
DCCLXII	Tumbercht	IX
DCCLXV	Beadulf	VI
DCCCII	Muca	XXII
DCCCXXIIII	Gutlac	XXVII
DCCCXL	Ealdmund	XVI
DCCCXLIX	Hereferth	XIIII
DCCCXC	Stitherd[p]	XI
DCCCCV	Ealdhun[q]	XXXIIII
DCCCCXXVII	Aelfric	XIIII
DCCCCXL	Dunstan	XXII
DCCCCLXII	Aelwardus	X
DCCCCLXXII	Sicgarus	XXVIII
MXVI	Beorhtred	XVI
MXXXIIII	Brichtwi	X
MLIII	Aethelward	XXVI
MLXXXII	Aegelnoth	XXIX
	Primus de Normannis	
MC	Turstinus	XIX
MCXVI	Herlewinus[r]	XIX
MCXXV	Sifridus	VI

[n] This whole chapter is omitted in M.
[o] *Glastoniensis* H.
[p] *Stidherd* H.
[q] *Ealdhum* H.
[r] *Herlwinus* H.

71. Names of the abbots of the church of Glastonbury.

Year of ordination	The British ones	Years of rule
460	St Patrick	
	St Benignus	
	Worgret	
	Lademund	
	Bregored	
Year of ordination	*The English ones*	*Years of rule*
670	Beorhtwald	10
680	Haemgils	25
705	Beorhtwald	7
712	Ealdberht	7
719	Ecgfrith	10
729	Coengils	16
743	Guba	2
744	Tyccea	6
746	Cuma	2
754	Wealdhun	32
762	Tunberht	9
765	Beaduwulf	6
802	Muca	22
824	Guthlac	27
840	Ealmund	16
849	Hereferth	14
890	Stihtheard	11
905	Aldhun	34
927	Aelfric	14
940	Dunstan	22
962	Aethelweard	10
972	Sigegar	28
1016	Beorhtred	16
1034	Brihtwig	10
1053	Aethelweard	26
1082	Aethelnoth	29
1100	Thurstan, first of the Normans	19
1116	Herluin	19
1125	Seffrid	6

MCLXXI	Henricus[s]	LI
MCLXXX	Robertus[t]	(VII)[u]
(MCLXXXX)	Henricus[v]	
(MCCXIX)	Willelmus[w]	(IIII)
	Robertus[x]	(XII)
(MCCXXXIIII)	Michael[y]	(XVIII)[z]

72. Bunde duodecim hidarum.

Et quoniam xii hide Glastonie maiori libertate pre ceteris terris suis sunt priuilegiate, expedit earum metas non ignorare.[160] Sciendum igitur quod inprimis incipit a la Brutascha apud Stretebrugge, in capite (australi)[a] eiusdem pontis, et tendit uersus orientem, in australi parte marisci, usque ad capud australe pontis de Baltenesberge; in parte boreali a dono Wlgari cum barba qui fuit operator eiusdem pontis tempore sancti Dunstani (abbatis),[b] et sic supra caucetum ultra Pinueslake per medium marisci usque ad domum Normanni apud molendinum de Baltenesberg'. Et sic inde sursum in uia usque in semitam que uenit de illa ecclesia, et postea sursum in Zeholt usque ad la[c] Lupiwite in orientali parte domus Hosgari Actaholt. Et inde in semitam que ducit per mediam extremitatem illius holte, recte usque ad pontem de Kineward in fossatum sancti Dunstani.[d] Et sic in riuulum qui uenit de Coleburi. Et ita ascendendo contra cursum aque usque ad domum Oswardi de la Burne. Et inde sursum contra la Burne usque ad curiam Ailmeri senescalli a la Brodelee. Et sic sursum de illa burna in uiam illam que iacet ante curiam suam. Et ita in australi parte illius ecclesie uersus orientem usque ad la Stoke in latam uiam. Et sic de uia eadem contra montem de Withelee in illam semitam que iacet in

[s] A later hand, probably of C15, responsible for all the additions to this chapter, adds *Bleys, episcopus Wyntonie*.
[t] *prior Wyntonie* added.
[u] All the bracketed entries are in the C15 hand.
[v] *de Soliaco prior Bermundsie* added.
[w] *capellanus dictus* added.
[x] *prior Bathone* added.
[y] *de Ambresbury* added.
[z] In the same C15 hand are named the following abbots together with the length of their rule:
Rogerus de Forde X; Robertus de Pederton XIIII; Iohannes de Tantone XVII; Iohannes de Cancia XIII; Galfridus Fromund XX; Walterus de Tantone XI dies; Adam de Sodbury XVI; Iohannes de Breynton VIII; Walterus de Monyngton XXXIII; Iohannes Chynnok XLV; Nicholaus Frome XXXVI; Walterus More XVIII; Iohannes Selwode XXXVII; Richardus Bere XXXI; Richardus Whytyng XV.
[a] Interlinear in a late C13 hand; in M.
[b] A later C13 marginal addition, incorporated in M but not in L.
[c] *la* om. H.
[d] *abbatis* added in the margin in a later hand and in the text of M.

1171	Henry	51
1180	Robert	(8)
(1190)	Henry	
(1219)	William	(4)
	Robert	(12)
(1234)	Michael	(18)

72. The boundaries of the twelve hides.

Since the twelve hides of Glastonbury are privileged to possess greater liberty than the rest of their lands it will be useful to know their boundaries. Let it be known that, beginning firstly at *La Brutascha* near Street Bridge, at the southern end of that bridge, they extend towards the east on the southern side of the marsh as far as the southern end of the bridge at Baltonsborough; thence in a northern direction from the home of the bearded Wulfgar, who was the controller of the bridge at the time when St Dunstan was abbot, and above the causeway on the other side of *Pinueslake* through the middle of the marsh to the house of Norman near the mill at Baltonsborough. Thence up along the path to the lane which comes from that church and then to *Zeholt* near the *Lupiwite* on the eastern side of the house of Hosgar Actaholt. Thence along the road which passes through the edge of the middle of that thicket straight to Kineward's bridge over St Dunstan's Dike. Thence to the brook which comes from Colebury. Then up stream as far as the house of Osward de la Burne. Thence upstream as far as the courtyard of Aylmer the steward at *Brodelee*. Then up from that stream along the path that lies before his courtyard and thence to the east along the broad road on the northern side of that church as far as *Stoke*. And then from that same road along the path, opposite the hill of *Withelee*, which lies on the northern side of *Chuleburn*, following it up to

australi parte de Chulebur'. Deinde in quandam semitam usque ad la Windeite et sic in diuisas de Bikenham et de Ferlege. Et sic descendendo[e] per medium parcem de Pilton' ultra uiam que extenditur supra pontem de petra in semitam illam que ducit ad Wottun'. Et sic in quadam semita usque ad Fulebroc. Et inde in australi parte illius ecclesie ultra riuulum usque Loffellegeche. Et sic descendendo[e] in moram usque ad Hochye et inde per mediam moram ultra la Soweie usque in diuisas fossati in parte boreali de Bachinwere. Et sic inde in ripam et ita in longum antiqui cursus aque usque ad pontem de Bledenye et sic descendendo[e] per medium illius pontis usque ad Litlenye que est diuisa de Martenesye. Et sic circa eamdem insulam usque ad Sadelby et inde in ripam et ita in longum cursus aque usque ad fossatum quod est inter moram de Stoke et Withtrichesham'[f] et sic in la Wynerdlak. Et sic per diuisas insule de Andredesye et de Draycote ascendendo contra montem usque ad la Horestone. Deinde in la wyarepathe et sic descendendo[e] usque ad superiorem Badecumbe. Et sic per diuisas de Ceddre usque ad la Grene Balle et ita ad Litlelakeweye. Inde ad la Ymerkyuel. Inde directe per medium alneti usque ad la Horewythege et ita usque ad Munekeneleghe, ita quod totum coopertum pertinet ad Ceddre, totum extra coopertum ad Glastoniam. Inde usque ad quamdam trenchiam que uocatur Bytwynenorde et sic ad la Scearpeorde, ita quod totum coopertum ibidem uersus orientem pertinet ad Glastoniam et extra coopertum (uersus occidentem)[g] pertinet ad Ceddre. Inde ad la[h] Nottepulle, ita quod totum coopertum remanet Glastonie, totum planum extra coopertum remanet Ceddre. Inde usque in Ylake et ita in longum de Ylake descendendo[e] usque ad Ywere. Et de Ywere in longum de Abbedesdith' ascendendo usque ad Langeby. Inde in cursum magne aque et ita in longum ipsius aque ascendendo contra orientem in diuisas de Wethmore et de Northilade usque ad Tunsingwere. Inde usque ad Kimpingmere. Inde usque ad Middelmede. Inde ultra montem usque ad Cumessam. Inde usque in la Lithlake. Deinde per mediam moram usque ad diuisas de Mere et de Poldune. Et sic per illas diuisas uersus orientem in australi parte illius more usque subtus Scerpham et sic inde subtus Hundewode. Inde uersus orientem usque ad la Brutasche quam posuimus primam bundam xii hydarum.[i]

73. Loca principalia infra xii hidas.

Loca que infra hos limites habentur et eodem gaudent priuilegio subiungemus. In primis ipsa insula Glastonie cum campis, siluis, pratis ac moris ad eam spectantibus. Deinde insula de Heorty cum specioso simul et spacioso auneto, cum pratis et paschuis uberrimis. Post hec magna pars de parco de Pilton'. Deinde Bikenham cum Stikelingh'. Post hec Witeleghe et Colebury cum toto Westpennard, campis, pratis et

[e] In each of these cases T reads *decendendo*; M has corrected some but not all.
[f] *Wihtricheshame* H.
[g] Interlinear in a later C13 hand; in M.
[h] *la* om. H.
[i] *hidarum* H.

Windeite and thence along the boundaries of *Bikenham* and *Ferlege*. Thence down through the middle of Pilton Park beyond the road which crosses the stone bridge along the path which leads to Wootton. Thence along that path to Fullbrook. Thence on the northern side of that church beyond the rivulet to *Loffellegeche*. Thence down into the marsh as far as *Hochye*, through the middle of the marsh beyond Zoy to the edge of the ditch on the northern side of *Bachinwere*. Thence onto the bank and along that ancient water-course to the bridge at Bleadney, thence crossing the middle of that bridge and going as far as *Litlenye*, which has been removed from Marchey. Thence around that island to *Sadelby*, onto the bank and along the water-course as far as the ditch which is between the marsh of Stoke-under-Ham and *Withtrichesham*, and thence to *Wynerdlake*. Then through the boundaries of the island of Nyland and from Draycot towards the hill as far as *Horestone*. Thence onto the *wyarepathe* and down to upper Batcombe. Thence past the boundaries of Elborough to the Green Ball and so to *Litlelakeweye*. Thence to *Ymerkyuel* and straight through the alder grove to *Horewythege* and so on to *Munekeneleghe*, the whole of which covert belongs to Elborough while everything outside it belongs to Glastonbury. Thence to a certain ditch called *Bytwynenorde*, thence to *Scearpeorde*, the whole of which covert to the east belongs to Glastonbury, while outside that covert (to the west) belongs to Elborough. Then to *Nottepulle*, the whole of which covert remains Glastonbury's while the plain outside the covert remains Elborough's. Thence to *Ylake*, descending from there to *Ywere*, thence along *Abbedesdithe* climbing up to Langby. Then down to the large water-course, climbing along its bank away from the east to the boundaries of Wedmore and *Northilade* as far as *Tunsingwere*. Thence to *Kimpingmere* and then *Middelmede*. Thence beyond the hill to *Cumessam* and thence to Leechlake. Thence through the middle of the marsh as far as the boundaries of Meare and Polden. Thence to the east past those bounds on the southern side of that marsh to below Sharpham and thence to below *Hundewode*. Thence towards the east as far as *La Brutasche* which we listed first in the boundaries of the twelve hides.

73. The main places within the twelve hides.

We subjoin the places which are contained within these boundaries and enjoy the same privileges. Firstly, there is the island of Glastonbury itself with the fields, woods, meadows and marshes belonging to it. Then the island of Hearty with its splendid and ample alder grove, its meadows and its very rich pasture lands. After these there is a large part of Pilton Park. Then *Bikenham* with Sticklinch. After these there are *Witeleghe* and Colebury with the whole of West Pennard and the

pachuis ad illa spectantibus. Deinde la Burne et Kineard cum campis suis et pratis. Postea quedam pars de Baltenesberge cum campis, pratis, pascuis largis et cum omni auneto et uniuersis moris uersus occidentem in parte boreali de Budeclee usque ad la Brutasca, que est in capite australi pontis de Strete. Deinde Edgarlegh' cum campis et pratis ad se spectantibus. Postea insula de Beokeri cum suis pertinenciis. De prenominata autem Brutaschia totus mariscus uersus occidentem qui[j] est in parte boreali de Hundeswode et de Scerpham usque ad diuisas de Poldon' et de Mere usque in la Liclake. Deinde insula de Mere et de Westye cum campis, pratis, boscis et moris. Deinde insula de Godenye cum suis terris et moris largissimis. Postea insula de Martenesye cum adiacenciis. Deinde insula de Padenbeorge et Norhthilade cum terris, pratis, pascuis et moris et boscis amplis ad eas spectantibus. Post hec insula de Andrewesye ceteras situ et loci amenitate antecellens, cum terris, boscis, pratis et moris largissimis. Hec sic cognominatur a sancto Andrea cuius ibidem habetur capella, sicut et Godenie propter capellam sancte Trinitatis et Martenesie a sancto Martino cuius ibidem est capella. Post supradicta est Badecumbe iuxta montem de[k] Munidop cum omnibus terris et pascuis super eumdem montem ad se pertinencibus. Hec omnia loca infra bundas duodecim hidarum contenta et ad Glastoniam pertinencia omni immunitate gaudent regie dignitatis a temporibus antiquis, confirmatumque est ecclesie Glastonie tam a regibus Britonum quam Anglorum et Normannorum. /

f17 *74. De Turstino, primo abbate de Normannis.*[1]

Expeditis quibusdam gracia quorum paululum digressum est, ad ordinem historie redeundum. Primus igitur abbas de Normannis fuit Turstinus[161] anno incarnacionis Dominice M^O^LXXXII^O^ quem Willelmus, ex duce Normannie factus rex Anglie, ibidem ex monacho Chadomensi abbatem constituit. Idem Willelmus, regno sue subiugato dicioni, quamplures ex suis conmilitonibus ex Glastonie feudauit possessionibus. Potest igitur connici ex hiis et precedentibus qualiter et per quos Glastoniense monasterium quondam opulentissimum suis sit terris pene nudatum, uidelicet per Aegelwardi et Aegelnoti dilapidacionem, per Danorum simul et Normannorum hostilem incursionem seu uiolentam oppressionem. Idem tamen Willelmus rex, ut iniuriam Glastonie prius illatam redimeret, quasdam terras, quas monachi suo iuri spectare dicebant set iniuste ablatas conquerebantur, eisdem auctoritate regia confirmauit in hec uerba.

[j] *que* T.

[k] *de* om. H.

[1] At the bottom of this folio is the following note in a C13 hand. It is not in M and there is no indication of where it is to be placed in the text: *Monasterium Glastonie, pre ceteris Anglie antiquius et quondam nobilius, nescio quo infortunio semper post aduentum Normannorum pessimis et infractum laboribus, nec in nouis edificiis nec in habitatorum compendiis profecit. Abbates enim rerum gloria elati, non religiosos set tirannos agunt, foris tumidi set inualidi, intus*

fields, meadows and pastures belonging to them. Then *La Burne* and Kennard Moor with its fields and meadows. Next a part of Baltonsborough with its fields, meadows and broad pastures together with the whole of its alder grove and all the marsh to the west on the northern side of Butleigh as far as *La Brutascha*, which is at the southern end of Street Bridge. Then Edgarley with the fields and meadows belonging to it. Next the island of Beckery with its appurtenances. Then the whole of the marsh which is to the west of *La Brutascha* and is on the northern side of *Hundeswode* between Sharpham and the bounds of Polden, Meare and Leechlake. Then the island of Meare and Westhay with its fields, meadows, woods and marshes. Then the island of Godney with its lands and substantial marshes. Next the island of Marchey with its adjoining lands. Then the island of Panborough and *Norhthilade* with the lands, meadows, pastures, marshes and broad woods belonging to them. After these the island of Nyland (*Andrewesye*), which surpasses the rest in its location and beauty, with its lands, woods, meadows and very broad marshes. This is so named from St Andrew whose chapel is located there, just as Godney is so named on account of the chapel of the Holy Trinity and Marchey on account of St Martin, whose chapel is there. Then there is Batcombe near Mount Mendip, with all the lands and pastures on that mountain which belong to it. All these places, which are contained within the boundaries of the twelve hides and belong to Glastonbury, have enjoyed every immunity of a royal dignity since ancient times and this has been confirmed for the church of Glastonbury by the kings of the Britons as well as the kings of the English and the Normans.

74. On Thurstan, the first Norman abbot.

Having explained those matters for the sake of which we digressed a little we must return to historical sequence. The first Norman abbot was Thurstan, a monk from Caen whom William, who had become King of England after being Duke of Normandy, established as abbot there in 1082. After William had subjected the kingdom to his authority he enfeoffed very many of his followers out of the possessions of Glastonbury. So it can be deduced from this and the earlier material how and through whom the once very rich monastery of Glastonbury was almost stripped of its estates, namely by the squandering of Aethelweard and Aethelnoth and the hostile assaults or violent oppression of the Danes and Normans. But the same king William, in order to repair the wrong earlier inflicted on Glastonbury, confirmed to the monks by his royal authority certain estates which, they complained, had belonged to them by right but had been unjustly taken from them. These were his words.

75. *(Carta regis Willelmi primi.)*[m]

Notum[162] sit tam presentibus quam futuris quod ego Willelmus, Dei gracia rex Anglie, uisis et cognitis cartis ecclesie Glastonie,[n] concedo eidem ecclesie in perpetuum ad uictum monachorum inibi Deo seruiencium pro salute anime mee quasdam terras quas calumpniabantur pertinere ad prefatam ecclesiam iure hereditario confirmo. Subnotantur autem terrarum nomina, uidelicet Mideltone, Fulebroc, Berges, Burniginton', Lim, Blakeford, Witon', testibus episcopo Willelmo Dunolmensi et archipresule Lanfranco et Thoma archiepiscopo et Wakelino[o] episcopo et Roberto[p] comite de Mauric' et multis aliis.

76. *De abbatibus de Muchelnie et Athelingie.*

Hiis[163] igitur ad instanciam abbatis Turstini sic patratis, eciam illud prosequamur qua efficacia uicinos abbates Muchalniensem et Ethilingensem sui iuris asseruit. Nam cum eos falsa delacione Gisonis Wellensis episcopi Lanfrancus archiepiscopus in generali concilio Anglie mordaciter impeteret, Muchaniensis, qui exercitacior esset in seculi rebus, respondit se in capitulo Glastonie iussu eiusdem loci et abbatis sui responsurum, ceterum extraordinarias accusaciones non timere. Ethelingensis autem iocul ariter eludens questionem minanti archiepiscopo baculum ei auferendum: 'Non curo,' inquit, 'quia meliorem habeo, nec tamen istum tibi trado.' Tum iussus abbas Turstinus, ut si sibi competere sciret causam ageret, surrexit loco sentencie dicende egitque multa et constanti facundia, memoriter retexens priuilegia regum a Kentuino et Ina regibus usque ad Eduuardum, quibus allegauit in eos abbates nullam iurisdictionem aliquem nisi Glastoniensem abbatem habere adeo ut in predictas ecclesias nullus debeat abbas intrare nisi fuerit electus a conuentu Glastonie. Tum cum archiepiscopus in regem conuersus dixisset se beati Dunstani nutriculam nolle minuere illeque retulisset nec se uelle matrem Domini contristare sed pro caucione futurorum episcopum Wellensem debere in Glastonie capitulo rem diffinire, resumpsit abbas sermonem, (dicens)[q] priuilegia ecclesie sue autentica esse, nullam cuiuslibet dignitatis personam causa iudicii Glastoniam debere uenire, sua ibi esse omnia et in ecclesiasticis et in secularibus rebus iudicia, facile fore ut inuictus princeps et sanctus archiepiscopus in re noua constituenda perpetua pulsarentur inuidia; ceterum quod antecessores sui habuissent integrum, se, qui in defensenda dignitate ecclesie eodem uigilaret spiritu, nequaquam omissurum. Quocirca episcopus Wellensis, si quid allegandum putaret, suo non regis uel archiepiscopi iussu

crudeles et incom(m)odi. Ad quod tam Turstini gesta abbatis quam aliorum precedencium et subsequencium predicant euidenter.

[m] In the margin in a later C13 hand; in M.

[n] *Glastoniensis* H.

[o] *W.* H.

[p] *Rob'* H.

[q] Not in T but supplied from John of Glastonbury: Carley, 190.

75. The charter of king William I.

Be it known to contemporaries and future generations that I, William, by the grace of God King of England, having seen and examined the charters of the church of Glastonbury, do grant and confirm to that same church in perpetuity, for the sustenance of the monks serving God there and for the salvation of my soul, certain lands which are claimed to belong to the church by hereditary right. The names of the estates are noted here and they are: Podimore Milton, Fullbrook, Berrow, Burrington, Lyme Regis, Blackford and Wootton. Witnessed by William, Bishop of Durham, Archbishop Lanfranc, Archbishop Thomas, Bishop Walkelin, Robert, Count of Mortain, and many others.

76. On the abbots of Muchelney and Athelney.

This charter was effected at the request of Abbot Thurstan and so let us also examine the efficacy with which he asserted his rights over the neighbouring abbots of Muchelney and Athelney. For when archbishop Lanfranc stingingly attacked them at a general council of England, as a result of a false accusation by Giso, bishop of Wells, the abbot of Muchelney, who was more practised in secular affairs, replied that he would make a response in the chapter of Glastonbury, when commanded by that place and its abbot, but that he did not fear such extraordinary accusations. But the abbot of Athelney jocularly dodged the inquiry by the archbishop, who was threatening to take his staff away from him, saying, 'I do not care because I have a better one; but just the same I am not handing this one over to you.' Then abbot Thurstan, who was ordered to undertake the case if he knew that it was appropriate for him to do so, rose in that place where judgements are given and pleaded with great and flowing eloquence, repeating from memory the privileges of kings from Centwine and Ine to Edward, by which, he affirmed, no-one except that abbot of Glastonbury had any jurisdiction over those abbots, so that no abbot ought to enter those churches unless he were chosen by the convent of Glastonbury. The archbishop turned to the king and said that he did not want to undermine the nurse-maid of the blessed Dunstan and the king replied that he did not wish to sadden the mother of God but that, to protect posterity, the bishop of Wells ought to determine the matter in the chapter of Glastonbury. The abbot then resumed his speech, saying that his church's privileges were authentic, that no person of whatever rank ought to come to Glastonbury to do justice, since all jurisdiction there, both in ecclesiastical and secular affairs, was his, that it could easily be that the victorious king and the holy archbishop were being impelled by ever-present ill-will to make a new arrangement, but that what his predecessors had maintained inviolate he, who defended his church's dignity with the same vigilant spirit, would by no means neglect. Wherefore the bishop of Wells, if he had any allegations to make, should come to Glastonbury at his command, not that of the king or the

Glastoniam ueniret. Quid plura? Optinuit causam abbas et quidem episcopus in capitulum uenit, sed purgantibus se abbatibus uictoria excidit et inglorius discessit.[r]

77. De translacione sancti Benigni.

Ad gloriam sane temporum Turstini pertinet beatissimi Benigni translacio, quam uirtutibus non incelebram alias stilus noster expediuit. Duo pallia, duo turribula, duo candelabra fecit.[164]

78. De discidiis inter Turstinum et suum conuentum et de cruce wlnerata.

Ipsius[165] autem tempore infortunium quoddam accidit quod omnino silencio preterire racio dissuadet, non ut acerbe rei commemoracio uideatur exprobacio, sed ut miraculum inde secutum deducatur in medium ad edificacionem audiencium. Discordie enim zizannia inter eumdem abbatem suumque conuentum dispersa fuisse refertur abbatisque[s] negligencie[t] impingitur causa discidii qui, dum conuentui multa de antiquis et approbatis consuetudinibus subtraheret, quedam eciam pro more sue patrie transmutaret. Licet super hiis priuatim frequenter requisitus publiceque fuisset redargutus, errata tamen corrigere dissimulabat presumptamque nullatenus exuit pertinaciam. Inter cetera eciam Gregorianum cantum aspernatus monachos compellere cepit[u] ut, illo relicto, cuiusdam Willelmi Fiscanensis cantum discerent et canterent. Hoc egre accipientes quippe qui iam tam in hoc quam in alio ecclesiastico officio secundum Romane morem ecclesie insenuerant,[166] insuper mores eiusdem tamquam alienigene nec de gremio ecclesie canonice instituti molestius forsitan tolerabant. Cum igitur die quadam mente turbida capitulum ingrederetur ac monachos super hiis et aliis negociis turbulencius alloqueretur nec eos sue uoluntati posset inclinare, confestim ira cecatus milites ac satellites suos phaleratos fecit accersiri. Quo uiso, monachi pauore uehementissimo correpti in fugam prout melius poterant uersi sunt ecclesiamque pro asilo subierunt, eiusdem hostia seris obstruentes. Sed ministri Belial irrumpentes (in)[v] templum absurdum perficiunt sceleris exemplum. Monachos eciam usque ad altare fugientes auxiliumque diuinum lacrimis profusis postulantes persecuti sunt, in eosdem arcu et sagittis iaculantes. Quidam eciam solaria inter columpnas erecta scandebant quo liberius innocencium sanguine animum saciarent maliuolum. Nec loci uel sanctorum potuit obsistere reuerencia donec unum ex monachis sacrum amplexantem altare lancea transfixum, alium ad altaris crepidinem sagittis confossum necassent ac XIIII[or] de aliis grauiter uulnerassent. Quapropter monachi tante necessitatis inportunitate compulsi demum

[r] *dicessit* T, M.
[s] *abbatisq.* H.
[t] A later C13 hand has interlined above *immo imprudencie*; not in M.
[u] In the margin N adds *note causa discordie*.
[v] Not in T but supplied from John of Glastonbury: Carley, 191.

archbishop. Need I say more? The abbot won his case and the bishop did indeed come to the chapter, but he had to depart ingloriously because victory escaped him when the abbots justified themselves.

77. On the translation of St Benignus.

To the glory of Thurstan's times belongs the translation of the most blessed Benignus which, as our pen has revealed elsewhere, was not celebrated without miracles. Thurstan was also responsible for two palls, two censers and two candlesticks.

78. On the discord between Thurstan and his convent and on the wounded cross.

However, in that abbot's time there occurred a certain misfortune which reason dissuades us from passing over in complete silence, not so that the recording of so grievous an affair may be seen as a reproach but so that the subsequent miracle might be publicly known, to the edification of those who hear it. For it is said that the tares of discord were sown between the abbot and his convent, the cause of the dissension being imputed to the heedlessness of the abbot who, at the same time as he removed many ancient and favoured customs from the convent, changed certain practices according to the custom of his own country. Although he had been frequently questioned about these in private and had been rebuked publicly concerning them he merely pretended to correct his mistakes and by no means abandoned his bold obstinacy. Among other things he even rejected the Gregorian chant and began to force the monks to abandon it and learn to sing the chant of a certain William of Fécamp. They undertook this reluctantly, especially since in regard to this, as to other ecclesiastical customs, they had grown up in the practice of the Roman church; moreover perhaps they tolerated his practices less readily because they were foreign, as it were, and had not been instituted canonically in the bosom of the church.

One day he came into the chapter in a turmoil and fiercely berated the monks about these and other matters without being able to bend them to his will. Forthwith he became beside himself with rage and had his soldiers and armed attendants summoned. At this sight the monks were seized with extreme fear and took flight as best they could, making their way to the church for sanctuary and blockading its doors with bars. But the servants of Belial burst into the temple and perpetrated unheard-of wickedness. They pursued the monks even up to the altar, where they had fled to beseech divine assistance with flowing tears, and assailed them with bows and arrows. Some of them even climbed onto the triforium galleries between the columns so that they might more easily sate their wicked souls with blood. Neither reverence for that place nor for its saints could hinder them until they had transfixed one monk with a lance as he was embracing the holy altar, killed another at the base of the altar by piercing him with arrows, and seriously wounded fourteen others. Whereupon urgent necessity compelled the monks at last to begin to defend

sese, prout poterant, defensitabant, aduersarios a choro propellentes.[167] Unus autem ex abbatis familia, in suo scelere ceteris pertinacior, cernens quemdam monachum crucem[w] argento coopertam manibus tenere ut ei defensionis clipeum prestaret, animo dedignanti in eumdem sagittam direxit. Sed, prouidente Deo, sagitta ymaginem Dominicam in cruce defixam subtus genua uulnerans, sanguinis riuulum ex eadem produxit,[x] qui de altari usque ad gradus, de gradibus usque ad terram descendens,[y] ulcionis diuine terrorem infaustis uiris incuciebat. Hoc uiso, sceleris huius perpetrator sui confusionem non sufferens, continuo amens est effectus, et ecclesia limina egressus corruit et fracta ceruice animam efflauit. Ceteri autem hoc intuentes, ne similia subirent supplicia, egredi monasterium festinabant. Sed equitatis diuine uirga eos pena non sinebat esse expertes quos in malignitatis perpetracione nouerat exstitisse consortes. Quidam enim intra, quidam extra, mentis corporisque inpotes effecti, penas non immeritas exsoluebant. Regi demum Willelmo primo querela super hoc delata, dum maxima fuisse patuit abbatis culpa, ab eodem rege in Normanniam ad monasterium unde uenerat redire compulsus est inglorius. (De monachis uero quamplures per episcopatus et abbacias iussu regis custodiendi disperguntur.)[z] Rege tamen mortuo idem Turstinus auxilio parentum suorum abbaciam Glastonie a filio suo Willelmo, dicto Rupho, quingentis libris argenti dicitur redemisse, et monasterium aliquot annis occupans et per eiusdem possessiones peruagatus, (longe ab ipso, ut dignus erat,)[a] misere uitam finiuit.[168] Cetera autem Turstini facta pocius miremur, non istud carpamus in quo, magis casu inpegit quam industria peccauit. Emulemur in eo feruorem religionis, non nullam pietatem in Deo, multam prudenciam[b] in seculo. Crux autem superius memorata, ab antiquis temporibus argento uestita, pro tanto miraculo conuentui uenerabilis populoque celebris habetur uulnerisque uestigia intuentibus adhuc ostendit manifesta. Acta sunt hec anno Domini M^{O}LXXXI°. Huius eciam rei testis est Orosius, Anglorum historiographus.[169]

79. De Herlewino abbate.

f18 Successit Herlewinus[170] anno incarnacionis M^{O}CI^{O} eque ut / Turstinus, Cadomensis monachus, clemencia et liberalitate iuxta insignis, quem Henricus primus, consenciente conuentu, ibidem abbatem constituit ubi et XIX annis prefuit. Is in nouitate aduentus pro parcitate uictus ignominie in regno Anglie est notatus. Et reuera strictius se agebat quam amplitudinis fortune sue intererat, non animi angustia sed pro gentili more patrie de qua uenerat. Uerumtamen ut dixi, pudore infamie respersus, ualuas curie quibus adueniencium arcebatur aditus a fundo eruit ut, patente noctibus perinde ut diebus accessu, nullus difficultatem causaretur

[w] A later C15? hand has added in the margin *predictam* and it is in M.
[x] In the margin a late C16? hand notes: *Haec non posuit in Gestis P nec in historia.*
[y] *decendens* T, M.
[z] added in the margin of T; in M.
[a] added in the margin of T; in M.
[b] *prouidenciam* H.

themselves as best they could and drive their opponents from the choir. But one of the abbot's servants, who was more determined in his wickedness than the rest, noticed a certain monk clutching in his hands a silver cross, which he was using as a shield to defend himself, and contemptuously aimed an arrow at him. But thanks to God's providence the arrow wounded below the knees the image of our Lord affixed to the cross, producing from it a stream of blood which, flowing down from the altar to the steps and from the steps to the ground, struck those unhappy men with the terror of divine vengeance. At this sight the perpetrator of the crime became unbearably confused and at once became mad, so that when he got outside the church he fell to the ground, broke his neck and died. As soon as the others saw this they hastened to leave the monastery lest they should suffer similar punishments. But the rod of divine justice did not allow them to escape retribution since it knew that they had been accomplices in the perpetration of evil. For some were affected internally and some externally, either their minds or their bodies being rendered impotent, and they paid a just penalty.

When a complaint about this was eventually made to king William I it was clear that the greatest fault lay with the abbot and he was compelled by the king to return ingloriously to the monastery in Normandy whence he had come. (Very many of the monks were dispersed at the king's order among bishoprics and abbacies to be watched over.) However, when the king died Thurstan is said to have redeemed the abbacy of Glastonbury with the help of his kin for 500 pounds of silver from his son William Rufus and to have occupied the monastery for a few years, wandering from estate to estate, before meeting a miserable end (far from there, as was appropriate). But let us admire Thurstan's other deeds rather than linger over this one, in which he stumbled accidentally but did not sin by design. Let us emulate his religious fervour, his considerable piety towards God and his great discretion in worldly affairs. The cross referred to above, covered in silver since ancient times, is venerated by the convent and renowned among the people on account of such a great miracle and still reveals clear traces of its wound to those who contemplate it. These events, to which Orosius, an historian of the English, bears witness, took place in 1081 AD.

79. On abbot Herluin.

Herluin succeeded in 1101 and was, like Thurstan, a monk of Caen, distinguished alike in kindness and generosity and was established by Henry I with the convent's approval as abbot there, where he ruled for 19 years. When he first arrived he was to his shame known throughout the kingdom of England for the parsimony of his way of life. And indeed he kept himself in closer check than the size of his fortune warranted, not out of meanness of soul but because it was the custom of the country from which he had come. However, filled with shame at the notoriety of which I have spoken, he completely removed the doors to his courtyard, which had prevented anyone from reaching him, so that, with free access at night as well as during the day, it would never be difficult to come to see him. To show how much

ingressus. Et ut ostenderet quantum infamiam parsimonie oderat, cunctos officiales conuocans hanc ab omnibus graciam precario munere depoposcit ut se in resumenda dapsilitatis fama iuuarent. Ianitori, si quemquam excluderet, cum fortunarum dispendio precisionem eciam auris comminatus. Eo factum est ut pro dapsilitate diceretur profusus, qui ante clamabatur astrictus. Fit enim fere in rebus mortalium ut auarus nominetur qui est prouidus, et qui est munificus nuncupetur prodigus. Ecclesiam a predecessore incoatam, quia magnitudini possessionum suarum non respondebat, solo tenus eruit et nouam incoauit in qua cccc^tas lxxx libras dispendit. Imaginem et crucem lxx marcis comparauit. Pro terris a tempore Normannorum ereptis cum mille marcas optulisset[c] regi, repulsam passus ad Terencianum dictum uerso animo: 'Faciamus', inquit, 'quod possumus si non possumus quod uolumus'.[171] Itaque datis c marcis argenti et duabus auri, maneriorum suorum mutilacionem resarciuit. Sex enim hidas in Pukelescyrce retrahens, ad xl extendit libras quod uix xvi ante ualuerat. Sexaginta marcis redemit terram quam Gaufridus de Magna Uilla tenebat in Wiltone. Terram de Cranemere recuperauit,[d] annuente rege Henrico, ut eam pro tribus hidis defensitaret. Milne et Lim de manibus Hardingi, Eadnothi filii, potentis tunc admodum et causidici, extorsit. Ab Ulrico, fratre Dunelmelsis[e] episcopi, quia parum succedebat sapiencia secularis, ecclesiastica communione priuato, Blakeford recepit. In Cumpton' hidam, in Soei aliam ad ecclesiam, quasi postlimino, redire fecit. Apud Walas terram decem librarum adquisiuit. Crucem opere mirabili et incomparabili fecit. Pallia ix, cappas ix, tapetum i, dorsalia v, albas iii, altare quod, cum Iohanni Cremensi[172] ostensum primo enormitate precii eius hebetasset animum, mox, si Rome haberetur,[f] centum marcis auri estimatum est,[g] (dedit ac)[h] monachorum officinas ampliauit. Clericos religionis uotum parturientes gratis recepit, nullo scilicet precio conuersionem eorum, ut quidam faciunt, nundinatus.[i] Pridie quam excederet missam cantans cordis contricione et lacrimarum fluuio se ipsum Deo uictimam fecit. Mox in capitulo cunctorum excessuum in monachos indulgenciam peciit et inpetrauit, accessisse se ad metam uite illis mirantibus uaticinatus. Sub ipso crepusculo de consilio medicorum pilulas sumpsit. Sed eis ante mediam noctem in tormentum transeuntibus, a monachis accurrentibus sacro unguine delibutus, in mera noctis diem clausit. Sepultus est iuxta Turstinum ad sanctum Andream.[j]

c Originally *contulisset* but corrected.

d A note at the foot of the folio in a late C16 hand reads *Terre de Crenmere erat xii hiderum, v, p15, col 4. Geldum erat nunc leue Huiusmodi relaxationes aliquot fecitS. Edw. ut patet in Doomesd.*; not in M.

e *Dunelmensis* H.

f *mox . . . haberetur*: the significance of this phrase is by no means clear.

g *esset* H.

h Lacking in T and supplied from John of Glastonbury: Carley, 199.

i *nundidatus* T; *nunditatus* M.

j A later C14 hand has added in the margin *Hic deficit carta Walkelini le Werreer de ecclesia de Wynford que sequetur infra, fere in fine libri*; not in M.

he hated his bad reputation for frugality he called together all his officials and, accompanying his request with a gift, entreated this favour of them all, that they should help him recover a good name for generosity. He threatened the doorkeeper with the loss of his property, even with the cutting off of an ear, if he were to shut anyone out. He so acted that he was said to be extravagant in his generosity, he who had previously been declared parsimonious. For it usually happens in human affairs that he who is careful is called greedy and he who is generous is deemed wasteful. Because the church left unfinished by his predecessor did not correspond to the extent of his wealth he completely levelled it and began a new one on which he spent 480 pounds. He provided an image and a cross for 70 marks. When he had offered the king 1000 marks for the lands seized at the time of the Normans he was refused but consoled himself with a saying of Terence: 'We will do what we can,' he said, 'if we cannot do what we wish.' And so he spent 100 silver marks and 2 gold ones on restoring his truncated manors. He recovered 6 hides at Pucklechurch, thereby increasing it in value from scarcely 16 pounds to 40 pounds. For 60 marks he redeemed land that Geoffrey de Mandeville held in Wilton. He regained land in Cranmore which, with King Henry's approval, was allowed to pass under his protection in return for 3 hides. He wrested Mells and Lyme from the hands of Harding, the son of Eadnoth, who was at the time a very powerful man and an advocate. From Ulrich, a brother of the Bishop of Durham, who had been cut off from communion with the Church he recovered Blackford because Ulrich's worldly wisdom failed him. He ensured the return to the church, as though naturally after a delay, of 1 hide at Compton Dundon and 1 hide at Zoy. He acquired land worth 10 pounds in Wales. He made a cross of marvellous and incomparable workmanship. He gave 9 palls, 9 copes, 1 carpet, 5 dossals, 3 albs and an altar which dumbfounded John of Crema when it was first shown to him by virtue of its great value and was considered to be worth 100 marks of gold if it were at that time in Rome. He also enlarged the monks' quarters. He accepted without charge monks who were fulfilling a vow of religion, not, that is, trading on their conversion for a profit as some do. While he was singing mass with a contrite heart and a flood of tears on the day before he died he offered himself as a victim to God. Then in the chapter he sought and obtained an indulgence for all his trespasses against the monks, prophesying to those who wondered at this that he had reached the end of his life. That evening he took some pills on the advice of his doctors but these began to torment him before midnight and, after being annointed with sacred oil by the monks who came running to him, he passed away during the small hours. He was buried next to Thurstan at the altar of St Andrew.

80. Consuetudines.

Consuetudines obseruate temporibus Turstini et Herlewini abbatum: In priuatis diebus, uidelicet Dominica, die Martis, die Iouis ac Sabbato tria generalia ad refectionem habuerunt fratres et duas pitancias. Ceteris uero tribus diebus, scilicet feria ii, feria iiii et vi duo generalia et tres pitancias. In diebus autem sollempnibus, quando fratres fuerunt in cappis, medonem habuerunt in iustis et similas super mensam et uinum ad caritatem et tria generalia et iiii uel v pitancias. In diebus uero in quibus in albis fuerunt, medonem similiter in iustis et similas super mensas et iii generalia et iii uel iiii pitancias. In precipuis autem festiuitatibus, id est Natali Domini, Pascha, Penthecoste, Assumpcione et Natiuitate sancte Marie et Dedicacione ecclesie, maior fuit quantitas in omnibus, secundum dignitatem festiuitatum.[173] In anniuersariis uero regum, episcoporum, abbatum et ducum qui Glastonie ecclesiam construxerunt debent fratres per singula altaria pro eorum animabus missas celebrare et maxime in communi conuentu honorifice coram positis ornamentis que huic ecclesie dederunt. Interim pauperes xiii pro eis reficiantur et postea in refectorio debent seruiri, sicut in festiuitatibus. De uestitu eorum ista est consuetudo: Unusquisque fratrum duas cucullas et duos froccos et duo stamina et duo femoralia habere debet et iiii caligas et peliciam nouam per singulos annos, et in cena Domini unusquisque diurnales sotulares et in hieme nocturnales et duo coopertoria ad lectum. Pedules uero decem, scilicet ad festiuitatem beati Michaelis ii, ad sollempnitatem Omnium Sanctorum iiii, ad festiuitatem sancti Martini ii, ceteras duas quando eis expedierit, habeant. Et hec est assisa: quando pro ceruisia uinum debent habere, unusquisque scilicet habere debet duas caritates in die. De minutis quere in texto.

81. De Sigfrido abbate.

Successit Sigfridus,[174] monachus Sagiensis, frater Radulfi archiepiscopi Cantuarie, anno incarnacionis Domini M^{o}CXX, similiter ab Henrico primo constitutus, qui et Glastoniam annis VI regebat. Is dedit pallium i, casulam, albam et priuilegium in hec uerba.

82. Priuilegium Calixti pape.

Calixtus[175] episcopus seruus seruorum Dei, dilectissimo filio Sigfrido Pelochino salutem et apostolicam benedictionem. Religiosis desideriis dignum est facilem prebere consensum ut fidelis deuocio celerem sorciatur effectum. Quamobrem nos, fili in Christo karissime, postulacionis tue desideriis benignius annuentes, beate Dei genitricis et gloriose semper uirginis Marie monasterium, cui annuente Deo presides, in ecclesie Romane tutelam protectionemque suscipimus et contra hominum peruersorum molestias eius priuilegio confouemus. Per presentis enim decreti paginam auctoritatemque statuimus ut quecumque ab apostolicis,[176] archiepiscopis,

80. Customs.

These were the customs observed in the time of Abbots Thurstan and Herluin. On some days of the week, namely Sunday, Tuesday, Thursday and Saturday, the brethren had three *generalia* and two *pitantiae* to eat but on the other three days, that is the second, fourth and sixth days, they had two *generalia* and three *pitantiae*. However, on holy days when the brethren were in copes they had cups of mead, fine wheaten cakes on the table, a measure of wine and three *generalia* and four or five *pitantiae*. On those days on which they wore albs they had a similar allowance of mead, fine wheaten cakes on their table and three *generalia* and three or four *pitantiae*. But on special festivals, that is Christmas, Easter, Pentecost, the Assumption and Nativity of the holy Mary and the Dedication of the church, there was a greater quantity for all, depending on the dignity of the festival. On the anniversaries of kings, bishops, abbots and ealdormen who helped build the church the brethren were obliged to celebrate mass for their souls at each altar, and, in particular, in the presence of the whole convent, to do so respectfully using the ornaments that they had given the church. At the same time 13 paupers were to be entertained on their behalves, after which they were to be served in the refectory as though it were a festival. This was the custom concerning dress: each of the brethren was to have two cowls, two frocks, two shirts of linsey-woolsey, two pairs of breeches, four pairs of stockings and a new pelisse every year, and on Maundy Thursday each was to have shoes for the day time and in winter for the night and two bed covers. They should also have ten pairs of slippers, two on the Festival of the Blessed Michael, four on the solemnity of All Saints, two on the Festival of St Martin and the other two when they considered it appropriate. And this is another ration: when they are to have wine in place of beer, each of them is to have two measures a day. For blood-letting see in the Gospel-book.

81. On abbot Seffrid.

Seffrid, a monk of Séez and brother of Ralph, archbishop of Canterbury, succeeded in 1120 AD, likewise appointed by Henry I, and ruled Glastonbury for 6 years. He gave 1 pall, a chasuble, and an alb and obtained a privilege in these words.

82. The privilege of Pope Calixtus.

Bishop Calixtus, servant of the servants of God, to his dearest son Seffrid Pelochin, greetings and apostolic benediction. It is proper to grant a ready consent to religious requests so that devout faith produces a speedy effect. Wherefore, dearest son in Christ, abundantly approving the desire behind your request, we do receive unto the care and protection of the Holy Roman Church the monastery of the blessed mother of God and glorious eternal Virgin Mary over which you preside with God's approval, and do support it in the face of the attacks of evil men with this privilege. By the deed and authority of this decree we order that whatever has been granted by legitimate bequest to our monastery by apostles, archbishops,

episcopis,[k] regibus et principibus aliisque fidelibus nostro monasterio largicione legittima collata sunt, quieta ei et integra conseruentur. Quecumque preterea futuris temporibus iuste canoniceque adquirere, Domino largiente, poteritis, firma tibi successoribusque tuis et illibata permaneant. Decernimus ergo ut nulli omnino[l] hominum liceat idem monasterium penitus perturbare, aut eius possessiones auferre uel ablatas retinere, uel minuere uel temerariis uexacionibus fatigare, set omnia integra conseruentur eorum pro quorum gubernacione et conseruacione collata sunt modis omnibus usibus profutura. Si qua autem ecclesiastica secularisue persona in futurum, hanc nostre constitucionis paginam sciens, contra eam temere uenire temptauerit, secundo tercioue commonita, si non satisfactione congrua emendauerit, potestatis honorisque dignitate careat reamque se diuino iudicio existere de perpetrata iniquitate cognoscat, et a sacratissimo corpore Dei et Domini nostri redemptoris Ihesu Christi aliena fiat et in extremo examine districte ulcioni subiaceat. Cunctis autem eidem loco iusta seruantibus sit pax Domini nostri Ihesu Christi quatinus[m] et hic[n] fructum bone actionis percipiant et apud districtum iudicem premia eterne retribucionis inueniant. Data Lateranis per manum Aimerici sancte Romane ecclesie cardinalis et cancellarii, Idibus Maii, indictione prima, incarnacionis Domini (anno)[o] M^oCXXIII, pontificatus domini Calixti secundi pape v^to. (Item[p] Wintoniensis episcopum Henricum, Cluniacensis ordinis monachum, inter antistites electos et sanctitatis honore preclares digne commemorandum duximus et conuersandum cuius animum quippe solidis formisque radicibus in Christo fundatum. Nec generositas regia nec illustris an(n)orum undique prosapia nec duplicitate dignitatis,[q] Glastoniensis scilicet sicut et Wintoniensis ecclesie, opulencia, caritate priuare potuit et humilitate, sed quanto maiorem in cunctis celsioremque pre ceteris ipsum gracia celestis extulerat, tanto humiliorem se in omnibus Deorum per omnia deuociorem mancipare curauit. Uerum non solum iste sed in multis scripturis multa predicabilia inseruntur de hoc Henrico episcopo quoque Wintonienses eius famam sugillando; ipsum duriorem asserant extitisse.)

83. De Henrico Blesensi, abbate Glastonie.

Is Sigfridus, Cicestrensis episcopus factus, habuit in Glastonia successorem anno M^oCXXVI Henricum,[177] fratrem Thebaldi Blesensis comitis, nepotem Henrici regis ex sorore Adela, qui eciam episcopus Wintonie non multo post factus est.

[k] *episcopis* om. H.
[l] *omino* T, M.
[m] *quatenus* H.
[n] *hii* H.
[o] *anno* om. T and supplied from copy of privilege contained in cartulary and printed in Watkin, 169.
[p] This is a later C13 marginal addition in T which is in the text in M before the last chapter. Om. H.
[q] *dingnitatis* T, M.

bishops, kings and other magnates should be maintained in place and undiminished. Moreover whatever you can acquire in the future rightly and canonically, through God's generosity shall remain firmly and completely with you and your successors. Therefore we decree that no-one at all be permitted to disturb that monastery internally or to take away its possessions, or to retain them if taken away, or to diminish them, or harass them with bold disturbances. Rather these ought to be preserved untouched for the unrestricted future use of those for whose government and maintenance they were bestowed. But if in the future any person, lay or ecclesiastical, who knows the content of this our decree, should dare to act rashly against it and, despite a second or third warning, does not suitably and satisfactorily make amendment, let him be deprived of rank, honour and power and let him know that he will stand before the Divine Judge accused of the wickedness he has perpetrated and let him be inimical to the Most Sacred Body of God and our Saviour the Lord Jesus Christ and let him be liable to severe revenge at the Last Judgement. But may the peace of our Lord Jesus Christ be with all those who serve that place justly, so that they may harvest here the fruit of their good acts and discover the reward of an eternal recompense at the Last Judgement. Given at the Lateran by the hand of Haimeric, cardinal and chancellor of the Holy Roman Church, on the 15th May, in the first indiction, in 1123 AD, the fifth year of the pontificate of our lord Pope Calixtus.

(We consider that Henry, bishop of Winchester and monk of the order of Cluny, ought to be worthily remembered among select bishops and those outstanding for their honoured sanctity and that he whose soul was solidly and firmly rooted in Christ ought to abide with them. Neither royal generosity nor an illustrious and ancient lineage nor the wealth of the double dignity of the churches of Glastonbury and Winchester could deprive him of charity and humility, but the higher he was raised through God's grace and the more eminent he became than others the more he endeavoured to subject himself humbly and devoutly in all his behaviour to all God's wishes. Besides this many writings contain various epithets about this Henry, bishop of Winchester, which scoff at his reputation; they assert that he was a harsh man.)

83. On Henry of Blois, abbot of Glastonbury.

After Seffrid was made Bishop of Chichester he was succeeded at Glastonbury in the year 1126 by Henry, brother of Theobald Count of Blois and nephew of king Henry by his sister Adela, who was also made Bishop of Winchester not much later.

Uir, preter natalium splendorem, pericia litterarum insignis, affabilitate uerborum comis, animi benignitate liberalis, cuius principia et processus quanto uobis emolumento fuerint et per hoc quanto fauore in os hominum uenerit nostis. De quo plura nec me dicere nec uos tederet audire, nisi consilium esset parcere admirabili eius uerecundie, habet enim hoc proprium, ut quamquam laudanda faciat, laudari tamen erubescat.

This man, of illustrious birth, is also distinguished in his knowledge of letters, kind and friendly in his address and noble in the kindness of his heart, a man whose origins and achievement have been of advantage to you, as you know, and have brought you great favour in the eyes of men. It would neither weary me to say more about him, nor weary you to hear more, but it would be advisable to spare his admirable modesty, for he has this characteristic, that he blushes to be praised although he does praiseworthy things.

Appendix: William's Original Text

DETAILED discussion of the authenticity of individual chapters of the *DA* is found in the notes to the text, but I offer here what I take to have been William's original version of chs 1-36. I do so because these chapters have been substantially amended or boldly interpolated and their original order tampered with so that a picture of what William originally wrote is obscured by the detailed argumentation of the notes. After the Preface William's original text continued thus:

Tradunt bone credulitatis annales, quod Lucius rex Britannorum ad Eleutherium, XIII loco post beatum Petrum papam miserit, oratum ut Britannie tenebras luce Christiane predicacionis illustraret. Mactus animi rex, magne prorsus laudis factum adorsus, ut fidem, quam tunc temporis pene omnes reges et populi persequerentur exibitam, ipse ultro appeteret uix auditam. De qua re, ut aliquid extrinsecus dicam, in eiusdem meriti laudem concurrit Ethelbirtus, multis annis post Lucium rex Cancie, qui predicatores ad se de Roma missos non turbido abegit responso, sed benigno excepit hospicio. Accessit benignitati sollers uerborum festiuitas, quod, etsi nollet uerbis eorum preproperum assensum apponere, tamen quia de longe uenerant ut que optime credebant ei communicarent, absurdum uideri posset si eis quicquam inferret molestie. Sunt ergo hii uiri amplissima recordacione digni, quorum alter Christianitatem prudenter inuitauit, alter libenter excepit. Uenerunt ergo, Eleutherio mittente, predicatores Britanniam, quorum in euum durabit efficacia, quamuis longe situs etatis consumpserit nomina. Horum fuit opera uetusta sancte Marie in Glastonia ecclesia, sicut fidelis per succidua secula non tacuit antiquitas. Sunt et ille non exigue fidei littere apud sanctum Edmundum reperte ad hanc sentenciam: Ecclesiam Glastonie non fecerunt aliorum hominum manus, sed ipsi discipuli Christi eam edificauerunt. Nec abhorret a uero, quia si Philippus apostolus Gallis predicauit, sicut Freculfus libro secundo, capitulo quarto, dicit, potest credi quod eciam trans oceanum sermonis semina iecit.

Ecclesia de que sane loquimur, que pro antiquitate sui celebriter ab Anglis Ealdechirche, id est Uetusta Ecclesia, nuncupatur, primo uirgea, nescio quid diuine sanctitatis iam inde a principio redoluit spirauitque in omnem patriam, quamuis ex deformi grandis reuerencia cultu. Hinc confluencium illuc populorum totis callibus unde, hinc opulentorum deposita pompa conuentus, hinc religiosorum et litteratorum frequens perendinacio. Nam, sicut a maioribus accepimus, Gildas, neque insulsus neque infacetus historicus, cui Britanni debent si quid noticie inter ceteras gentes habent, multum annorum ibi exegit loci sanctitudine captus.* Est ergo ecclesia illa omnium quas quidem nouerim antiquissima in Anglia, indeque cognomen sortita. In ea multorum sanctorum, quorum aliquos in processu notabimus, corporales seruantur exuuie, nec a beatorum cineribus uacat ullus fani ambitus. Adeo pauimentum lapide constratum, adeo alteris latera, ipsumque altare, supra et infra reliquiis confertissimis aggeruntur. Merito ergo dicitur celeste in terris sanctuarium tot sanctorum reconditorium. Quam felices, Deus bone, habitatores, quos ipsa loci reuerencia ad morum composicionem inuitat. Nullum de hiis crediderim deperire celo, quos corporibus egressos tantorum patronorum excipit laus uel excusacio. Ubi autem notare licet in pauimento, uel per trangulum, uel per quadratum, lapides altrinsecus ex industria positos, ex plumbo sigillatos, sub quibus quiddam archani sacri contineri si credo, iniuriam religioni non facio. Antiquitas et sanctorum congeries exciuit reuerenciam loco, ut uix ibi quis noctu presumat excubias agere, uix interdiu excrescens flegma proicere, illusorie feditatis conscius toto cohorreat corpore. Nullus inter contiguum cimiterium uel auem uenatoriam aduexit, uel quadrupedes induxit, qui sui uel rei possesse indempnis abierit. Ferro uel aqua examinandi si oracionem ibi deposuerunt, omnes quos presens memoria complectitur, uno excepto, de salute sua tripudiarunt. Si quis e uicino aliquod edificium locandum putasset, quod obumbracione sua lucem inuideret ecclesie, patuit ruine. Satisque constat homines illius prouincie nullum sanctius uel crebrius iuramentum habere, quam per ueterem ecclesiam, nichil magis uitantes, metu celeris uindicte, quam periurare. Labantem ueritatem dictorum que proposuimus plurimorum ueracissimorum hominum pro successu annorum fulciunt testimonia.

Quantum autem Glastonie ecclesia fuerit eciam primatibus patrie uenerabilis, ut ibi potissimum sub protectione Dei genitricis operirentur diem resurrectionis, multa sunt indicio quibus pro cautela fastidii abstineo. Illud quod clam pene omnibus est libenter predicarem, si ueritatem exculpere possem, quid ille piramides sibi uelint, que, aliquantis pedibus ab ecclesia uetusta posite, cimiterium monachorum pretexunt. Procerior sane et propinquior ecclesie habet quinque tabulatus, et altitudinem XXVIII pedum. Hec, pre nimia uetustate etsi ruinam minetur, habet tamen antiquitatis nonnulla spectacula, que plane possunt legi, licet non plene possint intelligi. In superiori enim tabulatu est ymago pontificali scemate facta. In secundo ymago regiam pretendens pompam, et littere: Her, Sexi et Blisyer. In tercio nichilominus nomina, Wemcrest, Bantomp, Winethegn. In quarto, Hate, Wulfred et Eanfled. In quinto, qui et inferior est, ymago et hec scriptura: Logwor, Weslicas, et Bregden, Swelwes, Hwingendes, Bern. Altera uero piramis habet XXVI pedes et III tabulatus, in quibus hec leguntur: Centwine, Hedde, episcopus, et Bregored et Beoruuard. Quid hec significent non temere diffinio, sed ex suspicione colligo eorum interius in cauatis lapidibus contineri ossa, quorum exterius leguntur nomina. Certe Logwor is pro certo asseritur esse, de cuius nomine Logweresbeorh dicebatur, qui nunc Mons Acutus dicitur; Bregden a quo

* At this point, I suggest, William incorporated details about the northern saints translated to Glastonbury. See n.55, p.194.

Brentacnol, et Brentemeirs; Bregored et Beorwald abbates eiusdem loci tempore Britonum; de quibus et de ceteris qui occurrere poterunt, ex hinc liberiori campo exultabit oratio. Iam enim abbatum seriem, et quid cuique, et a quo rege ad usus monasterii delegatum sit, sermo explicare contendet.

Ac primum de beato Patricio, a quo monimentorum nostrorum series elucescere cepit, pauca libabimus. Anglis Britannorum infestantibus pacem et Pelagianis eorum expugnantibus fidem, sanctus Germanus Autisiodorensis, ut alibi legitur, contra utrosque suppecias tulit. Illos enim alleluiatico cantu fudit, et istos euuangelicis et apostolicis tonitribus fulminauit. Inde in patriam meditatus reditum, Patricium ad familiare contubernium asciuit, eumdemque post aliquot annos Hyberniensibus, iubente Celestino papa, predicatorem misit. Ille munus iniunctum gnauiter executus, extremis diebus Britanniam remeans, priorem celsitudinem salutacionesque in foro respuens, super altare suum Cornubiam appulit; quod usque hodie apud incolas magne ueneracioni est, tum propter sanctitudinem et utilitatem, tum propter infirmorum salutem. Ita Glastoniam ueniens, ibique monachus et abbas factus, post aliquot annos nature cessit. Cuius assertionis omnem scrupulum absoluit uisio cuiusdam fratris, qui post obitum beati uiri, nutante memoria utrum ibi monachus et abbas fuerit, cum de hoc frequens uerteretur questio, tali confirmatus est oraculo. Resolutus enim in soporem, uisus audire quemdam legentem post multa eius miracula, hec uerba: 'Hic igitur metropolitani pallii decoratus est sanctitate; postmodum uero hic monachus et abbas factus est.' Adiecit eciam ut non integre credenti litteris aureis quod dixerat scriptum ostenderet. Excessit ergo Patricius anno etatis sue CXI, incarnacionis uero Domini CCCCLXXII, qui fuit annus ex quo in Yberniam missus est XLVII. Requiescit in dextro latere alteris uetuste ecclesie, in pyramide saxea, quam argento uestiuit posterorum diligencia.

Hinc Hyberniensibus mos inolitus ad exosculandas patroni reliquias locum frequentare. Unde et sanctum Indractum et beatam Brigidam illius terre non obscuros incolas illuc olim commeasse celeberrimus sermo est. Brigida quidem, que anno Domini CCCCLXXXVIII illuc uenerat post aliquantulam moram quam in insula, que dicitur Beokery, fecerat, domum reuersa, relictis ibidem quibusdam insigniis suis, uidelicet pera, monili, nola et textrilibus armis, que ibidem ad eius memoriam reseruantur. Indractum uero cum sociis ibidem martirizatum et sepultum, sicut alias stilus noster non tacuit; postea per Ynam regem de loco martirii in Glastoniensem translatum ecclesiam.

Anno Domini CCCCLX sanctus Benignus uenit Glastoniam. Hic discipulus sancti Patricii et successor in episcopatu eius tertius in Ybernia fuit, quemadmodum eorum gesta testantur. Hic igitur, angelo monente, patriam pontificiique dignitatem ex uoto deserens, uoluntaria peregrinatione suscepta, Glastoniam, Deo duce, peruenit, ubi et sanctum Patricium inuenit. Quis autem hic fuerit, et quomodo patria lingua dictus, non infacete exprimunt uersus qui in epitaphio sepulcri eius apud Ferremere scripti sunt.

Hoc patris in lapide Beonne sunt osse locata.
Qui pater extiterat monachorum hic tempore prisco.

Hunc fore Patricii dudum fortasse ministrum
Fantur Hybernigene, et Beonnam de nomine dicunt.

Quante autem apud Deum gracie fuerit, multis patet uirtutum indiciis; hoc eciam testantur eius insignia apud Fernigmere, data eius precibus aqua largissima et ex eius baculo arido ingens arbor uirens et frondifera. Hic itaque post inmensos agones in dicta insula beato fine quieuit ac post multorum curricula annorum, id est anno Domini M^{o} nonagesimo primo, Glastoniam honorifice translatus est.

Anno Domini DIIII sanctus Kolumkilla uenit Glastoniam. Quidam affirmant hunc sanctum uite sue cursum ibidem consummasse, sed utrum sic, aut inde repatriauerit, non diffinio.

Iam uero quanti eum locum penderit magnus ille Dauid Meneuensium archiepiscopus celebrius est quam ut nostro indigeat illustrari relatu. Is antiquitatem et sanctitudinem ecclesie diuino comprobauit oraculo. Dedicacioni enim eius intendens, cum episcopis septem, quorum primas erat, ad locum uenit. Paratis autem omnibus que officii usus exposceret, nocte precessura, ut putabat, festiuitatem, sompno indulsit. Omnes ergo sensus in quietem solutus, uidit Dominum Ihesum assistere causam aduentus blande sciscitantem. Quam cum ille incunctanter aperuisset, reuocauit eum a sentencia Dominus hoc dicto. Dedicatam a se dudum ecclesiam in honore sue matris, iteracione humana sacramentum temerari non oportere. Simulque cum dicto, uolam digito terebrare uisus hec, subiecit. Hoc haberet signum repeti non debere quod ipse anticipasset facere, set quia intencionis illius non tam fuerit audacia quam deuocio, penam non prolongandam. Denique mane futuro cum in missa, 'per ipsum et cum ipso et in ipso', dicturus esset, plenum ei salutis uigorem refundendum. Hiis terroribus antistes sompno excussus, sicut tunc sanie ulcerosa impalluit, sic postea prophetie ueritati applausit. Sed ne nichil uideretur egisse, aliam ecclesiam citato fecit et dedicauit opere. De hoc sane egregio et incomparabili uiro, utrum ibi obierit, an in sede propria uitam finierit, incertum habeo. Nam uiri religiosi recordatione digni eum cum beato Patricio esse affirmant; et Walenses, orationum frequentatione, et multiplici sermone, id proculdubio astruunt et corroborant, illud in medium proferentes Bernardum episcopum semel et secundo eum quesisse, et multis reclamantibus non inuenisse.

Sancti Patricii natiuitas, que anno Dominice incarnacionis CCCLXI fuit, aduentum beati Augustini in Britanniam ducentis triginta sex annis precessit. Cuius predicacionis commilitonem, Paulinum, ex archiepiscopo Eboracensi, Rofensem episcopum, asserit patrum tradicio, ecclesie contextum dudum, ut diximus, uirgee ligneo tabulatu induisse et plumbo a summo usque deorsum cooperuisse. Egit nimirum predicabilis uiri sollercia, ut nichil decederet sanctitati, et plurimum accederet ornatui. Et certe solet ecclesiarum cultus augustior quamlibet brutas mentes ad orandum illicere, quamlibet ceruicositatem ad supplicandum inflectere.

Anno Dominice incarnacionis sexcentesimo primo rex Domnonie terram, que appellatur Inesuuitrin, ad ecclesiam uetustam concessit, que ibi sita est, ob peticionem Worgret abbatis in quinque cassatis. Ego Mauuron episcopus hanc cartam scripsi. Ego Worgret eiusdem loci abbas subscripsi. Quis iste rex fuerit scedule uetustas negat scire, uerumptamen quod Britannus fuerit hinc presumi potest, quod Glastoniam lingua sua Yneswitrin appellauit, sic enim eam Britannice uocari apud eos constat. Worgret autem abbati, cuius nomen Britannicam barbariem redolet, successit Lademund at ei Bregoretd. Prelacionis eorum tempora sunt in obscuro set nomina illorum et dignitates in maiori ecclesia, prodente secus altare pictura, sunt in propatulo. Bregoredo successit Berthwald.

Anno Dominice incarnacionis sexcentesimo septuagesimo Ceonwalh, regni sui uicesimo nono, dedit Bertwaldo Glastoniensi abbati Ferramere, duas hidas, archiepiscopo Theodoro interueniente. Hic idem Bertwaldus, renitente rege, et diocesis episcopo, Glastonie renuntians, ad regimen monasterii Raculf secessit. Quocirca Bertwaldus, et fama religionis nominatissimus, et generis nobilitate precluus, quippe fratris Ethelredi regis Merciorum filius, et loci opportunitate Cantuarie proximus, Theodoro archiepiscopo decedente, illius successit cathedra.*

* There followed ch. 37. The rest of the original text can be visualised easily from the detailed notes.

NOTES

1: William of Malmesbury at Glastonbury

1 See the table in *MO*, 702.

2 Henry recorded his impressions in a short summary of his early activities at Glastonbury which is preserved in the earliest extant manuscript containing the *DA*. Henry's words are: . . . *inueni locum olim celeberimum priorum facta subsannantem, in tugurriis suis propinquam ruinam minantem, et, quod in praesenti pocius urgebat, monachos necessariis indigentes, et ecclesiam multis possessionibus et magnis uiduatam*. (*AD*, 305).

3 It was, Henry explains, my love of God and His mother that . . . *me compulit ut obsequium ei famulancium non desererem, remouerem hostes, dispersa congregarem. Ibid.*, 305-6.

4 The historian of the bishopric of Somerset describes Robert as expert in business and reports that Henry took him from Lewes to set the affairs of Glastonbury in order, *uti rebus abbatiae disponeret*. Hunter, *Ecclesiastical Documents* 23.

5 *MSD*, 7.

6 *GR*, 23-4.

7 *Ibid.*, 24.

8 Dunstan's biographer 'B' reports that St Patrick was buried at Glastonbury, (*MSD*, 10-11) a belief that, Finberg argues, derived from Dunstan himself ('St Patrick at Glastonbury', 76). On the liturgical evidence see *ibid.*, 72 and the Leofric Missal, Oxford, Bodleian Library, MS Bodley 579, fos 39, 39v, 40.

9 *Infra*, ch.31 and the chapters on the various West Saxon kings.

10 *GR*, 24.

11 The abbey maintained a record of the lands granted to it in a document known as the *Liber Terrarum*, which is no longer extant but the contents of which were listed, along with other records of charters, in the earliest manuscript of the *DA*, Cambridge, Trinity College, MS R.5.33 (724), fos 77r-78v. These lists are printed in *JG*, 370-9.

12 *Infra*, ch.66.

13 *Infra*, ch.74.

14 The account of the dispute is found *infra*, ch.78 and it was also reported by William in *GR*, 329 and *GP*, 197. Its notoriety is revealed by its being mentioned also in *ASC, sub anno* 1083, by Orderic Vitalis, *Ecclesiastical History* II, 271, and in the chronicle of John of Worcester, Oxford, Corpus Christi College, MS 157, fos 352-353.

15 *Infra*, ch.76 and for the course of the quarrel see *SHE*, 54-73.

16 See n.2 above, and *infra*, ch.74.

17 On the possibility of Glastonbury's importance in trade see M. Deanesly, ch.1. On the pre-Saxon settlement see H. M. Taylor and J. Taylor, 251-257 and C. A.

Ralegh Radford, 97-110. Compare the more cautious remarks by P. Rahtz, 'Glastonbury Tor', 111-122.

18 Taylor and Taylor, 251-257.

19 On St Patrick see R. P. C. Hanson. Note that 'B's Life of Dunstan provides evidence that St Patrick was being venerated at Glastonbury as early as the first half of the tenth century (*MSD*, 10-11). On the Irish scholars see Finberg, 'St Patrick at Glastonbury', 76-7 but note the more cautious assessment of an Irish presence by M. Lapidge, 'The Cult of St Indract at Glastonbury'.

20 P. H. Sawyer (*S*) collects the verdicts of modern scholars.

21 I have collected some of the references in my notes to charters, *infra.*

22 See *MO*, 117-118 for the general situation, 712 for knight-service and 702 for the wealth of monasteries.

23 Quoted by R. W. Southern, 249-250, a cogent summary of the dilemma of the monks confronted with the fact of the Conquest and a masterly analysis of their response. Similar sentiments are expressed by the Abingdon chronicler in the *Historia Monasterii de Abingdon*, in *Chronicon Monasterii de Abingdon*, 483-7.

24 See n.13 above.

25 On Lanfranc, see *The Life of St Anselm*, 50-53; on Warin see *GP*, 421.

26 See Southern, and also Leclercq, esp. 156-9. The possibility that cartularies and charter-chronicles flourished when monasteries were beginning to recover from a period of depression is raised in the discussion following R. H. Bautier, 853-5.

27 *GR*, 389. On Goscelin, see *The Life of King Edward*, 91-111.

28 On Osbert, see *The Letters of Osbert of Clare*, and A. Wilmart, 261-286. On Caradoc, see C. N. L. Brooke, 'The Archbishops of St David's, Llandaff and Caerleon-on-Usk', 201-242, especially 228-9, where he points out that it is 'coming to be more generally realised that forgery was a profession' and describes Caradoc as 'simply a professional hagiographer'.

29 A good example of the attempt to preserve local tradition is the case of Crowland, whose monks provided William with information about the translation of St Neot, incorporated by him in the *GP*, 321-2, and Orderic Vitalis with the same information, (II, xxiv-xxvi and 339-343).

30 For the possible motives of the monks see A. Gransden, 'The Growth of the Glastonbury Legends', especially 337-8 and the references cited there. Osbern's assertion is in his *Life of Dunstan* in *MSD*, 77-8 and William's criticism of it in *ibid.*, 251 and *infra*, ch.55.

31 *Infra*, 2.

32 *MSD*, 250, and 250, 252, 253 for subsequent remarks.

33 In his introduction to the *GR*, xxix-xxx. Apart from the passage indicated in the preceding note there is the following reference in *MSD*, 252, . . . *fraternitate qua vobis obnoxius sum obedientiam meam pulsatis* . . .

34 *The Monastic Constitutions of Lanfranc*, 114-5. On confraternity in English monasteries see *MO*, 475-479. Note William's appeal to the monks of Worcester, at the end of his *VW* (67) to offer masses for him on as many days as he has spent nights labouring for Wulfstan.

35 On the extent of William's travels see R. M. Thomson, 'The Reading of William of Malmesbury', 392-3. William was not slow to acknowledge hospitality when he encountered it; note his remarks about Winchester in *GR*, 516. See his praise of the monastery of Reading too in *GP*, 193.

36 Compare the opening of the present text with that of *VW*, 2-3.

37 *Infra*, 1-2. William defends in similar fashion the digression in *GR* on the history of the Franks, *nec multum a proposito elongabar* . . ., 69.

38 *MSD*, 412-422.
39 *Ibid.*, 416.
40 *Infra*, chs 23-25; the last of these chapters relates the rediscovery of the body after the fire of 1184.
41 See Thomson, 'Reading of William of Malmesbury', 369-70 & 392 and the same author's 'William of Malmesbury and the Letters of Alcuin', 154. Note also his partisanship in the Canterbury/York controversy: Gransden, *Historical Writing*, 176-7.
42 His plea that he had admirably fulfilled his other tasks is found *infra*, 2.
43 *Infra*, 3. Ch. 55 is devoted to St Dunstan but records only the lands given to the monastery during his abbacy, as opposed to the details supplied about Paulinus and David, for instance. William's use of the pronouns *uos* and *uobis* in ch. 83 suggests that at that time he had the monks in mind as his readers; the preface he added later.

2: Sources and Models for the *De Antiquitate*

1 *GP*, 196-8.
2 Besides the accounts of the Glastonbury relics and saints there is a version of the quarrel between abbot Thurstan and the monks varying from that in the *ASC, sub anno* 1083.
3 *GP*, 197.
4 *JG*, 370-5; on the manuscript see my chapter 5 below.
5 Keynes, 164-186; for the earlier date, *SHE*, 44-7, and Finberg, *Wessex*, 14.
6 Cf. the notorious Canterbury forgeries and the Book of Llandaff.
7 Keynes, 168-170.
8 *VSD*, 252.
9 Osbern's work, *VSD*, 250: and 'B's, *ibid.*, 252.
10 Thomson, 'Reading of William of Malmesbury', records these in his appendix and also notes that the *VSD* contains a reference to Aethelwold's English translation of the *Rule of St Benedict*, in a version with a prologue by the translator.
11 'B' remarks that Irish pilgrims frequented Glastonbury . . . *maxime ob beati Patricii junioris* (*senioris* in the MS that William apparently used) *honorem, qui faustus ibidem in Domino quievisse narratur. MSD*, 10-11. Osbern notes the legend too; *ibid.*, 75.
12 Leland refers to the lost *VP* in both his *Commentarii*, 36-40 and *Collectanea*, III, 273-6. John's account of Patrick is found in Carley, 73-87. It is interesting to note that Leland could find no trace of the third book of the *Life*, in which William would have dealt with the saint's return to England and his arrival at Glastonbury.
13 See Slover's article and *Four Latin Lives of St Patrick*, 22-4.
14 This is clear from Leland's summary. He notes that *Gul: Meld: frequenter citat librum Patritii de confessione . . ., Collectanea*, 273. Bieler overlooks this and so argues (*Four Latin Lives*, 24) that William must have known the *Life* by Muirchu; in fact everything that Bieler thinks is taken from Muirchu can be found in the *Confessio.*
15 The only reference to Glastonbury in the *Lives* available to William is the identification in the *vita tertia* of Patrick's burial place Dun Lecglaisse with Glastonbury, *Four Latin Lives*, 183.

16 Carley, 84-8 is clearly based on William's *Life*, as is revealed by its similarities to the relevant sections of *DA* and *GR*. The *Life* collected by John of Tynemouth, printed in *Nova Legenda Angliae*, 112-114, is certainly not William's although there are sufficient similarities to suggest derivation from a common tradition.

17 The incident is in *Four Latin Lives*, 141-2 and is repeated by John, (Carley, 84). The inscription on his tomb, recorded by William, (*GR*, 27) suggests that the monks had known the story earlier. See Finberg, 'St Patrick at Glastonbury', 82-3.

18 One is mentioned in the *DA*, chapter 13 and there is a fuller account in Carley, 85-6. None are related in the *GR* which contents itself with noting that there were some when the saint's body was translated (27).

19 For text and commentary see Lapidge, 'The Cult of St Indract at Glastonbury', 199-212. It is quite possible that the Old English Life was still extant in 1247 and was the volume in the library described as 'passionale sanctorum anglice script. vetust. inutil', *JG*, II, 436.

20 *DA*, chs11 & 15 and *GR*, 26-7 & 27-8.

21 *ASC, sub anno* 167 but the same information was available in Bede, *HE*, bk.1, ch.4 and in the *Liber Pontificalis*, both known to William.

22 *DA*, ch.2 and *GR*, 24. Freculph says of St Philip, *Philippus . . . Gallis praedicat Christum barbarasque gentes vicinasque tenebris et tumenti Oceano coniunctas ad scientiae lucem fideique portum deducit. PL* 106.1148. The library catalogue of Glastonbury lists a volume of Freculph in the library in the mid-thirteenth century.

23 *DA*, ch. 8 and *GR*, 26 draw on Bede, *HE*, bk.1, chs 17-22.

24 *GP*, 4.

25 The quotation comes from *GR*, 1; note also the remarks in *ibid.*, 58-67. Bede's *Historia Abbatum* is printed by C. Plummer, *Baedae Opera Historica*, (Oxford, 1896), I, 364-87.

26 *GP*, 328.

27 *DA*, prologue and chapter 32.

28 *Infra*, chs 67 and 54.

29 *Infra*, ch.8. Some visions are recorded.

30 As he does when treating of the reign of King Ine who occupies the centre of the stage because of his generosity to the church.

31 A. Gransden, 'The Growth of the Glastonbury Traditions', 337-8.

32 See Gransden, 'The Growth of the Glastonbury Traditions'; Sumption; and Rollason (esp. 79-86).

33 On 'chronicle-cartularies' see G. R. C. Davis, xiii and (for continental examples of the tenth and eleventh centuries) R. H. Bautier, 816-22.

34 On works produced at Durham and Evesham, see Gransden, *Historical Writing*, 111-122.

35 Hermann's work is in *Memorials of St Edmund's Abbey*, I, 26-92. There is an example of his use of charter evidence on 48.

36 Miracles: *Memorials of St Edmund's Abbey*, I, 58-9, 79-80, etc.; the bishop's claim, 60-67; the translation of relics, 84-5.

37 *VW*, 1 and 54.

38 R. M. Thomson ('William of Malmesbury's Edition of the *Liber Pontificalis*') has pointed out that William apparently did not know the late eleventh-century Passional from Worcester as had seemed likely. It is possible that he knew the Worcester copy of the epigrams and inscriptions compiled by bishop Milred of

Worcester; see Lapidge, 'Some Remnants of Bede's lost Liber Epigrammatum'. On William's searching out of historical material see Thomson, 'Reading of William of Malmesbury', 392-4 and note his contribution to the building up of the library at Malmesbury as reported in *GP*, 431.

39 See the comments by Thomson, 'Reading of William of Malmesbury', 393-4 and note the conclusion by R. I. Page, 87: 'Clearly William's and Florence's (episcopal) lists are closely related, though all that can be said on the basis of the present examination is that they share a common source.' For 'Florence' here read John.

40 *Hemingi Chartularium Ecclesiiae Wigorniensis*; see also N. R. Ker, 49-75.

41 See N. R. Ker and *Hemingi Chartularium*, 285 and 391, as well as the quote that follows.

42 *Hemingi Chartularium*, 282.

43 *Hemingi Chartularium*, 248-9 and 270-3.

44 *Hemingi Chartularium*, 405-8.

45 The last entry, on f.3v, reads: *Ecclesiam quoque sitam in villam que nominata Westbyria anno Dominice incarnationis MXCIII usibus monachorum Wigornensium concessit. Sed eam successor illius Samson episcopus abstulit.*

46 The list of the bishops of Worcester in this brief account is different from William's list in the *GP*, but this is not a decisive consideration.

47 f.1.

48 I have used the diplomatic edition (*The Text of the Book of Llan Dâv*). The date of its compilation cannot be determined exactly but W. Davies ('Liber Landavensis: its construction and credibility') argues that the core of it was composed between 1120 and 1129 and certainly no later than 1140. R. I. Jack believes that it was certainly completed before 1133 or 1134.

49 W. Davies, 'Saint Mary's Worcester and the Liber Landavensis', 460.

50 In C. N. L. Brooke, 'The Archbishops of St David's, Llandaff and Caerleon-on-Usk', 230.

51 These links are uncovered by Davies, 'St Mary's Worcester and the Liber Landavensis'.

52 The twelfth-century chronicle, conflated with a later one, is in *Chronicon Monasterii de Abingdon*, I. The text can be clarified by reference to F. Stenton, *The Early History of the Abbey of Abingdon.*

53 *Chronicon Monasterii de Abingdon*, I, 9 n.1.

54 The chronicler discusses the Danish invasions, for instance, (*Chronicon Monasterii de Abingdon*) 37-8 and the rule of abbot Cynatus on 59, n.1.

55 *Liber Eliensis*. (The date of composition and the authorship of the work are discussed on xlvi-xlix).

56 His sources are outlined in *Liber Eliensis*, xxviii-xlii.

57 That the author sought out information on his monastery's abbots is revealed by what he says about abbot Leofwin: *Huius vero mentionem in scriptis nostris nusquam reperimus, nisi tantum in cronico Anglico legitur . . .*, *Liber Eliensis*, 149.

3: The *De Antiquitate* and William's historical output

1 Southern, 23.

2 See Funkenstein, and the remark by Roger D. Ray in 'Medieval Historiography Through the Twelfth Century'.

3 See Hanning, 44-90.
4 *GP*, 70-2; for Eadmer see *MSD*, 237-8. On William's use of Eadmer see R. W. Southern, *St Anselm and his Biographer* (Cambridge, 1963), 247 and note; and for other examples of his harsh judgement of the pre-Conquest church see R. R. Darlington.
5 Dom. J. Leclercq, 156-62; the quotation is from 157.
6 The view of William. J. Brandt (see especially chapter 2); and note the remarks by R. W. Hanning on Brandt's book in his review of Lacroix, *L'Historien Au Moyen Age* in *History and Theory*, 12, 1973, 419-34.
7 Note the suggestive remarks by J. Campbell, 159-90.
8 *GP*, 4.
9 *Supra*, ch.1.
10 *GP*, 420 and *MO*, 105 & 114.
11 *GP*, 420-1 and E. J. Kealey, 112-114.
12 *GR*, 518.
13 *Infra*, 41.
14 This and the full account of the commissioning of the work are found in the letter to the Empress Matilda preserved in MS Troyes 924 *bis*. It is printed by E. Köngsen, 'Zwei unbekannte Briefe zu den Gesta Regum Anglorum'. On Queen Matilda as a patron see William's flattering remarks in the earlier letter in the same MS to King David of Scotland, *ibid.*, 212 and *GR*, 493-5. Note also the remarks by R. R. Bezzola, pt. 2, II, 422-6.
15 *GR*, 2.
16 The purport of the letters is that Queen Matilda's only fault was that she left their church without a pastor and that the monks hope that the Empress or the King will rectify that shortcoming. 'Zwei unbekannte Briefe', 212.
17 *GR*, 103-4.
18 *GR*, 103 & 283 for example.
19 *GR*, 69 & 358 are examples.
20 *GR*, 2 & 96-9.
21 *GR*, 259-60 & 518; see also 166.
22 *GP*, 277.
23 A concern that he would have learnt from Bede.
24 Southern, 255.
25 Thus he criticises Faricius in *GP*, 330-1 and Osbern in *VSD*, 250-2.
26 *VW*, 2. On William's customary approach of modifying his sources see R. M. Thomson, 'William of Malmesbury and the Letters of Alcuin', 151 and the references cited there.
27 *GR*, 389.
28 The sceptic was Osbern (*MSD*, 251) and William's comment is found *infra*, ch.55.
29 In his preface to volume 2 of *GR*, cxxxii.
30 *GR*, 29-31.
31 *GR*, 154.
32 *GR*, 173.
33 *ASC sub annis* 716 & 757; *GR*, 79-84; *GP*, 9-11.
34 *Councils*, 3, 350-87. *S*, 92.
35 See *GP*, 386-7, for example (speculation on abbot Aldhelm).
36 *DA*, ch.70.
37 *DA*, ch.35 and *GR*, 28-9.
38 *DA*, chs 38 and 51.
39 Thus Wealdhun is said to have ruled for 32 years because William had seen a grant to him dated 762 and one to his successor dated 794. *DA*, ch. 48.

40 *SHE*, ch. 2 (especially 26-7 for his judgement on William's calculations).
41 Knowles, Brooke and London, 7.
42 The editors of *Heads of Religious Houses* have devoted a special section to the problems of the pre-Conquest period (12-16); on difficulties of bishops' dates see M. A. O'Donovan, 23-44.
43 *GP*, 4.
44 *GP*, 186.
45 *GP*, 383-4.
46 *GP*, 298-9.
47 *DA*, ch. 32, and *GR*, 25-6.
48 *Radulphi de Coggeshall*, 36.
49 *DA*, ch. 35 and *GR*, 29.
50 *DA*, ch. 54.
51 Benignus, *DA*, ch. 33 and *GR*, 27. Note also Tyccea's inscription in *DA*, ch. 47.
52 See the quotation from Isidore cited by Funkenstein, 4; and on the vital role of orally delivered messages see the example of the delicate matter between Henry II and Frederick Barbarossa where the crux of the former's message is to be delivered by Herbert of Bosham personally, B. Smalley, *The Becket Conflict*, 60. On this whole question see now M. T. Clanchy.
53 Bede, *HE*, Preface. William remarks on the reliability of Bede and his informants in *GR*, 260-1 and on the authority of Luke and Gregory in *ibid.*, 357.
54 In *GR*, 104 and *BVM*, 63. There is a clear connection between the reliability of oral testimony and the holiness of the informant.
55 *VW*, 67.
56 *GP*, 327. It is the barbarous sound of their names that offends William.
57 *GR*, 344-5.
58 *GR*, 155.
59 *GR*, 161.
60 *GR*, 229.
61 *GR*, 447. Orderic Vitalis also distinguishes between oral and written evidence, as his remarks in book vi reveal (III, 282-4). On these remarks by Orderic see R. D. Ray, 'Orderic Vitalis and his Readers', esp. 24-5. Ray, however, seems to think that Orderic ought to be interested in the same facts as modern historians.
62 *GP*, 356-7. Note a similar defence of oral reports by the author of the *Liber Eliensis*, 30.
63 *MSD*, 10-11 ('B's' Life) and 75 (Osbern).
64 See the discussion in my chapter 2.
65 *GR*, 27.
66 *GR*, 28; the interpolated version is in *DA*, ch. 16.
67 William's account of Patrick is found in *GR*, 26-7 and *DA*, chs 8, 10 & 11. See also the discussion in my chapter 2 above and the references cited there.
68 The phrases *traditio maiorum GR*, 28 and *traditio patrum DA*, ch. 19 are given as the source for the account of Paulinus' restoration of the church at Glastonbury. William even warns of uncertainty about a church at Malmesbury said to have been built by Meildulf, *GP*, 345.
69 See 4 above.
70 William's account of Gildas is in *GR*, 24 and *DA*, ch. 7. Caradoc's *Life* is printed in *Gildas, De Excidio*, II, 395-413; see esp. 409-11.
71 Caradoc was probably at Glastonbury when William was, or at least soon after, C. N. L. Brooke, 'The Archbishops of St David's ', 230.

72 William's comments on the Arthur stories are in *GR*, 11. Evidence of political obligations influencing his historical presentation is given by R. B. Patterson.
73 The charter is in *DA*, ch. 65 and the introduction to it is in ch. 64. William's main account of the relations between Cnut and Edmund is in *GR*, 214-7.
74 *DA*, chs 49-51.
75 Modern accounts are found in *SHE*, 38 n3 and W. Levison, 249-51.
76 Bede, *HE*, bk.1, ch.4; *ASC sub anno* 167.
77 William's account is in ch. 2 *infra.*
78 *GR*, 24, with which compare ch. 2 *infra* where a later reader has tampered with the text and removed the expression of uncertainty about the hypothesis.

4: Forgery and the interpolations in the *De Antiquitate*

1 On the importance of the financial contributions of pilgrims, especially in the building of churches, see C. R. Cheney, and (more generally) J. Sumption.
2 A full account of the dispute is given by Adam of Domerham in *AD*, 352ff.
3 A. Gransden, 'The Growth of the Glastonbury Traditions'. Note that her claim that 'undoubtedly most of the interpolations were made soon' after the fire of 1184 (347) has had to be modified; see my ch.5.
4 See J. A. Robinson, *Two Glastonbury Legends*, 40-1, for an example of the way in which the prestige of Joseph of Arimathea was used.
5 *DA*, ch.2 and *GR*, 23-4.
6 *DA*, chs 1, 2 & 9. Note the comment in *GR*, 23-4, *quamvis longae situs aetatis consumpserit nomina* referring to the disciples sent by Pope Eleutherius.
7 On the date see my ch. 5 and the references therein.
8 On Joseph see Robinson, *Two Glastonbury Legends*, and V. M. Lagorio.
9 See n. 52 to ch. 2, *supra*, and M. Biddle *et al.*
10 Just as the British king was said to have been generous to Joseph and his followers and later to Phagan and Deruvian, *DA*, chs 1 & 2, so the Abingdon chronicler asserted that: *Obtinuit autem memoratus Abbenus a rege Brittonum, ad precum suarum instantiam, maximam partem Berroccensis provinciae . . . Chronicon Monasterii de Abingdon*, 2.
11 On the Westminster legend see *The History of Westminster Abbey*; *The Life of King Edward*, 113 and M. Bloch, 'La Vie de S. Edouard' (especially 83, n. 2 where Bloch points out that Osbert added another miracle to the received stories). The Glastonbury claim goes back as far as St Dunstan's biographer 'B', *MSD*, 7.
12 *HE*, bk.4, ch.19. The revised version is in the *Liber Eliensis*, 33 and the expulsion of the clerks by St Aethelwold is in *ibid.*, 74-5.
13 See Gransden, *Historical Writing*, 392-3.
14 See references in note 1, above.
15 See my ch.1. William's first reference to the *DA*, in his *VSD* where he announces his intention of writing it, reinforces the importance which the Glastonbury relics had assumed for him. *Quomodo autem et quo auctore reliquiae sanctorum ex Transumbranis Glastoniam sint advectae, in libro de Antiquitate eiusdem Ecclesiae accepta inserere non pigebit, si Deus mentem meam ad quod intendo direxerit. VSD*, 271.
16 On the popularity of these saints see Cheney, 351 & 357-8 and Sumption, 150-1 & 122.

17 The fire and its effects are described in *AD*, 332-4.
18 The events concerning St Dunstan are described in *DA*, chs 23-25.
19 *DA*, ch.7 insists that Gildas was buried before the altar although William in *GR*, 24 knows nothing of it; and *DA*, ch.16 records the translation of the remains of St David whereas in *GR*, 28 William declared: *De hoc sane egregio et incomparabili viro, utrum ibi obierit, an in sede propria vitam finierit, incertum habeo.*
20 See the remarks of Gerald of Wales (*Giraldi Cambrensis Opera*, IV, 49-51). The other outside chroniclers do not attribute the inspiration to Henry; see Gransden, 'The Growth of the Glastonbury Traditions'.
21 *DA*, chs 34 and 5. It only became necessary to identify Glastonbury with Avalon after the supposed exhumation.
22 See Gransden, 'The Growth of the Glastonbury Traditions', and W. A. Nitze.
23 *Chronicon Monasterii de Abingdon*, 7.
24 St David's altar in *DA*, ch.30 is an obvious example and note the crucifixes described in chs 26-28.
25 See *The letters of Osbert of Clare*, 87-8 and B. Smalley, 'Gilbertus Universalis and the "Glossa Ordinaria" ', 245.
26 Osbert's Life is printed by Bloch, and the earlier Life that he used in *Life of King Edward*, whose editor challenges (xxx-xli) Bloch's contention that Osbert was not dependent on the earlier anonymous Life.
27 The miracles are in Bloch, 112-20 and the translation on 121-3.
28 The changes are found in Bloch, 71, 73 & 110, with which compare the versions in the anonymous Life, *Life of King Edward*, 7, 10-11 & 79.
29 Ailred's Life is printed in *PL*, 115, 737-90; see for the changes mentioned coll.752-4 & 755-7 and *Life of King Edward*, xxxv-xxxvi. Analogous to Ailred's remarks about St Peter as a future patron are William's statement about the Glastonbury saints: *Nullum de his crediderim deperire caelo, quos egressos corpore tot patronorum excipit laus vel excusatio. GR*, 29, *DA*, ch.18.
30 See the discussion by B. W. Scholz.
31 Hence at St Edmund's the writings of Hermann, Osbert, an anonymous hagiographer, Geoffrey and Samson; on Canterbury see Sumption, ch.4.
32 *Liber Eliensis*, 231 and xxvii-xxxviii.
33 The letter (*MSD*, 412-22) is discussed in ch.1.
34 The quotation is from Robinson, *Two Glastonbury Legends*, 42. The manuscript is described by J. A. Bennett, 117-22.
35 *AD*, 445-7, 453.
36 *AD*, 425-36. Typical is the description of Glastonbury by the monks of Canterbury as *celebris olim religione et hospitalitate, ibid.*, 432.
37 These are the charters of Ine (*S*250), *DA*, ch.42 and *GR*, 36-9; of Edmund (*S*499), *DA*, ch.56, *GR*, 158-9; and of Edgar (*S*783), *DA*, ch.60, *GR*, 170-2.
38 *DA*, ch.60, *GR*, 171.
39 *DA*, ch.9.
40 See *Liber Eliensis*, 4 & 162 and the discussion of some of the problems in *ibid.*, 402-4. Note also E. Miller, esp. 8-14, 25-35 and 232-9.
41 In addition to the references in the previous note see also *Liber Eliensis*, xlix-l.
42 The charter in Bloch, 87-91 is an example. See the discussion in Scholz, and in M. Brett, 59-60 & 133.
43 These charters are *S*995, *S*1045 and *S*1046.
44 The Bury additions to the chronicle are in *Memorials of St Edmund's*, I, 340-56. The charters are on 340 & 342-4 and the account of Herbert's journey on 353-

4. An account of the struggle between the monastery and its bishop is given, with a document presenting the episcopal side, by V. H. Galbraith.

45 See the discussion in Morey and Brooke, 124-46 and for a study of a house which forged copies of many documents whose originals they still possessed see C. N. L. Brooke, 'Episcopal Charters for Wix Priory'.

46 See the lists in Keynes, 293-301.

47 These are the charters recorded in note 37 above. They were not incorporated in the *Liber Terrarum*, despite the fact that it was compiled not long before William's visit to Glastonbury, and their first recorded appearance was in the *DA* and then in the later recensions of the *GR*.

48 The story of king Arthur and Ider, *DA*, ch. 34, is concluded with the statement that the king established 24 monks at Glastonbury to pray for the soul of Ider and gave them lands to sustain themselves. A fourteenth century annotator identifies the actual estates involved. The charter of St Patrick records that Phagan and Deruvian were given 12 portions of land, *DA*, ch. 9.

49 On forgery at Westminster see T. A. M. Bishop and P. Chaplais; and P. Chaplais.

50 See *MO*, 425-6 and the figures he lists on 713-14 which show that Glastonbury fell from 72 in about 1160 to 50 in about 1200.

5: The Manuscripts of the *De Antiquitate*

1 Chs 3 and 30.

2 Ch. 25; for other revisions made after the fire see the notes to the appropriate chapters.

3 Ch. 34, parts of ch. 31 and ch. 5.

4 The charter is ch. 9 and Robinson's discussion of it is in *SHE*, 14-7. The dispute between Glastonbury and its diocesan bishop is described in *ibid.*, chs 3 & 6; see also *MO*, 327-30.

5 On the *History of the Holy Grail* see Loomis, 112-23. On the progress of the legend of Joseph at Glastonbury see Lagorio and, more generally J. A. Robinson, *Two Glastonbury Legends.*

6 The first two chapters show a dominance of present participles, seven most unclassical uses of the gerund, six subordinate clauses with *qui* and one each with *quia* and *cum*; the subjunctive is not used. The charter eschews the gerund, uses *cum* with the subjunctive nine times and has seven subordinate clauses with *quod*, three with *qui*, three with *ut*, one with *quoniam* and one with *nisi*. Chapter two claims that Phagan and Deruvian had dedicated a church to Saints Peter and Paul whereas the charter has them dedicating an oratory to St Michael.

7 For the propaganda associated with the exhumation see W. A. Nitze, and Gransden, 'The Growth of the Glastonbury Traditions', esp. 355-8.

8 The rewriting involved more than just interpolating marginal additions because sometimes the text had to be harmonised with the additions and sometimes sentences had to be reconstructed; note too the intelligent historical speculation in chapter 35. The section of the local history which takes the story of the monastery down to 1230 was copied into the Trinity MS by the scribe who wrote in 1247 while the rest of the history which carries the story down to 1290 is in a later hand. The same monk can hardly have been responsible both for the history down to 1230 and the continuation to 1290.

9 The accuracy of the Trinity text, especially where it can be compared with the *GR*, (23-9 and the relevant chapters of the *DA*, for example), demands that we postulate as few recensions between it and William's original text as are possible to account for it. That is why I suggest that the scribe of the Trinity MS was also the author of chapters one and two.

10 M. R. James, II, 198-202.

11 The catalogue is found on fols 102r-103v and is printed in Hearne, *JG*, II, 423-44.

12 Described in Hardy, *Materials*, iii, 150. See also H. O. Coxe, col. 529.

13 See *GR*, 28.

14 See *GR*, 158-9 and 170-2 and *DA*, chs 56 and 60.

15 This interpolation, which in M follows chapter one, is on 46 *infra*.

16 For examples of the way in which William adapted his own work see R. M. Thomson, 'William of Malmesbury and the Letters of Alcuin'. The variants between the two versions, which are noted in the text *infra*, amount to no more than changes in word order, the substitution of synonyms and the omission or addition of rhetorical phrases.

17 The speculations in CL (found in C fol. 87r as the relevant section of L does not survive) about the derivation of the name Glastonbury – *Glastinburi . . . que antiquitus a Britannis Yniswitrin nominabatur, ynis in Britannico sermone, insula Latine, wytrin Britannice, uitrea Latine, unde Yniswitrin insula uitrea quoque est ante Glastey, sed post aduentum Anglorum expulsis Britonibus, qui modo dicitur Wallenses, uocata est Glastengbury ex origine uocabuli, scilicet glasse Anglice, uitrum Latine et bury Anglice, ciuitas Latine, inde Glastyngbury, ut prescriptum est* – are taken from Caradoc's *Life of Gildas*, 410-12. The historiography of the life of Indract is inordinately complex. William's Life is lost but there does survive another twelfth century Life in Oxford, Bodleian Library, MS Digby 112 fols 98v-102v, and John of Glastonbury also preserved details from an earlier Life, (Carley, 123-6), presumed to be William's. John and L agree with William's *GR*, 27 in giving Indract seven companions against the nine of Digby; and John and L assert that the martyrdom took place at Shapewick whereas Digby says Hywic. However, John and Digby agree in attributing the martyrdom to the time of King Ine while L claims that it took place in Patrick's time; the *GR* is ambiguous, assigning the martyrdom to sometime after Patrick's death but claiming that the translation of his body by King Ine occurred *postmodum*. Even if the source of L's account (on fol. 8r) cannot be ascertained it is clear that he was using a work other than T – indeed he himself refers to a book *de gestis eorum* at Glastonbury.

18 The marginal additions on 46 and 68 of my edition, for instance, and the errors *fedeliores* (74), *angustior* (68), *recongnoscat* (100) and the mistaken date for the translation of Benignus on 62.

19 Among the saints whose relics are said to be at Glastonbury ch. 21 lists Selfrid; in T the original reading was Sigfridi but dots were placed below the Sig and Sel was written above; L reads Sigfridi (fol. 8r) while M reads Seifridi. In another case L has picked up a correction but M has not; the *Hic est Glasteing* on 9 reads in T *Hinc*, with a dot placed under the 'n'; L has made the correction but M has not. An intermediate manuscript would not have allowed such variations. To this evidence we can add that some of the marginal additions in T which were incorporated by M were in fact added to T after the copying of M as the hand that added them reveals. These additions, the notes on fol. 1v of T, 4 *infra*, for

example, are found in L from where M must have taken them. One of the later interpolators of T then added them to its margin.

20 The most notable example concerns the date of the translation of the remains of Benignus which took place in 1091. Both T and M read, in chapter 13, *anno nongentesimo primo* but L has corrected this to *anno M^O nonagesimo primo* and C reproduces this correct reading.

21 These manuscripts are:

London, British Library, MS Cotton Vesp.D.xxii, fols 2r-16r, V, a fifteenth century manuscript with extracts from the *DA*, based on M, preceding an edition of John of Glastonbury.

London, British Library, MS Cotton Titus A.xix, fols 19r-23r, a fifteenth century manuscript with a few extracts from the *DA* and other information about Glastonbury; probably based on T, and certainly contains nothing that could be William's original work.

London, British Library, MS Cotton Titus F. vi, fols 35v-44v, a sixteenth century manuscript with selected extracts from the *DA* based on T.

London, British Library, MS Cotton Vitellius C. ix, fols 255v-266r, a sixteenth century manuscript, partially burnt and remounted in a modern volume, which contains extracts from T.

London, British Library, MS Cotton Vitellius E. v, fols 131r-146v, a sixteenth century manuscript with extracts from the *DA* based on either T or M.

London, British Library, MS Harley 247, fols 11-11v, contains a copy of the charter of St Patrick, information on the churches of Glastonbury and a report on the benefactions of King Ine. It is not textually important.

London, British Library, MS Harley 258, fols 112v-120v, a sixteenth century manuscript with extracts from the *DA*. It appears to have been copied from V.

London, British Library, MS Harley 6148, fols 67-68v, a sixteenth or seventeenth century manuscript with a few extracts from the *DA* referring to Arthur, Joseph and some of the Glastonbury saints. It offers no important textual variants.

Cambridge, University Library, MS Mm. 3.27, a sixteenth century manuscript with extracts, sometimes complete, from the first 35 chapters of the *DA*. It seems to have been based on T, or another manuscript in that family, and is not textually important.

Oxford, Bodleian Library, MS Rawlinson B.201 (15503) is one of Hearne's transcripts.

Oxford, Bodleian Library, MS Bodley 957 (27593) is a seventeenth century manuscript copied from V.

I have seen all these manuscripts and verified that they have no independent textual value.

22 There is a description of this unusual manuscript by J. A. Bennett. On the custom of keeping schedules of miracles for shrines see *Life of King Edward*, xxxiii and on the advertising of miracles see Sumption, 152-3.

23 *AD*, a competent edition also based on T with some of M's variants noted. Hearne records the variants between his edition and Gale's.

24 T. Gale, *Scriptores quindecimi*, etc., (Oxford, 1691), 289-335; and reprinted in *PL*, clxxix, 1681-1734.

25 F. Lomax, *The Antiquities of Glastonbury by William of Malmesbury*, (London, 1908). I have not seen H. F. S. Stokes, *Glastonbury Abbey before the Conquest*, (Glastonbury, 1932) which includes, I believe, a translation of the *DA*.

NOTES TO THE TEXT

1 Henry of Blois, abbot of Glastonbury 1126-1171 and bishop of Winchester 1129-1171. On him see *DA*, ch.83. For *'viscera Christi'* see Philip., 1. 8 etc.

2 Compare the similar remarks in William's Preface to his *VW*, 2.

3 William's two books on St Dunstan are printed in *MSD*, 250-324. Compare his remarks in the Preface to Book 2 (*ibid.*, 288).

4 William echoes these words in the passage, in the later recensions of *GR* (23), in which he introduces the Glastonbury material.

5 On these works by William, which are no longer extant, see my ch.2 *supra* and the references cited therein.

6 There is another example of this unusual phrase in *GP*, 70.

7 Lucan, *Pharsalia*, IX, 726-7.

8 Cf. *GR*, 23; n.4 *supra*. The Preface I take to be William's own work, but before outlining my reasons for this belief let me say a few words about the problem of disentangling William's original text from its later accretions. The earliest investigators of the problem, who were drawn to the text because of its Arthurian material, were favourable to the authenticity of most of it; see G. Baist, R. Thurneysen, and F. Lot. The first scholar to appreciate the significance of the Glastonbury interpolations in the later recensions of the *GR* was Newell and he tried to assess the authenticity of the whole work, although his main interest was also Arthurian. His technique was pursued more rigorously by Robinson but he confined his investigation to the early part of the work; see *SHE*, 1-25. The guidelines laid down by these two scholars are the ones on which I base my own discussion of the authenticity of various parts of the *DA*, with the caveat made by Slover that care must be taken to appreciate the essentially different purposes of the *DA* and the *GR*. Not all material William incorporated in the former would have been considered appropriate for the latter; see C. H. Slover, 'William of Malmesbury and the Irish'.

There is no doubt that at least part of the Preface is William's work because of the parallels between sentences in it and in the *GR*; *supra*, n.4 and Newell, 466 to which should be added a correspondence earlier in the Preface: *Uerumtamen ne quid sedulitas mee desit officio eiusdem ecclesie uestre rudimentum et processum in huius libri auspicio repetens ab origine pandam*. These parallels reveal William searching through his own Preface to obtain a suitable introduction to the Glastonbury material that he had determined to insert into the *GR*. A lengthier parallel with the *VW* was noted above, *supra*, ch.1, n.35. Given the ample evidence that William had no hesitation in borrowing from one of his works for another – apart from the use made of the *DA* in the *GR* we can mention the dream of Brihtwold, *GR*, 272 and *GP*, 182 and the translation of Cuthbert, *GR*, 516 and *GP*, 274-5 – we can conclude that much of the Preface was certainly his work. For the rest there would have been little incentive for the monks to interpolate remarks about the overall aim of the work or for them to add the eulogy of Henry of Blois, from which William alone, as the author, might stand to gain.

Although these considerations, together with the style and unity of the Preface, convince me that it is William's work two possible objections must be countered. Newell considered that the Preface had been interpolated and quoted the following passage as evidence: *Unde, sicut estimo, non contemnende stilum dedi opere, qui beati Dunstani . . . uitam labore meo eterne mandaui memorie, duosque libros de hoc, uolentibus Glastonie fratribus filiis uestris, dominis et sociis meis, dudum integra rerum ueritate absolui.* He comments that 'William is not in the habit of such self-laudation; the passage is evidently falsified' (460, n. 5 and 466). This is not convincing because William was aware of his own ability and because this passage is laudatory rather of Dunstan, whose life demands the best that an author can produce, than of William. Besides the passage is reminiscent of one in *VW*, 3, which reads: *Unde non contempnenda sicut opinor cura successit animo beati Wlstani episcopi Wigornensis uitam nequaquam posteris inuidere; sed eam stilo qualicumque eterne mandare memorie.* Newell's objection then is untenable and the other objection, that there is a contradiction between the Preface and the Preface to the second book of his *VSD*, has already been resolved by Robinson, *SHE*, 4.

9 See *Acts* 1.14, 4.32 and 6.7.

10 Cf. Freculph in *PL* 106.1148.

11 The sentiments, as well as some of the language, in this account of the reception of the missionaries by the king is obviously based on Bede's account of the first contacts between King Aethelberht and the Gregorian missionaries, *HE*, bk.1, chs 25 & 26, a parallel to which William himself drew attention by comparing Lucius with Aethelberht in *DA*, ch. 2.

12 St Patrick's charter forms ch. 9 of *DA*; with the exception of the *Life of Dunstan* by 'B', printed in *MSD*, 3-52, it is impossible to determine what other *scripta seniorum* are meant, if any.

13 *Ibid.*, 6-7.

14 Ch.1 is clearly interpolated. This conclusion depends partly on a clarification of the relationship between the *DA* and the *GR*. In his earliest extant works William argued that King Ine had been responsible for the foundation of Glastonbury (*GP*, 196 and *GR*, 35, n.1) but he revised this opinion after visiting Glastonbury and incorporated these new views in later recensions of the *GR* by the simple expedient of copying directly from the *DA*. We can therefore compare the chosen extracts with the extant text of the *DA* and, if such a comparison reveal contradictions, we can justifiably doubt the text of the *DA*. In the present case we read in *GR* (23-4) that William was ignorant of the names of the disciples sent by Pope Eleutherius, but in ch.1 they are given names. These names became well known only after 1136 with the popularity of Geoffrey of Monmouth. With this in mind, together with the crude latinity of the chapter, the troubles at Glastonbury in the late twelfth century and the late association of Joseph of Arimathea with Glastonbury (my ch. 5 *supra*), we can dismiss all of ch.1 as a later interpolation. Hence the body of the work begins with the opening words of ch. 2, which also serve to introduce the Glastonbury sections in *GR*.

15 This passage, a marginal addition in T, was obviously written in the thirteenth century after Joseph's name became associated with Glastonbury. The references in it are to later Arthurian and Arimathean works, for the details of which see Carley, 352 (66.7-14 and 66.14-19).

16 William was familiar with four sources for the story of the alleged request of King Lucius: *ASC sub anno* 167; Bede, *HE*, bk.1, ch.4; *Liber Pontificalis*, 136; and *The Chronicle of Aethelweard*, 5.

17 The opening sentences of this chapter are clearly William's work, being found in *GR*, 23. It is difficult to be certain about the comparison between Lucius and Aethelberht (inspired in part by Bede's *HE*, bk.1, ch.25) because it is not to be found in the *GR* (which jumps from . . . *uix auditam.* to *Uenerunt ergo* . . .). I incline to attribute it to William principally because of the sophisticated historical perspective that it embodies. On the other hand one of the revisers reveals, in ch.35, that he is capable of thoughtful historical speculation; besides one might argue that the comparison would have suited the broad context of *GR* and that William would not have omitted it had it been his work.

18 The naming of the disciples, and most of the rest of the chapter which deals with their deeds, is obviously the work of a later reviser. To the arguments for rejecting ch.1, which are also relevant here, we can add that this chapter claims that the church dedicated to Saints Peter and Paul was constructed by Phagan and Deruvian whereas William, in a later recension of *GR* (36) identified King Ine as the builder of that church. It is likely that 'gestaque Britannorum' refers to Geoffrey of Monmouth's *HRB*, which names the missionaries sent to King Lucius as Faganus and Duvianus, (124-5). Note that the very last line of the *Life of Merlin*, almost certainly written by Geoffrey, remarks that the book he wrote is now known as the 'Gesta Britonum': ed. G. Clarke, (Cardiff, 1973), 134.

19 Much of the description of the church and its foundation is taken from the *Life of Dunstan* quoted in ch.1; see *MSD*, 6-7.

20 With this paragraph we return to William's own work, but in a modified form. The words *ergo restaurata* were obviously added by a reviser to make the passage consistent with an earlier, apostolic foundation. *DA*'s *apud sanctum Edmundum* is to be preferred to *GR*'s *in nonullis locis* on the grounds that it is likely that William discovered other copies after leaving Glastonbury and so revised his work in the *GR* to take account of that. The other alternative, that the reviser specified Bury, is possible but there seems no reason for him to have done so and so the authority of the *DA* should stand. The phrase *mittente scilicet sancto Philippo apostolo* is clearly interpolated to maintain consistency with the claim of an apostolic origin. The sentence in the *GR* describing speculations about St Philip as *opinionum naenias*, however, could well have been added by William when he wrote the *GR* because, although a reviser would have been tempted to revise it had it been in the *DA*, it seems just as plausible that William, out of respect for his hosts, tactfully excluded such a comment from the *DA* but considered it desirable in *GR*, 24.

21 This reference to Henry of Blois in the past establishes that this chapter was not William's work since Henry did not die until 1171. The letter on which the chapter purports to be based is no longer known.

22 Almost certainly the work referred to here is the *Historia Brittonum* of Nennius. The author has combined a number of passages from Nennius, ed. T. Mommsen: *filii autem Liethan obtinuerunt in regione Demetorum et in aliis regionibus, id est Guir Cetgueli, donec expulsi sunt a Cuneda et a filiis eius ab omnibus Britannicis regionibus.* (156); *Mailcunus magnus rex apud Britonnes regnabat, id est in regione Guenedotae, quia atavus illius, id est Cunedag, cum filiis suis, quorum numerus octo erat, venerat prius de parte sinistrali. . .* (205). In particular the author must have had access to a version of Nennius, BL, MS Harley 3859 or a

lost copy of it, which contained the court pedigrees of Hywel the Good. The relevant pedigree, not printed by Mommsen, reads (A. Wade-Evans, 111): *(I) udnerth map Morgen, map Catgur, map Catmor, map Merguid, map Moriutned, map Morhen, map Morcant, map Botan, map Morgen, map Mormayl, map Glast, unde sunt Glastenic qui uenerunt que uocatur Loytcoyt.* The identification of Glasteing as a swineherd could have been suggested by the *vita tertia* of St Patrick which contains a passage in which the saint encounters a huge grave whose occupant is raised from the dead and identifies himself thus: *Ego sum Glas filius Cais, qui fuit* (*fui* in some MSS) *porcarius Lugir regis Hirote* (*Four Latin Lives*, 165). See further Newell, 475-6. Note that according to the previous chapter this chapter too is based on the letter of the monk Godfrey, post-dating Henry of Blois.

23 Escebtiorne cannot be identified.

24 The authenticity of chs 4 and 5 can be considered together. Scholars have disagreed on their genuineness, with Newell and Robinson rejecting them as interpolations and Slover accepting them as William's work. Newell's argument – that the reference to the interpolated first chapter condemns this one – is not persuasive because it applies only to the ablative absolute that introduces ch. 4 and that could have been added by a later reviser, (475). Robinson regards the mythological character of the work as foreign to William but this can hardly be decisive when the *GR*, for instance, is full of such material, (*SHE*, 12). Slover, 'William of Malmesbury and the Irish', argues that William's familiarity with the sources of the chapters makes him the likely author, but surely a later monk could have had access to them too. I regard both chapters as interpolated principally because of the reference to Avalon, which we know was made only after the claim to possess Arthur's bones. Admittedly ch. 4 does not refer directly to Avalon but the detail of Glasteing having found his sow under an apple tree so conveniently allows the identification that it must be regarded as suspect.

25 On the name Ynswitrin see H. P. R. Finberg, 'Ynyswitrin' in his *Lucerna*, but note that he is mistaken in regarding the statement – that the British so named the island – as an interpolation, because it was included by William in *GR*, 29. See also L. H. Gray.

26 This chapter was incorporated by William into *GR*, 24, but the opening words of that version seem to record his intentions because the text as it stands here, with the English referring to the church as 'uetusta', is not coherent. *GR* correctly gives the old English name and reads: *Ecclesia de qua loquimur, quae pro antiquitate sui celebriter ab Anglis* Ealdechirche, *id est Vetusta Ecclesia, nuncupatur, . . .*

27 Incorporated in *GR*, 24 but without the last sentence asserting that Gildas was buried at Glastonbury. That sentence has surely been added to the *DA* because William takes care to note in the *GR* other saints who were buried at Glastonbury and to discuss the burial places of saints to whom he referred. Had he known that Gildas was buried at Glastonbury he would almost certainly have noted that fact in the *GR*. An approximately contemporary *Life of Gildas* was written for the monks by Caradoc of Llancarvan; on this see my ch. 3 *supra*. Notice the remarks about the MSS in Finberg, 'Ynyswitrin', 90.

28 Presumably Bede, *HE*, bk. 1, chs 13 & 20.

29 This chapter, with some variants, was incorporated in *GR*, 26. However, the material in *GR* is presented in a different order from the order of the same material in *DA*. It is unlikely that William revised the order (of all of chapters 8-32) for *GR* because he had made it clear enough, both in the Preface and in ch.

32, that he meant to proceed according to the succession of abbots, which is the idea that controls the material in *GR* but is far from being the case in the extant version of *DA* (the pledge in ch. 32 comes in the middle of the series of abbots). Hence a later reviser has tampered with the order of chapters 8-32 – and in doing so has left his mark by means of phrases that clumsily try to conceal it, such as the *Quo fere tempore antea* of this chapter or the *Set ut ad propositum redeam* of ch. 19. The order of *GR*, therefore, is to be taken as expressing William's intentions and so we must understand that the material on Patrick would have been preceded by material which, in the extant *DA*, follows it.

Some of the variants (between *DA* and *GR*) in this chapter itself seem to reveal the reviser's hand. Certainly the introduction *Quo fere tempore antea* was introduced to disguise the changed order and we should prefer to read, with *GR*, *Ac primum de beato Patricio, a quo monimentorum nostrorum series elucescere cepit, pauca libabimus.* The final sentence in the chapter (*Inde Glastoniam ueniens . . .*) ought also be regarded as the work of a later reviser because it refers to the forged charter of St Patrick, to which it is obviously intended to lead. Rather we should read, with the *GR*, *Ita Glastoniam ueniens, ibique monachus et abbas factus, post aliquot annos nature cessit.* The other variants are better explained by invoking William's habit of changing his own borrowings than by postulating a reviser making minute and inexplicable changes.

30 The following long interpolation found at the foot of folios 2v-4v in at least two fourteenth century hands, was obviously added some time after the appearance of the chronicle of Ranulf Higden (after the 1320s) who disturbed the Glastonbury monks by his reasoning about the two Saints Patrick. Carley (338) suggests that the long note may have been added to T by John of Glastonbury:

Sciendum quod Radulphus Cestrencis in nostro Patricio plurimum exorbitare non ignoratur, quippe qui sibi ipsi in sua descripcione contrariatur. Scribit namque in sua Policronica libro quinto Patricium Heberniensem apostolum inter cetera signorum suorum opera purgatorium quoddam ad terrorem incredulorum ibidem instituisse, et tamen libro septimo asserit illud purgatorium non fuisse Patricii Heberniencium apostoli, set cuiusdam Patricii abbatis quem libro quinto, ubi supra, dicit floruisse circa annum Domini octingentesimum quinquagesimum, et quia Hebernicos conuertere non potuit de Hibernia redisse et apud monasterium Glastonie in Anglia obisse, cum satis euidenter constet Hebernicos fuisse conuersos per sanctum Patricium a Celstino papa missum anno Domini quadringentesimo uicesimo quinto. Si ergo per priorem Patricium fuerunt Heberniensis conuersi per que cronica uel historias reperietur eos a fide postmodum discessisse quos Patricius secundus conuertere dicitur nequiuisse? Et si sic erat quod nequiuit quis, rogo, eos ad fidem in qua nunc sunt legitur postmodum conuertisse? Certe, prout in cronicis reperiri poterit, nullus. Certissimum est enim sanctum Patricium Heberniensium apostolum apud nos requiescere et nostri monasterii primum abbatem fuisse, tam ex scripturis antiquis quam eciam ex eiusdem sancti carta.

Anno Dominice incarnacionis tricentesimo sexagesimo primo natus est puer Patricius, patre Calipurno, matre uero Conches dicta, que soror fuit sancti Martini Turonensis archiepiscopi, ut testatur in sua cronica Martinus. Dictus est autem in baptismo Sucath, per sanctum Germanum Alticiodorensem episcopum cuius discipulatui se tradidit. Dictus est eciam Magoninus, et a Celestino papa Patricius, id est pater ciuium, appellatus est. Tradunt namque historie Constantinum et

Maximinum ac alios quosdam in Britania imperatores creatos, transito mari, omnem armatam et militarem manum abduxisse et inermes absque tutela Britones reliquisse. Hoc percipientes hostes circumabitantes, Hibernices et Picti, in Britannes omnis expertes milicie irruentes non ignobiles predas crebro abduxerunt. Quocirca inter ceteros captiuos eciam Patricium, iam sexdecim annorum adolescentulum, Hebernices rapuerunt. Latrunculorum ergo preda factus, uenditus est in seruum. Comparauit eum regionis illius quidam regulus, nomine Milchu, atque eum suo seruicio mancipauit. Denique durius quam herilis clemencie interesset agens cum adolescente suum eum subulcum instituit. Transierunt in hac seruitute sex anni continui. Demum angelico oraculo aurum sub cespite quodam inueniens domino tribuit ac seruitute liberatus patriam rediit atque parentes expeciit.

Illis diebus fides Britonum plurimum fuerat labefacta, tum propter Saxonum paganorum societatem, tum eciam propter Pelagianam heresim qua multis diebus infecti fuerant. Quapropter sanctus Germanus Alticiodorensis et sanctus Lupus Tricacinus episcopi, Britaneam mittuntur et catholicam fidem expugnantes euuangelicis atque apostolicis confutarunt auctoritatibus. Inde in patriam meditantes reditum, Patricium sanctus Germanus ad familiare asciuit contubernium. Cuius discipulatui duobus de uiginti annis non segniter insudans, Patricius scripturarum diuinarum leccione quidquid deerat plenitudini adiecit sciencie. Iamque quadragenariam etatem egressus, magistro ualefaciens suam presenciam Romane intulit curie inuenitque graciam in conspectu domini pape. Is erat Celestinus, a beato Petro quadragesimus quintus, anno Dominice incarnacionis quadringentesimo uicesimo quarto papatum ingressus. Ab eo Patricius Heberniam in opus euangelii missus anno Domini quadringentessimo uicesimo quinto, datus est illis gentibus doctor et apostolus. Ille opus iniunctum gnauiter executus, Hebernicos multis miraculorum signis atque portentis ad uiam ueritatis conuertit atque in fide catholica solidauit. Tandem Britaniam reuersus, pontificalem celsitudinem salutationesque in foro respuens, super altare suum Cornubiam appulit in portum, qui Hailemont dicitur, quod altare usque hodie apud loci ipsius incolas propter sanctitudinem et utilitatem atque infirmorum salutem in magna ueneracione seruatur. Inde Glastoniam ueniens anno Domini quadringentessimo quadragesimo nono, duodecim fratres anachoritice uiuentes ibidem reperiens congregauit, abbatis omnium uoluntate et eleccione, licet inuitus, suscipiens officium eosdem uitam agere docuit cenobialem. Per hunc enim religio monachorum in Glastonia sumpsit exordium, uitam ducencium monachorum more Egepciorum. Nondum enim exortum erat sidus aureum, scilicet pater Benedictus, quod orbem terre sua doctrina et exemplo foret illustraturum.

Et sciendum est quod duo sunt huius nominis sancti, quisque episcopus et confessor extitit, unus in Hebernia et ille, de quo nunc agitur, in Glastonia requiescens. Iste Patricius Hebernie requiescens in Hebernia extitit natus qui ibidem pontificauit circa annum Domini octingentesimum quinquagesimum qui eciam ibidem sepultus translatus est tempore regis Henrici secundi, filii Matildis imperatricis, cum sanctis Kalumkilla et Brigida, ut testatur Giraldus Cambrensis in Topographia Hebernie. Et quamquam sanctus Kalumkilla, qui eciam, secundum quosdam, Columbanus dictus est, et sancta Brigida cum hoc Patricio translati fuerunt, non tamen contemporanei fuerunt, nam sancta Brigida circa finem sancti Patricii maioris de quo superius actum est floruit. Superuixit enim eum, ut scribit Gildas, sexaginta annis uenitque Glastoniam anno Domini quadringentesimo octoagesimo circiter octauo. Sanctus uero Kolumkylla natus fuit quatuor annis ante obitum sancte Brigide succedenteque etate uenit ipse Glastoniam anno Domini quingentesimo circiter quarto. Hii namque ob uenerandas sui patroni Patricii reliquias cum nonnullis Hebernie nobilibus locum frequentauerunt. Hec uero sancta Brigida in quadam insula iuxta Glastoniam ubi erat oratorium in honore sancte Marie Magdalene consecratum, Bikery siue parua Hebernia dicta, aliquantulam moram per nonnullos annos traxit et, relictis ibidem quibusdam suis insignibus, pera, monili, nola et textrilibus armis que pro eius sanctitatis memoria ibi ostenduntur et adorantur, Heberniam rediit ibique non multo post in Domino quieuit sepultaque est in urbe Duniensi cum Patricio et Columbano simul modo una tumba, ut patet per epitaphium tumbe:

Hec sunt in duno tumulo tumulantur in uno,
Brigida, Patricius atque Columba pius.

31 In the *GR* (26) William gives the date 425, a date given by no other known source, and T probably originally agreed because the final X of CCCCXXX is written over an erasure. Leland's summary of William's *Life of Patrick* gives 430 (*Collectanea*, III, 274) the same date as given by the E version of the *ASC* with which William was familiar. *DA*, ch.10 gives 425.

32 Watkin, 'The Glastonbury "Pyramids"', shows that these names are derived from the names inscribed on the pyramids in the graveyard as recorded by William. . . . *in memoria eterna erant iusti*, Psalm 111:7.

33 *Non . . . eorum*, Mark 1.7. . . . *abiectus . . . habitare*, cf. Psalm 83:11.

34 Watkin, 'The Glastonbury "Pyramids"' (37, n.3) speculates that these names could have been taken from other monuments in the cemetery.

35 This chapter, containing the notorious charter of St Patrick, is obviously the work of a later reviser. It is not referred to elsewhere by William although it would have been ideal for the purpose of countering Osbern's claim that St Dunstan had been the first abbot of Glastonbury. Moreover, it refers to Phagan and Deruvian, of whose existence we know William to have been ignorant. We may add that Robinson has shown convincingly that the indulgences promised in the charter could hardly have been invented before the end of the twelfth century (*SHE*, 15). Finally the reference in the charter to the keeping of two copies of the charter indicates a date of composition after the fire of 1184 – why bother with the detail unless to counter a claim that the copy would have been destroyed in that fire? Why, too, would a vision be needed to resolve doubts about St Patrick (*GR*, 26-7 and *DA*, ch.11) if the charter had existed?

36 In *GR*, 26-7, the order of chapters 10 and 11 is reversed. The order of *GR* appears to be more flowing because the remarks about Patrick as abbot are followed by the proof of this and that by the report of his death; besides if ch. 10 follows ch. 8 (remembering that ch. 9 is certainly interpolated) then . . . *nature cessit* would be followed at once by *Excessit ergo Patricius. . .* which is hardly likely. The puzzle is why the reviser would bother to reverse the order; and the only solution that suggests itself is that he failed to grasp the principle behind the original order and decided that a chronological ordering was desirable. This hypothesis seems preferable to one that entails William radically reordering his work.

This is especially so since we know that the two chapters have been tampered with apart from the question of their order. Ch.11 identifies Glastonbury with Avalon and so reveals the work of a later reviser. Indeed it seems necessary to follow the *GR* account of Patrick's death rigorously because the diffuse chronological speculations in the *DA* version cover some of the ground already discussed in the account of the saint's career and are obviously introduced as a prelude to the reference to Avalon. Note too the reference to the fire of 1184 as a further example of the reviser's work.

37 With ch.11 too we should accept the *GR* version. The reviser has had to tamper with the first sentence because he had altered the order of chs 10 and 11. Hence he has produced a convoluted construction in which he has had to repeat the phrases *frequens questio* and *utrum ibi monachus et abbas fuerit.*

38 *GR*, 27 has a similar account of Bridget but there are variants. It does not record the date of her arrival at Glastonbury nor her presence on the island of Beckery. This can easily be explained by the suggestion that William considered that information irrelevant in *GR*. This is more likely given that the other variants suggest that William amended his account of her for *GR*. In *GR* William raises the possibility that Bridget had died at Glastonbury and he claims that her relics are preserved in honour of her sanctity. *DA* does not include either of these ideas, yet it is hardly imaginable that a later reviser would excise them given that they add to the lustre of the church. Ch.12 then should be accepted as William's work. On the name Beckery see Finberg, 'St Patrick at Glastonbury', 81-2; and on Bridget, whose name is in the calendar attached to the Leofric Missal, see J. L. Robinson.

39 The sentence on Indract in *GR*, 27, is slightly different from the version in *DA* but the text of the latter should be accepted as genuine since there is no plausible explanation of why a reviser would want to have altered it. Indract's death at Glastonbury seems to have been accepted by the eleventh century, although a date in the late tenth century is not impossible, Lapidge, 'The Cult of St Indract at Glastonbury', 183-4.

40 The chapter on Benignus is based presumably on William's lost *Life* of that saint and hence we should accept the *DA* version as his work on the grounds that he felt the need to eliminate some of the material as unsuitable for *GR*, 27. The date 901, however, is certainly wrong because *DA*, ch.77 ascribes the translation to the abbacy of Thurstan, which is compatible with the date 1091 given by L. John of Glastonbury explains *insignia* for us (Carley, 84-7).

Slover has pointed out, in 'William of Malmesbury's "Life of St Patrick"', 17-8, that there are similarities between this entry and Leland's summary of William's *Life of St Patrick.*

41 St Columba is not mentioned in *GR* but this chapter ought to be accepted as William's work because the uncertainty expressed about whether the saint died at Glastonbury is in William's style whereas an interpolator surely would not have introduced the possibility of doubt. Slover argues, less convincingly, that the Irish form of the saint's name is evidence that it is William's work; see C. Slover, 'William of Malmesbury and the Irish', 268-83.

42 The same story is told in *GR*, 27-8 with only minor variants, none of which ought to be preferred to the readings in *DA*. The story must be based on oral evidence because the eleventh century *Life* by Rhygyfarch (which William did not know anyway) ascribes the foundation of Glastonbury to St David but then has him leaving there and founding 11 other churches; A. Wade-Evans, (ed.), *Vitae Sanctorum Britanniae et Genealogiae*, (Cardiff, 1944), 15. It is clear that William was uncertain about the origins of the old church: in ch.2 he attributed its foundation to the disciples sent by Eleutherius, while allowing the possibility of an apostolic foundation, but here he combines a local legend about St David

with an account of an heavenly dedication similar to the one in the earliest *Life of Dunstan* with which he was familiar, (*MSD*, 7).

43 This chapter has been heavily interpolated and the version in *GR*, 28 ought to be regarded as William's genuine work. In the latter William notes that the place of St David's burial is uncertain whereas ch.16 has an account of how he came to be buried at Glastonbury. Moreover, the extant *DA* refers to St David as Bishop of *Rosina Uallis* but William knew his see as that of *Meneuensis*. One wonders, however, about the phrase *viri religiosi recordatione digni* in place of *quidam* in *DA* because one can hardly imagine the reviser downgrading the witnesses in this way. But with that possible exception the *DA* version of the chapter must be regarded as inauthentic.

44 This chapter must be regarded as interpolated since it continues the theme of the last which we know was not William's.

45 This chapter was reproduced more or less as it stands in *GR*, 24-5. But it would originally have followed ch.7 and has been displaced by a reviser (see n.29 *supra*). In fact, as I suggest below (n.55) there was probably additional material on the northern saints which preceded this chapter but which cannot now be recovered. This seems to be the best explanation of the different placement of the three sentences – *Merito . . . excusacio* – in the *DA* and the *GR*. *Pace* Newell, (480) it is not the case that these sentences are obviously in their proper place in *GR*, 25 & 29; they seem more suitably placed where they are in *DA*, given that they were in the context of an account of the many saints buried at Glastonbury. When William decided not to use the material on the northern saints in *GR* he relocated these sentences; this is a more likely hypothesis than one which has the reviser extracting them from their original context and grouping them together here. Why would he have done so? In two other cases where the two versions are different *GR* seems to record William's original work. *DA* refers to *ecclesia Glastoniensis* and *GR* to *ecclesia illa* and the change is surely due to the interpolator having spoken of the church of *Rosina Uallis* and this having made *illa* ambiguous. *DA* reads *In ea, preter beatum Patricium et alios de quibus superius dixi* where *GR* reads *In ea . . . quorum aliquos in processu notabimus*. Obviously the reviser of *DA* had to make this change because he had already mentioned some of the saints.

46 This chapter is reproduced almost exactly in *GR*, 28. Only one variant is clearly the work of the reviser and that is the introduction – *Set ut ad propositum redeam* – which was necessary because William's original order had been tampered with. The other changes ought to be attributed to William.

The chapter is based, as William makes clear, on oral evidence but the concept of Paulinus as a church builder is probably derived from Bede, who attributes the building of a stone church at Lincoln to him, *HE*, II, 16, and possibly a basilica at *Campodonum, ibid.*, II, 14.

47 This account of the translation of Indract is clearly misplaced here, violating as it does William's intention to maintain chronological order and having no connection with its surrounding chapters. It ought to be read, as it is in *GR*, 35-6, in the context of the treatment of King Ine. It is impossible, however, to reconstruct William's original language.

48 Aidan, Bishop of Lindisfarne was associated with Glastonbury as early as the tenth century as revealed by the Leofric Missal, (*English Kalendars before AD. 1100*, 44-55) and the Old English tract 'Resting Places of English Saints' in *Die Heiligen Englands*. On the former see C. Hohler; and on the latter D. W. Rollason.

49 Ceolfrith, Abbot of Wearmouth, was venerated at Glastonbury as early as the tenth century according to the Leofric Missal (25 September).

50 Benedict Biscop, founder of Wearmouth and Jarrow, who is not found in the Glastonbury calendars. *GR*, 328-9 has an account of the purchase of his remains and their translation to the abbey of Thorney.

51 None of these three, together with Ceolfrith and Benedict the subjects of Bede's *History of the Abbots of Wearmouth*, are recorded in the Glastonbury calendars; nor does William refer elsewhere to the fates of their relics.

52 Bede's name is found in the fifteenth century calendar from Glastonbury under 27 May, see *LC*. William refers nowhere else to Bede's remains, but surely he would have done so had he known that they were to be found at Glastonbury.

53 None of these three, two holy virgins and an abbot, are recorded in the Glastonbury calendars. Begu is probably the abbess Bugu who granted to the church three hides at *Ora*; see *DA*, ch. 40.

54 Hilda is recorded in *LC* under the date 17 November. Both the *GR*, 60 and the *GP*, 198 affirm that her relics were at Glastonbury.

55 The location of this chapter in the original *DA* and its genuine content are very difficult to determine. William was much concerned with the translation of these northern saints to Glastonbury. William promised to include an account of them in the *DA* (*VSD*, 271) and apparently did so, since he refers interested readers to this work for more information (*GR*, 56). I propose that the material was originally to be found preceding ch.18 (and following ch.7) because the whole thrust of that chapter is that Glastonbury is favoured by a rich collection of relics, an obvious conclusion to an account of the translation thither of the relics of the northern saints. Such an hypothesis also accounts for the displacement of three sentences from ch.18 (see n.45 *supra*).

It is equally difficult to determine whom William thought of as responsible for bringing the relics to Glastonbury. In *GP*, 198, he asserts that king Edmund initiated the translations, a view held by John of Glastonbury (Carley, 379). In *GR*, however, the relics are said to have been translated *tempore Danicae uastationis* (56), a description which is not altered in the later recensions of the *GR* despite modifications to its account of the relics including a reference to the *DA*. *GR* does not mention king Edmund in connection with the translations and, moreover, his reign is one of the few not plagued by Danish invasions, according to *GR* (157-60). It seems then that William changed his mind about that king's role in the translations. What of the claims in *DA* that the bones of the northern saints were brought to Glastonbury by Abbot Tyccea fleeing from the Danish attacks of 754? This is anachronistic and is not a mistake that William would have made because the earliest encounter with the Danes to which he refers was in the reign of Beorhtric, i.e. not before 786. No firm conclusion is possible, not even the negative one that the attribution of the translations to Tyccea is the work of a later reviser; because William might himself have held such a view, only to have additions made by a later interpolator who was mistaken about the dates of the Danish invasions. Probably William himself was uncertain.

Nor can we know what saints William thought had been translated to Glastonbury, except that Aidan, Ceolfrith and Hilda were among them and Benedict Biscop and Bede almost certainly were not. For the rest, what was originally William's work and what the contribution of enthusiastic later interpolators cannot be determined.

56 William refers to the death of Paulinus in *GP* (134) where he says that the saint was buried at St Andrew's.

57 In *GR* (407) William reports that the relics of St Urban were buried in Rome and in *ibid.* (408) that the head of Anastasius was to be found there too.

58 William refers to the burial of Daria at Rome in *GR* (405). John of Glastonbury attributes the relics of Ursula and Daria to the generosity of Henry of Blois, (Carley, 23 & 345).

59 This chapter is at least partially interpolated because of its references to the disciples of St Philip, Phagan and Deruvian, and Dunstan, David and Paulinus as being buried at Glastonbury. While some of the other names may have been listed by William it seems more plausible to argue that the whole chapter has been added by a later reviser, especially given the reference to the lack of complete knowledge *apud nos*, presumably referring to the Glastonbury monks and the later interpolator among them.

60 The interpolator is wrong here because *ASC* records the devastation of London *sub anno* 994 and the capture and martyrdom of Aelfheah *sub annis* 1011 & 1012. Possibly he based his account on *GR*, 187-8, in which William does not make the chronology clear.

61 As the 172 years that were said at the end of the last chapter to have lapsed since the translation indicate, this is the fire of 1184.

62 These three chapters concerning the purported translation and rediscovery of the remains of St Dunstan are certainly interpolated. The last chapter is specifically dated after the fire of 1184; and, besides, had William believed that the saint lay at Glastonbury he would surely have said so in his *VSD*. See also the remarks in my chapter 1 *supra.*

63 Chapters 26 to 29 were all interpolated later into *DA*. Aylsi's unfortunate encounter with the cross, given to the monastery by king Edgar, is reported by John of Glastonbury to have occurred after the fire of 1184 (Carley, 163). The second story, relating the incident with king Edgar and St Dunstan, was not mentioned by William in his *VSD* although it surely would have been had he known it. The incident which led to the wounding of the cross was reported by William in both *GR* (329-30) and *GP*, (197) but in neither place does he refer to this cross; moreover ch.78 (of *DA*) in which the wounded cross is more fully described has certainly been tampered with. The fire referred to in ch.28 was surely that of 1184. There are reasons for doubting that any of these chapters were written by William and in sum the case is irresistible.

64 Both Rhygyfarch and Gerald of Wales (*Giraldi Cambrensis Opera*, III, 377-404) relate this story but they do not connect the altar with Glastonbury. The account here is based closely on that of Rhygyfarch, (*Four Latin Lives*, 103-4), except for the references to Glastonbury.

65 It is this reference to Henry of Blois that clearly establishes that the chapter has been interpolated, although, in fact, William did not know the *Life of St David* by Rhygyfarch anyway.

66 The first sentence of this chapter, with minor variants, was incorporated into *GR* (25) where it introduces the description of the two pyramids. Some of the variants in *GR* might embody William's original text of *DA*. A reviser might well have changed *is locus* to *Glastonie ecclesia* because the interpolated account of St David would have made *is locus* ambiguous; he might also have added *et ad sepulturam desiderabilis* in order to introduce the list of nobles that he intended

to add. That list, making up the rest of the chapter, was surely interpolated both because William explicitly says that he is going to refrain from giving details and because some of the individuals named were certainly not thought by William to be buried there – Arthur, of course, but also bishop Lyfing who, according to *GP* (201) was buried at Tavistock. Note that, in accord with the reasoning explained in n.29 *supra*, this chapter must be understood to have originally been located after ch.18, as it is in *GR*.

67 On the much-debated question of the link between king Arthur and Glastonbury see Robinson, *Two Glastonbury Legends* and, more recently, G. Ashe.

68 The description of the pyramids in *GR* (25-6) notes that Centwine's name was inscribed on one of them.

69 William records in *GR*, 160, that Dunstan buried king Edmund in the northern part of the tower. Ch. 56 *infra* describes him as being buried to the left, not to the right.

70 Buried near king Edgar according to *GR*, 217.

71 There is an account of Edgar's burial and later translation in *GR*, 180-1; see also ch. 62 *infra.*

72 The burial of Brihtwold, bishop of Ramsbury (995 or 1005-1045), at Glastonbury and his generosity to that monastery are reported in *GR*, 182.

73 As noted above (n.66) William believed bishop Lyfing of Worcester (1031-1046) to be buried at Tavistock. Seffrid, bishop of Chichester (1125-1145), did not die until 1151.

74 At the bottom of the folio may be read the following passage taken from Gerald of Wales (*Giraldi Cambrensis Opera*, IV, 48-9). *Post bellum de Kemelen apud Cornubiam, interfecto ibidem Modredo, proditore nequissimo et regni Britannici, custodie sue deputati, contra auunculum suum Arthurum occupatore, ipsoque Arthuro ibi letaliter uulnerato, corpus eiusdem in insulam Auallonlam, que nunc Glastonia dicitur, a nobili matrona quadam eiusque cognata et Morganis uocata, est delatum, quod postea defunctum in dicto cimiterio sacro, eadem procurante, sepultum fuit. Propter hoc enim fabulosi Britones et eorum cantores fingere solebant quod dea quedam fantastica, scilicet que Morganis dicta, corpus Arthuri in insulam tulit Auallonlam ad eius uulnera sanandum. Que cum sanata fuerint, redibit rex fortis et potens ad Britones regendum, ut dicunt, sicut Iudei messiam suam, maiore* (*maiori* T) *eciam fatuitate et infelicitate simul hac infidelitate decepti.* A later hand adds beneath: *Super hac re quere plus postea tempore regis Ricardi.* Not in M.

75 William incorporated this chapter, almost verbatim, into *GR*, 25-6. Watkin discusses it and speculates as to the identity of the names in 'The Glastonbury Pyramids'. For the latest archaeological findings see Ralegh Radford.

Some of the variants in the *GR* version of the description of the pyramids probably record William's original work. The height of the pyramids is probably as recorded by *GR* because its better manuscript tradition makes it less likely to have been susceptible to the errors that could easily creep into the copying of Roman numerals. Centwine's name ought to be read before that of Haeddi, as in the *GR*, because William was trying to preserve a complete record of the pyramids, whereas the reviser obviously transferred the name to the interpolated section of the previous chapter. We should read *GR*'s *Bregored et Beorwald abbates eiusdem loci tempore Britonum* rather than *DA*'s *Beorwald nichilominus abbas post Hemgiselum* because the latter makes Beorhtwald, as the successor of Haemgils, an Anglo-Saxon whereas William described him as British. Note too that, as usual, the order of the *GR* is to be preferred so that this chapter must originally have followed, introduced by the previous one, ch.18.

76 This chapter is largely a fabrication of a later reviser because it refers to St Philip and Phagan and Deruvian and because it violates William's plans of chronological sequence by anticipating remarks on later abbots. The verses on Benignus and the two sentences that introduce them were incorporated by William in *GR* (27) but they have obviously been displaced from their original location (in the discussion of Benignus, *GR*, 27) by the reviser. On the verses see Finberg, 'St Patrick at Glastonbury', 82-3.

77 This story, the source of which cannot be determined (see the discussion in Carley, 363), was obviously interpolated after the purported discovery of Arthur's remains at Glastonbury. William indicates in *GR* (11) that he is interested in authentic history about Arthur and would doubtless have included this story had he known and believed it.

78 This charter and the discussion which follows it were included in *GR* (28-9) with minor variants. There is no reason not to assume that William himself made the changes. The inclusion in *GR* of the sentence pointing out the significance of the king's referring to the church of Glastonbury as *uetusta* would hardly have been omitted by a Glastonbury reviser but might easily embody an insight that occurred to William only when he was copying the Glastonbury material into *GR*. The explicit statement of abbatial succession is in accord with William's intentions in *DA* but must have been thought of as irrelevant to *GR*.

79 This plausible reasoning obviously represents the ideas of a thoughtful reader taking issue with William.

80 The charter here referred to, *S*227, is discussed by Robinson, *SHE*, 49-53, and is printed by Watkin, 644. On Abbot Brihtwold see Robinson, *SHE*, 27-9 and note too *ASC sub anno* 692.

Although the gist of this chapter has been incorporated into *GR* (29) the account as it stands here has obviously been heavily interpolated. A sentence has been added that implies that it was King Cenwalh who was converted by Birinus but William knew, and had stated (*ibid.*, 22) that the kings who had been converted were Cynegils and Cwichelm. Moreover the account of Abbot Brihtwold has been tampered with to eliminate the reference to his having left Glastonbury to become Bishop of Reculver. Probably the reviser was content that it be believed that the abbot had given up his rule at Glastonbury in order to become Archbishop of Canterbury but not that it be thought that he preferred Reculver to Glastonbury. The king's gift of Beckery, Godney, Marchey and Nyland in Somerset is not recorded in *GR*, except in the transcription of King Ine's charter, and so may have been added by the interpolator.

81 On Abbot Haemgils see Robinson, *SHE*, 29-31. The charter referred to, *S*1666, has been lost but was recorded in the *Liber Terrarum*.

With this chapter we have finished with that part of *DA* on which William based the first of the insertions about Glastonbury that he incorporated in *GR*. Hence there is no direct evidence for the authenticity of much of the rest of *DA*. We can, however, confidently assume that the material based on the Glastonbury charters is William's work both because they are used to pursue his stated aim of determining the succession of abbots and because some of the charters were subsequently incorporated by him into *GR*. As a matter of methodological principle, therefore, it will be assumed that all the charter material was included in *DA* by William.

82 The charter granting land at Quantock Wood, Som. and Creech St Michael, Som., *S*237, does not mention the 20 hides at Cary. Glastonbury held 15 hides at Quantock Wood according to *DB*.

The sentence affirming that King Centwine is buried in a pyramid could well have been interpolated, the reviser having extracted it from its rightful location in ch. 32. That this is so is confirmed by the statement that the pyramid is said to be in the monks' cemetery, as compared to the description in *GR* (25) of its bordering on the cemetery.

83 Baldred's charter granting land at Pennard, Som., *S*236, is printed in Watkin, 853. The monastery held 10 hides there in *DB*. There is no other record of the grant at Ludgersbury, now Montacute, Som.; Finberg, *Wessex*, 358. Baldred's grant of a fishery on the Parret is recorded in the *Liber Terrarum*; ch. 69 *infra* locates it at *Westwere*; *S*1665.

84 The charter by which Bishop Haeddi grants land at Leigh, Som., *S*1249 is printed in Watkin, 639. There were probably, in fact, two charters dealing with this property (see Robinson, *SHE*, 48-9) which would account for the discrepancy between the three hides in the extant charter and the six hides to which William refers.

85 King Ine's grant of land at Brent, Som., *S*238, is printed in Watkin, 979. The monastery held 20 hides there in *DB*.

There is a strong suspicion that the digression on Abbot Brihtwold has been interpolated. It fulfills the promise made in ch. 36 to elaborate on the details of his renunciation of the abbacy but since that promise was interpolated the mention of him here is suspect. This suspicion is confirmed by the use of the pronoun *noster* which suggests a Glastonbury monk as its author. Newell, 'William of Malmesbury', 495-7, offers a plausible explanation for the interpolation. The rest of the chapter can be taken to be William's.

86 There is a general grant of Ine's with exemption from dues and taxes for all the churches and monasteries of his kingdom, *S*245, printed in *GP*, 380-1 and there is a local adaptation of that, *S*246, printed in Watkin, 200. This chapter is based on the local adaptation.

87 On Abbot Beorhtwald see Robinson, *SHE*, 31-2, who notes that there is outside evidence for this abbot in the correspondence of St Boniface. There survives a charter of Ine to Beorhtwald, *S*248, granting land by the river Tone (at *Linig* in ch. 69), at Polden Hill, at Croscombe and by the river Sheppey (formerly Doulting), all in Somerset. There is a later charter granting land at Zoy, *S*251, Watkin, 903, where the monastery held 12 hides in *DB*. There is no other record of the land and fishery at *Escford*, which Finberg, *Wessex*, 373, suggests refers to a ford over the river Axe. There is no extant charter of the grant at Pilton, Som. but it was recorded in the *Liber Terrarum*, *S*1672, and the monastery held 20 hides there in *DB*.

88 No copies of Wilfrid's grants survive but there was a copy of the charter granting Wedmore, Som. in the monastery in 1247, *S*1674 and the grant at Clewer, Som. was recorded in the *Liber Terrarum*, *S*1675. See also *S*1668. Wilfrid is, of course, St Wilfrid who probably came to Glastonbury in c.681 after his explusion from Mercia. On abbot Ealdberht see Robinson, *SHE*, 34. The charter by which Forthhere, bishop of Sherborne (709-737), granted land at Bleadney, Som., *S*1253, is printed in Watkin, 640. There is no other record of abbot Ecgfrith or of the grant to him on the river Axe; see Finberg, *Wessex*, 377. The charter granting land at *Ora* does not survive but it was recorded in the *Liber Terrarum*,

*S*1673, and John of Glastonbury adds to the record of the grant *Yna rege consenciente et confirmante.* (Hearne, *JG*, 41, omitted from Carley).

89 The extant account of the churches at Glastonbury and their builders has been interpolated by a later reviser. The early builders are said to have included the disciples of Saints Philip and James and the twelve men from the north, none of whom were known to William. Moreover, it is clear from *GR* that William thought that the church built by Ine was only the second one there (*ecclesiam, huic vetustae ... appendicem, a fundamentis aedificavit*, 36). But even the reference to the church built by Ine has been altered. William would not have claimed that Ine had built the church for his brother Mul because he had carefully investigated Ine's family when writing *GP* and had affirmed that he had had no brother except Inigild (*ibid.*, 332). William begins his account of the reign of Ine in *GR* with a description of his attack on Kent in revenge for the burning of Mul but does not hint at any family relationship between them. Mul was, in fact, the brother of Caedwalla, as was recorded in the E version of *ASC* (known to William). All of this makes it most unlikely that the inscription was recorded by William; the purported inscription is, in fact, a pastiche (slightly modified) of two poems by Venantius Fortunatus, works unknown to William (Thomson, 'Reading of William of Malmesbury'). For the poems see the edition of F. Leo, *MGH*, AA iv, pt.i (Berlin, 1881, reprinted 1961), 56-7 & 40 and on knowledge of Fortunatus in England see R. W. Hunt.

If nothing survives as genuine from the account of the churches how then did William introduce his account of Ine's chapel and the great charter. We can do no better than suggest that the words in *GR* (35-6) are substantially what William wrote in *DA* and that any variants could only be guessed at.

90 Chapter 41 is not reproduced in *GR* but there are good reasons for thinking that it was written for *DA* by William. The second recension of *GR*, which omits most of the Glastonbury material, directs the reader to *DA* by saying of Ine's generosity to Glastonbury: *cui quantum splendoris adiecerit, libellus ille docebit quem de antiquitate monasterii eiusdem elaboraui.* It seems likely that the phrase *quantum splendoris* is a reference to this chapter. There was a precedent for William to include such material because Bede had included an account of similar gifts in his *Historia Abbatum.*

91 Aethelheard's grant of land at Polden Wood, Som., was in fact made after the death of Ine, as ch. 44 *infra* makes clear.

92 This charter, *S*250, was incorporated by William into *GR*, 36-9, although in a shorter form without the invocation and witness list. This is understandable because the more specialised work naturally called for a more complete copy of the charter. The whole chapter can be regarded as William's work.

93 An account of Ine's journey to Rome can be found in Bede, *HE*, bk. 5, ch. 7, and in *ASC sub anno* 726. Both of those sources, and William's own references in *GR* (39) and *GP* (332) refer to only one journey to Rome. The whole chapter was clearly interpolated by a later reviser whose purpose seems to have been to establish a papal confirmation for the king's charter and to make such a confirmation more convincing by maintaining that the king himself had obtained it.

94 On abbot Coengils see Robinson, *SHE*, 36. The charter granting Polden Wood, Som., *S*253, is the one anachronistically mentioned in Ine's charter. It is printed in Watkin, 372. There are no extant charters for the grants by the river Torridge, Dev., *S*1676 and at Brompton, Som., *S*1677, but they are both recorded in the *Liber Terrarum.*

95 This charter was copied by William into the third recension of *GR* (40) but there are variants between the two versions, the most significant of which is that this chapter gives the date 744 but *GR* the date 745. 744 is internally consistent because the next chapter refers to 745 as the following year, but the grant to which that next chapter refers was actually made in 746. The question cannot be confidently resolved but we suggest retaining the reading of *DA* and explaining the variants by William's apparent working methods – it is clear that he was not scrupulous to reproduce exactly his Glastonbury work and the date of the charter could easily have suffered from hurried copying. The charter, *S*257, is also printed in Watkin, 201.

96 On abbot Tunberht see Robinson, *SHE*, 36-7. The grant recording land at *Ure* (unknown) does not survive but it was recorded in the *Liber Terrarum*, *S*1678. Lulla's grant of land at Baltonsborough, Som., and *Scrobbamurht* (unknown), *S*1410, is printed in Watkin, 766, where the date is given as 746 and land at Lottisham and Lydford, Som. is also mentioned. Aethelbald's grants at two unknown locations do not survive but were recorded in the *Liber Terrarum*, *S*1679.

97 On abbot Tyccea see Robinson, *SHE*, 37. Note that a reviser has interpolated a phrase about a previous reference to Tyccea in connection with relics of the northern saints but the rest of the chapter is surely William's work, reflecting as it does his interest in recording sepulcral inscriptions. William refers to King Sigeberht, who ruled for only one year, in *GR*, 41. There is no extant copy of the agreement about land in the Polden Hills, Som. but it was recorded in the *Liber Terrarum*, *S*1680.

98 We know nothing of abbots Guba and Wealdhun apart from what *DA* tells us. On abbot Beaduwulf see Robinson, *SHE*, 38. No charters survive for the lands at Wootton, Som. or Houndsborough, Som. but the *Liber Terrarum* records a grant by Cynewulf which probably related to the former estate, *S*1684. The charters granting Elborough in Hutton, Som., *S*1681, Culmstock, Dev., *S*1687 & 1691, Culm Davy, Dev., *S*1683, *Cumtun* (Compton Dundon, Som.?), *S*1685, *Eswirht* (unknown), *S*1692 and Huntspill, Som., *S*1692 (see Finberg, *Wessex*, 397), do not survive but they were all recorded in the *Liber Terrarum.*

99 William refers here, of course, to his own *GR*.

100 For a discussion of the papal privilege and the royal confirmation, *S*152, see Robinson, *SHE*, 38 and Levison, 32 & 249-52. This chapter and the two subsequent ones to which it forms an introduction were not used in *GR* but bear all the hallmarks of William's own hand. The historical speculation about the political context of Glastonbury and about the identity of Cynehelm betray a thoughtful writer with a good knowledge of English history and the task of translating the charters required someone with the sort of linguistic skills William revealed in his translation of Coleman's *Life of Wulfstan.*

101 Isaiah 56.7 etc.

102 On the identity of the witnesses and on Cynehelm see Levison, 249-52 and Robinson, *SHE*, 38 n.3. Cynethryth, Aethelburh and Ceolflaed were probably Offa's widow and his daughters; Aethelheard was Archbishop of Canterbury and Hygeberht of Lichfield. Cynehelm was indeed the son of king Cenwulf but by the time that William began to write his life had become surrounded by legend; hence William's confusion.

103 The account of the succession of abbots becomes confused in this chapter. Ch. 48 referred to Beaduwulf ruling for 6 years and since a grant to him in 794 was

quoted this brings us to 800. This is indeed the date given for the beginning of the abbacy of Cuma but the problem is that there is no charter evidence for his existence. There is, however, mention in a charter of 802 of abbot Muca. Moreover, Muca, unlike Cuma, is mentioned in the tenth-century list of abbots compiled independently of the *DA*; see *SHE*, 26-53; and Muca also witnesses other charters, e.g. *S*270a. T originally attributed an abbacy of 22 years to Cuma (confirmed by M) but this has been altered to 2, presumably to maintain consistency with the existence of both Cuma and Muca. It seems likely that we have here a scribal error and that the 'ghost-word' (Robinson, *SHE*, 39) Cuma has been slipped into the text. This explanation still leaves an inexplicable inconsistency since there are 24 years between the end of the abbacy of Beaduwulf and the beginning of that of Guthlac in 824 but only 22 years allocated to the reign of Muca/Cuma.

The charter granting land by the Torridge does not survive but was recorded in the *Liber Terrarum*, *S*1693. The charter by which king Egbert granted land at Butleigh, Som. to his thegn Eadgils, *S*270a, is printed in Watkin, 762. A postscript to the charter reads: *Hanc cartulam reddidit Eadburth ad ecclesiam Glastingensem.* and among the witnesses is *Ego Muca abbas.* There is no other record of the sale of land by Abbot Guthlac to Eanulf; Finberg, *Wessex*, 404, suggests that Brunham could refer to Brompton Ralph, Som.

104 There is no other record of this land transfer at Doulting, Som. (Finberg, *Wessex*, 407). Glastonbury held 20 hides there in *DB*.

105 On King Aethelwulf's decimations, reported by William in *GR*, 109, see Finberg, *Wessex*, 187-213. The relevant charter, *S*303 is printed in Watkin, 202, but it does not mention *Occenefeld* (unidentified) or Downhead, Dev. The source for the decimations is the *ASC sub annis* 855-8.

106 The charters granting land at Clutton, Som., *S*1694, Hornblotton and Binegar, Som., *S*1699 and 1701 and Braunton, Dev., *S*1695 are no longer extant but they were all recorded in the *Liber Terrarum*. The charter granting land at Ditcheat and Lottisham, Som., *S*292, is printed in Watkin, 851 and the charter granting land at Winterbourne (Monkton), Wilts., *S*341, is printed in Watkin, 1236.

107 There are two sources, both known to William, which report the gift to Alfred of wood from the true cross, *ASC sub annis* 883 & 885 and Asser, 53-4. Hence it is probable that the whole chapter was William's work.

108 The charters granting land at Deverill, Wilts., *S*1713, *Weston* (? Weston, now Forscote near Radstock, Som.), *S*1711 and *Stoka* (? Stoke-under-Ham, Som.), *S*1717, do not survive but they were recorded in the *Liber Terrarum*. The other charters survive. They are: Winterbourne (? Monkton), Wilts., *S*399, Watkin, 1235; Wrington, Som., *S*371, Watkin, 1016; and Lyme Regis, Dor., *S*442, Watkin, 1062.

109 The chronology of the Glastonbury abbots has become very confused here and does not even correspond with the succession of abbots as presented by William in *VSD* (270) where Aldhun is said to have been succeeded by Aelfric and the latter by Dunstan. In this chapter it seems certain that the date for Stihtheard's succession ought to be 891 (not 981) and for Aldhun's 922 (not 992). In that case the sentences on those two abbots have probably been displaced (to be consistent with the incorrect dates) and ought to be relocated to the beginning of the chapter. This chapter would then be consistent with what we know William thought the correct order was, although in fact he was wrong; see Robinson, *SHE*, 40-4. William refers elsewhere to Athelstan's gifts of relics but either to

Malmesbury (*GR*, 150-1) or to his own foundation of Milton (*GP*, 186). On Athelstan as a relic collector see J. A. Robinson, *The Times of St Dunstan*, 71-80. The charter granting land at Compton, Som., *S*1705, has been lost but it was recorded in the *Liber Terrarum.*

110 The monks of Glastonbury wanted a refutation of Osbern's assertion that Dunstan had been the first abbot there (in his *Life of Dunstan, MSD*, 92).

111 William's *VSD*, 270, tells of Edmund's decision about Dunstan after he was saved from the brink of death.

112 The charter concerning land at Christian Malford, Wilts., *S*466, is printed in Watkin, 129. There is no other record of the estate at Kingston, Som. (Finberg, *Wessex*, 442) but the abbey had 8 hides there in *DB*. The charter for land at North Wootton, Som., *S*509, is in Watkin, 814. The charter granting land at Whatley, Som., *S*1726 has been lost but it was in the *Liber Terrarum*. There is no other record for the grant at Wrington, Som. but the abbey had 20 hides there in *DB*. The grant at Pucklechurch, Glos., *S*1724, has been lost but is in the *Liber Terrarum*. Finberg, *West Midlands* (96) points out that Pucklechurch was a royal residence and was probably left to the abbey as soul-scot but that the gift did not come into effect immediately. The charter for *Escford* (? on the river Axe), *S*1723 has been lost but it was in the *Liber Terrarum*. The charter for the lands at Damerham and Martin, Hants. and Pentridge, Dors., *S*513 is in Watkin, 1166. Lost is the charter for *Stane* (? Stone in East Pennard, Som.), *S*1725 but it was in the *Liber Terrarum*. The charter for lands at Buckland (Newton) and Plush, Dors., *S*474, is in Watkin, 1133. The charter for land at Okeford Fitzpaine, Dors., *S*1719, does not survive but it was in the *Liber Terrarum*. There is no other record of the grant at Hannington, Wilts., (Finberg, *Wessex*, 259) nor any other evidence that Aelfflaed was the widow of King Edward as the charters that do survive refer to her as *quaedam religiosa femina* (*S*474) and *amicabilis femina* (*S*399). There is no other record of the land at Kingston, Wilts. (Finberg, *Wessex*, 256). Lost are the charters for lands at Turnworth, Dors., *S*1729, and Yarlington, Som., *S*1731, but they were both in the *Liber Terrarum*. The charter for Grittleton, Wilts., *S*472, is in Watkin, 1201 where there is a note that Wilfrid left the land to Glastonbury after the death of his wife. The same note follows the charter granting land at Nettleton, Wilts., *S*504, Watkin, 1198. The charter concerning Tintinhull, Som., is no longer extant but it was recorded in the *Liber Terrarum*. The charter for Batcombe, Som., *S*462, is in Watkin, 844. The charter for Mells, Som., *S*481 is in Watkin, 823. The charter granting land at Abbotsbury, Dors., *S*1727, is lost but it was in the *Liber Terrarum*. There is an incomplete charter by which Edmund grants land at Langford, Wilts., *S*1811 and another charter granting land there to Wulfheah, *S*580 in Watkin, 326.

113 William attests elsewhere to Edmund's devotion to Glastonbury (*GR*, 158 and *GP*, 196-8) and there is no reason for doubting that the whole of this chapter was his work.

114 The rights referred to here are: jurisdiction over towns (? burglaries); right of holding the hundred courts; right of administering oaths; right of administering ordeals; right of doing justice on a thief taken within the estate in possession of stolen property; jurisdiction over housebreakers; jurisdiction over breaches of the peace; jurisdiction over those committing ambush (? on highways); right to tolls; and right to hold a court for those wrongfully accused of illegal possession of cattle or other goods. See Carley, 377 and Stenton, *Anglo-Saxon England*, 490-1.

115 Presumably the same gospel book in which, according to ch. 54 *supra*, the relics presented to the monastery by King Athelstan were recorded. It is no longer extant.

116 This charter, which William incorporated into the second and third recensions of *GR*, 158-9, is also printed in Watkin, 203; *S*499.

117 Note that in ch. 31 *supra* the king was said to be buried to the right.

118 The charter granting land at Badbury, Wilts., *S*499 is in Watkin, 1244. The charters granting lands at Christchurch, Hants., *S*1741, Tarnock and ? Stawell, Som., *S*1740, Nunney and Doulting, Som., *S*1742, *Hortone* (unidentified), *S*1743 and Camerton, Som., *S*1739 are all lost but were all recorded in the *Liber Terrarum*. There is no other record of the grant of 1 hide (as in ch. 69) at Elborough in Hutton, Som. (Finberg, *Wessex*, 465). The charter by which Eadred confirms the grant of Pucklechurch, *S*553, is in Birch, 887. This chapter and the next, being based on charter evidence can be taken to be William's work.

119 The charter by which Eadwig gives land at Panborough, Som., *S*626, is printed in Watkin, 638. The charter does not refer to the abbot by name and William seems to have obtained the name Aelsige from another charter, *S*625, in which it was probably interpolated; Watkin, 1199 & p ccxvi. For the abbots from Dunstan see Knowles, Brooke and London, 50-1.

120 None of these charters, concerning lands at Blackford, Som., *S*1757, Cranmore, Som., *S*1746, *Widecumbe* (unidentified), *S*1751, Stourton, Wilts., *S*1749, Yeovilton, Som., *S*1754, and Woodyates, Dors., *S*1753, survive but all were recorded in the *Liber Terrarum.*

121 The eulogy of king Edgar that characterises this chapter reflects William's attitude to that king as revealed in both the *GP*, 26, 40 etc., and the *GR*, 164-7 and the heavenly message that came to Dunstan at the time of his birth is reported similarly in the *VSD*, 289. The charter which was confirmed by the gift of an ivory horn was incorporated, in a fuller version, into the second recension of the *GR*, 167-8 n. 5. It is curious that the charter was abbreviated in the *DA*, where one would have thought the longer version more appropriate but it can hardly be postulated that a later reviser abridged a charter granting rights to his own monastery. This whole chapter, therefore, and the next one, can be taken to be William's work.

122 Some of these phrases are explained in n. 114 *supra*. The others have these meanings: *socam et sacam* is a vague phrase referring to the right of holding a court which one's tenants must attend (Stenton, *Anglo-Saxon England*, 487-90); *grithbrice* refers to a breach of the local peace; *hundred-setena* is absence from the local hundred; *ealle hordas bufan eorderam et beneorderam* is the right to all treasures above and below the ground; *flemeneferdere* is the right of exacting a penalty for the offence of harbouring a fugitive; and *utfangentheof* is the right to pursue a thief outside one's own jurisdiction and bring him to one's court for trial. See Carley, 382 and the *Oxford English Dictionary.*

123 Edgar's charter is also in *GR*, 170-2. *S*783. At about this point in T a hand of about 1300 has written another papal letter into the margin. The letter, not in M, has in fact been copied into T from the *GR*, 172-3. The letter, printed in its original version in *MSD*, was wrongly dated to 965 by William, who embellished his copy in the *GR* as a result of his researches at Glastonbury. See R. M. Thomson, 'William of Malmesbury and the Letters of Alcuin'. The absence of this letter (the text of which follows here) from the Glastonbury cartulary and from M suggests that there was no copy of it at Glastonbury and that it was not

originally included in the *DA* but was added by a later interpolator.

Iohannes episcopus, seruus seruorum Dei, Alurico inclito duci, amantissimo filio nostro spirituali, salutem continuam et apostolicam benedictionem. Relacione quorumdam fidelium comperimus te plurima agere mala in ecclesia sancte Dei genitricis Marie, que nuncupatur Glastingebury, que tocius Brytannie prima et ab antiquis primoribus ad proprietacem et tutelam Romani pontificis pertinere dinoscitur, et predia ac uillas, scilicet et ecclesias de Brente, de Pulton', quas, Ina rege dante operam, cum aliis ecclesiis quas adhuc iuste et canonice possidet, scilicet Souueie, Stret, Mereling, Budecal, Seapuuic, ab eius iure tua auida cupiditate diripuisse; et propter quod eidem loco propinqua heres habitacione illi semper nociuus esse. Oportunum autem extiterat ut tuo suffragio sancta Dei ecclesia, cui propinquus habitando effectus es, perplurimum accresceret et copia tui adiutorii proprietatibus ditaretur; set, quod nefas est, tuo decrescit inpedimento tuaque humiliatur oppressione. Et quia, licet indigni, non dubitamus nos beato Petro apostolo omnium ecclesiarum curam sollicitudinemque omnium suscepisse, ideo tuam ammonemus dilectionem ut pro amore apostolorum Petri et Pauli nostraque ueneracione ab ipsius loci cesses direpcione, nil de eius proprietatibus, ecclesiis, capellis, uillis et possessionibus inuadens. Quod si hec non feceris, scias te uice apostolorum principis nostra auctoritate excommunicatum et a cetu fidelium remotum perpetuoque anathemate submissum et eterno igni cum Iuda proditore perenniter mancipatum.

124 This privilege was incorporated into *GR*, 168-9. William's identification of the donor as John VIII is mistaken, as is Stubbs' suggestion John XIII (*ibid.*, 170). It was, in fact, issued by John XII. (Carley, 383). It is also printed in Watkin, 205, where it is erroneously dated 971. On abbot Aethelweard see Robinson, *SHE*, 41.

There is one interesting variant between *DA*'s and *GR*'s versions of this letter and it concerns the vexed question of the ordination of monks. Whereas *GR* asserts: *Ordinatio vero tam monachorum quam clericorum in arbitrio abbatis et conventus sit*, *DA* claims, more stridently, . . . *et se suosque, quos idoneos iudicauerunt, quocumque in Dorobernensi diocesi placuerit ad ordinandum dirigant.* The fact that the *GR* version is the one recorded in the abbey cartulary suggests that the *DA* version might be the work of a later reviser, probably at the time of the monastery's struggles with the bishop of Wells at the end of the twelfth century. However, it is not impossible that William was responsible for the variant himself. On the question of the pursuit of rights of independence and exemption see D. Knowles.

125 The charter for Sturminster Newton, Dors., *S*764, is in Watkin, 1095. There is no other record of the return of land at Marksbury, Som. (Finberg, *Wessex*, 506). The charter granting land at Podimore Milton, Som., *S*743, is in Watkin, 863. The charters for lands at Luccombe, Som., *S*1769, Blackford, Som., *S*1768, and High Ham, Som., *S*1773, do not survive but they were all in the *Liber Terrarum*. There is no other record of the land granted at Compton Dundon, Som. (Finberg, *Wessex*, 505), but *DB* reveals the abbey holding 5 hides there. The charters concerning lands at Wheathill, Som., *S*1770, Westbury-on-Severn, Glos., *S*1760, and Orchardleigh, Som., *S*1759, are no longer extant but they were recorded in the *Liber Terrarum*. The lands at Grittelton and Nettleton, Wilts., were referred to earlier (ch.55 and n.112). There is no other record of the land granted at Batcombe, Som. (Finberg, *Wessex*, 518). The charters for lands at

Cleeve, Som., *S*1766 and Durborough in Stogursey, Som., *S*1767, have not survived but they were recorded in the *Liber Terrarum*. There is no other record of the grant at Cranmore, Som., (Finberg, *Wessex*, 504). The charter granting land at Hannington, Wilts., *S*1763, does not survive but an entry in the *Liber Terrarum* refers to an estate there granted by Aelfwold who, Finberg (*Wessex*, 301) suggests, may have been Aethelflaed's husband. The grant of land at Idmiston, Wilts., *S*775, is in Watkin, 1195. The charter concerning lands at Stratton, Som., and Nyland, Som., *S*1761, has been lost but it was recorded in the *Liber Terrarum*. There is no record of the grants at Tintinhull, Som., and Mildenhall, Wilts., (Finberg, *Wessex*, 503 & 271). There is no other record of the grant at *Esseburn* (unidentified). The charter concerning Holton, Som., *S*1765 does not survive but it was in the *Liber Terrarum.*

126 The shrine for the relics of the two saints is also mentioned in *GR*, 181. The monks of Abingdon told a different story about their relics. *In cuius (Edgarus rex) tempore furati sunt monachi Abendoniae reliquias sancti Vincentii et caput Apollinaris et multas alias reliquias (a) monachis Glastonie* (*Chronicon Monasterii de Abingdon* ii, 280).

127 The translation is recorded in ch.66 *infra*. There is no reason to doubt that this whole chapter was William's work given the esteem in which he held king Edgar.

128 None of the charters granting lands at Aust Cliff, Glos., *S*1780, *Siteberge* (? Panborough, Som.), *S*1778, Pucklechurch, Glos., *S*1777, Wilton, Wilts., *S*1774, Hannington, Wilts., *S*1776 and a fishery, *S*1775, survive but they were all recorded in the *Liber Terrarum*. There is no other record of the grant at *Estun* (unidentified), (Finberg, *Wessex*, 655).

William is mistaken in having Beorhtred succeed Sigegar and omits the interesting Aelfweard (c.975-? 1009), some of whose letters survive and are found in *MSD*, 400-5. These letters are examples of the hermeneutic style practised in England in the tenth century, particularly at Glastonbury. See M. Lapidge, 'The hermeneutic style', esp. 96-7.

129 On abbot Brihtwig (c.1019-1024), who was bishop of Wells 1024-1033, see Knowles, Brooke and London, 51. William knew him as a bishop when he was compiling *GP* (194) but was not at that time aware that he had previously been abbot of Glastonbury.

130 On Cnut and his battles with Edmund see *GR*, 212-27. The account here may have been tampered with. The word *contudisset* implies that Edmund had the best of his struggles with Cnut but William's account in *GR*, 214-7, points to the opposite conclusion. Less significantly, *GR* omits the cause of Edmund's death and the gift of land that accompanied his body. If the text has been altered the original words are impossible to recover. There is no other record of the grant of land at Sturminster Newton, Dors. (Finberg, *Wessex*, 618).

131 William incorporated this charter, *S*966, into the *GR*, 225-6. It is also printed in Watkin, 206.

132 On abbots Aethelweard and Aethelnoth see Knowles, Brooke and London, 51. We know of at least one alienation of monastic property by the latter who granted 7 hides at Batcombe to his mother Aelfilla, *VCH*, ii, 85.

This chapter appears to be largely William's work. The account of the translation of king Edgar's body was incorporated almost verbatim into *GR*, 180-1 but there is one interesting variant. *GR* refers to the cure of one man, both blind and mad, but *DA* makes him two men by changing *sanato* (*GR*, 180) to *sanatis*. This certainly indicates that the last sentence about the cure of a well-known blind man has been interpolated, but one wonders about the story of the lunatic's cure. Of course, it could easily have been considered unsuitable for *GR* but the grammatical errors in the account (almost unique in T and therefore probably not the fault of the scribe) incline me to think that it too may have been a later interpolation. (Against this we have the style, which is more like William's than most of the interpolators', and the references in the account to the man being both blind and mad, a detail conforming to William's *sanato* and not to the interpolated *sanatis*).

133 Extracts from these lists were inserted by William in *GR*, 224-5 and undoubtedly *DA* originally contained lists similar to these. There are, however, reasons for suspecting that an interpolator has been at work. No mention is made of Brihtwold being bishop of Reculver, as well as archbishop of Canterbury, the same omission as in ch. 36 *supra*. Moreover Sigeric is described as bishop of Wells and Dunstan's third successor at Canterbury but *GR* (187 & 224-5) does not describe him as bishop of Wells and correctly says that he was Dunstan's second successor. It cannot be determined what William's original contribution consisted of.

For these later monks and bishops (the source of which was probably an eleventh century necrology, according to F. Birkeli who cites (28) the support of Dorothy Whitelock for his view) see, apart from the appropriate references cited in the chapters and notes where they are first mentioned, the list of monastic bishops in *MO*, 697-700. The archbishops are as follows: Brihtwold, archbishop of Canterbury 693-? 731; Athelm, consecrated bishop of Wells in 909, translated to Canterbury in 914 and died in 923 (on him see J. A. Robinson, *The Saxon Bishops of Wells*, 25ff & 56ff); Dunstan, bishop of Worcester 957-9, bishop of London 959-60 and archbishop of Canterbury 960-88; Aethelgar, bishop of Selsey 980-88 and archbishop of Canterbury 988-90, on whom see also *GP*, 32; Sigeric, bishop of Ramsbury 985-90 and archbishop of Canterbury 990-4; Aelfheaeh, bishop of Winchester 984-1005 and archbishop of Canterbury 1005-12, on whom see too *GP*, 33 and *GR*, 188; and Aethelnoth, archbishop of Canterbury 1020-38.

134 It is impossible to identify these bishops with any certainty, especially since we can by no means rely on the dates. The following identifications are suggested by an examination of the lists in F. M. Powicke. Eanfrith, bishop of Elmham 736 x 758-758 x 781; Aethelwine ?; Wigbeorht, bishop of Sherborne 793 x 801-816 x 824; Wigthegn, bishop of Winchester 805 x 14-833 (see *GP*, 160); Helmstan, bishop of Winchester 833-841 x 52; Tunbeorht, bishop of Winchester 871 x 77-877 x 79; Daniel, bishop of Cornwall 937 x 55-959 x 63 or Daniel, bishop of Rochester or Selsey 951 x 55-?; Aelfric, bishop of Ramsbury 970-81 (see Knowles, Brooke and London, 50).

135 Again certain identification is impossible. I have referred to the sources cited in the previous two notes. Sigegar, bishop of Wells 975-966 x 7 (see *GP*, 194); Brihthelm, elected bishop of Wells in 956, translated to Canterbury in 959 but deposed in the same year and then died as bishop of Wells in 973 – William refers to him as Brihtelm in the *GP*, 194; Aelfweald, bishop of Crediton 953-72 (see *GP*, 179); on Sigfrid, whose dates cannot be established exactly see Birkeli, 'Earliest missionary activities'; Aethelwold, bishop of Winchester 963-84 (see *GP*, 165-9); Wulfsige, bishop of Sherborne 992-1001, according to Knowles, *MO*, 700, or Wulfsige, bishop of Cornwall, 959 x 63-981 x 93; ? Aelfstan, bishop of London, 961-995 x 6 (see *GP*, 145); Aethelric, bishop of Sherborne 1001-9

(see *GP*, 179) or, less likely, Aelfric, bishop of Elmham 964 x 74-964 x 74 (see *GP*, 148); Cyneward, bishop of Wells 974-5 (see *GP*, 194); Aelfmaer, bishop of Selsey 1009-31 (see *GP*, 205); Brihtwig, bishop of Wells 1027-33 (see ch.63 *supra* and *GP*, 194).

136 Brihtwold was actually bishop of Ramsbury, 995 or 1005-1045. The mistake here does not brand the chapter as interpolated, however, because William himself made a similar mistake in his *GP* (181 and n.1 – the mistake was corrected but not before at least five other MSS had been copied) and may not have discovered his error until after he had written the *DA*. Brihtwold was renowned for his generosity to Glastonbury, as was well-known to William and reported by him in *GP*, 182. The report of the vision, however, is a later marginal interpolation, copied from *GR* (272) with the revealing variant *sanctum Edwardum* for *ipsum Edwardum* indicating that it post-dates the king's canonisation in 1161. The vision was also reported in *GP* (182) and both accounts were based presumably on that of the anonymous *Life* which William knew; see *Life of King Edward*, 8-9.

137 This chapter contains a summary of all the land grants recorded earlier but it has been compiled independently of the preceding chapters, as is indicated by certain discrepancies in the hidage of some estates and by the inclusion of one grant not recorded earlier. Yet it could be William's work. It exhibits a certain unity of purpose with the next chapter, which bears strong indications of having proceeded from William's pen. Moreover, the compilation seems to have been made before 1191, when Arthur became associated with the monastery, because the account of Arthur is a marginal interpolation.

138 See ch. 34, with the marginal note which identifies the lands that Arthur gave.

139 See ch. 35, although the number of hides is not specified there.

140 See ch. 36.

141 See ch. 37.

142 See ch. 38, where the location of the fishery is not specified.

143 See ch. 39, where the number of hides is specified as 10, a figure confirmed by the surviving charter.

144 See ch. 40, although the location of the estate on the river Tone is not specified there.

145 See ch. 40.

146 See ch. 46.

147 See ch. 47.

148 See ch. 48, where *Cumbe* (Culm Davy, Dev.) is said to have been granted by Sulca. This is probably correct since both Culmstock and Culm Davy were originally granted by Cuthbert, who passed the former on to Sulca and therefore, presumably, the latter too.

149 See ch. 52.

150 See ch. 53, where the number of hides at Doulting is said to be 20.

151 See ch. 54.

152 See ch. 55, although there 4 hides at Whatley and 21 at Wrington are specified. This confusion is preserved by John of Glastonbury who records 4 and 21 hides in one place (Carley, 146) and 10 and 20 hides in another (Carley, 50).

153 See ch. 57 where the hideages of the grants at Nunney and Elborough are not specified and the number of hides at Badbury is said to be 26, a confusion again preserved by John of Glastonbury (Carley, 51 & 151). The charter agrees with the 25 hides of this chapter. Ch. 57 also omits the grant of land at Pennard Minster,

Som., by the nun Aelfgyth. The charter survives, *S*563, and is printed in Birch, 903.

154 See ch.58, where the hideage at Stourton is omitted and the grant at Blackford said to be 3 hides – again John of Glastonbury has both figures (Carley, 151 & 152).

155 See ch.62. The grant at Horton was referred to in ch.57 where it was noted that the land was granted by king Eadred but passed over to Glastonbury only when the original donor's heir became a monk there, which must have been in the reign of Edgar. Ch.62 also referred to 6 hides at Blackford, not 5 as here – John of Glastonbury has both figures (Carley, 51 & 167). The earlier chapter refers to 17 hides at High Ham but John of Glastonbury quotes only 7 hides when he mentions the grant (Carley, 51 & 167). The surviving charter, *S*791, mentions 7 hides too and that must surely be the correct figure.

156 See ch.63.

157 See ch.64.

158 This chapter, containing material drawn from either charters extant in the twelfth century or the *Liber Terrarum*, seems to be William's work. This judgement rests mainly on the frank admission of the extravagant claims of the monastery, quite comprehensible if made by William but hardly likely to have proceeded from the pen of a local monk. The historical speculation about the apparent duplication of grants reads like William's work too. The first group of lands comes from a collection of old charters for lands that the monastery no longer held (so recorded in the *Liber Terrarum*). These are: Alhampton, Som., *S*1686; *Cinemeresforda* (either Quermerford in Calne, Wilts., or Kempsford, Glos.), *S*1688; *Leimucmere* (unidentified), *S*1698; Pilsdon, Dors., *S*1706; Portsbury, Som., *S*1707; *Litlantone* (unidentified), *S*1735; *Eatumberg* (unidentified), *S*1734; ? Shipham, Som., *S*1733; Brampford Speke, Dev., *S*498, (printed in Watkin, 980, the only charter of this group to survive); *Pendescliue* (unidentified), *S*1748; and Ubley, Som., *S*1771. The next group were all recorded in the *Liber Terrarum* but have subsequently been lost. These are: *Elonsanige* (unidentified), *S*1669; Monk Okehampton, Dev., *S*1696; Chelworth, Wilts., *S*1721; Worston, Som., *S*1710; Camel, Som., *S*1718 or *S*1755 or *S*1764; Rowberrow, Som., *S*1722; and *Peasucmere* (unidentified), *S*1750. The final group of grants refer to: Lydney, Glos., *S*1702; Lamyatt, Som., *S*1756; Hentsridge, Som., *S*1712 or *S*1736; Dulwich, Surrey, *S*747 (printed in Watkin, 1167, the only charter of the group to survive); Orchardleigh, Som., *S*1759; Piddle, Dors., *S*1730; ? Burton near North Coker, Som., *S*1709; Upavon, Wilts., *S*1720; and *Easaetencone* (unidentified), *S*1758.

159 For the early abbots in this list see Robinson, *SHE*, 26-53, for those between Dunstan and 1215 see Knowles, Brooke and London, 50-2 and for the later ones see *VCH*, 89-96. This chapter appears to have been added by a later reviser because the information in it does not correspond with the details given throughout the rest of the *DA*, a discrepancy it hardly seems likely William would have been responsible for given the emphasis he placed on ascertaining the correct succession of abbots.

160 On this inflated assessment of the twelve hides see J. A. Robinson, 'Memorials of St Dunstan in Somerset'. This chapter and the next are hardly likely to be the work of William. Such a detailed account of boundaries does not seem suitable to the task that he set himself. Moreover, references to the 'twelve hides' occur only in the first two chapters which are mainly the work of revisers. There is also

good evidence that the incorporation of West Pennard within the bounds indicates a date of composition after 1130; see M. M. Postan, esp. 263.

161 On abbot Thurstan see Knowles, Brooke and London, 51. There is no reason to doubt that this chapter was William's work, given his decision to continue his account of Glastonbury abbots up to Henry of Blois. The criticism of the Conqueror expressed here is less guarded than that expressed in *GR* (334-5) but is consistent with the latter.

162 This charter, concerning lands at Podimore Milton, Fullbrook, Berrow and Burrington in Somerset, Lyme, Dors., Blackford, Som., and Wootton, Wilts., was not included in any later Glastonbury cartularies.

163 There is no other record of this council. See M. Gibson, 142 and for the sort of dispute described here J. Sayers. It seems likely that the account was the work of William because a later reviser would not have been content to have Lanfranc describe Glastonbury as the *nutricula* of Dunstan (a word used by William in the Preface, however) but would surely have taken the opportunity to have the archbishop acknowledge that the abbey was also protected by the relics of the saint.

164 The reference here to (presumably) William's own (lost) *Life of Benignus* suggests that the chapter was his work. Note that the dating of the translation here corrects the erroneous 901 of ch.13. John of Glastonbury (Carley, 88) assigns the translation to the reign of William II, which conforms to the description in *GR*, 27, of it as *novae translationis.*

165 This notorious incident was also reported by William in both *GR*, 329-30 and *GP*, 197 but the account here differs to such an extent that it has clearly been altered by a later reviser, basing his account, as will be clear from the parallels cited in the notes, on the chronicle compiled at Worcester (on which see, most recently, V. Flint). In particular, this chapter presents the monks as driving their attackers from the church, whereas both *GR* and *GP* portray them as themselves being expelled. Note the reference to the bleeding crucifix already referred to in the interpolated ch.28. It is not possible to recover William's original account. The incident was also reported in the *ASC sub anno* 1083 and by Orderic Vitalis, *Ecclesiastical History*, II, 271. On the chant and resistence to changes see *MO*, esp. 553-5.

166 Cf. the account in the Worcester chronicle *sub anno* 1083 (CCC, Oxford, MS 157, f.352: *Hic inter cetera stultitie sue opera Gregorianum cantum aspernatus, monachos cepit compellere ut, illo relicto, cuiusdam Willelmi Fescannensis cantum discerent et cantarent. Quod dum egre acciperent, quippe qui iam tam in hoc quam in cetero ecclesiastico officio secundum morem Romane ecclesie insenuerant . . .*

167 Cf. Worcester chronicle, *sub anno* 1083: *Unum etiam monachum sacrum amplexantem altare lancea transuerberans interemit, alium ad altaris crepidinem sagittis confossum necauit, ceteri uero necessitate compulsi, scannis et candelabris ecclesie fortiter se defendentes, licet grauiter uulnerati, milites omnes retro chorum abegerunt.*

168 Cf. Worcester chronicle, *sub anno* 1083: *Cuius post mortem idem abbas tunc abbatiam suam a filio eius, rege Willelmo, quingentis libris argenti emit et, per ecclesie possessiones aliquot annis peruagatus, longe ab ipso monasterio, ut dignus erat, misere uitam finiuit.*

169 The reference to Orosius is puzzling given that the Worcester chronicle was the main source of the interpolator. The Glastonbury library catalogue noted that in 1247 the monastery had two copies of Orosius in Latin and one in English and

perhaps one of these was mis-titled. Even if that were so it could hardly have been the Worcester chronicle which dated the events 1083, not 1081 as here. Could Orderic Vitalis be meant?

[170] On abbot Herluin (1100-1118) see Knowles, Brooke and London, 51. There is no reason to doubt that the chapter was the work of William, particularly as it is more in his style than in the style of any of the interpolators.

[171] This commonplace, also quoted by William in the *HN*, 68, comes originally from Terence, *Andria*, 11305-6 but was included in sentence collections; no. 26156 in H. Walther, II, 4.

[172] On Cardinal John of Crema who was papal legate in 1125, and attended the consecration of Seffrid as bishop of Chichester see M. Brett, esp. 42-6.

[173] For the development of dietary customs, and especially the addition of the pittance to the allowance, an innovation first fully recorded at Glastonbury, see *MO*, 456-65. The *generale* was a dish of eggs or fish that was served to the whole table whereas the *pitantia*, a small dish of fish or eggs, was served to an individual monk or a pair of monks.

[174] On Seffrid Pelochin, abbot from 1120/1 until he was promoted to the see of Chichester in 1125, see Knowles, Brooke and London, 51.

[175] This papal privilege is also printed in Watkin, 169.

[176] The word *apostolicis* suggests the hand of a reviser and no doubt post-dates the blooming of the legend about the foundation of the church by the disciples of St Philip. Watkin's version omits the word and also reads *vestro* for the *nostro* of the next line, another clue that the reviser has tampered with the *DA* version.

[177] Henry was abbot of Glastonbury 1126-1171 and bishop of Winchester 1129-1171. See Knowles, Brooke and London, 51.

BIBLIOGRAPHY

(See also Abbreviations)

Primary Sources

The Antiquities of Glastonbury by William of Malmesbury, trans. F. Lomax, (London, 1908).
Asser's 'Life of King Alfred', ed. W. H. Stevenson, (Oxford, reprinted 1959).
The Chronicle of Aethelweard, ed. A. Campbell, (Nelson's Medieval Texts, 1962).
Chronicon Monasterii de Abingdon, ed. J. Stevenson, 2 vols, (RS, 1858).
Councils and Ecclesiastical Documents relating to Great Britain and Ireland, ed. A. W. Haddan and W. Stubbs, 3 vols, (Oxford, 1869-78).
Ecclesiastical Documents, ed. J. Hunter, (Camden Soc., O. S. viii, 1840).
The Ecclesiastical History of Orderic Vitalis, ed. M. Chibnall, vol. 2, (Oxford, 1969).
English Kalendars before A.D. 1100, ed. F. Wormald, (London, 1934).
Four Latin Lives of St Patrick, ed. L. Bieler, (Dublin, 1971).
Freculphi episcopi Lexoviensis Chronicorum Tomi Duo in *PL*, cvi, 917-1258.
Gildas De Excidio Britanniae, ed. H. Williams, Cymmrodorion Record Series, No. 3, (2 parts, London, 1899-1901).
Giraldi Cambrensis Opera, 8 vols, ed. J. Brewer et al., (RS, 1861-91).
Die Heiligen Englands, ed. F. Liebermann, (Hannover, 1889).
Hemingi Chartularium Ecclesiae Wigorniensis, ed. T. Hearne, 2 vols, (Oxford, 1723).
Flete's History of Westminster Abbey, ed. J. A. Robinson, (Cambridge, 1909).
The Letters of Osbert of Clare, ed. E. W. Williamson, (Oxford, 1929).
Liber Eliensis, ed. E. O. Blake, (Camden Soc., 3rd Series, xcii, 1962).
Liber Pontificalis, ed. L. Duchesne, vol. 1, (Paris, 1886).
Life of Merlin, ed. G. Clarke, (Cardiff, 1973).
The Life of King Edward the Confessor, ed. F. Barlow, (Nelson's Medieval Texts, 1962).
The Life of St Anselm Archbishop of Canterbury by Eadmer, ed. R. W. Southern, (Nelson's Medieval Texts, 1962).
Lucan, ed. and trans. J. D. Duff. Loeb Classical Library, (London, 1962).
Memorials of St Edmund's Abbey, ed. T. Arnold, 3 vols, (RS, 1890-96).
The Monastic Constitutions of Lanfranc, ed. D. Knowles, (Nelson's Medieval Texts, 1951).
'Nennius', *Historia Brittonum*, ed. T. Mommsen, MGH, Chronica Minora saec. IV, V, VI, VII, vol. 3, (Berlin, 1898, reprinted 1961).
'Nennius', *History of the Britons*, trans. A. Wade-Evans, (London, 1938).
Nova Legenda Angliae, ed. C. Horstman, (Oxford, 1901).
Radulphi de Coggeshall Chronicon Anglicanum, ed. J. Stevenson, (RS, 1875).
Sancti Dunstani Vita auctore B, ed. W. Stubbs in *MSD*, 3-52.
Sancti Dunstani Vita auctore Adelardo, ed. W. Stubbs in *MSD*, 53-68.
Sancti Dunstani Vita auctore Osberno, ed. W. Stubbs in *MSD*, 69-128.
The Text of the Book of Llan Dâv, ed. J. G. Evans and J. Rhys, (Oxford, 1893).

Venanti Honori Clementiani Fortunati presbyteri italici Opera Poetica, ed. F. Leo, *MGH* Auctores Antiquissimi iv, pt. i, (Berlin, 1881, reprinted 1961).
'La Vie de S. Edouard le Confesseur par Osbert de Clare', ed. M. Bloch, *Analecta Bollandiana*, XLI (1923), 5-131.
'*Vita Gildae* of Caradoc of Llancarvan', ed. H. Williams in Gildas *De Excidio Britanniae*, 395-413.
Vita Sancti Davidis by Rhygyfarch in A. Wade-Evans, ed., *Vitae Sanctorum Britanniae et Genealogiae*, (Cardiff, 1944).
'Zwei unbekannte Briefe zu den Gesta Regum Anglorum des Wilhelm von Malmesbury', ed. E. Könsgen in *Deutsches Archiv für Erforschung des Mittelalters*, 31 (1975), 204-14.

Secondary Works

G. Ashe, *The Quest for Arthur's Britain*, (London, 1968).
G. Baist, 'Arthur und der Graal', in *Zeitschrift für Romanische Philologie*, XIX (1895), 326-45.
R. H. Bautier, 'L'Historiographie en France aux xe et xie Siècles', in *La Historiografia Altomedievale*, Settimane di Studio, (Spoleto, 1970), 793-850.
J. A. Bennett, 'A Glastonbury Relic', *PSANHS*, XXXIV (1888), 117-22.
R. R. Bezzola, *Les Origines et la Formation de la Littérature Courtoise en Occident (500-1200)*, 2 vols, (Paris, 1960).
M. Biddle, H. T. Lambrick and J. N. L. Myres, 'The Early History of Abingdon Berkshire and its Abbey', *Medieval Archaeology*, 12 (1968), 26-69.
F. Birkeli, 'The Earliest Missionary Activities from England to Norway', *Nottingham Medieval Studies*, XV (1971), 27-37.
T. A. M. Bishop and P. Chaplais, eds., *Facsimiles of English Royal Writs to A.D. 1100*, (Oxford, 1957).
W. J. Brandt, *The Shape of Medieval History*, (New Haven, 1966).
M. Brett, *The English Church under Henry I*, (Oxford, 1975).
C. N. L. Brooke, 'The Archbishops of St David's, Llandaff and Caerleon-on-Usk', in N. K. Chadwick, *Studies in the Early British Church*, (Cambridge, 1958), 201-42.
C. N. L. Brooke, 'Episcopal Charters for Wix Priory', in P. M. Barnes and C. F. Slade, eds., *A Medieval Miscellany for Doris May Stenton*, (Pipe Roll Soc., 1962), 45-63.
J. Campbell, 'Bede', in T. A. Dorey, *Latin Historians*, (London, 1966), 159-90.
N. K. Chadwick, 'Intellectual Life in West Wales in the Last Days of the Celtic Church', in N. K. Chadwick, *Studies in the Early British Church*, (Cambridge, 1958), 121-82.
P. Chaplais, 'The Original Charters of Herbert and Gervase, Abbots of Westminster', in P. M. Barnes and C. F. Slade, *A Medieval Miscellany for Doris May Stenton*, (Pipe Roll Soc., 1962), 89-110.
C. R. Cheney, 'Church Building in the Middle Ages', reprinted in his *Medieval Texts and Studies*, (Oxford, 1973), 346-63.
M. T. Clanchy, *From Memory to Written Record, England 1066-1307*, (London, 1979).
H. O. Coxe, *Laudian Manuscripts*. Bodleian Library, Quarto Catalogue Reprints, (Oxford, 1973).
R. R. Darlington, 'Ecclesiastical Reform in the Late Old English Period', *EHR*, LI (1936), 385-428.

W. Davies, 'Liber Landavensis: its construction and credibility', *EHR*, LXXXVIII (1973), 335-51.
W. Davies, 'Saint Mary's Worcester and the Liber Landavensis', *Journal of the Society of Archivists*, 4 (1972), 459-85.
G. R. C. Davis, *Medieval Cartularies of Great Britain*, (London, 1958).
M. Deanesly, *The Pre-Conquest Church in England*, (London, 1961).
G. H. Doble, 'Saint Indract and Saint Dominic', *Somerset Record Society Publications*, 57 (1942), 1-24.
H. P. R. Finberg, *The Early Charters of Wessex*, (Leicester, 1964).
H. P. R. Finberg, *The Early Charters of the West Midland*, (Leicester. 1972).
H. P. R. Finberg, 'St Patrick at Glastonbury', in his *West Country Historical Studies*, (Newton Abbot, 1969), 70-88.
H. P. R. Finberg, 'Ynyswitrin', in his *Lucerna*, (London, 1966), 83-94.
H. P. R. Finberg, 'Sherborne, Glastonbury and the Expansion of Wessex', *TRHS*, 5th Series, 3 (1953), 101-22.
D. J. V. Fisher, 'The Early Biographers of St Ethelwold', *EHR*, LXVII (1952), 381-91.
V. Flint, 'The Date of the Chronicle of "Florence" of Worcester', *Revue Bénédictine*, LXXXVI (1976), 115-19.
A. Funkenstein, 'Periodisation and Self-Understanding in the Middle Ages and Early Modern Times', *Medievalia et Humanistica*, new series, 5 (1974), 3-23.
V. H. Galbraith, 'The East Anglian See and the Abbey of Bury St Edmunds', *EHR*, XL (1925), 222-8.
M. Gibson, *Lanfranc of Bec*, (Oxford, 1978).
A. Gransden, 'The Growth of the Glastonbury Traditions and Legends in the Twelfth Century', *JEH*, 27 (1976), 337-58.
A. Gransden, *Historical Writing in England c.550-c.1307*, (London, 1974).
L. H. Gray, 'The Origin of the Name of Glastonbury', *Speculum*, 10 (1935), 46-53.
R. W. Hanning, *The Vision of History in Early Britain*, (New York, 1969).
R. W. Hanning, review of B. Lacroix, *L'Historien Au Moyen Age* in *History and Theory*, 12 (1973), 419-34.
R. P. C. Hanson, *St Patrick. His Origins and Career*, (Oxford, 1968).
C. Hohler, 'Some Service-Books of the Later Saxon Church', in *Tenth Century Studies*, ed. D. Parsons, (London, 1975), 68-83.
R. W. Hunt, 'Manuscript evidence for knowledge of the poems of Venantius Fortunatus in later Anglo-Saxon England (with an appendix "Knowledge of the poems in the earlier period" by M. Lapidge)', *ASE*, 8 (1979), 279-95.
R. I. Jack, *Medieval Wales*, (Sources of History, 1972).
M. R. James, *Catalogue of Western Manuscripts in . . . Trinity College Cambridge*, 4 vols, (Cambridge, 1900-1904).
E. J. Kealey, *Roger of Salisbury, Viceroy of England*, (Berkeley, 1972).
N. R. Ker, 'Hemming's Cartulary', in *Studies in Medieval History Presented to F. M. Powicke*, (Oxford, 1948), 49-75.
S. Keynes, 'Studies on Anglo-Saxon Royal Diplomas': unpublished Fellowship thesis for Trinity College, 2 vols, (Cambridge, 1976).
D. Knowles, 'Essays in Monastic History', *The Downside Review*, 50 (1932), 201-31 & 396-436.
D. Knowles, C. N. L. Brooke and V. London, *The Heads of Religious Houses in England and Wales 940-1216*, (Cambridge, 1972).

V. M. Lagorio, 'The Evolving Legend of St Joseph of Glastonbury', *Speculum*, 46, (1971), 209-31.
M. Lapidge, 'The Cult of St Indract at Glastonbury', in *Ireland in Medieval Europe: Studies in Memory of Kathleen Hughes*, ed. D. Whitelock, R. McKitterick and D. N. Dumville, (Cambridge, 1981), 179-212.
M. Lapidge, 'The hermeneutic style in tenth-century Anglo-Latin literature', *ASE*, 4 (1975), 67-111.
M. Lapidge, 'Some Remnants of Bede's lost Liber Epigrammatum', *EHR*, XC (1975), 798-820.
J. Leclercq, *The Love of Learning and the Desire for God*, (New York, 1962).
J. Leland, *Commentarii de Scriptoribus Britannicis*, ed. A. Hall, (Oxford, 1709).
J. Leland, *De Rebus Britannicis collectanea*, ed. T. Hearne, (London, 1774).
W. Levison, *England and the Continent in the Eighth Century*, (Oxford, 1946).
R. S. Loomis, *The Development of Arthurian Romance*, (London, 1963).
F. Lot, 'Glastonbury et Avalon', *Romania*, 1898, 526-64.
E. Miller, *The Abbey and Bishopric of Ely*, (Cambridge, 1951).
A. Morey and C. N. L. Brooke, *Gilbert Foliot and his Letters*, (Cambridge, 1965).
W. W. Newell, 'William of Malmesbury on the Antiquity of Glastonbury', *PMLA*, XVIII (1903), 459-512.
W. A. Nitze, 'The Exhumation of King Arthur at Glastonbury', *Speculum*, 9 (1934), 353-61.
M. A. O'Donovan, 'An interim revision of episcopal dates for the province of Canterbury, 850-950', 2 parts, *ASE*, 1 (1972), 23-44 & 2 (1973), 91-113.
R. I. Page, 'Anglo-Saxon Episcopal Lists', *Nottingham Medieval Studies*, 2 parts, IX (1965), 71-95 & X (1966), 2-24.
R. B. Patterson, 'William of Malmesbury's Robert of Gloucester', *American Historical Review*, 70 (1965), 983-97.
M. M. Postan, 'Glastonbury Estates in the Twelfth Century', reprinted in his *Essays on Medieval Agriculture and General Problems of the Medieval Economy*, (Cambridge, 1973), 249-77.
F. M. Powicke, *Handbook of British Chronology*, (London, 1961).
C. A. Ralegh Radford, 'Glastonbury Abbey', in G. Ashe, *The Quest for Arthur's Britain*, (London, 1968), 97-110.
P. Rahtz, 'Glastonbury Tor', in G. Ashe, *The Quest for Arthur's Britain*, (London, 1968), 111-122.
R. D. Ray, 'Medieval Historiography through the Twelfth Century: Problems and Progress of Research', *Viator*, 5 (1974), 33-59.
R. D. Ray, 'Orderic Vitalis and his Readers', *Studia Monastica*, 14 (1972), 17-33.
J. A. Robinson, *Somerset Historical Essays*, (London, 1921).
J. A. Robinson, *The Times of St Dunstan*, (Oxford, 1923 reprinted 1969).
J. A. Robinson, 'Memorials of St Dunstan in Somerset', *PSANHS*, 62 (1916), 13-23.
J. A. Robinson, *The Saxon Bishops of Wells*, (British Academy Supplementary Papers, no.4, 1918).
J. A. Robinson, *Two Glastonbury Legends*, (Cambridge, 1926).
J. L. Robinson, 'St Brigid and Glastonbury', *Journal of the Royal Society of Antiquaries of Ireland*, 83 (1953), 97-9.
D. W. Rollason, 'Lists of Saints' Resting Places in Anglo-Saxon England', *ASE*, 7 (1978), 61-93.
J. Sayers, 'Monastic Archdeacons', in C. N. L. Brooke et al., *Church and Government in the Middle Ages*, (Cambridge, 1976), 177-203.

B. Scholz, 'Two Forged Charters from the Abbey of Westminster and their Relationship with St Denis', *EHR*, LXXVI (1961), 466-78.
C. H. Slover, 'William of Malmesbury and the Irish', *Speculum*, 2 (1927), 268-83.
C. H. Slover, 'William of Malmesbury's Life of St Patrick', *Modern Philology*, XXIV (1926), 5-20.
B. Smalley, *The Becket Conflict and the Schools*, (Oxford, 1973).
B. Smalley, 'Gilbertus Universalis, Bishop of London (1128-34) and the Problem of the "Glossa Ordinaria"', *RTAM*, VII (1935), 235-62.
R. W. Southern, 'Aspects of the European Tradition of Historical Writing: 4. The Sense of the Past', *TRHS*, 5th Series, 23 (1973), 243-63.
F. M. Stenton, *Anglo-Saxon England*, 3rd edn., (London, 1971).
F. M. Stenton, *The Early History of the Abbey of Abingdon*, (Oxford, 1913).
J. Sumption, *Pilgrimage, an Image of Medieval Religion*, (London, 1975).
H. M. Taylor and J. Taylor, *Anglo-Saxon Architecture*, (Cambridge, 1965).
R. M. Thomson, 'The Reading of William of Malmesbury', *Revue Bénédictine*, LXXXV (1975), 362-402.
R. M. Thomson, 'William of Malmesbury's Edition of the Liber Pontificalis', *Archivum Historiae Pontificae*, 16 (1978), 93-112.
R. M. Thomson, 'William of Malmesbury and the Letters of Alcuin', *Medievalia et Humanistica*, new series 8 (1977), 147-161.
R. Thurneysen, 'Zu Wilhelm von Malmesbury', *Zeitschrift für Romanische Philologie*, XX (1896), 316-21.
H. Walther, *Lateinische Sprichwörte und Sentenzen des Mittelalters in Alphabetischer Anordnung*, (Göttingen, 1963-70).
A. Watkin, 'The Glastonbury "Pyramids" and St Patrick's "Companions"', *The Downside Review*, 65 (1947), 30-41.
A. Wilmart, 'Les compositions d'Osbert de Clare en L'honneur de Sainte Anne', in his *Auteurs Spirituels et Textes Dévots du Moyen Age Latin*, (Paris, 1971), 261-86.

INDEX